Advancing Pluralism in Teaching Economics

The complex economic problems of the 21st century require a pluralist, real-world oriented and innovative discipline of economics that is capable of addressing and teaching these issues to students. This volume is a state-of-the-art compilation of diverse, innovative and international perspectives on the rationales for and pathways towards pluralist economics teaching. It fosters constructive controversy aiming to incite authors and commentators to engage in fruitful debates.

This volume addresses a number of key questions: Why is it important for a social science to engage in pluralistic teaching? What issues does pluralist teaching face in different national contexts? Which traditions and practices in economic teaching make pluralist teaching difficult? What makes economics as a canonical textbook science particular and how could the rigid textbook system be innovated in a meaningful way? What can we learn from school education and other social science disciplines? Through examining these issues the editors have created a pluralist but cohesive book on teaching economics in the contemporary classroom drawing from ideas and examples from around the world.

Advancing Pluralism in Teaching Economics offers a valuable insight into the methodology and application of pluralist economics teaching. It will be a great resource for those teaching economics at various levels, as well as researchers.

Samuel Decker is an economist and activist based in Berlin, Germany. He works as scientific assistant for the online learning platform Exploring Economics (www.exploring-economics.org/en/). He holds a master's degree in "Political Economy of European Integration" and is an active member of the student movement for pluralism in economics.

Wolfram Elsner was Professor of Economics at the University of Bremen, Germany from 1995 until he retired in 2016. He has also worked as head of local economic development, head of the Planning Division of the Ministry of Economic Affairs of the State of Bremen, and as Director of the State of Bremen Government's economic research institute, 1986 to 1995. He was president of the European Association for Evolutionary Political Economy, 2012–2016.

Svenja Flechtner is an Assistant Professor of Pluralist Economics at the University of Siegen, Germany. She has been a research assistant at Europa-Universität Flensburg and Freie Universität Berlin. From 2014–2018, she was a council member of the European Association for Evolutionary Political Economy.

Routledge Advances in Heterodox Economics

Series Editors: **Mark Setterfield**, *The New School for Social Research, USA* and **Peter Kriesler**, *University of New South Wales, Australia*

Over the past two decades, the intellectual agendas of heterodox economists have taken a decidedly pluralist turn. Leading thinkers have begun to move beyond the established paradigms of Austrian, feminist, Institutional-evolutionary, Marxian, post Keynesian, radical, social, and Sraffian economics, opening up new lines of analysis, criticism, and dialogue among dissenting schools of thought. This cross-fertilisation of ideas is creating a new generation of scholarship in which novel combinations of heterodox ideas are being brought to bear on important contemporary and historical problems.

Routledge Advances in Heterodox Economics aims to promote this new scholarship by publishing innovative books in heterodox economic theory, policy, philosophy, intellectual history, institutional history, and pedagogy. Syntheses or critical engagement of two or more heterodox traditions are especially encouraged.

35. Inequality and Uneven Development in the Post-Crisis World
Edited by Sebastiano Fadda and Pasquale Tridico

36. Keynes and The General Theory Revisited
Axel Kicillof, Translated by Elena Odriozola

37. Microeconomic Theory
A Heterodox Approach
Authored by Frederic S. Lee, Edited by Tae-Hee Jo

38. The Economics of Law, Order, and Action
The Logic of Public Goods
Jakub Bożydar Wiśniewski

39. Advancing Pluralism in Teaching Economics
International Perspectives on a Textbook Science
Edited by Samuel Decker, Wolfram Elsner and Svenja Flechtner

For more information about this series, please visit www.routledge.com/series/RAHE

Advancing Pluralism in Teaching Economics

International Perspectives on a Textbook Science

Edited by Samuel Decker, Wolfram Elsner and Svenja Flechtner

Routledge
Taylor & Francis Group
LONDON AND NEW YORK

First published 2019
by Routledge
2 Park Square, Milton Park, Abingdon, Oxon OX14 4RN

and by Routledge
52 Vanderbilt Avenue, New York, NY 10017, USA

First issued in paperback 2020

Routledge is an imprint of the Taylor & Francis Group, an informa business

British Library Cataloguing-in-Publication Data
A catalogue record for this book is available from the British Library

Library of Congress Cataloging-in-Publication Data
Names: Decker, Samuel, 1990- editor. | Elsner, Wolfram, editor. | Flechtner, Svenja, 1985- editor.
Title: Advancing pluralism in teaching economics : international perspectives on a textbook science / edited by Samuel Decker, Wolfram Elsner and Svenja Flechtner.
Description: 1 Edition. | New York : Routledge, 2019. | Series: Routledge advances in heterodox economics | Includes bibliographical references and index.
Identifiers: LCCN 2018019545 (print) | LCCN 2018035211 (ebook) | ISBN 9781315177809 (Ebook) | ISBN 9781138037625 (hardback : alk. paper)
Subjects: LCSH: Economics–Philosophy. | Pluralism.
Classification: LCC HB71 (ebook) | LCC HB71 .A237 2019 (print) | DDC 330.0071–dc23
LC record available at https://lccn.loc.gov/2018019545

ISBN 13: 978-0-367-58690-4 (pbk)
ISBN 13: 978-1-138-03762-5 (hbk)

Typeset in Bembo
by Integra Software Services Pvt. Ltd.

Contents

Contributors

Frank Beckenbach is Professor of Environmental and Behavioural Economics at the Economics Department of the University of Kassel, Germany.

Sudipta Bhattacharyya is Professor of Economics at the Department of Economics and Politics at the Visva-Bharati University in Santiniketan in West Bengal, India.

Ian Coelho de Souza Almeida is a PhD candidate in Economics at the Federal University of Minas Gerais, Brazil.

Shuanping Dai is Junior Professor at the Institute for East Asian Studies and Mercator School of Management at the University of Duisburg-Essen, Germany.

John Davis is Professor Emeritus of Economics at Marquette University and at the University of Amsterdam.

Samuel Decker graduated in political economy at the Berlin School of Economics and Law and is engaged in the *Netzwerk Plurale Ökonomik* (German-speaking Network for Pluralist Economics).

Sheila Dow is Emeritus Professor of Economics, University of Stirling, UK, and Adjunct Professor of Economics, University of Victoria, Canada.

Wolfram Elsner is Professor of Economics (retired) at *iino – Institute for Institutional and Innovation Economics*, University of Bremen, Germany. He was EAEPE-President from 2012–2014 and 2014–2016 and is managing editor of the *Forum for Social Economics*.

Ben Fine is Professor of Economics at the School of Oriental and African Studies, University of London, holding honorary positions at the Universities of Johannesburg (Senior Research Fellow attached to the South African Research Chair in Social Change) and Rhodes University (Visiting Professor, Institute of Social and Economic Research).

Svenja Flechtner is Assistant Professor of Pluralist Economics at University of Siegen, Germany.

Rafael Galvão de Almeida is a PhD candidate in Economics at the Federal University of Minas Gerais, Brazil.

Silja Graupe is Professor of Economics and Philosophy and Vice President of Cusanus Hochschule in Bernkastel-Kues, Germany, an innovative university she co-founded in 2014 dedicated to promoting creativity and social responsibility.

Jakob Kapeller is a philosopher, who has accidentally become an economist. He is currently acting as the head of the Institute for Comprehensive Analysis of the Economy (ICAE) and a member of the Department of Economics, both located at Johannes Kepler University Linz, Austria.

Philipp Kortendiek is a student of social sciences education and French language education at the University of Duisburg-Essen, Germany.

Jens Maesse is Assistant Professor at the Institute of Sociology, Justus-Liebig University of Giessen, Germany.

Astrid Schwabe is an Assistant Professor of public history and history didactics at Europa Universität Flensburg, Germany.

Till van Treeck is Professor of Socio-Economics and managing director of the Institute of Socio-Economics at the University of Duisburg-Essen, Germany.

Janina Urban is currently a researcher at the Institute for Societal Development in the field of New Economic Thinking in Duesseldorf, Germany.

Hadrat Yusif is a Senior Lecturer in the Department of Economics at the Kwame Nkrumah University of Science and Technology, Kumasi, Ghana.

Referees

The editors wish to thank the following who contributed to the volume as anonymous reviewers of individual chapters.

Emrah **Aydinonat**
Bruno de **Conti**
Peter **Dorman**
Ben **Fine**
Alan **Freeman**
Claudius **Gräbner**
Carsten **Herrmann-Pillath**
Steve **Keen**
Jan **Priewe**
Manuel Ramon **Souza**
John P. **Watkins**
Jakob **Kapeller**
Caroline **Ruiner**
Leonhard **Dobusch**

Economics and its teaching at a critical juncture

Introduction

Samuel Decker, Wolfram Elsner and Svenja Flechtner

1. Crisis and the changing face of the economics mainstream – but not in teaching

It has become a widespread statement that the financial crisis of 2007/2008 marked a turning point in the external and internal assessment of the state of the economics discipline. And indeed – the critique of the dominant mainstream of economics that till then was a concern of specialised and marginalised critical, heterodox circles within the discipline, became an issue of public interest. The nagging question of the Queen of England, why "no one saw it coming", i.e. why the "queen of social sciences" could not anticipate, recognise, and characterise the most severe financial and economic crisis since 1929, and the role of mainstream economic theory, models, and policy advice in causing the crisis in the first place, exposed the discipline to an unprecedented degree of criticism (e.g. Bertocco 2017; Chun 2017; Payson 2017).

A scientific discipline the ruling mainstream of which was incapable of seeing "it" coming and even acknowledging it, when it was already there, must have a problem with its higher education and teaching as well. As the critical economics student movement that constituted itself as an international initiative stated: "It is not only the world economy that is in crisis", their public letter, signed by more than 60 student initiatives from more than 30 countries in 2014 concluded, the "*teaching of economics is in crisis, too*" (ISIPE 2014, emphasis added).

Besides this new and unprecedented cooperation among critical economics students and the cooperation between that new "students movement" and long-standing dissenting lecturers, "heterodox" academic networks and associations, in their quest for a pluralist teaching, even high-rank policy-makers (e.g. Merkel 2014; Blanchard et al. 2010), top central bank managers (e.g. A. Haldane of BoE in Marriner 2017), and prominent mainstream economists (e.g. Romer 2016) have joined the criticism of the mainstream, its textbook culture, and its teaching practice.

This might indicate that the very functionality of economics for the political and economic system in general and its higher-education system in particular has come into question. However, the intensity of this criticism (from the rapidly growing literature on pluralism in economics, e.g. Garnett et al. 2010; Courvisanos et al. 2016), with the resonance even within the mainstream and among broad areas of practitioners (e.g. Mason 2016), should not lead to the conclusion that some pluralism in economics is already guaranteed in any way – or even underway.

While some argue that mainstream economics has made substantial steps towards pluralism in terms of research, theorising, modeling, and methodologies (e.g. Colander 2000; Colander et al. 2011; Davis 2008; Colander 2010; Fontana 2014; Fontana 2017), other observers have pointed out that this applies to ever more specialising, fragmentising, diversifying, and complexity-oriented research and methodologies, but certainly does not apply to the largely standardised (if not petrified) and orthodox higher mass teaching and textbook writing (e.g. Colander 2015; Elsner and Lee 2010; Elsner 2013, 2017), and that thus non-mainstream approaches still have stayed marginalised particularly in teaching (e.g. Abramovitz et al. 1992; Gechert et al. 2017; Vallet 2017). Even if some innovative teaching concepts and methodologies have entered discussion, the day-to-day practice of economics teaching has not essentially altered. In view of teaching contents and methods, economics has certainly not moved towards a pluralist discipline that broadens cognition and insights and enables students, non-ideological practitioners, and the general public, or even well-meaning policy-makers, to solve the complex and critical challenges today's and future societies are facing.

The remarkable persistence of mainstream economics in everything, except perhaps research and methods, does not imply that the financial crisis had no impact at all on the discipline. However, whether we may look back one day on that as a turning point for the better, a pluralist teaching in this case will depend on how successfully alternative approaches in teaching can be built, institutionalised, and interconnected in a long-term transformative project. As the dust seem to have settled after the crisis and its Great Recession, the current phase and the discussions, institutions, and alliances that emerged from it, might turn out to be critical in shaping the long-term development of the discipline. Ten years after the crash, economics teaching seems to be at a critical juncture.

2. Challenges for pluralist teaching – and the content of this volume

Though need and demand for a pluralist transformation of higher education in economics appear to be more broadly established today than before, such transformation faces immense challenges. Three key challenges of teaching pluralist economics appear to have to be addressed in order to generate a more favourable terrain for a pluralist economics teaching:

- first, to move from the mere need and articulated demand for pluralism in economics to a more concrete and real-world scientific programme

- second, to overcome the dominance of a few universities and countries in the Global North in shaping the discipline and imposing its mainstream's unified perspective as a one-size-fits-all device on (nearly) a global scale
- third, to critically reflect upon and develop alternatives to the highly standardised and normalised system of economics textbooks and to develop and establish alternative networks and platforms for teaching contents.

The present volume addresses these challenges in three parts.

The first part of the book – *Why Pluralism is important for (teaching) a serious Social Science: Foundations* – deals with the task of developing a robust *meta-theoretical* conceptualisation of pluralism and pluralist teaching, given the vague and undetermined nature of the concept of pluralism at first sight.

Sheila Dow (Pluralist economics: Is it scientific?) analyses and debunks the objection frequently put forward that a pluralist discipline diminishes scientific standards and develops her concept of a "structured pluralism". In the second chapter, *Frank Beckenbach* (Monism in modern science and competitive pluralism) deciphers modern science as a social subsystem loosely coupled to the rest of society and sketches the way in which monistic economics was generated within this subsystem during and after WWII. This is contrasted with the view that monism in economics has eroded recently and a dominant orthodoxy would no longer exist. A necessity for, and the modes of pluralism are concluded from this and the basic features of a heterodox alternative are outlined and applied to teaching. Further, *Jakob Kapeller* (Pluralism in economics – Epistemological rationales and pedagogical implementation) dissents with the alleged diversity of mainstream economics and develops an epistemological and pedagogical foundation for pluralism in economics. He provides concrete suggestions for organising pluralist economic teaching. *Ben Fine* (In and against orthodoxy: Teaching economics in the neoliberal era) develops insights into his lifelong experience of teaching non-mainstream approaches in a faculty environment that is dominated by mainstream economics. He addresses crucial issues regarding the relation between mainstream and non-mainstream approaches in teaching economics and elaborates "how presentation of the mainstream can be the critical starting point for both exposing its deficiencies and opening the way for alternatives". *Astrid Schwabe* (An Outsider's Perspective: What can economics teaching learn from history didactics?), finally, lays out the concepts of "historical consciousness", "historical culture" and "learning history", and derives commonly held criteria for history education. These criteria are shown to support critical historical thinking based on the different interpretations of the past, which in turn are "central for conveying critical thinking in students".

Taken together, these contributions offer mainly meta-theoretical but also some pedagogical answers to the question of how pluralist economics is indispensable for teaching a serious social science, which then may contribute to societal learning, cognition, and problem-solving.

The second part – *International Perspectives on Pluralist Teaching* – intends to move away from the one-sided, western-centric viewpoint that characterises both mainstream economics and the economics teaching debates. Note that the formation of mainstream economics has been intrinsically linked to the emergence of the scientific hegemony of the USA at the beginning of the 20th century as well as to "the standardizing power of a few elite US universities" (Heise 2016, 4; also, e.g. Milonakis 2017; Arnsperger and Varoufakis 2006; O'Boyle and McDonough 2017; Reinert et al. 2016). The modern division of labour among the social sciences and the development of their respective assigned perspectives and biases during the 20th century have originated from a few universities and countries in the Global North. Reclaiming a true pluralist and transdisciplinary economic science therefore may have to take the form of a decentralisation and internationalisation of creating and disseminating economic knowledge.

Rafael Galvão de Almeida and *Ian Coelho de Souza Almeida* (Issues in Teaching of Economics and Pluralism in Brazil) offer an insight into teaching economics in Brazil, where pluralism in economics is no abstract demand, but has in parts already become reality. History of Economic Thought has been a mandatory teaching field in Brazil, and the official Brazilian journal ranking system gives a greater weight to heterodox journals. Both factors support a plural environment. The authors have conducted a survey among professors of economics and show that they see a necessity of rethinking the teaching of economics, while preserving pluralism. In considerable contrast to that, *Sudipta Bhattacharyya* (Economics Education through India's Problematic Trajectory from Pluralism to Neo-Liberalism and to "Hindutva") draws a worrying picture of the development of economics teaching in India in recent years. The trend towards neo-classicism and neoliberalism that compromises teaching in India since the 1990s has accelerated recently under far-right governments. In China, on the other hand, pluralism is not achieved yet with a general coexistence of different schools, as *Shuanping Dai* (China's Idiosyncratic Economics: An Emerging Unknown Monism Driven by Pluralism) explains, but so far two paradigms (neoliberal neoclassicism and Marxist political economy) are fighting for hegemony in economics, which today, however, is virtually dominated, in the Chinese universities, by US-trained neoliberal neoclassicists. But future plural interaction seems to have some chance under the recent political environment that requires operationalisation and application of the real-world criterion of "Chinese characteristics", which might tend to discard "one-size-fits-all" unified neoliberal-neoclassical prescriptions for academia, and economic research and teaching in particular. In a similar vein, the perspective provided by *Hadrat Yusif* (The need for an independent perspective: Teaching economics in Ghana) states that the conflict in teaching economics in Ghana is not one between one unified dominant mainstream paradigm vs. pluralism, but between concepts that are applicable in the African context and those that are not. *Philipp Kortendiek* and *Till van Treeck* (Teaching the euro crisis: What do students in Germany and France learn about the causes of Europe's economic crisis?), finally, complement the previous contributions in a twofold way: first, they concentrate on economic teaching in schools – an issue that is (mistakenly) largely ignored so far by the pluralism debates in economics; second, they exemplify that different perspectives in teaching, and in this case, divergent economic positions towards the eurozone, do exist even between countries and regions in the Global North.

Due to the relatively stable and quasi-monopolised orthodox canon of a few million-selling textbooks and their central role in reproducing the mainstream pattern, economics is often described as a canonical "textbook science". The dual challenge for the realisation of pluralism then consists in making the standardising role of the rigid and simplistic textbook system visible, and on the other to develop alternative textbooks, as well as new networks and platforms for teaching plural contents. This defines the issues of Part III, *Economics Textbooks: Failures and New Pathways.*

Silja Graupe ("Waging the War of Ideas": Economics as a Textbook Science and Its Possible Influence on Human Minds) analyses mainstream textbooks and characterises them as simplistic, ideology-laden and often purely rhetorical free-market propaganda. *Jens Maesse* (The schoolmaster's voice in the field of economics: How professional identities are formed by textbook culture discourses) analyses the "textbook culture" in economics as a sociological phenomenon of a scientific community. *Wolfram Elsner* (Why textbooks must, and how they can change into a complex real-world economics: The example of a fundamentally new complexity-economics micro-textbook) questions David Colander's recent thesis that economics textbooks must, but will not change, since the self-reproduction of the mainstream and its teaching are firmly institutionalised and petrified. Elsner provides the example of two recent "post-2008" textbooks (Elsner 2012; Elsner et al. 2015), their radically alternative, institutional, evolutionary and complexity perspectives (along with the orthodox view), and explains the ways how they could be realised, particularly the latter one that appeared in a top "conservative" publishing house, which has not previously been known for publishing heterodox textbooks. *Janina Urban* (What can we learn from school economics education?) concludes this part by presenting the *Beutelsbacher consensus* which provides three criteria that any published teaching material – and in particular, textbooks – for school education in Germany must respect. The critical teaching of economics disciplines, the prevailing textbook culture of which remains in stark contrast to these criteria, could certainly benefit in terms of inviting students to evaluate and ponder different approaches to economic problems.

3. Pluralism, the mode of faster and broader cognition and insight – also in teaching and learning

There certainly exist more issues than those discussed above which prevent a transformation of economic thought and teaching practice and that would deserve our attention. We just may mention, for instance, the structures of publishing that tend to favour orthodoxy (Kapeller 2010; D'Ippoliti 2017), the entanglement between business journalism and orthodoxy, and the orthodox entrenchment of political consulting through the exclusion of other perspectives by leading neoliberal governments (e.g. Rodrik 2015; Turchin 2017).

The central idea behind the present volume and the forthcoming follow-up volume "*Principles and Pluralist Approaches in Teaching Economics. Towards a Transformative Science*" is that teaching represents both one of the least developed realms of the discipline and one of the most crucial fields of leveraging the transformation towards pluralism. Dismissing tens of thousands of young academically trained economists and business people worldwide each year from academia, often with a simplistic world view in mind and no sufficient understanding of complex structures, evolutionary process, lasting tensions, historical time, unintended consequences, persistent adverse mechanisms and resulting structures, unpredictability of system motions, non-linearities, path-dependence, emerging idiosyncratic dynamic system properties, or the relevance of strategies in populations, is a true tragedy of this particular discipline. The student initiatives for pluralism are of course right in targeting the form and content of teaching as the primary grievance in economics.

To be sure, the contributions in this volume just present and continue an ongoing debate rather than a ready-made formula to implement pluralist teaching. We are standing on the shoulders of many others who have already paved ways of critical and pluralist teaching up to this point (e.g. Mearman 2007; Mearman 2014; Fullbrook (ed.) 2008; Reardon (ed.) 2009; Lee 2010; Schneider and Underwood (eds.) 2013). As we will point out in the conclusion, pluralism in economics is a long-term transformative project with theoretical and methodological issues going on and difficult tasks of implementation ahead – and without any guarantee of success. In this process, there should not dominate one specific understanding of pluralism and no blindness regarding the weaknesses and open questions of the concept itself. Pluralism should be understood as a critical questioning method and process – also towards itself.

For instance, we included two contributions that mark contrary positions in the debate. The comment by *John Davis* (Explaining difference and diversity in an increasingly complex economics) recapitulates the position in favour of some differentiation, diversification, and fragmentation – and in parts some pluralism arising – of the mainstream. *Samuel Decker* (Towards a critical and transdisciplinary economic science?) in contrast rejects the understanding that mainstream economics is on a road to some pluralism and rather examines the capacities of a more fundamentally pluralist economics to challenge a dominating orthodoxy.

With the contributions in this volume, we intend to make methodological, conceptual, and practical knowledge and expertise available that will be needed in order to transform economics teaching and in this way advance pluralism as well as broader and faster cognition and insights in economics. Promoting a plurality of theoretical and methodological approaches in economics research is not sufficient, since economic thought has been under public critique and obviously is overdue for change already. What is needed is an intensified discussion about how an economics education can educate graduates of economics that are able to deal with the manifold challenges of the 21st century, and about the elaboration of ideas, initiatives, institutions, and practical tools and ways of teaching that pave the way for those practical challenges. In this way, the present volume may be seen as a considerable step forward over the current critical pluralism literature.

Acknowledgments

We are thankful to our co-organisers and the funders of the conference "Teaching Economics in the 21st Century", from which this volume emerged. The conference took place at the Berlin School of Law and Economics on 26–28 November 2015. It was jointly organised by the Institute for International Political Economy (IPE), Forschungsstelle für wissenschaftsbasierte gesellschaftliche Weiterentwicklung (FGW), Netzwerk Plurale Ökonomik, the World Economics Association (WEA), the European Association for Evolutionary Political Economy (EAEPE), Arbeitskreis Politische Ökonomie (AK PolÖk), the Research Network Macroeconomics and Macroeconomic Policies (FMM) and Vereinigung für Ökologische Ökonomie (VÖÖ).

References

Abramovitz, M. et al. (1992): 'Plea for a Pluralist and Rigorous Economics', *American Economic Review* 82(2), XXXV.

Arnsperger, C. and Varoufakis, Y. (2006): 'What Is Neoclassical Economics? the Three Axioms Responsible for Its Theoretical Oeuvre, Practical Irrelevance And, Thus, Discursive Power', *Post-Autistic Economic Review* 38, 2–12.

Bertocco, G. (2017): *Crisis and the Failure of Economic Theory. The Responsibility of Economists for the Great Recession*. Cheltenham, UK: Edward Elgar.

Blanchard, O., Dell'Ariccia, G. and Mauro, P. (2010): 'Rethinking Macroeconomic Policy', *IMF Staff Position Note* SPN/10/03. Available at https://www.imf.org/external/pubs/ft/spn/2010/spn1003.pdf, accessed on 31 January 2017.

Chun, C.W. (2017): *The Discourses of Capitalism. Everyday Economists and the Production of Common Sense*. London: Routledge.

Colander, D. (2000): 'The Death of Neoclassical Economics', *Journal of the History of Economic Thought* 22(2), 127–143.

Colander, D. (2010): 'Moving beyond the Rhetoric of Pluralism. Suggestions for an 'Inside-The-Mainstream' Heterodoxy', in Garnett Jr., R.F., Olsen, E.K. and Starr, M. (eds): *Economic Pluralism*, 36–47. New York: Routledge.

Colander, D. (2015): 'Why Economics Textbooks Should, but Don't, and Won't Change', *European Journal of Economics and Economic Policy: Intervention* 12(2), 229–235.

Colander, D., Holt, R. and Rosser, J.B. (2011): 'The Complexity Era in Economics', *Review of Political Economy* 23(3), 357–369.

Courvisanos, J., Doughney, J. and Millmow, A. (2016): *Reclaiming Pluralism in Economics*. Abingdon, UK: Taylor & Francis.

D'Ippoliti, C. (2017): "Many-Citedness': Citations Measure More than Just Scientific Impact', Institute for New Economic Thinking *Working Paper* No. 57.

Davis, J.B. (2008): 'The Turn in Recent Economics and Return of Orthodoxy', *Cambridge Journal of Economics* 32(3), 349–366.

Elsner, W. (2012): *Microeconomics of Interactive Economies. Evolutionary, Institutional, and Complexity Perspectives. A 'Non-Toxic' Intermediate Textbook*. Cheltenham, UK: Elgar.

Elsner, W. (2013): 'State and Future of the 'Citadel' and of the Heterodoxies in Economics: Challenges and Dangers, Convergences and Cooperation', *European Journal of Economics and Economic Policies: Intervention* 10(3), 286–298.

Elsner, W. (2017): 'Complexity Economics as Heterodoxy. Theory and Policy', *Journal of Economic Issues* 51(4), 939–978.

Elsner, W., Heinrich, T. and Schwardt, H. (2015): *Microeconomics ofonomies. Evolutionary, Institutional, Neoclassical, and Complexity Perspectives*. Oxford: Elsevier/Academic Press.

Elsner, W. and Lee, F.S. (2010): Editors' Introduction to 'Evaluating Economic Research in a Contested Discipline. Rankings, Pluralism, and the Future of Heterodox Economics', *Studies in Economic Reform and Social Justice*, Repr. of a Special Issue of *The American Journal of Economics and Sociology* 69(5), 1–12.

Fontana, M. (2014): 'Pluralism(s) in Economics: Lessons from Complexity and Innovation', *Journal of Evolutionary Economics* 24(1), 189–204.

Fontana, M. (2017): 'Just Another Niche in the Wall? How Specialization Is Changing the Face of Mainstream Economics', *Cambridge Journal of Economics*. doi:10.1093/cje/bex003

Fullbrook, E. (ed). (2008): *Pluralist Economics*. London, New York: Zed.

Garnett Jr., R.F., Olsen, E.K. and Starr, M. (2010) (eds): *Economic Pluralism*. New York and Abingdon: Routledge.

Gechert, S., Niechoj, T., Stockhammer, E., Truger, A. and Watt, A. (2017): 'Towards Pluralism in Macroeconomics? 20th Anniversary Conference of the FMM Research Network', *European Journal of Economics and Economic Policy* 14(2), 125–130.

Heise, A. (2016): 'Pluralism in Economics. Inquiries into a Daedalean Concept', Zentrum für Ökonomische und Soziologische Studien, *Discussion Papers* No. 51. Available at https://www.econstor.eu/bitstream/10419/141825/1/860401677.pdf, accessed on 1 February 2017.

ISIPE International Student Initiative for Pluralism in Economics (2014): 'An International Student Call for Pluralism in Economics', May 5 2014. Available at http://www.isipe.net/, accessed on 1 February 2017.

Kapeller, J. (2010): 'Citation Metrics: Serious Drawbacks, Perverse Incentives, and Strategic Options for Heterodox Economics', *American Journal of Economics and Sociology* 69(5), 1376–1408.

Lee, F.S. (2010): 'A Heterodox Teaching of Neoclassical Microeconomic Theory', *International Journal of Pluralism and Economics Education* 1(3), 203–235.

Marriner, K. (2017): 'Bank of England Says Economists in 'Crisis' after Crash and Brexit', *money marketing*, 6 January 2017. Available at https://www.moneymarketing.co.uk/bank-england-says-economists-crisis-crash-brexit/, accessed on 20 February 2018.

Mason, J.W. (2016): 'When We Turn to Concrete Economic Questions, There Isn't Really a 'Mainstream' at All', *Evonomics*, 26 July 2015. Available at http://evonomics.com/economist-mason-turn-concrete-economic-questions-isnt-really-mainstream/, accessed on 20 February 2018.

Mearman, A. (2007): 'Teaching Heterodox Economics Concepts', The Economics Network (ed), *The Handbook for Economics Lecturers.* Available at https://www.economicsnetwork.ac.uk/handbook/printable/heterodox.pdf, accessed on 20 February 2018.

Mearman, A. (2014): 'Teaching Political Economy', in Schroeder, S.K. and Chester, L. (eds): *Challenging the Orthodoxy*, 39–56. Berlin: Springer.

Merkel, A. (2014): Rede Von Frau Bundeskanzlerin Merkel Zum 5. Treffen Der Nobelpreisträger. Available at http://www.bundesregierung.de/Content/DE/Rede/2014/08/2014-08-20-lindau.html, accessed on 2 February 2017.

Milonakis, D. (2017): 'Formalising Economics: Social Change, Values, Mechanics and Mathematics in Economic Discourse', *Cambridge Journal of Economics* 41(5), 1367–1390.

O'Boyle, B. and McDonough, T. (2017): 'Bourgeois Ideology and Mathematical Economics – A Reply to Tony Lawson', *Economic Thought* 6(1), 16–34.

Payson, S. (2017): *How Economics Professors Can Stop Failing Us. The Discipline at the Crossroads.* London: Lexington.

Reardon, J. (ed). (2009): *Handbook of Pluralist Economics Education.* London: Routledge.

Reinert, E.S., Ghosh, J. and Kattel, R. (eds). (2016): *Handbook of Alternative Theories of Economic Development.* Cheltenham, UK: Edward Elgar.

Rodrik, D. (2015): *Economics Rules: The Rights and Wrongs of the Dismal Science.* New York: Norton.

Romer, P. (2016): 'The Trouble with Macroeconomics', Talk delivered on 5 January 2016 as the Commons Memorial Lecture of the Omicron Delta Epsilon Society. Available at https://paulromer.net/wp-content/uploads/2016/09/WP-Trouble.pdf, accessed on 1 September 2017.

Schneider, G. and Underwood, D. (2013): Introduction to '*Teaching Social Economics*', Special Issue, *Forum for Social Economics* 42(1), 1-4.

Turchin, P. (2017): 'What Economics Models Really Say. A Review of Economics Rules: The Rights and Wrongs of the Dismal Science by Dani Rodrik (Norton, 2015)', *Cliodynamics* 8, 80–84.

Vallet, G. (2017): 'Rethinking Economics for a Pluralist Approach', in Rochon, L.-P. and Rossi, S. (eds): *A Modern Guide to Rethinking Economics*, 50–68. Aldershot, UK: Elgar.

Part I

Why pluralism is important for (teaching) a serious social science

Foundations

1 Pluralist economics

Is it scientific?

Sheila Dow

1. Introduction

The purpose of this chapter is to address any nagging doubt that supporting pluralism in economics makes it unscientific. By science I mean a systematic procedure for establishing reliable knowledge, involving evidence-based enquiry and critical thinking.[1] Can pluralism deliver reliable knowledge? What I will argue is that it is inevitable that different ideas will co-exist in economics, not just about theory, but also as to what constitutes reliable knowledge, i.e. different theories of understanding: different approaches understand the evidence of experience differently, apply different types of logic to it and put different emphases on the purpose of the exercise being prediction or explanation. If this is the case, then the search for reliable knowledge inevitably entails plurality. *Support* for such a plurality – pluralism – arises from two main sources. One is that it is helpful to have a variety ofanalyses to illuminate different aspects of a complex, evolving reality, making economics at a disciplinary level more reliable. The other is the need for economists to be able to recognise the limitations of their chosen approach relative to alternatives, and to explain and defend that approach in debate, making economics within each approach more reliable. As a corollary, restriction of economics to one approach is a less reliable basis for knowledge of the economy.

There is a long tradition of economists aspiring to science on a par with the physical sciences, an aspiration apparently met by the inclusion of economics in the Nobel prize system. Nobel prizes for the physical sciences are awarded for breakthrough discoveries which open up new possibilities for enquiry or change the way scientists think about their subject. But the context is one of disciplines which are viewed as having a shared understanding of the range of possibilities at any point in time and a shared understanding of their subject. Even when there is revolutionary change, either a new paradigm replaces the old one, or the old one is absorbed into a new synthetic paradigm. Thomas Kuhn's (1970[1962]) theory of revolutions in the physical sciences involved one dominant paradigm succeeding another.

Kuhn (1970[1962]) argued that each paradigm has its own view as to what constitutes reliable knowledge, i.e. what constitutes science. Later Kuhn (1999) explained the flash of insight he experienced as a graduate student which set him off on this path. He had been taught that Aristotle had been wrongheaded on astronomical subjects. But Kuhn tried to read Aristotle himself from the author's perspective and discovered new realms of meaning which revealed Aristotle's wisdom in his own context. Kuhn used this insight to explain why each succeeding dominant paradigm is incommensurate with the previous one, i.e. there is insufficient common ground by which to compare them directly.

Applying Kuhn's ideas to economics has always been controversial, not least because of differences in interpretation. For example Blaug (1992, chap. 2) sees Kuhn's absence of over-riding criteria for good science as unacceptably relativistic, undermining the methodological monism which Blaug supports. On the other hand Fullbrook (2001) argues that this relativism is in fact anti-pluralistic in protecting the mainstream from challenge from alternative paradigms. Indeed economics does not seem to fit Kuhn's pattern of a succession of dominant paradigms, but rather the persistence of a dominant paradigm even in the face of the type of anomaly which was supposed to spark a revolution. Mainstream economics rather has adapted (within its own framework) in order to be persuasive that it is addressing anomalies as they arise. This strategy has been successful in large part because of the rhetorical success of presenting itself as the most scientific approach (see McCloskey 1983). Thus for example Romer (2015, 89) defines science in terms of consensus on 'true' theoretical and empirical statements, while he defines insistence on differences within economics as (unscientific) politics.

But we can in fact use Kuhn's insight to understand the *co-existence* of incommensurate paradigms in economics. Kuhn was always reluctant to discuss the social sciences, considering them immature (implying that consolidation into a single dominant paradigm would only come with maturity). But now even the prospect of unified physical sciences has been questioned. Thus Cartwright (1999, 1) characterises both physics and economics as a 'patchwork'. There is good reason then to expect the co-existence of incommensurate paradigms as the norm rather than a transitional state. In what follows, we explore why this is so and consider different approaches to understanding reliable knowledge; this forms the basis for a pluralist position on economics. We then consider what this pluralism entails for generating and using reliable knowledge, i.e. for economic research, for economic policy making and for teaching economics. In the process we distinguish between methodological pluralism (arguing for the co-existence of several approaches), pluralist methodology (arguing for the use of a range of different methods) and theoretical pluralism (arguing for a range of theories, whether or not within a single approach or employing a single method).

2. Establishing reliable knowledge: different paradigms

The thinking in economic methodology which dominated up to the 1970s borrowed from the philosophy of science the idea of drawing a distinction between science and non-science. Central to this philosophy was the notion of empirical testing, such that only those theories which were testable were to be regarded as scientific, everything else being unscientific. Further, testing would identify the best theories. Popper (1959) argued that simply confirming theories with evidence did not produce reliable knowledge – only showing that a proposition was falsified allowed any definitive conclusions. Blaug (1992) was influential in promoting this approach within economics. Theories would be derived by means of applying deductivist (classical) logic to assumptions which were taken to be true. They would then be tested against the evidence, seeking to identify any falsification, and those theories which performed best would be the ones regarded as most reliable. This is a monist methodological approach: there is conventional agreement about the best methodology.

But while this approach served the purpose of developing and presenting economics as a science on a par with the physical sciences,[2] the philosophy of science was moving on from logical positivism. Caldwell (1982) details how the logistical problems with empirical testing made logical positivism unworkable. In particular, according to the Duhem-Quine problem, if evidence contradicts a conclusion based on theory, it is impossible to pin down exactly what accounts for the failure and thus what needs to be changed, ranging from particular datasets to the precise mathematical formulation of theory. Further, it was shown to be impossible to rid economic methodology of (untestable) metaphysical content (Boland 1997, 80–82).

Nevertheless mainstream economics continued to espouse some form of logical positivism and the corresponding general approach to methodology. Its merits are taken for granted and only given explicit expression, if at all, in introductory textbooks. Mankiw and Taylor's (2006) textbook is unusual now in making their methodological approach explicit. They offer a clear statement of logical positivism in a way which used to be more commonly found in the introductions to textbooks. They give their purpose as teaching students to 'think like an economist' (Mankiw and Taylor 2006, 19–21). They explicitly classify economics as a science on a par with the physical sciences in that they employ 'the scientific method' of developing theories on the basis of simplifying assumptions and testing them. There are of course debates within econometrics as to different methods of empirical testing, and the sources of evidence have widened in recent years to include survey evidence and the results of experiments. But the methodological approach still stands, based on a logical positivist philosophy of science, distinguishing between science and non-science.

Science according to Mankiw and Taylor is 'dispassionate', echoing the prevalent mainstream view that the economic researcher engages in positive science, but only then do policy makers derive normative conclusions by applying their separate value systems. Further science, according to this view, is cumulative, becoming more robust the more theory is developed and the more datasets are used for testing. It is now widely understood that mainstream economics actually defines the subject of economics according to this methodology, i.e. according to logical positivist principles of what constitutes reliable knowledge. As Becker (1976, 5) put it: 'what distinguishes economics as a discipline from other disciplines in the social sciences is not the subject matter but its approach'. This has allowed a form of imperialism whereby economics extends into the traditional subject matter of other disciplines by applying the mainstream economic method. Lazear (2000) puts it as follows:

> Economics is not only a social science, it is a genuine science. Like the physical sciences, economics uses a methodology that produces refutable implications and tests these implications using solid statistical techniques. In particular, economics stresses three factors that distinguish it from other social sciences. Economists use the construct of rational individuals who engage in maximising behavior. Economic models adhere strictly to the importance of equilibrium as part of any theory. Finally, a focus on efficiency leads economists to ask questions that other social sciences ignore. These ingredients have allowed economics to invade intellectual territory that was previously deemed to be outside the discipline's realm.
>
> Lazear (2000)

Because mainstream economics is presented as a technical, positivist exercise, it has increasingly protected itself from popular challenge. This was something which Adam Smith associated with the physical sciences rather than the social sciences. He noted that the physical sciences were protected from public challenge:

> Natural philosophers, in their independency upon the public opinion, approach nearly to mathematicians, and, in their judgments concerning the merit of their own discoveries and observations, enjoy some degree of the same security and tranquillity.
>
> Smith (1976[1759], III.2.20)

But moral philosophy (from which political economy was emerging) was different:

> A system of natural philosophy may appear very plausible, and be for a long time very generally received in the world, and yet have no foundation in nature, nor any sort of resemblance to the truth ... But it is otherwise with systems of moral philosophy and an author who pretends to account for the origin of our moral sentiments, cannot deceive us so grossly, nor depart so very far from all resemblance to the truth.
>
> Smith (1976[1759], VII.ii.4.14)

As mainstream economics became synonymous with the deductive mathematical method, in an effort to become more 'scientific', the scope for departing from resemblance to the truth increased. Indeed, as Earle et al. (2016) argue, the combination of the increasing power of economics in political argument with its presentation as a specialist technical discipline has created what they call an econocracy: something which discourages public engagement. But the evident failings of mainstream economics to predict the recent crisis or to prevent much of its social impact have encouraged more forceful challenges within public discourse. This has encouraged other approaches to reliable knowledge in economics.

It has been a persistent theme in critiques of mainstream methodology to challenge the validity of the assumptions on which the deductivist structure is built (the assumptions of rational, fully-informed choice by atomistic agents). But this has become a major research programme within New Keynesian economics which has gained widespread attention. Departures from these assumptions are explored: behavioural biases, cognitive limitations, asymmetric information and other-regarding behaviour. However this approach has simply refined the assumptions, certainly in the direction of greater realism, but still with rational economic man as the benchmark. Agents are still depicted as constrained optimisers, but facing more complex constraints. Logical positivism and the empirical testing of deductivist theory still prevail. What Colander (2000) has identified as a general pluralist development within mainstream economics is in fact theoretical pluralism, not methodological pluralism.

There have been more fundamental critiques which conclude that even modified rational optimising assumptions are far from being self-evident and are in fact false. All assumptions by definition involve some departure from reality, but the argument is that rational economic man is not a simplification of real individuals but rather a fiction. By implication any conclusions derived deductively from such assumptions are unreliable. A logical positivist would argue that the proof was in the empirical testing. In fact Popper was happy to accept that economics made assumptions which had not been empirically supported, such that falsification was limited to the propositions deduced from them. But even this has invited further critique. First, the normal practice is to seek *confirmation* from the data, which is less reliable than seeking falsification. Second, it is long established that any test is applied to a complex structure of assumptions and formulations which make it impossible to identify what has been falsified if the evidence contradicts the hypothesis (the 'Duhem-Quine' problem discussed above).

But third, there has been a critique of the whole notion of 'facts' independent of theory at one level or, at another level, what Searle (1995) calls the 'deep background' of the researcher at another level. This social and individual background influences, at a subconscious level and from an early age, how we observe and interpret the real world. Different approaches to reliable knowledge in economics thus start from different understandings of the subject matter (different ontologies). Thus for example the state of unemployment is regarded variously within different communities in economics as damaging dignity, reducing income, encouraging dependency on the state, or as voluntary leisure, depending on how the commentator understands the world. A further example is money which is variously regarded as a technical input into exchange, a subjective perception of liquidity, and as a social relation. Boland (1997, chap. 5) criticises the mainstream strategy of treating metaphysical assumptions (like the maximisation hypothesis) as if they were tautologies, i.e. logically true. As metaphysical presuppositions they are part of an economist's 'deep background' which generally is unacknowledged.

Corresponding to different ontologies are different views as to what constitutes a good argument and relevant evidence, i.e. as to what constitutes reliable knowledge (including what the 'facts' are and what is meant by 'facts'). This is what Kuhn (1970[1962], postscript) defined as the disciplinary matrix by which each paradigm is identified. Each paradigmatic community in economics builds up knowledge from the shared world view.[3] Thus for example an Austrian economist focuses on the individual in a competitive environment, particularly the individual entrepreneur, and builds evidence drawn from case studies which focus on the subjective understanding of the situation. Since the focus is on variety of experience at the individual level, there is a limit to the scope for general theorising. Institutionalists, on the other hand, focus on the nature and role of institutions over long periods of time. While human agency plays a part, as well as institutional change, the focus is more on persistence of institutions, drawing on time series data. Post-Keynesians occupy a middle ground between the two in the sense of focusing on the interplay between structure and agency and between the short run and the long run. Mathematical models may be used as partial (i.e. incomplete) arguments contributing to a broader structure of argument where the closures required of models are examined in the relevant context, in combination with use of other methods.

Lawson (2004) argues that non-mainstream schools of thought reflect different interests, which result in different lines of questioning, rather than different ontologies. But it is hard to support the idea that an Austrian and a Marxist, for example, understand the nature of the economy in the same way (Dow 2004b). Nevertheless distinctions between ontologies (or indeed paradigms) are not absolute, but rather useful as categorisations by which to understand the discipline and as a basis for mutual understanding. The boundaries of paradigms are permeable and evolving, and yet they hold enough in common for communication to be effective in promoting scientific activity. Different ontologies and all they entail render paradigms incommensurate; each has its own take (none of which can be regarded as 'correct') on a common reality. But it is this common reality which ensures that incommensurability is not complete.

Heterodox approaches have in common an understanding of the economic system as being open, in the sense that non-deterministically evolving structures, interrelations and creativity mean that there is no scope for universal laws with respect to the economic system. Deductive logic applied to assumptions taken to be 'true' in some sense can only at best analyse those segments of an open system which can, with justification, be regarded as somewhat closed. Any element of openness in the real economy limits the reliability of logical positivism as a basis for knowledge (Dow and Chick 2005); certainly it cannot claim to be the most reliable basis for knowledge. As Lawson (1997) explains, logical positivism is a closed-system epistemology which implies a closed-system ontology, even though many mainstream economists would agree that the economy is in some sense open.[4]

An open-system ontology has profound implications for the possibilities for knowledge, not just of economic agents but also for economists. An open system does not yield categorical knowledge but rather uncertain knowledge. It was one of the major contributions of Keynes (1973a[1921]) to develop a theory of how we (in ordinary life as well as in science) establish grounds for belief under uncertainty, to provide the basis for action. He argued that we aim for reliable knowledge by drawing on a range of types of evidence and argument, including conventional and expert argument.[5] But since the resulting judgements cannot be taken as true, they are subject to discrete shifts, e.g. as expert opinion or conventional opinion shifts. Rather than using classical logic (deduction from a set of axioms) we employ 'human logic', i.e. employing multiple strands of argument, using different methods, and with multiple starting points. We cannot demonstrate our own view to be correct, but rather need to persuade by means of argument which employs reason, evidence and rhetoric. As Keynes (1973b, 470) put it: 'In economics you cannot convict your opponent of error; you can only convince him of it.' Keynes was forceful in argument and argued for meritocracy in government. Nevertheless argument was necessary since inevitably what is regarded as reliable may differ from person to person and from social group to social group.[6]

Indeed, since a closed system of mathematics allows only for very limited argument and application, mainstream economists can be observed to rely on a wide range of methods in what McCloskey (1983) calls their 'unofficial discourse'. In practice, they employ a pluralist methodology. But the 'official discourse' of academic publication still requires that arguments conform to the closed-system norm of mathematical deductivism. As we have seen, this requirement of the official discourse is used to demarcate science from non-science, an important element of the power relations which operate within the discipline. Publication, funding, hiring and firing are increasingly built on metrics with respect to the official discourse. It is a major issue, which pluralism would address, that the operation of this official discourse in parallel to the very different unofficial discourse is not widely recognised within the mainstream, far less justified methodologically (Dow 2007).

But while in institutional, sociological terms one view on the official discourse can be enforced, Kuhn argued that there is no basis in philosophy of science for an overarching authority to establish what constitutes reliable knowledge in any discipline. But the absence of one set of rules for science does not mean no rules, simply a range of sets of rules. Further, since science proceeds on the basis of scientific communities, there is in practice a limit to the number of approaches which can be sustained. Individual scientists must be able to persuade *some* of their fellows of the worth of their research (even if only for publication and hiring purposes), and so need to be able to communicate within one approach or another. The outcome is what I have termed 'structured pluralism' (Dow 2004a), whereby any discipline operates within a fairly limited range of paradigms, according to the number of communities which can be supported. The alternative of complete relativism is, I would argue, not logistically feasible. Pursuing knowledge is a social activity which requires successful (even if imperfect) communication, which would be precluded by the infinite number of paradigms of complete relativism. With a limited number of paradigms, there is scope for *some* understanding across paradigmatic divides as a basis for *some* communication, such that debate is possible.

In economics there is no question that there is a variety of views as to what constitutes reliable knowledge and no ultimate arbiter (supported by philosophy of science) to decide which is best. Each approach to economics thus adopts systematic procedures to produce knowledge which is reliable according to the approach from which it came. We have just argued against the view that only a monist approach is scientific. The question at issue now is whether it is *more* scientific to focus on only one approach which the majority regard as most scientific or to foster a range of approaches, i.e. pluralism.

At a general level, a biological analogy supports the argument that a pluralist approach is more robust, a better basis for building scientific knowledge. Biological diversity is seen as a robust strategy for addressing unforeseen developments within which one strain or another may be more resilient. The same applies to economics: some schools of thought are more attuned to addressing particular circumstances than others. For example, a Post-Keynesian/Minsky approach focuses on the potential for financial and economic instability and was thus well-placed to predict and explain the likelihood of crisis. Economics is more robust if there is a range of approaches on hand with which to address new developments as they arise. But it also provides a range of perspectives by which to understand, analyse and, through policy, change our common economic reality.

We seek below to argue further that pluralism is the best route to reliable knowledge by considering pluralism in turn in the practice of economic research, in policy advice and in education.

3. Being a (methodological) pluralist economist

What does pluralism actually mean for scientific practice? It is important to recognise the different levels at which pluralism can apply. So far we have been discussing methodological pluralism, the argument for a range of methodological approaches to economics. But there is further the question of a pluralist methodology, i.e. one of the range of methodological approaches which advocates using a particular range of methods simultaneously. Mathematical formalism (the requirement that all argument be expressed within a commensurate formal, mathematical system) is one example of a monist methodology, the official discourse of mainstream economics. But other approaches have reasoned grounds for making limited use of formal mathematical models as partial arguments alongside arguments using other methods or for not using formal modelling at all. Models may be used as aids to thought or as the basis for analysing long data series, while empirical work may be addressed to establishing stylised facts rather than predictions. The range of methods used reflects the understanding of the nature of the subject matter and the methodological approach supported by the relevant school of thought.

Within a pluralist methodology, the question arises as to the role of different methods of scientific enquiry and how to combine the outcomes of applying different methods. First, we need to consider the context in which different methods are employed. Within logical positivism there is an apparently straightforward process of deducing propositions from self-evident axioms and testing them against objective data. But neither pure deduction nor pure induction is possible in practice: the subject matter and the truth-value attached to axioms derive from experience, while the derivation of observations from experience is not independent of theoretical priors. An alternative methodology drawing on Keynes's human logic is retroduction, by which experience (using some methods for representing it) combined with imagination yields ideas about possible causal relations which can then be exposed to analysis and further evidence using a range of methods.[7] Rather than linear deduction, which is vulnerable to any problems with the axioms on which it builds, this approach uses what I have referred to as a 'Babylonian' approach,[8] which builds theories on a range of arguments with different starting points. This is a mechanism for increasing weight of argument, a concept developed by Keynes (1973a[1921]). If deductive argument and evidence are insufficient to demonstrate the truth of a proposition, at least we can have more confidence in the proposition the more relevant evidence we have. This provided the basis for our discussion of a pluralist methodology which produces a range of types of reasoning.

The different arguments within this process can be combined by means of triangulation. As Downward and Mearman (2007) explain, triangulation in fact applies at a range of levels to contribute different perspectives to a retroductive analysis of any economic question. While the concept of triangulation originally derives from methods in navigation and surveying, '[i]n social research in its broadest sense, triangulation implies combining together more than one set of insights in an investigation' (Downward and Mearman 2007, 80). Triangulation can be applied at the level of data, whereby different types of evidence can be drawn from official statistics, survey evidence etc. It can also apply to investigators: different research teams drawing on different disciplines and different skill sets. Similarly, considering a problem simultaneously from the point of view of different theories enhances understanding. Finally, there can be triangulation in the sense of drawing on different versions of the same method, or of drawing on different methods (e.g. qualitative and quantitative research).

Understanding what a pluralist methodology means for practice within one paradigm is one thing; understanding what methodological pluralism means for practice is quite another.[9] It is a matter of awareness of 'otherness' which requires sufficient knowledge of alternative approaches to allow communication (just as some knowledge of a foreign language helps us understand our cultural surroundings better when we visit a foreign country) (see further Kaul 2007). But further it challenges us to be ready to defend our own choice of approach over others. It is through the ability to be aware of alternatives and also the requirement to be able to justify one's approach that pluralism provides a more robust and thus more reliable range of knowledge about the economy. The discipline benefits from having a range of approaches with different comparative advantages for addressing different types of problem. But it also benefits from the scope for creative cross-fertilisation of ideas between approaches. Thus, even if in a pluralist environment mainstream economics were to continue to dominate, it would be a more robust approach for having explicitly made its case in relation to alternatives (which requires acknowledging and understanding alternatives) than the current situation where its dominance is due to the exercise of power.

Since the subject matter is complex, accounting for the multiplicity of approaches, inevitably any one approach provides only partial knowledge. Since there are no universal extra-paradigmatic criteria, it is a matter of argument which approach provides the most reliable knowledge. Further, the subject matter being open, each approach needs to be able to adapt to changing circumstances and be able to justify these adaptations. At the same time, as understanding of other paradigms develops and as circumstances change, there may be merit in paradigms borrowing from each other, although inevitably these borrowed ideas take on a different form within another paradigm. Fostering a range of approaches therefore ensures that economists continue to be aware of the limitations of their own approaches as well as their capacities, and to be able to introduce new ideas as a result of debate. Where mainstream economists have maintained some awareness of debate outside the mainstream, they have proved to be adept at absorbing ideas and transforming them for compatibility with the mainstream framework. But pluralism continues to be stifled by the general mainstream unwillingness to engage in debate about, and defend, the mainstream approach itself, or even acknowledge that other approaches might have their own legitimacy.

We can summarise the implications of methodological pluralism by drawing up some positive heuristics and some negative heuristics (a list of 'dos' and 'don'ts').

Positive heuristics:

- Respect the legitimacy of alternative approaches and have an understanding of them.

- Be prepared to justify your own approach relative to others.
- Be prepared to adapt your approach as events unfold and as a result of debate.
- Be open to drawing on other approaches for ideas, even if they turn into something else in your approach.

Negative heuristics:

- Don't dismiss arguments from alternative approaches out of hand.
- Don't insist that all economists follow your chosen approach (but argue).
- Don't attempt to pick elements from different approaches simultaneously without ensuring that they fit into a coherent methodological and theoretical framework.
- But don't always focus on the meta-methodological level.

These heuristics can be seen in terms of courteous academic behaviour; indeed one of the arguments for pluralism is the ethical argument for mutual respect (Screpanti 1997). But it is more than an ethical argument about good behaviour, it is an ethical argument about knowledge. If no one approach can claim truth and the survival of the discipline rests on nurturing a range of approaches, then the ethical argument concerns honesty about the limitations of any one approach. In order to function as economists we must choose an approach; our research would be incoherent if we jumped from one approach to another, unless the result was a new synthetic approach. But the onus is on each economist to engage in debate about the relative merits of the different approaches, being able to defend her chosen approach, but also able to understand enough about alternative approaches to engage in more-or-less effective communication.

4. Being a pluralist policy maker

A policy maker is in a different position, generally drawing on economic advice as an outsider to the discipline. A pluralist policy maker is aware of different approaches. She will normally be drawn to one approach which corresponds to her ontology. Further, since ideology is embedded in world view (Fine 1980), the approach employed will reflect a political position. But, as a pluralist, the policy maker would know that there are other claims to reliable knowledge. The concept of weight of argument (which we discussed above in relation to pluralist methodologies) can be applied by the policy maker to methodological pluralism, i.e. a range of methodological approaches. If arguments from a range of perspectives all point to a particular policy action, the policy maker can take that action with greater confidence. If however the advice conflicts, the policy maker has to weigh up the justifications offered by the advisers, taking account of their ideological underpinnings; if they also are methodological pluralists, the advisers will understand the obligation to make their case. The policy maker in turn has to be able to express a case publicly for the action chosen. The choice, of course, will reflect political realities, but rather than separating the policy decision from economic theory as requiring different methods ('arts' as opposed to positive science; see Colander 1992), economics would be more effective if it built theory on institutional and political realities – a return to political economy (Milonakis and Fine 2009).

Pluralism thus provides the policy maker with a more robust basis for policy making by providing a range of foci on a complex reality, provided by policy advisers better able to present and defend the underpinnings of their advice in relation to alternatives and to be honest about limitations. Some approaches will come to the fore in particular circumstances, just as others will prove to be less relevant. As Elliassen, Hauge and Rajić (2015) discuss, focusing on only one approach carries the risk of huge policy mistakes. Thus for example the liberalisation of formerly-planned economies ran into all sorts of problems because much of the analysis had ignored institutional considerations particular to those economies (as is standard in mainstream analysis, which presents itself as having universal application).

In terms of the process by which the policy maker arrives at a conclusion, Downward and Mearman (2008) show how triangulation applies at this level too. Using the Bank of England as a case study, they show how the decision-making process draws on different types of data, using a range of types of investigator and theory, in a process of triangulation. Indeed triangulation is applied through governance structures, such as policy making by committee. However a tension arises between requiring investigators and committee members to have a shared ontology, facilitating a unified decision-making process, on the one hand, and seeking full triangulation between different ontologies, potentially requiring conflict resolution, on the other. A truly pluralist approach to policy advice would engage with different paradigms. This would require the effort being made by all to communicate meaning as effectively as possible (given the inevitable degree of incommensurability between paradigms) and to be able to understand each other's paradigm sufficiently to engage in effective debate.

While a unitary policy maker (such as a Prime Minister) holds an ontology which accords with that of the relevant political party, political parties (like research paradigms) have permeable and evolving borders, and yet provide the basis for a (more or less) reasonably cohesive community. But successful democratic government involves recognising other approaches in the form of other parties, as well as recognising the more general plurality within society. This could involve recognising plurality where some groups are more vulnerable than others and therefore more in need of protection by the state. Or it could involve recognising the greater power wielded by some sections of society, e.g. the financial sector. This power can take the form of lobbying for deregulation, or the more diffuse form of market sentiment. The latter can create the problems which governments have to address (such as the recent crisis) but can also constrain government policy (as in the case of market sentiment favouring austerity policies). Governments themselves are thus subject to the power of external forces to which they must pay attention. Nevertheless, while a particular political approach to policy inevitably reflects awareness of the significance of other groupings' analysis, and government rhetoric may not be consistent with policy practice, government must adopt one approach or another (see further Dow 2012b).

5. Pluralist education in economics

But it is difficult to advise researchers and policy advisers on pluralism if the economics education system is geared to promoting monism. This monism in economics education is all the more insidious in that it discourages critical thinking. Kuhn (1970[1962]) explicitly discussed the role of education in propagating paradigms; textbooks provide exemplars to train students to 'think like economists', something which is reinforced by assessment procedures (see further Graupe, this volume). Not only are students launched on their careers as economists ill-equipped to engage in pluralism, but they have actively been discouraged from doing so. The most important implication of our discussion of pluralism in economics therefore is that it requires a pluralist approach to economics education.

As the G-Science (2016) statement pointed out, science involves critical thinking. So scientific education in economics needs to include training in critical thinking. This requires two important and related elements: first, it requires the capacity to debate; and second, it requires knowledge of different schools of thought as input to debate. Both of these require the basic starting point that students are encouraged and trained, indeed required, to form their own views about economics.

A pluralist curriculum which covers different approaches to economics signals that no one approach can lay claim to truth and that all economic theory is contestable (see Betz, this volume, for a case study). It is not necessary to cover all schools of thought, particularly at the earlier stages of the programme. It is sufficient to present at least two approaches to demonstrate that economic knowledge can be built up in different ways, each of which can be defended on its own terms. Preferably there would be more than two approaches in order to avoid the misleading impression that one is 'right' and the other 'wrong' – in any absolute sense rather than from the perspective of one approach or the other.[10] It only requires students to have a sense of 'otherness' to accept a pluralist approach (Panther, this volume). For those students who already have this sense, what is required is an economics programme which does not 'unteach' it.

An effective way of teaching about different schools of thought is to teach through debate (Dow 2003). This was an early demand of the French student group out of which grew the Post-autistic Economics movement. Students can be pointed towards debates in the literature in order to promote understanding of different approaches. But students themselves can learn the facility of critical thinking by engaging in debates as part of the curriculum, where students are encouraged to take different stances on approach (including as devil's advocate).

As well as covering the content of (some) different schools of thought, the curriculum also needs to provide material on the history of thought and methodology (Dow 2009). History of thought is important in three respects. First, it is hard to understand the modern array of schools of thought without understanding how they arose and developed and who were the key figures in their development. Second it is important to understand, not only why their importance waxed and waned, but that economics should not be thought of as going through an inexorable process of improvement. It is this view within the mainstream, that modern economics encapsulates the best of past thought, which has justified the marginalising of history of thought education as being only of antiquarian interest. Third, the history of thought provides invaluable material for future developments in economics, showing how different ideas were developed to address particular problems in the past and how they worked out.

Even more fundamental is that a pluralist curriculum includes material on the methodology of economics. Differences between schools of thought are associated with methodological differences, so students need some understanding of how to appraise different methodologies (as well as economic theories). The capacity and skills for critical thinking need to be learnt for application to methodology. But, further, an understanding of methodology is fundamental to understanding the whole rationale for a pluralist curriculum, and how it can be applied during subsequent careers. As future practising economists, students will need to be equipped to make their own choice of approach. This requires understanding what each approach involves, but also why one approach may come more naturally than another (because of otherwise unacknowledged ontology and epistemology). They will also need to be equipped to justify their choice of approach and engage in debate with others. All of this requires methodological awareness, something more evident in the other social sciences but increasingly absent in economics.

This is not to argue necessarily for separate courses in history of thought and methodology, although these could be specialist options. Preferably all pluralist teaching should incorporate elements of history of thought and methodology into the fabric of content in particular fields, something which used to be the norm in previous generations of education in political economy. This of course requires that the educators themselves are equipped with an education in history of thought and methodology. There might therefore need to be a transitional phase of specialist courses until it was reasonable to expect teaching staff to be equipped to teach economics in a historical and methodologically-aware way.

Finally, while mainstream economics has been presented as a technical discipline to which values are only added later by politicians, it is accepted in most other schools of thought that economics is a moral discipline. If different values are embedded in different schools of thought, then these need to be brought to the fore and be addressed in debate. Part of a pluralist education means education in the moral responsibilities of economists. One of these responsibilities is to be honest about the values being applied in theory on which policy advice is based. A further responsibility is to be honest about the limitations of economics. If no one approach can be demonstrated as the best, then advice needs to reflect this, requiring the advisor to justify her position in relation to alternatives. This moral responsibility goes well beyond the conventional discussion of economists' ethics in terms of plagiarism, conflict of interest etc. Many students choose to study economics as a means to understanding the economy in order to change it for the better. Pluralist economics education therefore needs to train students in understanding their moral responsibilities and how to fulfil them.

6. Conclusion

It has been argued here that pluralism should not be dismissed as being unscientific. Far from it. In fact pluralism provides a much richer understanding of the concept of reliable knowledge in economics, and why and how schools of thought differ as to what that means. To restrict economics to one, inevitably limited, monist approach is to restrict the scope for reliable knowledge, reducing the scientific capacity of the discipline. Further, without the obligation which pluralism imposes to explain and defend one's own approach, economic theory from any one approach is weaker and less capable of constructive evolution.

Pluralist practice has many challenges, which we have explored here for economic researchers, advisors and policy makers. To meet these challenges, economists require an appropriate, pluralist education. This should include exposure to different schools of thought, training in critical thinking and debate, education in the history of thought and in methodological awareness. Thankfully, thinking and practice are advancing rapidly on pluralist economics education, due in large part to the excellent work of the international student movement.

Acknowledgment

This chapter has benefitted from comments by the editors and by two referees.

Notes

1 This definition draws on the G-Science Academies Statement 2016.
2 This purpose arose towards the end of the nineteenth century, coinciding with the marginalist revolution, and was given further impetus in the period after World War II (Mirowski 1989; Blaug 1999).
3 There has been a series of accounts of different schools of thought since the 1980s, see e.g. Dow (1985); the most up to date will be the new Rethinking Economics volume *Rethinking Economics – An Introduction to Pluralism,* currently under preparation; see http://www.rethinkeconomics.org/home/rethinking-reader/

4 This discussion of openness needs to be distinguished from the idea of an open economy, where the closed system may be expanded to include the foreign sector, or the idea of stochastic processes, where the nature of deviations from the norm as pre-specified in the structure of the disturbance term.
5 See further Runde and Mizuhara (2003) on Keynes's philosophy and economics.
6 This was the sense in which Keynes regarded probability as subjective.
7 This is Newton's 'experimental philosophy', which the Scottish enlightenment philosophers used for developing political economy, and which has found its most recent expression in critical realism.
8 The term follows from Richard Feynman's discussion of the non-Euclidean nature of Babylonian mathematics; see further Dow (2012a).
9 Triangulation between methodological approaches, or paradigms, is problematic, unless the object is to arrive at a new, synthetic, approach.
10 This is a matter of debate, whether non-mainstream schools of thought present themselves as the only alternative to mainstream economics (i.e. they too are monist). But a pluralist presentation of an alternative involves argument designed to persuade of its superiority, while respecting that it is reasonable to come to a different view from a different perspective.

References

Becker, G. S. (1976): *The Economic Approach to Human Behavior*. Chicago: University of Chicago Press.

Blaug, M. (1992): *The Methodology of Economics: Or How Economists Explain*. Cambridge: Cambridge University Press.

Blaug, M. (1999): 'The Formalist Revolution or What Happened to Orthodox Economics after World War II?', in Backhouse, R. E. and Creedy, J. (eds.), *From Classical Economics to the Theory of the Firm: Essays in Honour of D P O'Brien*. Cheltenham: Edward Elgar, 257–280.

Boland, L. (1997): *Critical Economic Methodology*. London: Routledge.

Caldwell, B. J. (1982): *Beyond Positivism: Economic Methodology in the Twentieth Century*. London: George Allen & Unwin.

Cartwright, N. (1989): *Nature's Capacities and Their Measurement*. Oxford: Oxford University Press.

Cartwright, N. (1999): *The Dappled World: A Study of the Boundaries of Science*. Cambridge: Cambridge University Press.

Colander, D. (1992): 'The Lost Art of Economics', *Journal of Economic Perspectives* 6 (3), 191–198.

Colander, D. (2000): 'The Death of Neoclassical Economics', *Journal of the History of Economic Thought* 22 (2), 127–143.

Dow, S. C. (1985): *Macroeconomic Thought: A Methodological Approach*. Oxford: Basil Blackwell.

Dow, S. C. (2003): 'The Relevance of Controversies for Practice as Well as Teaching', in Fullbrook, E. (ed.), *The Crisis in Economics: The Post-Autistic Economics Movement: The First 600 Days*. London: Routledge, 132–134.

Dow, S. C. (2004a): 'Structured Pluralism', *Journal of Economic Methodology* 11 (3), 275–290.

Dow, S. C. (2004b): 'Reorienting Economics: Some Epistemological Issues', *Journal of Economic Methodology* 11 (3), 307–312.

Dow, S. C. (2007): 'Variety of Methodological Approach in Economics', *Journal of Economic Surveys* 21 (3), 447–465.

Dow, S. C. (2009): 'History of Thought and Methodology in Pluralist Economics Education', *International Review of Economics Education* 8 (2), 41–57.

Dow, S. C. (2012a): 'The Babylonian Mode of Thought', in King, J. (ed.), *The Elgar Companion to Post Keynesian Economics*. Cheltenham: Edward Elgar, 15–19.

Dow, S. C. (2012b): 'Policy in the Wake of the Banking Crisis: Taking Pluralism Seriously', *International Review of Applied Economics* 26 (2), 161–175.

Dow, S.C. and Chick, V. (2005): 'The Meaning of Open Systems', *Journal of Economic Methodology* 12(3), 363–381.

Downward, P. and Mearman, A. (2007): 'Retroduction as Mixed-Methods Triangulation in Economic Research: Reorienting Economics into Social Science', *Cambridge Journal of Economics* 31, 77–99.

Downward, P. and Mearman, A. (2008): 'Decision-Making at the Bank of England: A Critical Appraisal', *Oxford Economic Papers* 60, 385–409.

Earle, J., Moran, C. and Ward-Perkins, Z. (2016): *The Econocracy: The Perils of Leaving Economics to the Experts*. London: Rethinking Economics.

Elliassen, R. L., Hauge, J. L. and Rajić, I. (2015): *Fit for a Fix: Why the Economics Curriculum Needs a Pluralist Revamp*, Anglia Ruskin University and University of Cambridge. Mimeo.

Fine, B. (1980): *Economic Theory and Ideology*. London: Edward Arnold.

Fullbrook, E. (2001): 'Real Science Is Pluralist', *Post-autistic economics newsletter*, 5 (March), http://www.paecon.net/PAEtexts/Fullbrook1.htm, accessed 11 April 2017.

G-Science Academies. (2016): Statement: *Nurturing Future Scientists*, https://royalsociety.org/~/media/about-us/international/g-science-statements/2016-nurturing-future-scientists.pdf?la=en-GB, accessed 1 August 2016.

Kaul, N. (2007): *Imagining Economics Otherwise: Encounters with Identity/Difference*. London: Routledge.

Keynes, J. M. (1973a[1921]): 'A Treatise on Probability', in *Collected Writings*, Vols. VIII. London: Macmillan for the Royal Economic Society.

Keynes, J. M. (1973b): 'The General Theory and After: Preparation', in *Collected Writings*, Vols. XIII. London: Macmillan for the Royal Economic Society.

Kuhn, T. S. (1970[1962]): *The Structure of Scientific Revolutions*. Chicago: Chicago University Press.

Kuhn, T. S. (1999): 'Remarks on Incommensurability and Translation', in Rossini, R., Sandri, G. and Scazzieri, R. (eds.), *Incommensurability and Translation*. Aldershot: Elgar, 33–38.

Lawson, T. (1997): *Economics and Reality*. London: Routledge.

Lawson, T. (2004): 'Reorienting Economics: On Heterodox Economics, Themata and the Use of Mathematics in Economics', *Journal of Economic Methodology* 11 (3), 329–340.

Lazear, F. P. (2000): 'Economic Imperialism', *Quarterly Journal of Economics* 115 (1), 99–146.

Mankiw, R. G. and Taylor, M. P. (2006): *Economics*. London: Thomson.

McCloskey, D. N. (1983): 'The Rhetoric of Economics', *Journal of Economic Literature* 21, 481–517.

Milonakis, D. and Fine, B. (2009): *From Political Economy to Economics: Method, the Social and the Historical in the Evolution of Economic Theory*. London: Routledge.

Mirowski, P. (1989): *More Heat than Light: Economics as Social Physics, Physics as Nature's Economics*. Cambridge: Cambridge University Press.
Popper, K. (1959): *The Logic of Scientific Discovery*. New York: Basic Books.
Romer, P. M. (2015): 'Mathiness in the Theory of Economic Growth', *American Economic Review: Papers & Proceedings* 105 (5), 89–93.
Runde, J. and Mizuhara, S. (2003): *The Philosophy of Keynes's Economics: Probability, Uncertainty and Convention*. London: Routledge.
Screpanti, E. (1997): 'Afterword', in Salanti, A. and Screpanti, E. (eds.), *Pluralism in Economics*. Cheltenham: Edward Elgar, 298–307.
Searle, J. (1995): *The Construction of Social Reality*. New York: Simon & Schuster.
Smith, A. (1976[1759]): *The Theory of Moral Sentiments*, Glasgow edition edited by Raphael, D. D. and Macfie, A. Oxford: Oxford University Press.

2 Monism in modern science

The case of economics

Frank Beckenbach

1. Introduction

Taking into account the features of the modern science of economics, it is not self-evident to postulate pluralism even if there should be a consensus about a dominating school of thought. What is going on in economics is – at least to a large part – determined by the economists themselves and they possibly agree that a dominant paradigm makes participation in the scientific discourse easier. Hence, it seems to suggest itself that postulating pluralism needs a foundation that comes from outside, such as ethical or even political considerations. In this contribution I will not (at least not immediately) pursue this argument; instead pluralism will be legitimised by analysing the social practices in the science of economics itself. In this view, pluralism is an auto-correction of scientific procedures required in specific situations for purposes defined within economics. It will be argued that generating and diffusing radically new economic knowledge is a task of modern science (like economics) and that in specific situations this can only be guaranteed by pluralism. In that situation, pluralism has to be competitive in that it explicitly tries to confront and overcome the established knowledge.

Against this backdrop, it seems appropriate to reflect on the specificity of modern science in general before analysing how economics fits into this framework. For deciphering the specificity of modern sciences (in general and especially economics) as well as for figuring out the necessity of pluralism in terms of concepts, methods, and syllabi, modern complexity theory offers helpful heuristics. The basic idea, which can be used for both tasks, is that in complex systems there are self-generated procedures for reducing the very large potential state space by building sub-parts, the elements of which are densely related whereas the sub-parts as a whole are coupled in a loose manner. This idea of "near-decomposability" (Simon 1996) can be used as a heuristic for understanding social subsystems in modern societies like science or the economy. But because the internal relations in economics as a science are based on the construction and diffusion of knowledge mainly within science there may be a lack of correspondence (isomorphism) between the features of the economy and the knowledge about the latter circulating in economics. To (re-)establish this correspondence (isomorphism) contrary to the simplifications being actually dominant in modern economics can be considered as the main feature of a heterodox challenge in economics.

Correspondingly this elaboration starts by deciphering modern science as a social subsystem being loosely coupled to the rest of society (Section 2). Based on that, the way in which modern (monistic) economics was generated within this subsystem will be sketched (Section 3.1). This is contrasted with the views that this monism would have been eroded in recent times due to imports from other sciences into economics (Section 3.2). Conclusions as regards the necessity as well as the mode of pluralism are drawn from this discussion (Section 4). Perspectives for a heterodox alternative and its role for fostering pluralism are sketched in Section 5.

2. Features of modern science in general

2.1 Complexity and functionally differentiated science

The asserted features of science in modern societies strongly depend on the way society itself is conceptualised. Depicting it as a network of activities ($A_1 \ldots A_n$) the basic explanatory variants of a dominant dependent variable, of a dominant independent variable, and of complete interdependence may be distinguished (see Figure 2.1). It can be expected that in these cases the role and features of science (comprising one or several of these activities) differ considerably.

Complexity theory assumes that beyond these basic cases there are structures of interdependencies between activities which are crucial for the survival of the system as a whole. A prominent example of such a structure is "near decomposability" (Simon 1977, 1996, 2002). According to this view, complex systems survive by building clusters of internal activities which are linked more intensely than the clusters themselves. Hence, these clusters are rather robust against changes in the other clusters coupled to them. If the coupling of the clusters is circular in some way, a system as a whole can be separated from its environment (see Figure 2.2).

In such a context, science in general (and economics as a special case) can be understood as a social subsystem being differentiated against other subsystems (such as, for example, the economy, politics etc.) *firstly* by a special orientation schema specific for that subsystem ("Leitdifferenz") and *secondly* within that subsystem by a net of dense relations related to this orientation schema (contrary to the loose relations to the orientation schemata of other subsystems) (Luhmann 2003). Hence, apart from the "functional differentiation" of science as a whole, there is an operational differentiation within science (in terms of different disciplines, administrative roles etc.). In that view, scientists generate insightful knowledge being eager that this knowledge is perceived, modified and distributed by other scientists.[1] In that sense, science is indeed about a specific way of communication generating further opportunities for

X	A1	A2	A3	A4	A5	A6
A1	0	0	0	0	0	1
A2	0	0	0	0	0	1
A3	0	0	0	0	0	1
A4	0	0	0	0	0	1
A5	0	0	0	0	0	1
A6	0	0	0	0	0	0

X	A1	A2	A3	A4	A5	A6
A1	0	0	0	0	0	0
A2	0	0	0	0	0	0
A3	0	0	0	0	0	0
A4	0	0	0	0	0	0
A5	0	0	0	0	0	0
A6	1	1	1	1	1	0

X	A1	A2	A3	A4	A5	A6
A1	1	1	1	1	1	1
A2	1	1	1	1	1	1
A3	1	1	1	1	1	1
A4	1	1	1	1	1	1
A5	1	1	1	1	1	1
A6	1	1	1	1	1	1

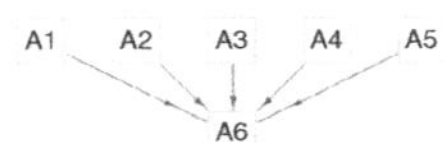

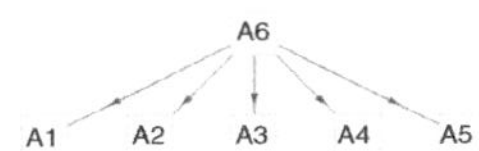

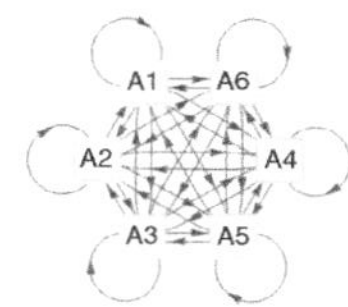

Figure 2.1 Basic cases for activity dependence. “0” indicates that the row element is not (or only marginally) influencing the corresponding column element; “1” indicates a strong influence. Dominant dependent variable (left), dominant independent variable (middle) and complete interdependence (right).

X	A1	A2	A3	A4	A5	A6
A1	1	1	0	0	0	0
A2	1	1	(1)	0	0	0
A3	0	0	1	1	0	0
A4	0	0	1	1	(1)	0
A5	0	0	0	0	1	1
A6	(1)	0	0	0	1	1

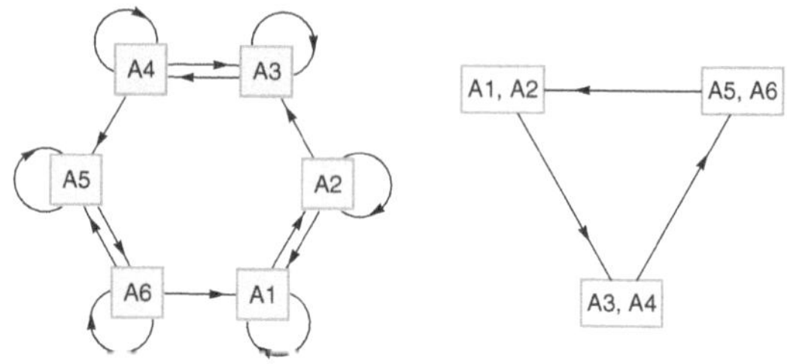

Figure 2.2 Near-decomposability and modularisation in a circular system. Activity dependence in binary terms with modules in blue and interfaces in red (left), system graph of all elements (middle) and of simplified modules (right).

such a communication.[2] Hence, a self-referential process of opening up possibilities to connect with other researchers is at the heart of modern science. This is realised by research collaborations, conferences, journal contributions and books as well as by institutional forms of scientific communication and – not least – the allocation of money. Linked to this process of generating, modifying and diffusing knowledge is a process of acquiring scientific reputation at the level of scientists. These observations imply that the main drivers for the processes in science are originated in science itself: neither being dominated by interests outside science nor dominating other fields of social activities is – according to this view – the main feature of modern science.

Even though the structure of near-decomposable sub-systems is already an institutionalised form of reducing uncertainty for the system as a whole, the former remains a feature within every sub-system and that means within science. Hence, if one suggested option for new insightful knowledge becomes accepted by a larger group of scientists, this reduces the remaining uncertainty because possibilities to connect to this option are becoming calculable. Taking into account the recursive nature of scientific operations, this is then tantamount to a "lock in" of these knowledge options in that the probability that scientists pick it up is higher the more it is already accepted. Whereas the creation of such a path might be accidental (or pushed from outside the science at stake) the consolidation of such a path is endogenously produced by feedback or "amplifiers": the efforts to get scientific perception are economised due to economies of scale and scope as well as to network externalities; furthermore the amount of scientific perception and reputation does increase, and the switching costs to other knowledge options are getting more important (path dependency in science; Peacock 2009). This first-order path dependence of singular research trajectories (related to a specific research topic, belief, methods etc.) can be condensed to a second-order path dependence if these singular research trajectories are bundled up by assigning a common denominator to them. This is tantamount to a generation of "paradigms" or "research programmes" in modern science.[3] If such a paradigm is becoming dominant against competing paradigms, science is in a stage of monism (Dusek 2008 for the epistemological dimension).[4]

Such a modern type of self-referential science is not "coming out of the blue". Rather it is an arduous result of a conflict-laden historical process (Wilholt 2012, 209; Mirowski 2004, 51). At least three prerequisites of modern science are worth mentioned here: *firstly*, a constitutional guarantee for the freedom of scientific research, *secondly*, an autonomy of science institutions (in administrative as well as fiscal terms) in relation to the state authorities and, *thirdly*, the (more or less) unconditional financial alimentation of science institutions and activities by the state.[5] Based on these achievements, a scholarship which was in former times predetermined by religious and/or political tasks – even if there were different degrees of personal independence and integrity – has been substituted by a profession only dedicated to generate and diffuse insightful knowledge in modern societies (Schülein and Reitze 2012).

Conceptualising science in this way as a "functionally differentiated subsystem" (Luhmann 2003; see also Luhmann 1992, 271) does not mean that science is operating in an autarchic manner. On the one hand, it needs elements it cannot produce itself. Apart from material inputs like paper, computer and electricity it needs a human input in terms of educated individuals. Additionally, it needs something it can observe and reflect about (and this has to be accepted by other scientists). Nevertheless, the way this observation and reflexion takes place is to a large degree determined from inside science. On the other hand, the subsystem of science is loosely coupled to the rest of society in that the products of science are used in other subsystems and scientific research is inspired by the other subsystems. Hence science is prone to being influenced by these subsystems (as well as influencing them) (Luhmann 1992, 293). Rather than being a heuristic device for strictly demarcating isolated subsystems, the idea of "near-decomposability" offers the perspective of autonomous but co-evolving subsystems, i.e. sub-systems that have their own strong internal dynamics but being nevertheless influenced by other sub-systems.

2.2 Insufficiency of usual explanations of what is going in science

This way to view science, as part of a modern society being composed (at least to a large part) of self-organised subsystems, is in a way a departure from the usual explanations of what science is and how it evolves. In this respect, three approaches can be distinguished: the epistemological approach, the sociology of science approach and the social system approach.

According to the *epistemological approach* the scientific observer and the observed reality can be separated and scientific evolution is tantamount to the approximation of both. Criteria according to which this approximation should be judged are suggested; in that sense this is a normative approach to scientific progress. Logical positivism (Mill 2006[1872]) as a first variant of this approach is strictly focussed on empirical observability and suggests methods for transforming observed circumstances into scientific explanations. According to critical rationalism (Popper

1989), such a procedure cannot be successful in terms of verification because the explanans is already laden with pre-empirical beliefs or theory content. Hence, scientific progress cannot be defined positively but only negatively: explanations are valid as long as there is no counter proof for what is suggested by the explanation.

The obvious explanatory gaps of the epistemological approach as regards the observable dynamics in modern science are the background for the *sociology of science approach*. Although scientific observer and observed reality are still considered as separate entities in this approach, scientific evolution is not considered as an increasing progress in terms of insights and knowledge but rather as a discontinuous (non-linear) process. This is due to the social organisation of science which is taken into account as an element of the explanans for what is going on in science. Hence, there is a switch from a normative to a descriptive perspective on science. The most prominent variant of this approach is originated from Kuhn (1970). Kuhn observes that knowledge in modern science is organised in the form of "paradigms" meant as a bundle of problems as well as concepts and methods for dealing with these problems shared by many scientists. These paradigms are the outcome of scientific competition between different attempts to relate problems, concepts and methods making one of them dominant in the course of time.[6] This dominance holds until an increasing number of contradicting "anomalies" are observed and a new paradigm is established by a conflict laden process. This suggested procedural dichotomy between routine (reign of paradigm) and revolution (switch of paradigms) has been differentiated by Lakatos (1978) who tries to bridge the ideas of Popper and Kuhn (Hands 2001, 110). In his view, a paradigm is not a monolithic whole but composed of a "hard core" of basic assumptions as well as beliefs and a "protective belt" of auxiliary hypotheses in which the scientific work of testing and refuting is carried out.

Enhancement of perspective and generalisation of what is observed in the sociology of science approach defines the social *system approach*. In this approach, scientific observer and observed reality are no longer strictly separated entities, but strongly depend on each other in that the observed reality is itself considered as a social construction (in terms of observation and communication) the genesis of which can be observed by science (in terms of second- and even higher-order observations). Scientific activities, as well as their results, are explained by their broader social embeddedness or, to put it the other way round, the rules of science are to a large part determined by the rules governing the society at large. Hence, the evolution of science is not only non-linear but also a succession of progress and retrogression (e.g. in forgetting insights) is possible. In such a framework, a combination of descriptive (what is going on?) and normative (what is an outside observer expecting?) points of view is possible. A crude variant of this approach has been put forward by Marx and was later specified by Marxists (e.g. Bernal (1939), Hessen and Grossmann as documented in Freudenthal and McLaughlin (2009)) and proponents of the "Frankfurt School" (e.g. Horkheimer 1933, Horkheimer 1937). According to this variant, science in capitalism is characterised by being subsumed under economic interests determining the direction as well as the speed of scientific research. Especially in the social sciences, this implies a more or less conscious orientation of research(er) towards the requirements of these interests. Social science is then dichotomised in simply legitimising of what appears to the observer, on the one hand, and in demystifying these appearances and clarifying the hidden causes on the other hand.

Considering science as an operationally closed and functionally differentiated subsystem is radically different from these approaches – although it is a specification of the social system approach by means of complexity theory and by integrating insights of the sociology of science in terms of paradigms and research programmes. It turns aside from these usual ideas about science and its development: this is so because the reality of science is assumed to be scientific communication, because there is no dichotomy between scientific observer and observed reality and an attempted approximation between both. Science is not subsumed but self-referential. In that sense, science is not primarily about "truth"; rather it is about appropriateness for the scientific community. This does not exclude that the acceptance of scientific insights within science may be influenced by practical problem solving being fostered by these insights.

3. Modern economics

3.1 Development of economics towards monism after World War II

Economics as a social science has specificities which are not observable in the natural sciences. Generally – as in every social science – it should be expected that a consensus about acceptable knowledge is more difficult to achieve because the possibilities for exact observation and experimentation are more limited and hence the spectre for "creative construction" of insights is greater. In that sense economics can be regarded as a "moral science":

> I . . . want to emphasise strongly the point about economics being a moral science. I mentioned . . . that it deals with introspection and with values. I might have added that it deals with motives, expectations, psychological uncertainties. One has to be constantly on guard against treating the material as constant and homogeneous. It is as though the fall of the apple to the ground depends on the apple's motives, on whether it is worth falling, and whether the apple wanted to fall, and on mistaken calculations on the part of the apple as to how far it was from the centre of the earth.
>
> Keynes (1973[1983], 300)[7]

Attempts have been made to understand the recent development in this "moral science" of economics by using the aforementioned approaches for explaining the evolution of science (with the exception of the social system approach): logical positivism, critical rationalism und the sociology of science (Hands 2001). But exactly due to the "moral" nature of economics it turns out that the traditional explanations for scientific development are only of limited explanatory value when applied to social sciences in general and to economics in particular. Specifically, the epistemological approach is applicable for social sciences (such as economics) only in a limited way.

> Returning to the idea that economists are unable to rule out various assumptions that may lead to similar conclusions, the issue for us is how to choose between two (or more) theories, *none* of whose premises can be verified exactly as either holding or not, and none of which can easily be disentangled via either observed data or giant natural experiments.
>
> Athreya (2013, 16)

Rather, the constructions used for getting insights in economics should be judged on a plausibility basis (e.g. by avoiding contradictions to the knowledge communicated in other sciences) without sharp discrimination criteria being applicable. Hence, in economics a type of "organised storytelling (...) to persuade others" (ibid., 13) is going on. This constructive storytelling can be linked to the limits for directly observing the causal elements, especially if inner states of individuals are involved.

Hence, to conceptualise economics as an operational specification within functionally differentiated modern science can be used as a starting point for understanding the development of economics after World War II ("modern economics"). Obviously economics is a specialised modern science: it is separated from other social sciences (operational specialisation), it is not dominated by outside interests nor is it dominating other social sub-systems.[8] The nature of scientific communication is mostly self-referential (Buiter 2009, 2). Accordingly, a multitude of singular path creations and consolidations (combining topics, methods and beliefs) could be observed in recent times (e.g. theory of production, market form theory, growth theory). Based on that, peculiarities of modern economics can be identified which distinguish its development from other social sciences.

i Originating in science policy in the United States and afterwards diffusing into the whole western world, a second order path creation and consolidation has taken place after the 2nd World War II[9] thereby synthesising several hitherto separated singular paths to a paradigm especially by elaborating a unified and consistent formal treatment for the state spaces of households and firms as well as for the way they operate in these state spaces and the information requirements involved. In this process economics became a mathematically constructed science almost completely isolated from empirically meaningful explanation.[10] Correspondingly, the properties of an overall equilibrium for these entities have been specified in terms of existence, uniqueness and stability (Hicks (1962[1939]), Samuelson (1947), Koopmans (1957), Arrow and Hahn (1971); for an overview cf. Weintraub 1993, 59; Ingrao and Israel 1990, 217).[11]

ii This was accompanied by strengthening the autonomy of economics in separating the economic knowledge from the social neighbour disciplines. Whereas before the World War II it was not unusual to link knowledge from psychology, sociology and political science to economic knowledge proper (as can be easily verified by taking into account the classical economist, the early neoclassicals as well as the different schools in pre-war economics), after the war this was substituted by an attempt to figure out a "pure economics". References to psychological knowledge were obliterated in the construction of the homo oeconomicus, references to sociology were obliterated by the devising of methodological individualism and references to political science obliterated by elaborating welfare theory (and later on public choice). According to the concept sketched above, this is another step in operational differentiation within the social sciences.

iii The final component of post-war economics was a switch to a performance-driven science. The basic idea behind this switch is the mapping of scientific quality into quantity by figuring out frequency measures on different levels. This mapping is used as an allocation device for resources as well as reputation in the realm of science. That means the more knowledge options that are accepted and diffused the more these options will be rewarded. This can be read as an explicit acknowledgement of the self-referential nature of scientific communication. Conversely, this nature is further strengthened by these procedures.

To summarise, synthesising different paths to a consistent paradigm, strengthening the autonomy of this paradigm and finally the frequency dependence of resource allocation triggered a strong 2nd order path creation and stabilisation in economics after the war.[12]

3.2 Orthodox mainstream – a straw man?

A lot of authors (Colander 2000; Colander et al. 2004; Davis 2006; Vromen 2007; Hodgson 2013) pretend that a part of the recent post-war development in economics has been a new kind of pluralism. According to this diagnosis, concepts originating from outside economics have been imported and assimilated by the latter and thereby generated new fields of economic research eroding the borders of mainstream economics. Hence, the old-fashioned mainstream is assumed not to exist anymore.[13]

The following new concepts and the corresponding research are mentioned in this context:

- In the realm of microeconomics, property right and transaction cost economics hinting at the role of institutions and information asymmetries, game theory as a concept taking systematically into account the activities of

others as a determining factor for own pay off, behavioural as well as experimental economics with its orientation towards observations (instead towards axioms) and by hinting at the violation of many rationality standards – at least in the lab;
- In the realm of macroeconomics the taking into account of multiple equilibria, complexity economics using formalisms for analysing non-linear system with emergent properties, and finally evolutionary economics focussing not only the biological foundation of behaviour but also the dynamics of populations composed of heterogeneous elements (Colander et al. 2004, 496; Davis 2006, 1; Vromen 2007).

This is a rather disparate assembly of recently upcoming strands in economics which needs further qualification as regards the new plurality hypothesis mentioned above. *Firstly*, complexity economics as well as evolutionary economics are up to now heterodox side streams. This can be derived not only from their basic conceptual ideas which are explicitly based on criticising the post-war paradigm in economics mentioned above.[14] Furthermore the nature of this side stream is obvious if one looks at quotation frequencies in economic journals as well as books. *Secondly*, the remaining concepts and research fields can each be divided into one (bigger) part, the focus of which is to harmonise the enhancement and complication at stake with the paradigmatic state of the art in post-war economics and another (smaller) part in which perspectives beyond this realm are at the centre of research (Dobusch and Kapeller 2009). This last part is not yet fully discussed as regards its implications for a non-mainstream economics.

The background for this easing of the "old-fashioned" specification of neoclassical economics seems to be a particular field of research which has been hyped recently: experimental game theory and behavioural economics (Vromen 2007, 70; Arnsperger and Varoufakis 2006, 9). If this is the case, the question arises of whether the conceptual and methodological enhancements arrived at in this specific field of research can be considered as pars pro toto for economics as a whole. At least the experimental underpinning of theory building confines this kind of research to areas in the economy which are accessible for experiments and excludes those, which are not.[15] Hence it can hardly be classified as being representative of the whole discipline. Apart from that, the knowledge gained in the field of behavioural and experimental economics has not yet successfully passed the test of being canonically consistent. Whereas the "old-fashioned" constructs of neoclassical economics (selfish perfectly informed individuals, maximisation of goals under well specified constraints and Pareto-equilibrium) are complementary to each other and by this constitute(d) a paradigmatic whole, this is no longer the case if the suggested relaxation of these constructs is assumed. How behaviourally enriched individuals interact in the market and what kind of outcome they are able to generate is by no means answered through this research.[16] The more the scientific mapping of individuals diverges from *homo oeconomicus*, the more ad hoc assumptions are necessary to ensure mutual compatibility of individual decisions and – even more ambitious – any kind of equilibrium. Hence, even for this specific part of economics it is not shown that the modifications of the standard definition of neoclassical economics can be synthesised into a consistent concept being a challenge for the mainstream. In picking up the notions suggested for the development of modern science above it can be asked if the new singular paths of economic discourse are still compatible with the second order path dependence and the corresponding paradigm emerging in economics after World war (being a nice embellishment) or not (being a conceptual alternative).

Accordingly, behavioural/experimental economics is ambiguous as regards its implications for modern mainstream economics. One part is focussed on divergences from the rationality standards determined by the expected utility concept in terms of "anomalies". Here the main focus is on the robustness of these effects and, in case of robustness, on how to mitigate them in such a way that the mentioned rationality standards can be re-established (e.g. Sunstein 2014; Mirowski 2013, 256; Berg and Gigerenzer 2010). The other part is based on the assumption that these violations not only persist but furthermore are often "ecologically" rational in that they are adequate for m decision situations ("fast and frugal heuristics"). This can be considered as a starting point for figuring out a behaviourally informed concept of economic agent (Gigerenzer 2011; Beckenbach 2015). The same can be observed in the other fields of modern economic discourse mentioned above. Most of transaction cost economics is devoted to the task of enhancing incentive structures and efficiency criteria in such a way that the usual rationality and equilibrium assumptions still apply. Most of game theory is focussed on the modification of the equilibrium concept (especially by including Nash equilibrium) and on figuring out the conditions of achieving it in different game situations. Hereby Pareto efficiency still remains the reference idea.

Taking the abovementioned ambiguity of the new discourses in economics into account it seems plausible to diagnose a shift to a modified axiomatic structure of neoclassical economics still allowing to draw borderlines between neoclassical and non-neoclassical economics (Arnsperger and Varoufakis 2006, 7): important parts of the "hard core" of modern neoclassical economics remained untouched by this new research. Such parts are the basic worldview behind most components of modern economics, a sample of characteristic methods as well as the opinion of leading institutions (Dobusch and Kapeller 2012, 1038). Moreover, the basic tenets (or axioms) for the "new mainstream" have to be complemented and specified. Accordingly, the complete structure of the mainstream (or modern neoclassical economics) can be summarised as follows.

The basic worldview is focussed on the notion of *scarcity as the distinctive foundation of economics*. This is often stated explicitly but sometimes it is taken as an implicit background assumption. The limitation of such an approach is obvious: scarcity as an individual relation between limited means and unlimited ends not only excludes situations with satiation but is furthermore mediated by social processes (e.g. market operations and technology configurations) and therefore cannot explain anything in itself. Finally, such an approach to economics is *eo ipso* ignorant against the different historical forms in which scarcity manifests itself and is dealt with.[17] This is tantamount to explaining and legitimising the specificities of modern (capitalist) market economies by referring to circumstances which are much more general in terms of historical validity. Hence, the level of generality in the explanans and the explanandum systematically diverge, or to state it differently, there is an incorrect identification of necessary and sufficient condition in scientific explanation.[18] The specific social conditions which have to be dealt with here remain hidden behind the suggestive use of more general and universal considerations. Hence, there is a basic ignorance against "social forms" (Marx) or historic specificities in the economy (Hodgson 2001) in this ideology of scarcity (Mathaei 1984).

There are multiple – partly relaxed – tenets (axioms) (TN), the endorsing of which are still typical for a large part of modern economics. They can be grouped as follows: [19]

- *Action theoretic tenets* are (TN_1) a given stylized state space[20] in which agents can operate and (TN_2) an ability of the agents to attain all information relevant for their action;
- Action is only derived from decisions; the corresponding *decision theoretic tenets* are (TN_3) the idea that any decision is structured by preferences, i.e. a subjective ordering of available decision alternatives, (TN_4) a separation of this ordering from constraints, (TN_5) a clear distinction between cause and effect (unidirectional two-level explanation) and – by taking into account the action theoretic tenets – (TN_6) a maximisation rule as regards the decision alternatives;
- Interaction is modelled by starting from the individual, i.e. by pursuing (TN_7) the *methodological individualism*[21];
- (TN_8) Interaction is subordinated under supposed *equilibrium conditions* in that the former is simply the fulfilment of the latter. This might be complicated by introducing a moderate dose of rationality restriction.[22]

Corresponding to this sort of analysis there is a *sample of methods* which are typical for the mainstream: generally a preference for (convex) set theory, calculus and especially maximisation methods as well as methods of game theory and finally econometric methods for the data fitting.[23]

Finally, organisational features have to be mentioned as a component of mainstream economics: *accepted academic practices* as well as *established institutions* are essential here.

Hence, contrary to the hypothesis of a new pluralism, it seems more appropriate to characterise the current situation as an on-going dominance of a modern neoclassical mainstream (see also the chapters by Kapeller and Dow in this volume). Its core has been partly modified and partly it is accomplished by side-streams mainly engaged in integrating new subject matter. According to the subject matter at stake, either different specifications of action theoretic and decision theoretic tenets are suggested giving the postulation of equilibrium conditions a greater importance (like in modern microeconomics) or the latter are relaxed and more emphasis is put on maintaining the former (as in modern macroeconomics). To put it in terms of Lakatos' research programmes, the research in experimental as well as behavioural economics can be qualified at most as driving the neoclassical research programme towards becoming partly "degenerative" in that it includes a threat for some traditional core axioms because neither their generality nor their complete compatibility can be guaranteed anymore.[24] Whether this threat can be fended off remains to be seen. Two options for such a defence can be derived from analysis above: (i) constructing protective belt mechanisms for re-establishing the traditional axioms (e.g. giving homo oeconomicus a new chance by way of "nudging"); and (ii) relaxing and generalising the axioms in such a way that they are still compatible with each other and remain valid for the whole realm of economics.

4. Need for and varieties of pluralism

4.1 Need for pluralism

Usually the need for pluralism is derived from normative considerations in that the adherents postulate it without qualifications as a basic requirement of scientific research.[25] From an analytical point of view this is not convincing, if this postulate is unconditional, because pluralism (of whatever kind) is not a general prerequisite for the working of a modern science as proposed in Section 2.1. Hence, the question is whether there are analytical arguments in favour of pluralism taking into account the observable social practices in modern science.

According to the concept sketched above, a multitude of perspectives, methods etc. is a general condition for reproducing a functionally differentiated scientific activity. In a situation with no paradigm or where multiple paradigms govern the scientific activities, postulating pluralism as a norm is not necessary. Contrary to that, in a situation where one paradigm dominates and is protecting itself against its erosion (situation of monism), it is necessary to establish pluralism as a procedural norm of scientific communication.[26] Postulating pluralism under these conditions can either have an instrumental meaning if it is seen as a measure to foster scientific progress by establishing alternative methods and perspectives; or it is meant as realising a principal (permanent) feature of scientific activities taking into account that there might be no consensus about the existence of monism (see also the chapters by Dow and Kapeller in this volume).

Considering research, the development of economics especially after the World War II has manifested that a "normal science" can get stuck into one paradigm or narrowly defined research programme. Reduction of uncertainty and transparent opportunities for building up reputation make these fixations popular among scientists. But at least in three respects the task of modern science can be threatened by such a development. *Firstly*, according to the specific Leitdifferenz which is the backbone for the modern autonomy of science, the main task of scientific activities is to generate and diffuse new insightful knowledge. This task can be fulfilled only in a limited way if scientists are orientated to an established ensemble of knowledge. At least radically new knowledge is then impossible.[27] *Secondly*, science in general and especially economics is evolutionary in nature: new and unexpected possibilities of scientific observation as well as unforeseen explanation requirements make a given and accepted knowledge stock vulnerable to change (Veblen 1898; Georgescu-Roegen 1966, 3, 92; Dow 2008, 83). Focussing and preserving such knowledge runs the risk of blocking this evolutionary nature. *Thirdly*, if establishing a paradigm/research programme is coupled with a higher degree of autonomy, in that the science at stake gets (more) independent of neighbour sciences, such a (more or less) complete decomposability contradicts the near-decomposable nature of the real world. Ignoring the isomorphism with the real subject-matter is not a problem in itself, as long as it is accepted in the science. But for logical reasons it generates problems of internal inconsistency and – at least in the long run – of legitimacy of that science.[28] *Fourthly*, in a "moral science" (in the sense of Keynes quoted above) scientists have to care for self-reflectivity: the focus they choose, as well as the generalisations they make in their theories, have to be questioned every time because in a social science like economics acceptance of knowledge is not necessarily legitimated by empirical observation. Economic knowledge is a construction, the main and first purpose of which is to enable scientific communication; therefore the appropriateness of these constructions for getting insights need on-going reflections (Dow 2008, 81). A dominating paradigm (monism) is tantamount to abolishing such a self-reflection.

Related to scientific research is the instruction/vocational training as a part of science. Here, not only is the education of scientists themselves the problem. Rather, in modern societies with large fields for applied sciences, science has to deliver knowledge and methods for instrumental qualifications. Against this backdrop, instruction and education as a part of the institutions of science (especially universities) have some specificities from which requirements for this part of scientific activities can be derived. Its main focus is not on specialised (rather quickly devalued) knowledge but on self-reflectivity, meta-qualifications and general problem solving abilities (Weehuizen 2007, 155; Garnett et al. 2010, 219). Hence, there is a necessity not only to offer a consistent educational perspective in methodological terms but also for presenting different concepts to structure and handle knowledge. This is an implication of delivering meta-qualifications and of the varieties of problems which have to be solved later on in the job. Hence, multiple perspectives are a generic feature of scientific instruction and vocational training at least in education/instruction related to uncertain environments. Here, pluralism is not only necessary as a safeguard against missing the task of science (as in the case of monism) but rather an indispensable permanent feature.[29]

4.2 Complementary vs. competitive pluralism

Considering the current state of economics in research as well as instruction/education there seem to be good reasons for establishing pluralism without referring to the normative constructions of the epistemology of science. A straightforward way to implement that pluralism would be to complement monistic mainstream economics by revitalising the components it has skipped when becoming dominant (complementary pluralism). First of all, that would imply to (re-)consider the contributions psychology, sociology and political science could offer for solving problems in economics or at least to correspondingly broaden the perspective of economic analysis. Additionally, institutionalising self-reflection in economics in terms of giving the history of economic thought, epistemology and ethical considerations in economics a greater importance would be a part of such a complementary pluralism. Finally, broadening the spectre of subject-matters of economics by focussing on important but neglected or inadequately treated topics (like justice, gender, environmental degradation) is an essential element of this kind of pluralism.

Even though such an enhancement would create an environment for relativising mainstream economics, the latter would remain untouched in its essential elements. Given a situation of monism, there is additionally a need for competitive pluralism. The focus of this kind of pluralism is to figure out concepts and theories having the same subject matter as mainstream economics but that do not share any (or most) of the tenets of the latter. This does not exclude that similar methods are used if they are promising in terms of new insights.[30] Accordingly, such a competitive pluralism should demonstrate the possibility of enhancing the knowledge base of mainstream economics e.g. by showing a higher level of generality, and/or more plausibility and/or higher empirical evidence.[31] The main goal of such a competitive pluralism is to erode the current mainstream (monism) in economics. Whether this may lead to a new mainstream in the future remains an open question.[32]

5. Features of a heterodox economics[33]

Although the features of mainstream economics may be a starting point for explaining the heterodox alternative, the latter is not conceptualised as a simple antithesis to the neoclassical mainstream (whatever may be its precise status quo). According to the specificity of knowledge and insights in science in general, and particularly to the post-war situation in economics (cf. Sections 2.1 and 2.2 above), there is a need for a competing paradigm, the components of which are consistent with each other. Guidelines for figuring out such a paradigm can be suggested: availability of concepts, primary focus on plausibility and empirical support instead of generality, precision and elegance (Vromen 2007, 87); moreover, finally, conceptual openness towards the neighbouring sciences. In such a context, the modern neoclassical concept turns out to be a special case with limited explanatory power. Contrary to what Vromen presumes, this is not an all-aspect-all-theories approach (ibid. 2007, 72) but focuses on the main topics of microeconomics and macroeconomics.

Going beyond the homo oeconomicus construct as well as methodological individualism (TN_7) is an implication of taking bounded rationality seriously. No simple (static) aggregation of autonomous entities is possible if technological as well as behavioural interdependencies are acknowledged as a normal state of the art. Rather, the (past) results of interaction are a determining factor for (actual) individual decisions: there is a recursive aggregation including an explanation of the individual by the outcome of economic interaction. This is of special importance if the outcome of interaction cannot be deduced from individual properties (emergent phenomena and recursive downward causation). In such a perspective, institutions as (temporarily) frozen and sanctioned interaction outcomes are an essential part of economic analysis. Hence, the catchword here is at least recursive methodological individualism or even a combination of methodological individualism and methodological holism.

Heterodox approaches leave maximising behaviour (TN_6) and methodological instrumentalism behind. In this respect, the neoclassical vision is composed of two assumptions: a stylised state space (e.g. convexity, continuity) (TN_1) and consistency requirements as regards the decisions in this state space ($TN_{2\text{-}5}$). Besides didactical reasons, there is no need to transfer these assumptions into the realm of a heterodox approach which is oriented towards a "plausible" mapping of observable state spaces as well as decision procedures. Hence, the main topic of the heterodox approach is to relate different state spaces with the selection of appropriate decision procedures. Neither "difficult" (large, complex or even uncertain) state spaces nor sub-conscious ways of deciding and acting (e.g. routines) are excluded. In such a context, two features come up which are alien to the modern neoclassical approach: *firstly*, the criterion for rationality of actions is no longer the same for all individuals but rather determined on the individual level by way of selecting an action mode or by pursuing an experience-dependent aspiration level; *secondly*, constraints and choices are no longer independent from each other because preferences may be influenced by those constraints or changing the constraints may guide the way to act (e.g. in the case of innovation).

Even though stylising the state space of agents is indispensable for any modelling attempt, in a heterodox approach this state space configuration is not determined by a mathematical formalism which is chosen a priori (i.e. without considering the problem at stake). Additionally, it is not necessary to include state space properties in the agent's knowledge of their possibilities to act. Exploration and exploitation as procedures for creating a state space and making use of it are essential features of a heterodox approach. Two elements are becoming important then for discriminating between different options to act: *firstly*, observing, gathering, assessing and retrieving information about own activities; and *secondly* the influence of observable activities of others. The way this discrimination between different options takes place largely depends on the specific economic context (e.g. it is different in households and firms) but in any case it is not appropriate to consider deliberate (preference-driven) decisions as the only way to tackle this discrimination requirement: "fast and frugal heuristics" (Gigerenzer 2011) are also an essential element here.

Even if the Pareto-optimum as the "old" device for equilibrium construction and evaluation has been loosened to mere compatibility requirements (as in the case of Nash equilibrium) or simply to market clearing processes, it is still an essential feature of the modern neoclassical research programme to postulate various sorts of equilibrating procedures (TN_8). Contrary to that, the charm of the heterodox approach is the absence of any such kind of a priori postulates. According to the heterodox perspectives sketched so far, a true bottom up explanation of the economic outcome is intended. That means, "plausible" agents as well as "plausible" interaction modes determine the order of economic activities as a whole without superimposing restrictions guaranteeing a desired structure of this outcome.[34] Hence, it is not per se excluded that economic activities generate equilibrium but this is a special case in the spectrum of possible types of order (including cycles with single or multiple periodicities, chaos, statistical power law etc.) implying any time-dependent "regular" variation of state variables. To sum up, individual discrimination, social discrimination and how both are mediated by prices as well as institutions is another essential part of a heterodox approach.

Contrary to the general features of the neoclassical research programme mentioned above, the heterodox programme is sensitive to the historical specificity of the modern market economy. If considering the economic practices as "social forms", a scientific endeavour which migrated to economic sociology in recent times, this should be re-introduced in economic analysis itself. The self-referential and self-propagating nature of these social forms not only puts further limits on a simple means-ends approach in economics but is also critical of the popular view that the wellbeing of the consumer is the ultimate goal of economic activity in our times. In such a context, money plays an essential role and has to be one of the core subjects of heterodox concepts. It is not simply a veil on mutual preference articulation but an essential mechanism for making them comparable. Accordingly, to explain the supply and demand of money (in its different forms) endogenously should have a prominent part in heterodox analysis (on the micro as well as the macro level).

Finally, to concede the embeddedness of the economy and accordingly to focus interdisciplinary concepts is an important feature of the heterodox approach. The multi-mode approach to economic decisions necessitates collaboration with psychology; the role of norms, institutions as well as the emergence of social action necessitates collaboration with sociology; deciphering uncertainty and instability and the corresponding adaptation requirements induced by a vulnerable ecological environment necessitate collaboration with ecology etc.

6. Conclusions and perspectives

The persistent narrowness in the scope of orthodox mainstream economics is not accidental. It seems to be a supposed result of the general reproduction dynamics of the modern science of economics and a consolidation of a particular path backed by this reproduction dynamics. If such a particular path is dominating, in that the drivers for closing and sealing off this path are stronger than the drivers for eroding and decomposing it, economics is running the risk of monism. In that case, the task proper of science to generate and disperse new insights and knowledge is threatened and pluralism becomes an obligatory medicine. If the self-reflectivity of economics (the blocking of which is often an element of path domination) is sufficiently sensible for this threat or if interventions from other social subsystems (like politics) are required, an element of therapy cannot be anticipated here.

Whereas in research postulating at least competitive pluralism is a requirement only in a specific situation (monism), in education pluralism in both its competitive as well as its complementary form is indispensable. Variety of perspectives, of concepts, and methods is a necessary element of preparing students for the real world complexities of economic life (see Elsner, Heinrich, Schwardt 2015). That this does not necessarily end up in an omnium-gatherum of educational elements should have been demonstrated by the suggestions above. Absence of such a broad approach simply generates an education failure.

Acknowledgments

In elaborating this article I benefited from discussions with Jakob Kapeller and Ingo Barens as well as from an anonymous referee report; of course I am alone responsible for anything written here.

Notes

1 Insightful knowledge is meant here as a specific type of knowledge beyond tacit nature on the one hand and purely instrumental orientation on the other hand.
2 Apart from being similar to other functionally separated activities in society, science is specific in terms of contents and procedures related to producing and diffusing insightful knowledge.
3 There are similarities and differences between the drivers for creating as well as for consolidating path dependence and paradigm in science on one side and economy on the other side (Dosi 1988; Kuhn 1970; Peacock 2009).
4 According to Kuhn (1970) this is the usual state in "normal science".
5 This is at least true for basic scientific research due to a lack of private interest to engage therein.
6 Kuhn does not explain how these paradigms come about. Path-dependence, especially second-order path dependence as suggested above, is an explanatory option for this offered by modern complexity theory.

7 Keynes borrowed the apple metaphor from Montague (1899). According to the latter, all sciences which are not related to physical observations are classified as "moral". (I thank Ingo Barens for this hint).

8 Neither the idea that economy is becoming a hegemonic subsystem subsuming science nor the counter-hypotheses about science itself subsuming other subsystems are compatible with this view – notwithstanding the eminent influence of economic interest groups on economics (Bernal 1965; Mirowski 2002) and the "performative" role of modern economics (Callon 2006).

9 Creating and stabilising this meta-path in the United States was heavily influenced by the activity of institutions like Cowles Commission (according to which "science is measurement"), Econometric Society, Rockefeller Foundation on the one hand and externally created reputation-hotspots in the selection of Nobel prize winners in economics on the other hand. The difference between the United States, Britain and France regarding the institutional conditions is analysed in Fourcade (2009). This kind of institutional influence on establishing a dominant conceptual path in economics has to be separated from institutional influence directed to create a "neoliberal" policy orientation e.g. by the Mont Pelérin Society. It has been shown, that the conceptual background for this policy framing is rather ambiguous (Mirowski 2013, 50).

10 Hence, the analysis of Kuhn being mainly based on taking into account empirically oriented natural sciences is only of limited value for explaining the specificity as well as the robustness of the modern paradigm in economics.

11 This was intended also as a way to overcome the separation between microeconomics and macroeconomics the main source of which was the work of Keynes. In that sense the "neoclassical synthesis" as well as the "dynamic stochastic equilibrium models" are two stages of getting rid of the "aberration" resulting from Keynes' contributions and of re-establishing the general equilibrium frame work as a backbone of all economics (De Vroey 2016).

12 Dobusch and Kapeller (2009, 877) show that network effects, economies of scale and scope as well as sunk costs and the mainstream bias in performance-dependent resource allocation play an important role in generating this quasi-monistic structure in post-war economics. Such a diagnosis of strong paradigm domination (monism) in post-war economics is in sharp contrast to the smooth diffusion models of competing paradigms suggested recently by several authors (e.g. Colander et al. (2004, 458); Davis (2006)).

13 The arguments for backing this assessment are quite disparate and mostly assuming what should be shown (e.g. Colander (2000, 135); Colander et al. (2004, 486); Vromen (2007, 68); Davis 2006).

14 This assessment does not contradict the fact that former adherents of 'The Economy as an Evolving Complex System' return to the realm of neoclassical economics (Blume and Durlauf 2006, 2). Human beings and their thinking are no exception from evolving complexity, including retrogression.

15 The realm of this research is even more constrained if it is taken into account that there is a common sense between experimental economists about the necessary design for experiments (e.g. excluding intransparent situations and deception, including monetary reward etc. (Camerer 2011).

16 According to the experimental orientation, mostly interaction in small groups by applying stylised settings is investigated. But even in this stylised interaction environment an equilibrium outcome – even one with multiple equilibria – is not guaranteed (Fehr and Falk (2002, 708). Other examples for the resulting ambiguity are postulating (Akerlof and Shiller 2015) or modelling (Spiegler 2014) market mechanisms compensating for the irrationality of economic "Phools".

17 Scarcity as the main focus of economics has been put forward by Robbins (1935, 15). This has been an early signpost for the research in favour of a paradigmatic

pure science of economics (ibid., 64, 70) which took place later on and which eliminated the "statesmanlike vagueness in the description of the postulates" (Koopmans 1957, 136) inherent in Robbins' suggestions. Some aspects of this conformity between Robbins' early definition of economics and its later axiomatisation are analysed by Backhouse and Medema (2009).

18 The most prominent example in this respect is the explanation of prices by referring to the notion of scarcity. In almost every textbook on microeconomics you can find a type of reasoning starting from the phrase "If there is no scarcity, there are no prices" and deriving from that the conclusion "Prices have to be and can be explained by scarcity" (e.g. Schotter 2009, 5; Colander 2006, 9; Pindyck and Rubinfeld 2001, 4). The same is true for research monographs (e.g. Debreu 1959, 33). Even if scarcity (in whichever form) should be a necessary condition for prices coming into existence, the former is by no means a sufficient condition for explaining the latter.

19 The literature only mention parts of these tenets: e.g. Hodgson (2013, 7) discusses TN_3, TN_4, TN_7 and TN_8. Arnsperger and Varoufakis (2006) refer to TN_3, TN_6, TN_7 and TN_8.

20 Stylised is meant here not in the sense that inessential features can be neglected in a scientific abstraction but rather as a requirement of formal/mathematical manipulation. One example is the convexity assumption.

21 If methodological individualism is proposed in strict terms by taking the individual and only the individual as explanans and interaction as well as all sorts of economic structures as explanandum this methodological device can only be maintained by smuggling in unexplained elements (Hodgson 2013, 31). Most prominent are "homogeneous", "representative" or "rationally expecting" individuals. Furthermore TN_1 already supposes some preordering not derivable from individual action.

22 The way to use the equilibrium concept can be illustrated by referring to Blanchard (2009, 27).

23 Some authors additionally refer to mathematical formalism per se as an essential mainstream feature (Lawson 2015; Dow 2008). In this general form this argument cannot be substantiated: there are also heterodox concepts using mathematical formalisms (e.g. evolutionary economics complexity economics and – to a part – Post-Keynesian economics). Rather, it is a special type of mathematical formalisation (calculus and optimisation algorithms) and a specific way to attribute semantic contents to formalisms which is typical for the modern mainstream (Dow 2008, 80).

24 This corresponds to Dow's distinction between „ "official discourse" and "unofficial discourse" (Dow 2008, 79).

25 Mostly these postulates are specified in terms of epistemological, ontological and methodological requirements (Dow 2008; Dobusch and Kapeller 2012, 1041).

26 Especially in modern differentiated science with disciplinary operational self-referential dynamics this could mean: unmasking pseudo-pluralism.

27 There is no simple analogy between pluralism as an essential feature of scientific progress and pluralism implied in dispersed new knowledge-gaining procedures in the market (as e.g. Polanyi (1962) contends). Due to the different approval procedures in science, there is a stronger reluctance against diverging or new insights and a higher importance of path-dependency etc.

28 A straightforward example is economic policy: if it is conceptualised in the closed framework of (welfare) economics, no convincing recommendations for solving real world problems can be given.

29 This is in sharp contrast to the narrow-mindedness of mainstream education and hints to its disorienting role as regards instruction and education (Vromen 2007, 74; Hodgson 2013, 5 for an overview).

30 Hence, appropriate mathematics has its place in such an endeavour (contrary to what Lawson (2015) is proposing).

31 This is not a plea for heterodox monism because the superiority of a concept/theory cannot be stated objectively (Dow 2008, 85 and the contribution of Dow in this volume). Rather, it is a plea for competing constructions of economic knowledge.

32 In that sense this kind of pluralism is fundamentally different from the idea of "interested pluralism" favoured by Dobusch and Kapeller (2012, 1043): it is not assumed that a dominant paradigm situation can be transformed (by the goodwill of the dominant players in science) into an overarching "ideal speech situation" à la Habermas. Rather pluralism is a contest which has to be organised by dissenters alone on the level of arguments, methods and practices. What happens if this contest situation is neglected (by not caring for marking the essential differences) can be studied by considering e.g. the fate of the journal "ecological economics" which started as a dissenting journal (in a sense assuming an "ideal speech situation") and which is dominated now by the neoclassical mainstream.

33 The following ideas are meant as a trigger for elaborating alternative concepts (and selecting appropriate methods) which can only take place in scientific communication. In that sense some features of future concepts are suggested; this does not exclude that only some of them might be appropriate when these concepts are specified – or that other features may then become more important.

34 "Plausible" here refers to a type of scientific knowledge which does not contradict insights from other sciences and which is in conformity with direct observability.

References

Akerlof, G.A. and Shiller, R.J. (2015): *Phishing for Phools – the Economics of Manipulation and Deception*. Princeton: Princeton University Press.

Arnsperger, C. and Varoufakis, Y. (2006): 'What Is Neoclassical Economics? The Three Axioms Responsible for Its Theoretical Oeuvre, Practical Irrelevance and, thus, Discoursive Power', *Panoeconomicus* 1, 5–18.

Arrow, K.J. and Hahn, F.H. (1971): *General Competitive Analysis*. Amsterdam: North-Holland.

Athreya, K.B. (2013): *Big Ideas in Macroeconomics*. Cambridge: MIT Press.

Backhouse, R.E. and Medema, S.G. (2009): 'Robbins's Essay and the Axiomatization of Economics', *Journal of the History of Economic Thought* 31(4), 485–499.

Beckenbach, F. (2015): 'Innovative Behavioral Approaches to Analyse the Incentives of Environmental Instruments – A Survey', in Beckenbach, F. and Kahlenborn, W. (eds.), *New Perspectives for Environmental Policies through Behavioral Economics*. Berlin: Springer, 15–68.

Berg, N. and Gigerenzer, G. (2010): 'As-If Behavioral Economics: Neoclassical Economics in Disguise?', *History of Economic Ideas* 18(1), 133–165.

Bernal, J.D. (1939): *The Social Function of Science*. London: Routledge.

Bernal, J.D. (1965): *Science in History*. London: C.A. Watts.

Blanchard, O. (2009): 'The State of Macro', *Annual Review of Economics* 1, 209–228.

Blume, L.E. and Durlauf, S.N. (2006): *The Economy as an Evolving Complex System III*. Oxford: Oxford University Press.

Buiter, W. (2009): *The Unfortunate Uselessness of Most 'State of the Art' Academic Monetary Economics*, MPRA Paper No. 58407. Munich University Library.

Callon, M. (2006): 'What Does It Mean to Say that Economics Is Performative?', in MacKenzie, D. and Muniesa, F. (eds.), *Do Economists Make Markets? On the Performativity of Economics*. Princeton: Princeton University Press, 311–357.

Camerer, C.F. (2011): 'The Promise and Success of Lab-Field Generalizability in Experimental Economics: A Critical Reply to Levitt and List', Working Paper. California Institute of Technology. Available at http://dx.doi.org/10.2139/ssrn.1977749, accessed 30.08.2017.

Colander, D. (2000): 'The Death of Mainstream Economics', *Journal of the History of Economic Thought* 22(2), 127–143.

Colander, D. (2006). *Microeconomics*. Boston: McGraw-Hill.

Colander, D., Holt, R.P. and Rosser, J.B. Jr. (2004): 'The Changing Face of Mainstream Economics', *Review of Political Economy* 16(4), 485–499.

Davis, J.B. (2006): 'The Turn in Economics: Neoclassical Dominance to Mainstream Pluralism', *Journal of Institutional Economics* 2(2), 1–20.

De Vroey, M. (2016): *A History of Macroeconomics from Keynes to Lucas and Beyond*. Cambridge: Cambridge University Press.

Debreu, G. (1959): *Theory of Value. An Axiomatic Analysis of Economic Equilibrium*. New Haven: Yale University Press.

Dobusch, L. and Kapeller, J. (2009): 'Why Is Economics Not an Evolutionary Science? New Answers to Veblen's Old Question', *Journal of Economic Issues* 43 (4), 867–898.

Dobusch, L. and Kapeller, J. (2012): 'Heterodox United vs. Mainstream City? Sketching a Framework for Interested Pluralism in Economics', *Journal of Economic Issues* 46(4), 1035–1057.

Dosi, G. (1988): 'Sources, Procedures and Microeconomic Effects of Innovation', *Journal of Economic Literature* 26(3), 1120–1171.

Dow, S.C. (2008): 'Plurality in Orthodox and Heterodox Economics', *Journal of Philosophical Economics* 1(2), 73–96.

Dusek, T. (2008): 'Methodological Monism in Economics', *Journal of Philosophical Economics* 1(2), 26–50.

Elsner, W., Heinrich, T. and Schwardt, H. (2015): *The Microeconomics of Complex Economies: Evolutionary, Institutional, and Complexity Perspectives*. Oxford: Elsevier.

Fehr, E. and Falk, A. (2002): 'The Psychological Foundation of Incentives', *European Economic Review* 46(4–5), 687–724.

Fourcade, M. (2009): *Economists and Societies – Discipline and Profession in the United States, Britain and France, 1890s to 1990s*. Princeton: Princeton University Press.

Freudenthal, G. and McLaughlin, P. (2009, eds.): *The Social and Economic Roots of the Scientific Revolution – Texts by Boris Hessen and Henryk Grossmann*. Berlin: Springer.

Garnett, R., Olsen, E.K. and Starr, M. (2010, eds.): *Economic Pluralism*. London: Routledge.

Georgescu-Roegen, N. (1966): *Analytical Economics – Issues and Problems*. Cambridge: Harvard University Press.

Gigerenzer, G. (2011, ed.): *Heuristics: The Foundations of Adaptive Behavior*. New York: Oxford University Press.

Hands, W. (2001): *Reflection without Rules*. Cambridge: Cambridge University Press.

Hicks, J.R. (1962[1939]): *Value and Capital: An Inquiry into Some Fundamental Principles of Economic Theory*. London: Oxford University Press.

Hodgson, G.M. (2001): *How Economics Forgot History: The Problem of Historical Specificity in Social Science*. London: Routledge.

Hodgson, G.M. (2013): *From Pleasure Machines to Moral Communities – An Evolutionary Economics without Homo Oeconomicus*. Chicago: University of Chicago Press.
Horkheimer, M. (1933): 'Materialismus Und Metaphysik', *Zeitschrift Für Sozialforschung* 2(1), 1–33.
Horkheimer, M. (1937): 'Traditionelle Und Kritische Theorie', *Zeitschrift Für Sozialforschung* 6(2), 245–294.
Ingrao, B. and Israel, G. (1990): *The Invisible Hand: Equilibrium in the History of Science*. London: MIT Press.
Keynes, J.M. (1973[1983]): 'Letter to R.F. Harrod', in Moggridge, D. (ed.), *The Collected Writings of John Maynard Keynes*, Volume XIV. London: Macmillan.
Koopmans, T. (1957): *Three Essays on the State of Economic Science*. New York: McGraw-Hill.
Kuhn, T.S. (1970): *The Structure of Scientific Revolutions*. Chicago: University of Chicago Press.
Lakatos, I. (1978): *The Methodology of Scientific Research Programmes: Philosophical Papers*. Cambridge: Cambridge University Press.
Lawson, T. (2015): *The Nature and State of Modern Economics*. London: Routledge.
Luhmann, N. (1992): *Die Wissenschaft Der Gesellschaft*. Frankfurt a.M.: Suhrkamp.
Luhmann, N. (2003): *Theory of Society*. Stanford: Standford University Press.
Mathaci, J. (1984): 'Rethinking Scarcity: Neoclassicism, NeoMalthusianism and Neo-Marxism', *Review of Radical Political Eoncomics* 16(2–3), 81–94.
Mill, J.S. (2006[1872]): *A System of Logic: Ratiocinative and Inductive*. Indianapolis: Liberty Fund.
Mirowski, P. (2002): *Machine Dreams: Economics Becoming a Cyborg Science*. Cambridge: Cambridge University Press.
Mirowski, P. (2004): *The Effortless Economy of Science?* Durham: Duke University Press.
Mirowski, P. (2013): *Never Let a Serious Crisis Go To Waste – How Neoliberalism Survived the Financial Crisis*. London: Verso.
Montague, F.C. (1899): 'Sciences, Moral and Political', in Palgrave, R.H.I. (ed.), *Dictionary of Political Economy*. London: Macmillan, 367–368.
Peacock, M.S. (2009): 'Path Dependence in the Production of Scientific Knowledge', *Social Epistemology* 23(2), 105–124.
Pindyck, R.S. and Rubinfeld, D.L. (2001): *Microeconomics*. London: Prentice Hall.
Polanyi, M. (1962): 'The Republic of Science: Its Political and Economic Theory', *Minerva* 1, 54–74.
Popper, K. (1989): *Logik Der Forschung*. Tübingen: Mohr.
Robbins, L. (1935): *An Essay on the Nature and Significance of Economic Science*. London: Macmillan Press.
Samuelson, P.A. (1947): *Foundations of Economic Analysis*. Cambridge: Harvard University Press.
Schotter, A. (2009): *Microeconomics: A Modern Approach*. Mason: South-Western.
Schülein, J.A. and Reitze, R. (2012): *Wissenschafstheorie Für Einsteiger*. Wien: Facultas.
Simon, H.A. (1977): 'The Organization of Complex Systems', in Patte, H.H. (ed.), *Hierarchy Theory: The Challenge of Complex Systems*. New York: George Braziller, 1–27.
Simon, H.A. (1996): *The Sciences of the Artificial*. Cambridge: MIT Press, 183–216.
Simon, H.A. (2002): 'Near Decomposability and the Speed of Evolution', *Industrial and Corporate Change* 11(3), 587–599.
Spiegler, R. (2014): *Bounded Rationality and Industrial Organization*. Oxford: Oxford University Press.

Sunstein, C. (2014): *Why Nudge? The Politics of Liberterian Paternalism.* New Haven: Yale University Press.

Veblen, T. (1898): 'Why Is Economics Not an Evolutionary Science?', *Quarterly Journal of Economics* 4, 373–397.

Vromen, J. (2007): 'In Praise of Moderate Plurality', in Groenewegen, J. (ed.), *Teaching Pluralism in Economics.* Cheltenham: Edward Elgar, 64–94.

Weehuizen, R. (2007): 'Interdisciplinarity and Problem-Based Learning', in Groenewegen, J. (ed.), *Teaching Pluralism in Economics.* Cheltenham: Edward Elgar, 155–188.

Weintraub, E.R. (1993): *General Competitive Analysis: Studies in Appraisal.* Ann Arbor: The University of Michigan Press.

Wilholt, T. (2012): *Die Freiheit Der Forschung – Begründungen Und Begrenzungen.* Frankfurt a.M.: Suhrkamp.

3 Pluralism in economics

Epistemological rationales and pedagogical implementation

Jakob Kapeller

1. Introduction

Economics has a strong tradition as a separate and autonomous subfield in social research: internally, it is tied together by a specific vision of economic decision-making and economic interactions, where the former is based on instrumental rationality, while the latter are conceived as equilibrating processes leading mostly to socially efficient outcomes. Hence, the standard economic approach builds on the conceptual pillars of scarcity, optimisation and, mostly efficient, equilibria. While this dominance of a single theoretical approach has often been understood as an indicator of the high quality, intellectual coherence and practical usefulness of standard economics (e.g. Lazear 2000), other authors emphasize the internal diversity and corresponding incoherence *within* the standard economic approach (e.g. Hausman 1992; Bowles and Gintis 2000).

This dominance of a single approach to economic issues is especially relevant in the context of teaching economics, as it allows for the introduction of a set of highly standardized economic textbooks, which, so to say, codify the established knowledge using different degrees of analytical and mathematical complexity. This tradition of highly influential textbooks in economics thereby goes back to the 19th century (e.g. John Stuart Mill's *Principles of Political Economy*, published in 1848) and has had a strong impact on both the development of the economic discipline as well as the evolution of public debates on economic issues. This crucial role of textbooks for establishing and transmitting economic knowledge to a larger audience has thereby long been recognised. Paul A. Samuelson – the author of the most popular economics textbook of the 20th century – once framed this insight in the following iconic way: "I don't care who writes a nation's laws – or crafts its advanced treaties – if I can write its economics textbooks." (Samuelson, cited after Skousen 1997, 150)

In this paper, I try to sketch a different view on the teaching of economics, which recognises its societal impact and is conceptually more strongly coined by a pluralist and inclusive approach to economic thought. In doing so, I first introduce three basic epistemological arguments on how a pluralist conception of science can contribute to an improvement of existing practices in research and teaching (Section 2). Hence, I implicitly assume that the potential epistemological merits of a pluralist approach also provide some guiding clarifications for a pluralist teaching of economics. Additionally, I will assess and compare different diagnoses regarding the relative openness of mainstream economic research, to ask how far current mainstream economic practices, which often come with an increasing variety of models, can be considered pluralist (Section 3). This section serves to show that there is indeed a connection between theoretical and methodological diversity on the levels of teaching and research in economics as such diversity is significantly lagging behind model variety. Finally, I will try to delineate some suggestions on how to practically implement a pluralist approach to economic research (Section 4) and economic teaching (Section 5) drawing on the foundations developed in the foregoing sections.

2. Pluralism in economics: epistemological rationales

The search for more and more general and inclusive theories of increasing range and explanatory power is a central aim of science. Theories of strong generality, such as Newtonian mechanics and Darwin's theory of evolution, distinguish themselves by summarising and systematising existing knowledge, and by their potential to allow for new prognoses, insights and theories. Against the backdrop of the broad applicability of these theories, the aim of discovering increasingly far-reaching theories, and, in this way, steadily improving our knowledge, seems dominant. The impression arises that the "final objective" of every science is, primarily, the construction of a universal and inclusive theory of the respective subject area.

> The ultimate aim of a science is to establish a single, complete, and comprehensive account of the natural world (or the part of the world investigated by the science) based on a single set of fundamental principles.
>
> Kellert et al. (2006, x)

Such an interpretation – the search for a "universal" theory as the "ultimate" aim of science, and the related aspiration to thoroughly explain some subject by means of a fixed set of statements, i.e. a single theory, that is as general as possible – falls short on several levels. First, such an interpretation is based on too simplistic and abridged a notion of the precise function of this search for increasingly comprehensive theories within the development of science. Second, such an approach is in danger of underestimating the complexities and multifacetedness of social reality. As a third point, such a view can lead to a subversion of typical practical requirements for the critical evaluation of theories, which typically afford to consider competing explanations for some phenomena in roughly equivalent proportions. In total, therefore, three arguments arise against a monistic conception of science and the associated interpretation of the aim to create increasingly general theories as "monistic", which will be illustrated in the following in greater detail (see also Beckenbach's chapter in this volume).

2.1 The fundamental argument: there is no such thing as a "most general" theory

The fundamental argument can be traced back to the more general idea of fallibilism, which states that every empirical hypothesis and, because of that, every theory is fallible (Popper 2002[1959]). Fallibilism refers to the fact that in the area of empirical science (in contrast to purely formal analysis), proving that some insight is a 'certain truth' is impossible from the point of view of logic, as we always lack a means to definitely confirm the correctness of the underlying hypotheses, even if the data speaks in its favour. This ambiguity in the scientific process is sometimes called the "asymmetry between falsification and verification" and has led people to speak of the "corroboration" instead of the "confirmation" of hypotheses (again following Popper 2002[1959]).

Moreover, striving for "certain" knowledge can lead one astray when certainty is wrongly interpreted as a criterion of quality, as, ultimately, "all certainties of knowledge are manufactured and, as such, worthless for the assessment of reality" (Albert 1991, 30, authors' translation). Since we do not have a suitable apparatus for "certain" reasoning at our disposal, we are condemned to always presuppose our own fallibility. From the point of view of critical rationalism, this logical limitation is the reason that every form of empirical scientific theory is potentially flawed and revisable.

When put in the context of the search for increasingly general theories, this argument leads straight to the conclusion that the idea of a "most general" or "complete" theory is misleading, as, due to the fundamentally fallible character of our knowledge, we can never fully rely on the validity or completeness of a theory. Even if we had found such a "most general theory", we could never prove this finding beyond doubt. Hence, those proponents of mainstream economics who propose, like Becker (1976) or Lazear (2000), that standard economics offers such a 'most general' theory are clearly led astray by their own conceptual convictions.

This means that the quest for increasingly comprehensive theories has to be understood differently. In the best possible case, this search augments our knowledge gradually; however, in this way, it does not have a final, all-encompassing goal. From this follows that the search for increasingly comprehensive theories has to be understood as a process, first and foremost, which is desirable, because it can contribute to a continuous improvement of our knowledge (without ever reaching perfection). The search for increasingly comprehensive theories is an open aim, not a closed one; in this sense, the journey is the destination. Especially, the existence of actual or allegedly general theories in a certain field should not per se preclude the emergence or sustaining of alternative theories, as long as the latter also strive for empirical accuracy. This latter aspect is especially important as individual participation in different research programs is often coined by self-reinforcing feedback effects, which can contribute to paradigmatic dominance and theoretical monism within a given field (Sterman and Wittenberg 1999; Dobusch and Kapeller 2009).

2.2 The empirical argument: the complexity of reality

Empirical reality as examined by the social sciences is multifaceted, dynamic and diverse. For this reason, social and economic phenomena often cannot be explained by a single argument as these phenomena have several causes, which bring forth only a conjoint effect. Conversely, most social phenomena also yield different effects and, hence, have different implications and properties depending on the researcher's specific perspective and questions on the subject. To disentangle observed patterns with respect to the most important mechanisms underlying these patterns is one of the prime tasks of social research – an argument that is also partially recognized by those standard economists, who do not shy away from questions of "external validity", i.e. the issue of whether past empirical results can be applied beyond their original research context (e.g. Deaton 2010). To illustrate the complexity originating from this setup, I suggest considering the example of increasing income inequality.

Observable since the 1980s, the increase in income disparity in most OECD countries (Atkinson 2007) has a number of fundamentally different causes. Globalisation, regional competition and the race for the best location put pressure on domestic income policies. Increased flexibility of labour regulations, successively relaxed taxation of corporate profits as well as top labour incomes (Egger et al. 2016) further fostered the resulting divide between increasing salaries at the top and stagnating or even declining wages in the lower parts of the income distribution. At the same time, unions are regressing in their degree of organisation, and, as a result, have little to counter these developments. Additionally, technological evolution increases the educational requirements of employees (e.g. Card and DiNardo 2002), which renders education into an amplifier of existing inequalities. Hence, even a short and superficial discussion reveals several drivers of increasing inequality and provides a series of partially related causes relevant for adequately addressing this issue. Moreover, this increase in income disparity is not only complex on the level of causes, but also connected to vastly different effects and consequences. Increasing inequality leads to a deterioration of physical and mental health in the entire population (Wilkinson and Pickett 2007), to reduced domestic demand and increased indebtedness (Kapeller and Schütz 2014), and increases the labour supply (Bowles and Park 2005) as well as the instability of the financial markets (more play money on the upper, as well as more nonperforming loans on the lower end of the income spectrum). Additionally, rising income inequality has implications for the behaviour of the political system (Gilens and Page 2014), may foster dynastic intergenerational patterns (Piketty 2014), and so forth.

Multifacetedness, therefore, means the necessity to consider a substantial number of different layers – influencing factors and consequences of economic phenomena – that have to be considered when looking at an economic issue in its entirety. As it seems highly unlikely that social-scientific theories will be found that incorporate all those different aspects, the advantage of a pluralistic approach can be seen especially clearly: in this frame, existing theoretical approaches are at best partially suited to understand the observed phenomena and processes – they are "partial theories" that, in the ideal case, deliver empirically valid explanations for a part of the envisaged subject area. "Economics is", then, "by necessity, a multi-paradigmatic science" (Rothschild 1988, 13), which needs a variety of different conceptual perspectives – as opposed to a variety of models all based on the same fundamental perspective, as is the case in contemporary standard economics (see also Elsner 1986).

Different theories pertaining to the same area are not necessarily antagonistic from this perspective, but often are of complementary character, as they only study the treated phenomena from one specific angle. This feature may actually be constructively exploited to address different economic situations and problems across time and space by giving priority to those theoretical arguments which align well to the problems under study. In this vein, it seems natural that a multitude of theoretical approaches is necessary in order to somewhat adequately depict this multifacetedness of social reality.

The philosopher of science Ronald Giere (1999) suggests thinking of the usage of different maps made for different purposes (e.g. hiking maps for hikers, road atlases for drivers, etc.) as a metaphor for the necessity of using different theories to fully assess a certain subject. In order to do justice to the complexity and multifacetedness of reality, it is, therefore, reasonable to look for different theories in order to address social phenomena as comprehensively as possible, and, as a result, to be able to supply differentiated statements about a certain topic of interest.

2.3 The practical argument: how to choose between competing theories?

A core problem in science is to offer suitable methods and criteria for organising the relative evaluation of competing theories and hypotheses, i.e., to distinguish the relative success of several rival explanations, differentiating between better and worse theoretical arguments. The established answer to this problem is the suggestion to examine competing explanations via the principle of critical tests (Popper 2002[1959]; see Hands 2001; for the more specific case of economics), that is, to simply assess the quality of different theories by comparing how well they stand up to a confrontation with empirical facts, also considering the variety and intensity of the employed tests.

A practical condition of this relative assessment is to proceed without prejudice when selecting theories to be tested empirically, and treat and consider every available explanatory approach (i.e. each relevant theory) equally. Pluralism in theory choice is a practical prerequisite of empirical research endeavours, not only in the sense that current studies should not be biased by past judgements, but also to actually ensure a critical attitude in testing. Otherwise, "monism of theories [...] can easily have the consequence of using facts only for the illustration or backup of the predominant theory, and interpreting them in a compliant way" (Albert 1991, 61, authors' translation).

In this way, the principle of critical evaluation is often subverted in current economics, however, as it implies "not only the search for contrary factual findings, but primarily also the search for alternative theoretical conceptions as necessary" (Albert 1991, 62, author's translation). Different hypotheses about a topic of research must not have a priori authority over others, since all hypotheses should be evaluated according to the same epistemic principles (Popper 2002[1959]). By implication, this presupposes a balanced representation of all available and relevant hypotheses in academic discourse. Although the pluralist principle to consider all hypotheses in equal measure is surely rather an ideal than a strict requirement, it seems especially essential when, as it is in the social sciences, the number of reliable theories with a broad range of applications is low.

In summary, three central arguments arise against a monistic conception of science, and against the ensuing aspiration to fully explain a given subject area via one theory that is as general as possible. First, the fundamental argument implied that the aim of finding a single all-encompassing theory for any subject can never be achieved and, hence, a certain variety in theorising seems necessary – especially when we come to the edge of established knowledge. Second, the empirical argument refers to the multifacetedness of social phenomena, and emphasies (the danger of) blind spots resulting from a purely monistic approach to explaining said phenomena. Finally, the practical argument relates to a basic methodological tenet that seems to be at least potentially endangered by an attitude that is too monistic in its theoretical perspective.

3. Pluralism in economics: competing assessments

While from the point of view of epistemology, pluralism appears as an indeed promising guiding concept for research, there has been little note about the actual character and orientation of economics' current praxis. If one consults the literature relevant to this issue, at least two positions can be determined. The first position focuses on the paradigmatic dominance of neoclassical theory (Dobusch and Kapeller 2009), and subsequently diagnoses a generally unfounded discrimination of non-neoclassical, so-called "heterodox" economic theories. In doing so, the first position characterizes the economic "mainstream" theory as largely monistic.

> The confrontation of heterodoxy versus mainstream in fact draws its existence and justification from the present condition of the regime of science, which is characterized by an obvious privileging and support of a

> neoclassically shaped mainstream at universities, research institutes and international economic organizations.
>
> Rothschild (2008, 25, authors' translation)

The exclusion of heterodox economists from the employment (Lee 2004) and publication market (Hodgson and Rothman 1999; King 2002), the homogenous character of economics education (Hill and Myatt 2007; ISIPE 2014) as well as the non-reception of heterodox approaches in the area of mainstream economics as identified by citation analyses (e.g. Kapeller 2010) count as central evidence for this line of argument.

However, an alternative view on economics' current praxis emphasises the internal theoretical diversity of the neoclassical mainstream, and detects the conceptual core of this paradigm in a commitment to a "model-oriented building of theories".

> Those standard classifications convey a sense of the profession as a single set of ideas. In our view, that is wrong; it is much more useful to characterize the economics profession as a diverse evolving set of ideas, loosely held together by its modeling approach to economic problems.
>
> Colander et al. (2004, 486–487)

Here, Colander et al. ascribe an inherently pluralist character to mainstream economics. In essence, there is a reference to the multitude of different models, assumptions and model results that – as is suggested – does not fit with the allegation of a one-sided or monistic theoretical orientation. Nonetheless, Colander et al.'s statement is not very specific with regard to the exact role of core building blocks of standard economic theory, i.e. scarcity, optimisation and equilibrium, within the core "modelling approach" of the economic mainstream. In the following, this position will be investigated more precisely from the point of view of theory of science in order to answer the question of whether or to what extent the broad variety of models in neoclassical economics constitutes a product of its alleged pluralist character.

3.1 The variety of mainstream economics and the principle of axiomatic variation

The standard perspective in economics, which is largely based on neoclassical economic theory, goes hand in hand both with the exclusion of alternative theoretical approaches and with the self-perception of increasing internal variety. In this section, the second observation in particular will be explained with reference to "axiomatic variation" (Kapeller 2013).

In the context of the position proposed by Colander et al. (2004), Colander (2000) describes "modern applied microeconomics" as "a grab bag of models with a model for every purpose", and refers to the large variety of different model variations within neoclassical economics. The crucial question that needs to be answered is whether this large variety of models actually results in a true variety of theories within the neoclassical school – as Colander et al. posited – or whether they play a different role in the discourse of neoclassical mainstream.

At its core, the method of "axiomatic variation" that is observable within the neoclassical development of models rests on the idea of modifying single axioms of a model, removing them or adding new ones in order to create a new variation of an already established model to address a novel problem or a prevailing criticism. In this way, a perpetual expansion of the neoclassical spectrum of theories ensues as scientists are provided with the means to generate new puzzles within an already existing theoretical edifice.

Using axiomatic variation – like in a cloning laboratory – a whole number of variations of a model can be generated without any relevant constraint. However, while most parts of the "genetic make-up" of such a variation will indeed resemble well-established patterns of argument, some specific characteristic is usually inserted into a new model to distinguish the latter from their model of origin.

In this context, an "axiom" is simply to be understood synonymously to "model assumption". It follows that an economic model consists of a series of axioms A_1 to A_n. In the case of the modification of single axioms, an existing model M gives rise to a new model M^*. Taken on its own, the concept of axiomatic variation is not unique, as it is applied in the area of natural sciences in a similar fashion. However, contrary to natural sciences, neoclassical economics does not rigidly distinguish between law-like statements and auxiliary hypotheses in its theoretical considerations (Albert 1994), which makes it difficult to judge whether practices in these two fields are really akin. Most importantly, law-like hypotheses will stay constant across all model-variations associated with a certain theory: Newtonian models will always incorporate the argument that force equals mass times acceleration, while other assumptions introduced into Newtonian models might well vary as they describe different contexts of application.

In contrast, an important pattern in modern economics is that it is possible to alter all occurring axioms of an established model, including axioms that may very well be perceived as statements of law. Hence, this aspect differs strongly from the practice of natural sciences, where variations in the axiomatic setup of specific assumptions only concern the respective situational assumptions, meaning those auxiliary hypotheses that are used when applying more general, law-like statements to a specific problem. For example, Newton's law of universal gravitation ($F_1 = Gm_1m_2/r^2$) is valid both on Earth and the Moon, but its valid application requires a modification of auxiliary hypotheses (practically speaking: different numerical values for m_1 have to be inserted in the above formula; cf. Bunge 1967).

However, in the field of neoclassical economics, this possibility of variation is not explicitly restricted to the sphere of auxiliary hypotheses (whatever it may be) – rather, all axioms of a model can be varied without second thought, as already observed by Daniel Hausman more than twenty years ago.

> First, not all microeconomic models employ all [microeconomic] laws, even when they are relevant to the explanatory tasks at hand. Not only are there models [. . .] that leave out laws that have no implications for the case at hand, but there are also microeconomic models that incorporate contraries to some of the fundamental laws of microeconomic theory. For there are models with satiation, models with increasing or decreasing returns to scale, models without profit maximization, even models without completeness and models without transitivity. It is as if physicists sometimes supposed that force is proportional to acceleration and in other models took force to be proportional to acceleration squared.
>
> Hausman (1992, 52)

Therefore, the insufficient differentiation between law-like statements and auxiliary hypotheses within neoclassical economics constitutes a fundamental reason for the large variety of economic models, and for the accompanying flexibility of the dominant neoclassical paradigm when it comes to accommodating all kinds of empirical evidence. It also makes clear that the core assumptions of neoclassical economics – scarcity, rationality and equilibrium – are best understood as influential metaphors: they coin the style and direction of research overall, but are not necessarily binding concepts, when it comes to the formulation of specific models and arguments.

A prime example of this flexibility of neoclassical theory can be found in the works of George Akerlof, especially in his famous argument on asymmetric information and the associated "market for lemons" (Akerlof 1970). In the context of his engagement with the neoclassical standard model, Akerlof exchanges the axiom of "complete information" for that of "asymmetrical information", in which relevant information about products is distributed unequally between supplier and demander. In this way, Akerlof tries to explain, for example, why suboptimal results of allocation may emerge in competitive markets, taking the market for second-hand cars as his prime example. From Akerlof's example, it becomes clear that via axiomatic variation, different and contradictory variations of a model can coexist without problems. In this interpretation, the standard model M contains the assumption of "complete information" (A), and explains those cases in which markets function efficiently (E). The alternative model (M^*) contains the contrary assumption of "incomplete and asymmetric information" (A^*), and explains those cases in which markets do not function efficiently ($\neg E$).

Formally speaking, for every model M with the assumption A and result E, there exists an alternative model $M^\star$ with an alternative assumption $A^\star$, leading to a contrary result $\neg E$. This simple formula captures the essence of axiomatic variation in mainstream economic models.

Akerlof's example already gives a hint as to why the principle of axiomatic variation as established in economic discourse is well suited to grant immunity against criticism. Specific criticism of the assumption of "complete information" and its implications can be repelled by reference to the alternative variation of the model that contains the assumption of "incomplete" or "asymmetrical" information. The same is true for possible criticisms of the standard account of market efficiency within neoclassical theory. For the most part, this possibility of immunisation against critique has to be judged independent from Akerlof's clearly identifiable quest for a more realistic theory. The flexibilisation and accompanying immunisation of neoclassical theory via the method of axiomatic variation is, hence, often more of a by-product, that emerges without the explicit intention for immunisation and thereby independent from the specific motives and intentions of single authors.

From an epistemological viewpoint such concerns about immunisation could only be remedied by a greater degree of precision. Specifically, the decisive question is whether the assumption of "complete information" is regarded as a statement of law or an auxiliary hypothesis within neoclassical models: if the assumption is interpreted as an auxiliary hypothesis, two *complementary* market theories emerge (one for "standard markets" and one for "markets for lemons"). Their existence would require as detailed as possible a specification of their respective areas of application, which, strictly speaking, must not overlap. However, if the axiom is interpreted as a statement of law, two *competing* models of the markets emerge, one being the standard model, the other being an alternative theoretical description of the market that postulates unequally distributed information as an essential property of markets, and, hence, comes to very different conclusions regarding the properties of market outcomes. While both cases would represent good scientific practice, the reluctance to differentiate between law-like statements and auxiliary assumptions leaves it open as regards which of the two cases actually applies. Moreover, further conditions for both interpretations – the specification of separate domains of application in the former case and the evaluation of the relative merits of both assumptions in the latter case – are not fulfilled.

In sum, this raises doubts with regard to Colander et al.'s (2004) claim that an increase in the number of models actually signifies an increase in intellectual diversity in economics: if the increase in variety contributes to the accommodation of empirical observations simply by adding additional conceptual flexibility – instead of revisions in canonical knowledge and received wisdom – such efforts can culminate in an immunisation against critique. In the next section, I will try to elaborate this argument in greater detail and put it in an adequate historical context.

3.2 Axiomatic variation and immunisation against critique

The flexibility of mainstream economic theory attained due to axiomatic variation contains the potential for extensive immunity against criticism. On a fundamental level, at least two principles of immunisation against critique can be identified in this context:

1. The strategy of "evasion": Due to the existence of several model variations with different assumptions and results, any empirical criticism can be evaded by always referring to alternative models to which the respective criticism does not apply.
2. The strategy of "assimilation": Here, singular "interesting" assumptions or results from competing theories are being carried over into the neoclassical theoretical structure and, hence, are being "reproduced" by it.

First, the strategy of "evasion" shall be considered. The core thought of axiomatic variation has been elucidated already; namely the possibility to alter some part of the entirety of axioms within a model M at will in order to obtain an alternative model M^*. Via this option, any empirical criticism of neoclassical standard models can be "evaded". However, the illustration of only two model variations, as made in the preceding chapter, is too simple. The neoclassical research area is much more characterised by the fact that there is a continuous expansion of the relevant model population (Colander et al. 2004).

Examples for such a "strategy of evasion", besides the "market for lemons" (Akerlof 1970), include a lot of research in behavioural economics where experimental deviations from the standard model's predictions are often rationalised via axiomatic variation, mostly by assuming some idiosyncratic preference structure (e.g. Fehr and Schmid 1999).[1] Another example is provided by the theory of financial markets which, besides "efficient allocation", also offers a wide range of highly volatile bubble models (see, for example, De Long et al. 1990). If this strategy is pursued consistently and the associated outcomes are all attributed to the single approach of mainstream economics, then it seems barely possible to undertake serious endeavours of falsification, since all possible results (simplified: E and ¬E) are present within different model populations anyway. While this strategy creates problems of consistency when appraising the state of (some field in) economics from an aggregate viewpoint, but nonetheless allows for and facilitates immunisation against critique by providing the opportunity to evade dealing seriously with contradictory empirical evidence.

The second immunisation strategy discussed here can be termed as strategy of "assimilation", and is applied predominantly in the discussion and integration of arguments originating from alternative theoretical paradigms. The basic idea is that in the process of axiomatic variation, single assumptions or outcomes found in alternative theories can be transferred into the neoclassical theoretical structure. It is a process of assimilation with the aim of strengthening or extending neoclassical theory by trying to absorb an attractive or interesting aspect from a competing paradigm. An especially well-known example of such absorption of ideas took place in 1937, when John Hicks moulded elements of Keynes' General Theory with more traditional arguments and thereby created the well-known IS-LM model (Hicks 1937). Mainly, Hicks adopted Keynes' axiom of a demand-driven macroeconomic equilibrium (Palley 1996, 34). Other assumptions, such as that of fundamental uncertainty (Keynes 1937, 213f), were not considered in Hicks' IS-LM model. By this example it becomes obvious how single assumptions from a seemingly attractive competing theory can be transferred seamlessly into neoclassical theory. Even in the 21st century, macroeconomic lectures still traditionally teach the term of "neoclassical synthesis" as a refined version of Hicks' model. Similarly, the New-Keynesian argument on involuntary unemployment arising from a lack of flexibility on labour markets ("sticky wages") originated from the aim to replicate a central result of the General Theory – namely the possibility of involuntary unemployment – without making use of the Keynesian mechanism of effective demand in determining employment (e.g. Modigliani 1944).

A second example of the transfer of a theory from a competing paradigm is the integration of Schumpeter's concept of "creative destruction" into the neoclassical theoretical system. Schumpeter sees the concept of "creative destruction" as a permanent process of change of economic events that is propelled by new technologies and forms of organisation, as well as by changes in market policy and strategy (Schumpeter 1993[1950]). Through this perpetual process of change – the process of "creative destruction" – existing industries and technologies are gradually being exchanged for alternative, modern concepts, which increase macroeconomic productivity. The neoclassical approach adopts Schumpeter's notion of "creative destruction", but only in a very specific manner. While Schumpeter aims to analyse the effect of technological change, and the shifts in the economic process emerging from these changes, the neoclassical approach uses the factor of technological change as a blanket explanation for all unanticipated economic changes. Not the causes and effects of dynamic economic processes are being studied; only a respective "catch-all" variable is being introduced (in the form of the well-known "Solow residual"), which provides a parameter for statistically "explaining" exogenous deviations from equilibrium as effects of technological change. Hence, "creative destruction" is used as a placeholder in modern economics to justify circumventing the study of those aspects in economic development that Schumpeter originally thought to be most interesting.

These two examples of Keynes and Schumpeter illustrate how the assumptions of alternative paradigms are partly or only symbolically being assimilated by the neoclassical theory corpus through axiomatic variation (for a more detailed depiction, see Kapeller 2012, chapter 7).

Returning to the original question, namely whether the neoclassical school actually creates a system of inner theoretical variety as proposed by Colander et al. (2004), I would argue that this claim has to be approached with substantial scepticism based on the above considerations. At first glance, the neoclassical theoretical structure seems to have a variety of different theories at its disposal; however, this diversity is not real, as the generated model variations ultimately consolidate the dominant role of the standard models as encapsulated in economic textbooks, which serves as a prime heuristic and blueprint for the general style of modelling in modern economics. In this way, the process of axiomatic variation also turns into an instrument for the immunisation of a monistic-neoclassical approach, instead of contributing to the effective broadening of economic discourse.

4. Pluralism in economics: suggestions for research practice

In contrast to the practice of axiomatic variation prevalent in mainstream economics, one could also ask whether the ideas of 'pluralism' and theoretical openness can actually be useful when it comes to composing research questions and venues, or in short, whether pluralism may serve as a suitable conceptual guide when developing research strategies.

In addressing this perspective, I would like to emphasise that pluralism is, first and foremost, about openness and the absence of prejudice (which, of course, does not imply the absence of judgement; Dobusch and Kapeller 2012). One obvious strategy for taking demands for openness and pluralism seriously is to develop something akin to a modest, comparative assessment of different economic theories or traditions. Such an assessment should be comparative, not only because it should aim to include different economic arguments and traditions, but also because it tries to assess the similarities and differences of competing approaches, not in a single brush, but rather within a nuanced analysis paying attention to different spheres of economic theorising (theories of economic behaviour vs. theories of monetary policy, for instance). Such an approach allows for focusing on how different economic theories align in detail. Additionally, such an assessment should be modest insofar as it refrains from early judgements and prioritisations, but at first looks for potential complementarities or synergies across different theories: while most traditions know some argument or assumption, which can hardly be reconciled with alternative approaches, conflicts in other branches or spheres of theorising are often much less intense. A prime example for such a constellation is the relationship of post-Keynesian and Austrian economics, which is coined by often opposing stances on policy issues, while some parts of their theoretical analysis, e.g. on the role of uncertainty in determining investment (Lawson 1996) or on the importance of endogenous money creation, can often be reconciled. A pluralist approach urges a stronger focus on these potentials for synergy and complementarity to better address the many faces of social reality and to contribute to a more integrated understanding of economic issues.

In past works, Dobusch and Kapeller (2012) have addressed the question of whether pluralism can serve as a suitable principle for organising and devising research strategies in greater depth, and suggested the following basic heuristic as a blueprint for constructively doing economics from a pluralist vantage point (see Table 3.1). Taking the outcomes of a comparative assessment of different economic approaches as described above as a starting point (see column 2 in Table 3.1), our heuristic suggests possible strategies for further work based on these outcomes.

Table 3.1 Strategies for comparing theoretical statements of different economic paradigms

#	Comparison between theoretical statements	Pluralist research practices / strategies		
(1)	→← Identical			
(2)	↗↖ Convergent	(a) Integration (1)–(3)		
(3)	↑↑ Compatible		(b) Division of labour (3)–(4)	
(4)	OO Neutral			(c) Diversification (b)+(d)
(5)	↖↗ Divergent	(d) Test of conflicting hypotheses (5)–(6)		
(6)	←→ Contradictory			

Source: Dobusch and Kapeller (2012, 1051). Reprinted with permission from Taylor & Francis.

Examples of the successful or potential application of the routines depicted in Table 3.1 can be found in the history of economic thought as well as more recent works and developments. An illustrative example relating the former is that of Schumpeter and Keynes: although both of these authors make similar arguments on the passionate character of entrepreneurial decision-making (Keynes 1937; Schumpeter 2006[1912]) or the nature of finance as a sphere coined by its own inner logic, which could well be integrated in a single account (identity and/or complementarity in Table 3.1), they tend to disagree in other aspects, e.g. when it comes to evaluating technological change: for Keynes, the main effect of technological change is to increase labour productivity and, hence, to create unemployment given that demand stays constant (see, e.g., Keynes 1930, where he speaks explicitly about "technological unemployment"). Schumpeter on the other hand emphasises that innovation could take various forms, including the creation of new products or wholly new markets, where some of these forms lead – in contrast to the traditional Keynesian view – to an increase in demand instead of merely boosting labour productivity (Schumpeter 2006[1912]). In this specific respect – the expansionary nature of innovations in capitalism – Schumpeter is much closer to Marxian authors, who, like Rosa Luxemburg (1913), argue that the expansionary nature of capitalism can take on very different forms depending on the relevant social and historical context. In this example, the stepwise comparison of the arguments brought forward by Keynes and Schumpeter mirror closely the piecemeal and topic-based strategy of modest comparison advocated above, which, in turn, allows for a nuanced, sectoral assessment of the relative alignment of both authors. This short example also allows for making an argument on how to resolve the underlying conflict, namely by allowing for different forms of innovation, where some contribute to technological unemployment, while others contribute to the emergence of new markets and, hence, additional demand. In this view, the theoretical conflict between Keynes and Schumpeter is rationalised as an opportunity for introducing an argument about the potential complementarity of their – originally opposed – arguments (see also Dosi et al. 2010). The resulting concept – a typology of innovations, where innovations are grouped in different types with regard to their specific economic effects – can even be further extended, e.g. to cases like international tax evasion of large corporations, where innovation is understood as a new way to circumvent an existing social obligation (e.g. Kapeller et al. 2016).

Examples can also be taken from current theoretical discourses. Let us take, for instance, the case of increasing household debt and its relation to the recent crisis: here, microeconomic arguments from institutional economics suggest that increasing inequality and increasing costs of living are a suitable starting point for explaining the rise in household debt. The resulting arguments are in turn merged with a Keynesian approach to aggregate demand and/or a Minskyan view on finance, to arrive at a fuller picture with regard to the economic mechanisms giving rise to the great financial crisis (e.g. Zezza 2008; Kapeller and Schütz 2014). Similarly, arguments from institutional consumer theory can also be expressed in the language of standard economics, which enriches the predictive capabilities of the latter (e.g. Bowles and Park 2005). Another example which focuses less on the complementarity and integration of different economic approaches, but, rather, makes use of diversification as a general principle is the incorporation of complexity economics and agent-based modelling in macroeconomic debates. Although both of these approaches can be understood as formal offsprings of evolutionary/institutional economics as well as general network theory, these approaches manage to bring new forms of data (Tacchella et al. 2012), new methods (Cristelli et al. 2015) as well as new capabilities of model-building (e.g. Epstein 2007) into the macroeconomic discourse, thereby enriching the latter, without disqualifying more traditional approaches. Quite to the contrary, some of these works – which are partially produced and published in natural science – are unknowingly located in the tradition of heterodox trade theory, which emphasises the role of accumulation, sectoral specialisation and path-dependency as in Latin-American structuralism or the international economics of Nicolas Kaldor (1981) and Joan Robinson (1979).

The main purpose of these examples is to put some actual flesh on the bones laid out in Table 3.1 and, thereby, to make tangible the underlying argument about the possible role of "pluralism" as a cornerstone for the conceptualisation of research strategies. However, they hopefully aid in another task, namely to develop an intuition on the difference between the pluralist approach suggested here and the routine of axiomatic variation practised in mainstream economics. Aside from a series of nuances, the main aim here is to align and critically compare different approaching ex-ante supposing an equal footing of these various approaches, while the mainstream practice of axiomatic variation assigns primacy to established models and then aims to incorporate novel ideas into these established modes of thinking.

5. Pluralism in economic teaching: some suggestions

Pluralism in economic education is often harder to implement than pluralism in economic research. The main reason for this is that academic teaching is closely intertwined with the aim of providing students – also those students who do not major in economics – with an adequate overview on the subject under consideration. In providing such an overview, teaching only a single approach is often beneficial in terms of pedagogical simplicity compared to a more diversified approach, which aims to provide a variety of conceptual and theoretical perspectives to illuminate those issues. Hence, there is a scarcity-related argument ("student attention is scarce!") for focusing only on the dominant perspective, which, ironically, focuses on problems emerging from scarcity. Moreover, economics teaching is strongly coined by a set of standardised economics textbooks, which aim to set out the canonical knowledge in economics to students and lay readers alike. As these textbooks are mostly founded on the perspective of mainstream economics and, thereby, set an informal standard, more diverse and pluralist approaches to economic education are automatically considered as "non-standard" and unconventional and, hence, have a hard time gaining legitimacy (see also Graupe's and Maeße's chapters in this volume).

Nonetheless, the basic idea of pluralism – to acknowledge and integrate various different perspectives on a given subject in a common debate – seems well suited to serve as an organising principle of economic teaching for at least three reasons. First, the general structure of a pluralist approach as understood here, that is, an approach aiming for a patient and constructive comparative assessment of competing theories and approaches in economics, can be utilised as a starting point for an "introduction into economic controversies". Such an introduction could provide students with the ability to anchor and contextualise different economic arguments with regard to their theoretical and historical origins. Second, introductory lectures in economics often shape the mindset of students – especially the large majority of students who only attend a few courses in economics before delving into other subjects – with regard to what is a sound economic argument or a sound public policy and, hence, come with a significant load of responsibility for course instructors (e.g. Fullbrook 2011). A pluralist take on introductory economics would possibly try to make different approaches and perspectives to economic problems accessible and, thereby, better equip students to understand how economic development is impacted by different actors, constraints and social interests and, hence, support them in developing balanced arguments on public policy issues. Finally, such an approach would suit the main principle of intellectual modesty – fallibilism – as courses and underlying materials would no longer suggest that "the main economic problems are already solved and one has, simply, to accept and apply the available solutions" (Albert 1998, 153, author's translation), but rather point to the contested character of economic knowledge.

Finally, such a problem-oriented and pluralist approach to economic education might also foster interdisciplinary thought. Taking the issue of social mobility and social stratification as an example, one possible approach is to contrast Thomas Schelling's "checkerboard model of racial segregation" (1969), where social stratification in spatial contexts is the result of individual preferences, with the theory of social stratification as developed by Pierre Bourdieu (1984). Bourdieu is counted among the most important authors continuing the theoretical heritage of Thorstein B. Veblen;he forcefully argued that social advantage might come in different forms (hence, his differentiation of different forms of capital) with differing degrees of persistence.

A concept for economic teaching – especially the development of introductory and intermediate courses in economics – which makes use of all these potential advantages is a problem-oriented "social issues" approach (Grimes 2009), which focuses on different economic problems and questions and then delineates different answers to these questions and contextualises these answers historically and theoretically. Such a take on teaching economics could make good use of a grid comparing different economic approaches along various spheres of theorising as suggested in the foregoing section to selectively present specific answers given to core economic problems in different periods of time and different theoretical contexts. A selective presentation makes good sense as it takes into account that different economic traditions often focus on different questions and, at the same time, allows straightening pedagogical presentations accordingly. In what follows, I will provide some examples of different economic problems and illustrate how they could be approached from a pedagogical viewpoint.

5.1 Example 1: unemployment

A core problem in economic thought is the question of unemployment, which has broader social ramifications and, hence, is easily recognised as such a core problem by outsiders or newly introduced students. One possible take on this question would be to develop a typology of explanations for unemployment reaching from a purely neoclassical explanation – which basically states that all unemployment is voluntary due to the properties of efficient markets and rational individuals – to a simple post-Keynesian point of view, emphasising that employment is, eventually, always demand-constrained. Intermediate views are provided by the neo-Keynesian account (starting with Modigliani 1944), which basically sides with the neoclassical view, but assumes that "wage rigidity" prevails on labour markets, making the latter less efficient, and Hicks' interpretation (1937) that aggregate demand only matters in the short-run, a view conserved by the success of the IS-LM model. The pedagogical presentation of said typology could be anchored either in economic history and the history of economic thought, which often is much more apt for interdisciplinary audiences, or in a comparative discussion of different economic models (as in Palley 1996).

5.2 Example 2: poverty

My second example relates to the issue of distribution, but suggests introducing a more specific focus on poverty. In this context, one could compare mainstream economic approaches, institutional-evolutionary theories of consumption and more hands-on empirical research to give a nuanced perspective on the problem of poverty. A simple arrangement to facilitate a comparative discussion in this context would be to introduce the two main definitions of poverty – relative and absolute poverty – and ask what different economic theories can say about these criteria. In this context, relative poverty is attained when a household receives less than some share (typically: 60%) of average income, while the definition of absolute poverty relates to the fulfilment of basic needs, like shelter, clothing, heating, food and social inclusion.

Based on these considerations, one can explain why neoclassical standard theory will consider relative definitions of poverty to be arbitrary and absolute definitions of poverty to be largely meaningless (as preferences are private and uniform, there is no such thing as a basic need in the standard model), while concepts from evolutionary and institutional concepts – like social emulation (Veblen 1970 [1899]) or the distinction between needs and wants (Witt 2001) – might provide a theoretical foundation for said concepts. Conversely, one could organise a similar discussion around the issue of wealth, taking some data from Piketty (2014) or others and suggesting different theories, like institutional accounts of social stratification, Marxian theory of class and exploitation and older dynastic models from mainstream theory (e.g. Meade 1964), to explain the observed patterns.

5.3 Example 3: the role of nature

Another example relates to the role of nature in economic processes and could start by juxtaposing classical political economy, where natural resources – especially agricultural land (Ricardo 1815) – were considered to be the main source of wealth aside from human labour – to more recent approaches, where land and nature are conceptually supplanted by capital and technology in macroeconomic analysis (following Cobb and Douglas 1928), and turned into a subject of microeconomic analysis. Based on these historical foundations, one could try to introduce students to current cleavages in economic thought on the role of nature by confronting Pigou vs. Georgescu-Roegen, i.e., by comparing the technologically optimist, market-focused view of environmental economics with the more long-term and aggregate perspective of Georgescu-Roegen, which more strongly emphasises the primacy of ecological foundations in economic activities (e.g. Georgescu-Roegen 1973).

5.4 Example 4: price formation

My fourth example relates to a major topic in mainstream economics: the issue of price formation in (more or less) competitive markets. For starters, it seems helpful to make clear that the focus on price formation inherent in modern economics is already based on the implicit premise that price formation illuminates the most important properties of markets. While this premise might well be rejected and replaced with other key aspects of market behaviour – namely that markets allow for the introduction of innovations (Schumpeter 2006[1912]) or serve as an arena for exercising power (Rothschild 1971) – it seems important to point out that even in the event of accepting this focus on price formation, introducing a certain theoretical variety is still possible. Possibly the most obvious way to do so is explicitly suggested by Robert Prasch (2008), who introduces a distinction between "gravitating" and "escalating" behaviour of prices, where the former follows the iconoclastic description of gravitating prices by Smith (2003[1776], Book I), which serves as a forerunner of traditional supply-and-demand analysis. The latter case of escalating prices, however, is based on historical studies of speculation (e.g. Kindleberger and Aliber 2005 [1978]) and discusses the possibility of positive feedback in pricing formation ("to buy when prices rise") leading to escalating prices, also studied in some mainstream models of financial instability (e.g. De Long et al. 1990).

These short sketches should suffice to illustrate this specific implementation of a pluralist approach to economic education which makes use of a problem-oriented approach, i.e., which aims to put different economic questions centre stage. While the preparation of such courses might indeed prove to be ambitious, as lecturers actually have to cover a certain variety of fields from different theoretical perspectives, students would surely receive an introduction that provides an anchoring of economic questions within their everyday experiences. Hence, it might well turn out that the workload associated with preparing such a course is indeed substantial, but also comes with a non-negligible advantage, namely that of doing one's job at least roughly right.

6. Conclusion

In this chapter, I tried to show how a pluralist conception of economics might translate into concrete suggestions for organising economic research and teaching. In distilling these suggestions, I focused on a series of epistemological rationales pointing to the potential contribution of a pluralist conception of science. Such an approach is in dire need of complementary views, which explore the idea of pluralist economic education from the perspectives of pedagogy, public policy, political relevance or the job market, to finally arrive at a fuller image of pluralist economic education. In doing so, one should also incorporate some of the great works out there which already try to synthesise different streams of economic thought in the form of pluralist introductory or intermediate texts (a collection of such works is provided in the 6th edition of the *Heterodox Economics Directory*; Kapeller and Springholz 2016).

Acknowledgments

I want to thank Claudius Gräbner and Leonhard Dobusch for helpful comments.

Note

1 Hence, behavioural economics exploits the flexibility of preferences to retain the assumption of rational optimisation. Notwithstanding this observation, we should add that the assumption of optimisation is surrendered in other context. For instance, the bubble models mentioned above refer to "rules of thumb", which determine behaviour instead of optimisation.

References

Akerlof, A. (1970): 'The Market for 'Lemons': Quality Uncertainty and the Market Mechanism', *Quarterly Journal of Economics* 84(3), 488–500.

Albert, H. (1991): *Traktat Über Kritische Vernunft*. Tübingen: Mohr.

Albert, H. (1998): *Marktsoziologie Und Entscheidungslogik*. Tübingen: Mohr.

Albert, M. (1994): *Faktorpreisausgleichstheorem*. Tübingen: Mohr.

Atkinson, A.B. (2007): 'The Distribution of Earnings in OECD Countries', *International Labour Review* 146(1–2), 41–60.

Becker, G.S. (1976): *The Economic Approach to Human Behavior*. Chicago: Chicago University Press.

Bourdieu, P. (1984): *Distinction: A Social Critique of the Judgement of Taste*. Cambridge, MA: Harvard University Press.

Bowles, S. and Gintis, H. (2000): 'Walrasian Economics in Retrospect', *Quarterly Journal of Economics* 115(4), 1411–1439.

Bowles, S. and Park, Y. (2005): 'Emulation, Inequality, and Work Hours: Was Thorsten Veblen Right?', *The Economic Journal* 115(507), F397–F412.

Bunge, M. (1967): *Scientific Research* (Book II). Berlin: Springer.

Card, D. and DiNardo, J.E. (2002): 'Skill-Biased Technological Change and Rising Wage Inequality: Some Problems and Puzzles', *Journal of Labor Economics* 20(4), 733–783.

Cobb, C.W. and Douglas, P.H. (1928): 'A Theory of Production', *The American Economic Review* 18(1), 139–165.

Colander, D. (2000): 'The Death of Neoclassical Economics', *Journal of the History of Economic Thought* 22(2), 128–143.

Colander, D., Holt, R.P. and Rosser, J.B. Jr. (2004): 'The Changing Face of Mainstream Economics', *Review of Political Economy* 16(4), 485–499.

Cristelli, M., Tacchella, A. and Pietronero, L. (2015): 'The Heterogeneous Dynamics of Economic Complexity', *PLoS ONE* 10(2), 1–15.

De Long, B.J., Shleifer, A., Summers, L.H. and Waldmann, R.J. (1990): 'Positive Feedback Investment Strategies and Destabilizing Rational Speculation', *Journal of Finance* 45(2), 379–395.

Deaton, A. (2010): 'Instruments, Randomization, and Learning about Development', *Journal of Economic Literature* 48(2), 424–455.

Dobusch, L. and Kapeller, J. (2009): 'Why Is Economics Not an Evolutionary Science? New Answers to Veblen's Old Question', *Journal of Economic Issues* 43 (4), 867–898.

Dobusch, L. and Kapeller, J. (2012): 'Heterodox United Vs. Mainstream City? Sketching a Framework for Interested Pluralism in Economics', *Journal of Economic Issues* 46(4), 1035–1057.

Dosi, G., Fagiolo, G. and Roventini, A. (2010): 'Schumpeter Meeting Keynes. A Policy-Friendly Model of Endogenous Growth and Business Cycles', *Journal of Economic Dynamics and Control* 34(9), 1748–1767.

Egger, P., Nigai, S. and Strecker, N. (2016): 'The Taxing Deed of Globalization', Unpublished working paper. Available at https://www.econ.uzh.ch/dam/jcr:2fa30260-bd17-48ea-bedd-83985a38a022/draft_35.pdf, accessed on 6 September 2017.

Elsner, W. (1986): *ÖKonomische Institutionenanalyse – Paradigmatische Entwicklung Der ÖKonomischen Theorie Und Der Sinn Eines RüCkgriffs Auf Die ÖKonomische Klassik Am Beispiel Der Institutionenanalyse (Property Rights)*. Berlin: Duncker & Humblot.

Epstein, J.M. (2007): *Generative Social Science: Studies in Agent-Based Computational Modeling*. Princeton, NJ: Princeton University Press.

Fehr, E. and Schmidt, K.M. (1999): 'A Theory of Fairness, Competition and Cooperation', *Quarterly Journal of Economics* 114(3), 817–868.

Fullbrook, E. (2011): 'Toxic Textbooks', INET Blog, Available at https://www.ineteconomics.org/ideas-papers/blog/edward-fullbrook-toxic-textbooks?p=ideas-papers/blog/edward-fullbrook-toxic-textbooks, accessed on 9 August 2016.

Georgescu-Roegen, N. (1973): *The Entropy Law and the Economic Process*. Cambridge, MA: Harvard University Press.

Giere, R.N. (1999): *Science without Laws*. Chicago: Chicago University Press.

Gilens, M. and Page, B.I. (2014): 'Testing Theories of American Politics: Elites, Interest Groups, and Average Citizens', *Perspectives on Politics* 12(3), 564–581.

Grimes, P.W. (2009): 'Reflections on Introductory Course Structures', in Colander, D. and McGoldrick, K.-M. (eds.), *Educating Economists – the Teagle-Discussion on Re-Evaluating the Undergraduate Economics Major*. Cheltenham: Edward Elgar, 95–98.

Hands, D.W. (2001): *Reflection without Rules*. Cambridge: Cambridge University Press.

Hausman, Daniel M. (1992): *The Inexact and Separate Science of Economics*. Cambridge: Cambridge University Press.

Hicks, J.R. (1937): 'Mr. Keynes and the Classics: A Suggested Interpretation', *Econometrica* 5(2), 147–159.

Hill, R. and Myatt, A. (2007): 'Overemphasis on Perfectly Competitive Markets in Microeconomics Principles Textbooks', *Journal of Economic Education* 38(1), 58–76.

Hodgson, G.M. and Rothman, H. (1999): 'The Editors and Authors of Economics Journals: A Case of Institutional Oligopoly?', *The Economic Journal* 109(453), F165–F186.

ISIPE. (2014): 'An International Student Call for Pluralism in Economics', Available at http://www.isipe.net/open-letter/, accessed on 5 May 2016.

Kaldor, N. (1981): 'The Foundations of Free Trade Theory and Their Implication for the Current World Recession', in Los, J., Kula, W., Hagemeyer, H., Bobrowski, C. and Assorodobraj-Kula, N. (eds.), *Studies in Economic Theory and Practice*. New York: Elsevier, 213–222.

Kapeller, J. (2010): 'Citation Metrics: Serious Drawbacks, Perverse Incentives and Strategic Options for Heterodox Economists', *American Journal of Economics and Sociology* 69(5), 1376–1408.

Kapeller, J. (2012): *Modell-Platonismus in Der Ökonomie - Zur Aktualität Einer Klassischen Epistemologischen Kritik*. Frankfurt am Main: Lang.

Kapeller, J. (2013): 'Model-Platonism in Economics: On a Classical Epistemological Critique', *Journal of Institutional Economics* 9(2), 199–221.
Kapeller, J. and Schütz, B. (2014): 'Debt, Boom, Bust: A Theory of Minsky-Veblen Cycles', *Journal of Post-Keynesian Economics* 36(4), 781–813.
Kapeller, J., Schütz, B. and Tamesberger, D. (2016): 'From Free to Civilized Trade: A European Perspective', *Review of Social Economy* 74(3), 320–328.
Kapeller, J. and Springholz, F. (2016): *Heterodox Economic Directory*, 6th edition. URL: http://heterodoxnews.com/hed/, accessed on 10 August 2016.
Kellert, S.H., Longino, H.E. and Waters, K.C. (2006): (eds.) *Scientific Pluralism*. Minneapolis, MN: University of Minnesota Press.
Keynes, J.M. (1930): 'Economic Possibilities for Our Grandchildren'. URL: http://www.econ.yale.edu/smith/econ116a/keynes1.pdf, accessed on 10 August 2016.
Keynes, J.M. (1937): 'The General Theory of Employment', *Quarterly Journal of Economics* 51, 209–223.
Kindleberger, C.P. and Aliber, R.Z. (2005[1978]): *Manias, Panics, and Crashes – A History of Financial Crises*. London: Wiley.
King, J.E. (2002): *A History of Post-Keynesian Economics since 1936*. Cheltenham (UK): Edward Elgar.
Lawson, T. (1996): 'Hayek and Keynes: A Commonality', *History of Economics Review* 25 (1), 96–114.
Lazear, E.P. (2000): 'Economic Imperialism', *Quarterly Journal of Economics* 115(1), 99–146.
Lee, F.S. (2004): 'To Be a Heterodox Economist: The Contested Landscape of American Economics, 1960s and 1970s', *Journal of Economic Issues* 38, 747–763.
Luxemburg, R. (1913): 'The Accumulation of Capital', Available at https://www.marxists.org/archive/luxemburg/1913/accumulation-capital/, accessed on 10 August 2016.
Meade, J.E. (1964): *Efficiency, Equality and the Ownership of Capital*. Cambridge, MA: Harvard University Press.
Modigliani, F. (1944): 'Liquidity Preference and the Theory of Interest and Money', *Econometrica* 12, 45–88.
Palley, T.I. (1996): *Post-Keynesian Economics: Debt, Distribution and the Macro Economy*. London: Palgrave-Macmillan.
Piketty, T. (2014): *Capital in the 21st Century*. Cambridge, MA: Harvard University Press.
Popper, K.R. (2002[1959]): *The Logic of Scientific Discovery*. London: Routledge.
Prasch, R.E. (2008): *How Markets Work: Supply, Demand and the Real World*. Cheltenham: Edward Elgar.
Ricardo, D. (1815): *An Essay on Profits*. London: John Murray.
Robinson, J. (1979): 'Reflections on the Theory of International Trade', in Robinson, J. (ed.), *Collected Papers*. Blackwell: Oxford, 130–145.
Rothschild, K.W. (1971): *Power in Economics*. Harmondsworth: Penguin.
Rothschild, K.W. (1988): 'Micro-Foundations, Ad Hocery and Keynesian Theory', *Atlantic Economic Journal* 16(2), 12–21.
Rothschild, K.W. (2008): 'Apropos Keynesianer', in Hagemann, H., Horn, G. and Krupp, H.-J. (eds.), *Aus Gesamtwirtschaftlicher Sicht: Festschrift Für Jürgen Kromphardt*. Marburg: Metropolis, 19–29.
Schelling, T.C. (1969): 'Models of Segregation', *American Economic Review* 59(2), 488–493.
Schumpeter, J.A. (1993[1950]): *Kapitalismus, Sozialismus Und Demokratie*, 7th text edition. Tübingen and Basel: Francke.

Schumpeter, J.A. (2006[1912]): *Theorie Der Wirtschaftlichen Entwicklung*, Reprint of first version. Berlin: Duncker & Humblot.

Skousen, M. (1997): 'The Perseverance of Paul Samuelson's Economics', *Journal of Economic Perspectives* 11(2), 137–152.

Smith, A. (2003[1776]): *The Wealth of Nations*. London: Bantam.

Sterman, J.D. and Wittenberg, J. (1999): 'Path Dependence, Competition, and Succession in the Dynamics of Scientific Revolution', *Organization Science* 10(3), 322–341.

Tacchella, A., Cristelli, M., Caldarelli, G., Gabrielli, A. and Pietronero, L. (2012): 'A New Metrics for Countries' Fitness and Products' Complexity', *Nature: Scientific Reports* 2(723), 1–7.

Veblen, T.B. (1970[1899]): *The Theory of the Leisure Class*. London: Allen and Unwin.

Wilkinson, R.G. and Pickett, K.E. (2007): 'The Problems of Relative Deprivation: Why Some Societies Do Better than Others', *Social Science & Medicine* 65(9), 1965–1978.

Witt, U. (2001): 'Learning to Consume – A Theory of Wants and the Growth of Demand', *Journal of Evolutionary Economics* 11(1), 23–36.

Zezza, G. (2008): 'U.S. Growth, the Housing Market, and the Distribution of Income', *Journal of Post-Keynesian Economics* 30(3), 375–401.

4 In and against orthodoxy

Teaching economics in the neoliberal era

Ben Fine

1. Contexts

I have been teaching heterodox economics as a heterodox, Marxist economist for more than forty years. This offers ample experience on which to assess the challenges that continuing this endeavour of designing and delivering teaching materials poses. It is taking place within a discipline that has become increasingly if not absolutely intolerant of alternatives to what is, in many if not all respects, its own increasingly narrow orthodoxy. But my own situation is and has been idiosyncratic and leads me to be hesitant about drawing lessons of general applicability, an issue to which I will return. Specifically, I have only taught in roughly equal measure, with at most occasional sorties elsewhere, at two institutions – Birkbeck College and the School of Oriental and African Studies, both part of the University of London – literally within a stone's throw of each other. I have also only taught, again with minor exceptions, at postgraduate level and within dedicated economics departments (as opposed to providing economics for interdisciplinary courses). I joined Birkbeck in the early 1970s when it was setting up to be pluralist (although it has gone mainstream over the past two decades), and left for SOAS in 1992 to join what was becoming probably the leading and largest collection of heterodox economists in the UK if not the world. It is also relevant that I only studied economics as a postgraduate, following a maths degree, and this undoubtedly smoothed both my understanding of orthodoxy in technical terms and my acceptability to orthodoxy, if increasingly limited, as a heterodox economist, not least as I had gained a modicum of academic respectability through publications in leading journals albeit at the expense of "playing the game". In general, I have been confined to teaching core micro and macro courses, again with occasional exceptions in taking responsibility for optional courses, for example in Marxist economics, the history of economic thought, and interdisciplinarity through focus on "economics imperialism".

In light of this personal trajectory, I see my situation as having been extraordinarily favourable in relative and absolute terms in being able to teach heterodoxy with some degree of freedom. I am mindful that others will not enjoy the same advantages, especially given the increasing intolerance of the orthodoxy that is not only analytical in substance but also institutionalised in who appoints and is appointed, what they have to teach, what they are allowed to research, and what is recognised in teaching and research as academically acceptable. Opportunities are almost certainly greater in the teaching of economics other than in economics departments but I do not have the experience and knowledge to comment on how this affects what can, and should be taught, and how. Some hopes might be placed for the pluralist teaching of economics other than in economics departments but I am not in a position to assess its potential nor what and how it might best be delivered.

However, despite my circumstances, influence of the orthodoxy has still hung heavily on what can be done by way of alternatives. Put crudely, you cannot just teach what you like. In offering an economics degree from within an economics department, you are going to have to cover much of the material that is taken as sacrosanct by the orthodoxy; otherwise you are to some degree doing your students a disservice. In any case, without wishing to make a virtue out of necessity, it would be disarming not to train students in orthodoxy as this is what they will confront in whatever way they deploy the economics that they have gained. It is imperative to have a strong command of orthodoxy even though this is both increasingly demanding (especially given the technical requirements of the discipline), crowding out room for alternatives, and desperately unfair as orthodoxy tends to have no, less or at most distorted knowledge of heterodoxy, as well as subjecting it to dogmatic dismissal. There is also the strategic issue of not abandoning economics to the economists, however deficient they might be considered as they are hardly going to fade and die even in the presence of alternatives prospering elsewhere.

In short, teaching economics almost inevitably involves primarily teaching the orthodoxy, a conclusion that is more likely to irk heterodox (teach different) than pluralist (teach more) economists. Paradoxically, though, my position is highly critical of a pluralist stance if it merely sees the orthodoxy as one approach to be taught amongst others. For this fails to acknowledge inequality within the discipline and that other approaches cannot be taught on an equal basis.

In other words, we teach orthodoxy because we have to and it is hegemonic, and not just because it is one approach amongst others. In addition, the orthodoxy is so pervasive, especially for those who have just a minimal degree of exposure to the discipline, that it often serves as a starting point for how the economy is conceived and the problems that it is deemed to pose (even though these are far from intuitive for those who have not been exposed to an economics education). The standard axioms of consumer choice, for example, are remarkably counter-intuitive to the uninitiated (i.e. against all personal experience) but become unquestioned and second nature once taught and adopted. So, from my perspective, the issue is not so much in the first instance what we teach but how we teach it critically, with the orthodoxy as a point of departure.

Even this concession raises a number of stumbling blocks. First, students have mixed backgrounds and knowledges of orthodoxy itself and, because economics is often taught and learnt by rote through models and their technical derivation and properties, the orthodoxy has to be relearnt both for its inner properties and for these in light of broader considerations. Students may have spent more time going through the mechanics of models than in understanding their rationale other than on their own terms in application.

Second, this means that technically demanding material cannot be avoided, some of which is essential whilst some can be chosen for honing such skills as well as allowing for critical content to be revealed. Most economics textbooks are disproportionately mathematical in content, difficult to follow and negligent of the motivation for, and significance of, one assumption or other, and model or other, after another. So the difficulty here is to offer some select technical material without its becoming at the expense of substantive content and serving purely as a goal in its own right.

Third, economics now covers a vast and growing weight of subject matter, both within and between topics. So, once again, as with technical material, a judicious choice has to be made across breadth and depth of material to be presented. This is necessary in order both to offer sufficient coverage of orthodoxy, its basic principles and applications, and to allow space for criticism.

Fourth, by the same token, some opportunity can be taken to offer alternatives. These too must be judiciously chosen for their importance in illustrating differences with the orthodoxy, whether by topic, principle, method, conceptualisation, theory, policy implications or by ready appeal to "realism". In short, the goal is to introduce students to alternative ways of thinking, often ways that were the orthodoxy but have now been discouraged and excluded from the core curriculum, rendering the idea of alternatives and alternative thinking to the orthodoxy both counterintuitive and subject to resistance, if not incomprehension.

Fifth, then, this is to compensate for the unavoidable fact that the vast majority of economics students, even those entering postgraduate study or academic careers, are unaware of methodological issues, of the history of their own discipline, of knowledge of alternatives to the mainstream, and of longstanding criticisms of the mainstream which are rarely acknowledged let alone countered (if they can be). This too adds to the weight of material that might be covered as well the difficulties of communicating it and its importance.

Last, one of the problems in teaching economics is that the technical demands can be so heavy upon students that they take up an undue weight of care and attention, in complete disproportion to the significance of what is being communicated. It takes a moment to say that maybe utility maximisation is neither the only motivation of consumers nor the best way to look at consumption, but it takes much longer and is more demanding to explain that the existence of utility functions depends upon a set of axioms – that preferences be binary, reflexive, transitive, complete and continuous. But which of these is the more important? Of course, ease of expression and learning is far from the only or main criteria of what it is important to cover and how, but there are clearly some trade-offs to make, to employ the vernacular. I am endlessly surprised how students of economics are accomplished in the techniques they have been taught without simultaneously having developed conceptual understandings and a keen sense of what is important or not, in terms of both what is within the material and what is not.

Over the years, I have found ways of addressing, if not overcoming, these difficulties of what to teach and how through including topics, and ways of presenting them, that compromise across the various demands and obstacles detailed above. In addition, I have just drafted a text for each of microeconomics and macroeconomics from which I draw below in illustrating how alternatives might be taught within and around the orthodoxy.[1] But I am acutely aware that my own journey through what I teach and how, and in what context, will be very different from that of others who are themselves liable to be differentiated from one another. and so there are no templates for alternative courses. It is important that they be carefully constructed, reflecting detailed investigation and preparation. Indeed, preparing properly to teach is as demanding as undertaking research, and unrecognised research it is for the teacher of heterodoxy who must both command and exceed the limits of orthodoxy in imaginative, original and informed fashions.

2. History of economic thought as a starting point...[2]

One of the most astonishing characteristics of orthodoxy is its almost absolute ignorance of its own history. This goes far beyond getting it wrong (e.g. Adam Smith anticipated general equilibrium with his invisible hand when, in Smith's hands, it had nothing to do with general equilibrium), alongside decline of the history of economic thought as a field within the discipline on the implicit Whiggish grounds of its dismissal on since theory and methods could only have improved. Students tend to be highly receptive to the idea that economics is uniquely deficient in this regard, that it is important to understand how something came to be the way it is to understand what it is, and to feel they have been short-changed in their previous education. All of this can be used to motivate attention to how economics came to be the way it is,[3] a history that can be told in a number of different ways, not least by both chronology and theme.

For economics in general, a starting point can be the division between classical political economy and neoclassical economics and the passage through the marginalist revolution of the 1870s, of which most students are unaware. The contrast between the two broad approaches can be drawn to bring out elements of heterodox alternatives, ranging across: methodological individualism (of a special type, reduced to utility maximisation) versus methodological holism (to introduce systemic or structural analysis, and classes, and what these mean to students for whom there is lack of familiarity with the terms let alone the concepts); subjective versus objective theories of value; interdisciplinarity; deductivism versus inductivism; and equilibrium and efficiency versus prospects for capitalism.[4]

As a result, the marginalist revolution of the 1870s can be seen as a staging post in the rise of orthodoxy, with the next steps being the Keynesian revolution of the 1930s, the formalist revolution of the 1950s, the monetarist counter-revolution of the 1970s and the subsequent market (and other) imperfections reaction that takes us almost to the present day. Each of these stages of development of the discipline can be usefully laid out for teaching purposes in explaining the nature and origins of current orthodoxy (what was put in and what was taken out and how). For microeconomics in particular, the passage from marginalist to formalist revolutions bypassed the Great Depression and the rise of macro. It can be seen as concerning itself with two questions alone: how to extract the maximum information for the forms taken by supply and demand curves given individuals are pursuing self-interest through the market (and demand does not necessarily go down with price), and how to aggregate across such individuals to generate a simultaneous general equilibrium.

We know, and need to teach, that these problems were solved by Hicks-Slutsky-Samuelson (the first- and second-order conditions for optimisation) and Arrow-Debreu, respectively, (with the latter establishing existence and efficiency properties of general equilibrium in light of the two fundamental theorems of welfare economics). For the former, not least through duality approaches to optimisation, it follows that everything hinges upon given utility and production functions, and what can be dubbed the core technical apparatus (TA) of the orthodoxy. The use of production and utility functions in particular as the key components of the TA have been taken as sacrosanct within the mainstream both for the narrowly defined analysis of supply and demand and for their projection onto any number of other problems (as with economics imperialism, see below). All of the technical apparatus is, though, readily inserted within what can be called a technical architecture (and another TA), of preoccupation with optimisation, equilibrium and efficiency. The two together can be hammered home by referring to TA^2 as continuing to form the foundations of the current orthodoxy,[5] so much so that it can be both taken for granted, augmented or, perversely, even dispensed with to suit (see below on "suspension").

But as important as the derivation of TA^2 itself is how it was derived. Here, again as a teaching device, it is useful to refer to an "implosion". Essentially, the results became the goal in and of themselves and any sacrifice was acceptable to achieve them in terms of method, conceptualisation, assumptions and, even realism. Thus, preferences (and so the nature of individuals and goods) are taken as given, motivation is single-minded, prices are taken as given, there are no economies of scale and scope, and so on. The narrowness of the scope of analysis is an important motivational device in teaching (the reasons for) lack of realism.

Each of the sacrifices made in this implosion is essential in order to get to TA^2. Further, TA^2 was consolidated following what is known as the formalist revolution of the 1950s (when, as the next stage in its development, economics began to become heavily mathematical). A virtue is made out of necessities in constructing TA^2 that goes far beyond the rationale of deriving the results themselves. The methods, conceptualisations, theories and assumptions turn from a means to an end into the end themselves becoming the starting point for all economic analysis, promoting standard assumptions and mathematical methods. This is an important point for students grappling with the notion that the orthodoxy is warranted by its supposedly superior methods (which they are not) and emulation of the physical sciences (which it does not, given the latter's heavy dose of empirical realism).

Students also need to know that the distinction between macroeconomics and microeconomics derives from the 1930s, with the rise of Keynesianism and the perceived inability of the evolving TA^2 to be able to deal with the Great Depression as a systemic failure (of effective demand for Keynes). It is also imperative for students to be aware that in the inter-war period, there were other traditions of economics as strong as those informing micro and macro, if not stronger. Not least of these was the original "old" institutional economics with its inductive (if still theoretical) preoccupations with topics such as the rise of trade unions, monopolised corporations, distribution, and the regularity of cyclical movements, with a corresponding reliance upon economic history and socio-economic analysis as opposed to mathematical modelling.

As a result, by the time of the formalist revolution, there was a tripartite division of the discipline into micro, macro and a disparate collection of other applied fields considered more or less unamenable to micro/macro analysis as such – thus, for example, the old or classical development economics drew more upon economic history and inductive methods. Although both micro and macro rapidly established their positions and increasingly mathematical forms through textbook teaching, macroeconomics (especially through IS/LM) was seen as distinct from and, to a large extent, more prestigious than micro. Even so, it is important to highlight the distinction between the economics of Keynes and Keynesian economics as it was to become in the neoclassical synthesis, not least with an initial embrace of mathematical methods and modelling if not exclusive dependence on optimising agents at the expense of systemic analysis.

But, having imploded upon its core TA^2, micro was ready to explode, not only across economics but other disciplines too in what can be termed economics imperialism. This is a topic, not least in reflecting interdisciplinarity, that should be prominent in the teaching of economic theory. It raises issues of what is the scope of economic analysis both in principle, or logically, and historically (attending to what has been considered the scope of subject matter, content and methods of the discipline through time). For the history underpinning the creation of TA^2 was one of confining analysis to one aspect of human behaviour (a reduced notion of utility and its maximisation) to one application, the market through supply and demand (and with very special assumptions to operationalise the exercise). Logically, though, despite this historical confinement of microeconomic principles, their application logically is not constrained in subject matter at all. Utility maximisation after all makes no reference to supply, demand, the market and so on. Accordingly, whilst the history of TA^2 points to confinement of its scope of application, its logic paradoxically suggests otherwise.

In short, what might be termed the historical logic of economics imperialism points to the historical limits imposed in deriving and applying TA^2 but its logical potential for wide scope of application once established. Indeed, this is exactly what has happened since the formalist revolution with an explosion of TA^2 across both economics and social science more generally. It begins analytically by applying utility maximising and the like as if in the presence of markets even where they are absent, with early examples being human capital theory, cliometrics (or the new economic history) and public choice theory (polemically, for students, the choice between apples and pears is identical to that between war and peace). Students should also understand that the non-market factors that have been excluded to be able to establish TA^2 are subsequently, arbitrarily and perversely brought back in to be explained by its application.

The leading exponent of economics imperialism in what I have termed its first phase is Gary Becker. Without exception, his work never refers to money and finance nor to unemployment. But economics imperialism in its second phase, which follows the monetarist counter-revolution in macroeconomics as discussed below, continues to rely upon TA^2 but adds the wrinkle of allowing for markets to work imperfectly as a result of asymmetric information (Stiglitz, but initiated by Akerlof's market for lemons) or increasing returns to scale (Krugman primarily for trade and geography and otherwise much less prominent as such).[6] This phase of economics imperialism understands the non-market as the collective, rational response to such market imperfections – that is why the state, institutions, customs or apparently irrational behaviour exist. The result is to give rise to a whole range of new fields straddling economics and the other social sciences as well as rejuvenating older applications of the first phase of economics imperialism, also incorporating into microeconomics those applied fields that previously had an independent existence (the new development economics, trade theory, industrial economics, etc.).

These developments across microeconomics have their counterparts in macroeconomics. Until the monetarist counter-revolution, Keynesianism reigned supreme although the IS/LM framework was at times complemented by other interpretations such as the reappraisal and post-Keynesianism. These are worthy of coverage in highlighting differences in schools of thought in how the economy is conceived. Indeed, in presentational terms, it is judicious across all teaching to treat the orthodoxy with respect in the sense of not designating it as right or wrong as such but to see alternatives as offering different ways of understanding how the economy works. This involves highlighting for each what is present as well as what is absent, the tensions and errors that these create on their own terms let alone those from other perspectives, and the structures, processes, relations and agencies involved (the latter highly reduced in case of orthodoxy in view of its individualism and deductive methodology).

Thus, as neatly captured by Coddington's notion of the reappraisal as reductionist, it can be seen as a generalisation of general equilibrium in which optimising agents are both resource and exchange constrained, analytically captured through the device of fixed price models. Quite apart from smoothing the transition through the monetarist and new classical counter-revolutions that explicitly subordinated macroeconomics to (market-imperfection) microeconomics, ultimately taking the form of the New Consensus Macroeconomics, the reappraisal neatly captures the effective demand aspect of Keynesianism. Yet it entirely discards its systemic elements, itself heavily reduced as previously mentioned relative to Keynes himself by the IS/LM framework (Keynes' views on mathematical modelling, methodological individualism, expectations and uncertainty, animal spirits, and the nature of a modern financial system all need to be brought to the fore although appeal to the authority of Keynes has diminished just as he has increasingly been misrepresented, and rejected).

Post-Keynesianism, on the other hand, goes in the opposite direction highlighting to students in a relatively easy manner the systemic nature of macroeconomic analysis, providing opportunity to introduce elements of structure (wages and profits), relations (capital and labour), processes (monopolisation) and agency (sources of demand through consumption or investment), as well as emphasising the endogeneity of the monetary system (opening, especially in the wake of the Global Financial Crisis, GFC, the impact of the financial system on effective demand through speculation, investment, consumption and distribution). In addition, methodological considerations can be introduced through dividing the school into two camps: one that builds models on foundations that differ from the orthodoxy as opposed to another that emphasises the fluid and uncertain character of the macroeconomy, and the corresponding vanity involved in reducing the macroeconomy to a model, however well it is constructed and estimated.

To some degree, the narrative of the history of macroeconomics has been disrupted by shifting to the alternative narrative of comparison of schools of thought. Running the two simultaneously, if coherently and clearly, is no bad thing, particularly if also offering a broader vision of the trajectory of macroeconomics to its present state, or at least until the GFC. Here two themes can be emphasised. One is how the short and long runs are related to one another. Macroeconomics, with exceptions that prove the rule (such as growth theory and real business cycles), has increasingly been reduced to investigating short-run deviations around (given) long-term trends. This can be shown to be the consequence of illegitimately conflating three different notions of the long run itself: the passage of time, equilibrium and the relative speed of adjustment of variables, as much a theoretical as an empirical matter.

Second, macroeconomics has increasingly converged on general equilibrium although in two entirely different and independent ways (over and above its being the distant and forgotten long run around which the short run moves, with presumption of the existence of a unique, stable and efficient epicentre). One is to rely upon microfoundations and methodological individualism, in the even more extreme form of representative agents. The other is through Walrasian consistency across markets (which, for example, has profound implications in the form of Ricardian-type equivalence results and what the state can and cannot do).

These two themes allow the journey to the contemporary state of macroeconomics to be traced, although they need to be complemented by significant events along the way, including: excision of monopoly and corporate power, distribution of income and wealth, class struggle, technical change, and broader economic and social conditions and the role of the state, from the analysis; reduction of Keynes to IS/LM; Patinkin's real balance effect to make money matter but not very much and in limited ways; the reduction of uncertainty to expectations; substitution of rational for adaptive expectations; reduction to representative individuals; and reduction of macro to supply and demand with more or less randomly distributed more or less sticky markets, more or less informationally known.

3. ...to the Global Financial Crisis and back again

Such narratives across micro and macro allow the more recent developments within the discipline to be explained in the wake of the GFC. On the one hand, much can be made of the failure to anticipate or even to allow for such eventualities, not least with absurdities of the various versions of the efficient market hypothesis to the fore for which financial markets and their interaction with other markets are presumed to ground out the best of all possible worlds. On the other hand, the response to it has been minimal for which the contrast with the 1930s (Keynesianism) and the 1970s (monetarist counter-revolution) can be drawn. This does not mean that orthodoxy has stood still. Rather, it has entered a new phase of economics imperialism that even more extensively straddles and incorporates into itself the subject matter and topics of other disciplines. It does so through what I have called suspension, both holding onto and letting go (of TA^2) at the same time. So confident is the discipline in TA^2 in itself and as at the core of the discipline, that it has now become applied in conjunction with whatever else it pleases from wherever it pleases and to whatever it pleases. This is so, as observed previously, despite the bringing back in what was previously necessarily assumed away, and inconsistent with, TA^2, in order to establish it in the first place. The most obvious example is alternative behavioural assumptions. But much the same applies to any number of variables of grander or lesser scale from non-optimal behaviour to institutions and the like.

Such developments can be used to expose the strengths and weaknesses of the orthodoxy. Why is it and how is it that such factors can be brought into account now when they were shunned previously, not least Simon's bounded rationality and even game theory when it was first established (as it implies that individuals cannot see themselves as isolated and independent of one another)? The strengths derive from the orthodoxy's institutional capacity both to retain its core principles as well as to contradict them. By the same token, it opens analytical weaknesses not only through inconsistencies and lack of rigour (which have in practice rarely been a problem for the discipline) but also from the methods, concepts and theories that have been traditionally deployed by other disciplines in addressing the widening subject matter of economics. In addition, the weaknesses of the orthodoxy are exposed by its failure to be able to explain the economy on the basis of its own economic principles although this can be projected as a strength in terms of drawing upon other disciplines and non-economic factors if only on its own terms.

The orthodoxy's weaknesses can then be exposed through an account of its own history but equally opening up opportunities for alternatives. For the latter, in the wake of the GFC, the most obvious starting point is the self-confessedly impoverished treatment of finance within macro. Across the other social sciences, and within heterodoxy, the crisis itself and the conditions that underpinned it, have given rise to the astonishingly rapid and extensive emergence of the concept of financialisation. But the concept of financialisation is notable for its absence from orthodox economics, and for the good reason that it is totally incompatible even with a suspended TA^2. For it involves structures (location of finance within the economy), relations (of power over economy and society), agencies (other than individuals, not least those within the financial system) and processes (the expansion and proliferation of financial markets and assets).

As a result, covering the concept of financialisation is a very powerful counterweight to orthodoxy. But it also carries two further significant implications for the direction in which teaching can go. One is to see it as revealing only the tip of the iceberg of the deficiencies of the orthodoxy, most obviously because of the crisis itself. This opens up the rationale for highlighting how other major issues of systemic importance have been overlooked or mistreated even if not brought to the fore, such as distribution (Piketty as the exception that may have limited lasting impact), corporate behaviour and power (where are multinationals in micro and macro?), the role of health, education and welfare in economic performance, and the sources and impact of technical change.

The other issue is to dissolve or at least to turn upside down the relationship between micro and macro, perversely since the thrust of orthodoxy is to reduce macro to micro. On the one hand, how are we to understand and address microeconomic questions in the absence of locating them within their macroeconomic context (for example, corporate behaviour without consideration of shareholder value, the sources of technology, the making of markets, and so on)? On the other hand, the division between micro and macro is arbitrary, an artificial creation of the evolution of economics as opposed to the economy itself. Indeed, the socialisation of the economy in practice runs against the increasing reliance upon microeconomics in principle within orthodoxy. Questioning the separation between micro and macro is not identical to, but allows for consideration of, issues of conflict and power that have long been absent from orthodoxy.

A striking way to illustrate these points and many that have come before is through growth theory and its own trajectory from Harrod-Domar through old and new versions. Growth theory has itself gone through phases of prominence but, when in favour, it is generally located within macro for obvious reasons. Yet its substantive content is exclusively microeconomic. Indeed, and to some degree perversely, Solow's growth model is microeconomics projected to macroeconomic two decades before the New Classical Economics celebrated such. It draws upon the simple production function for the vast majority of its substantive content, and has subsequently paved the way for any number of microeconomic projections onto macroeconomics through new growth theory. One way to teach this is through exposing the weaknesses of old growth theory, not least in terms of its reliance upon steady-state balanced growth, full employment and perfectly working markets, and how new growth theory either fails to resolve these or adds a few weaknesses of its own. These include, in the case of the eponymous Barro-type regressions, the reduction of the history of growth for all times and places to what is effectively a Cobb-Douglas production function for growth across any set of variables you care to include. The result is as incoherent as for the measurement of total factor productivity. The latter involves treating as the residual all of the deviations from the assumptions of the one sector model – not least relative price changes, imperfect competition, lack of full employment, and economies of scale and scope. Having putatively calculated TFP, orthodoxy proceeds to explain it precisely by those factors that have been assumed away in measuring it, whether that be corruption, recessions, trade union strength or whatever.

But underpinning growth theory is the ubiquitous production function. As is well-known to heterodox economists, even if of decreasing prominence from its heyday in the sixties, this is totally flawed on its own terms in light of the Cambridge Capital Critique. The best way to put this is in the simple following terms. The properties or deductions derived from a one-sector model do not in general carry over to models of more than one sector. This does itself open up a number of other inner criticisms of the orthodoxy that totally undermine its intuitions and credibility ranging over the assumption of the existence of a unique, stable, efficient equilibrium, the theory of the second best, and the theory of comparative advantage (requiring full employment, only two sectors, perfect competition, etc.).[7] These exercises from within orthodoxy themselves demonstrate to students that mathematical techniques take precedence over their results since, despite the latter's thrust, orthodoxy presumes that they do not prevail.

Such inner criticisms also open the potential for other alternative avenues. First is the conceptualisation of production itself as a simple relation between inputs and outputs, for which Marxist labour process theory offers a critical point of departure. Second is the assumption of given technologies as opposed to theories of technological change for which there are various theories and factors from which to choose. A good starting point is Adam Smith's division of labour from which his peculiar components theory of price derives. A growing division of labour allows for rising wages as a component part of price. The details – and errors pointed out by Ricardo in taking the constituent components of price as independent of one another, even though they are bound by net output – need not detain us. Rather, what is important is that Smith is seeking to construct a theory of value in a context in which productivity is changing, something that at most is unsatisfactorily addressed, if not assumed away, by orthodoxy through comparative statics. Indeed, the only other major theorist to incorporate technical change into value theory in this way is Marx. Although Marx's value theory has often, controversially and narrowly, been interpreted through a static theory of equilibrium price in the form of the so-called transformation problem, it is more fully and appropriately understood as a theory of technical change through which the system of exchange is exposed to deep underlying tensions as it seeks to accommodate the accumulation of capital as productivity evolves differentially across sectors (Fine and Saad-Filho 2016).

Apart from questioning the separation between micro and macro, exploring the relationship between value theory and productivity change allows for coverage of classical political economy, not least because it incorporates broader considerations of various interpretations of falling profitability, the stationary state and crises. Producer theory, though, also offers the opportunity to consider competition as a topic. Within the orthodoxy, despite its common origins in TA^2 with consumer theory – production and utility functions are essentially equivalent – there is a richness of analysis, albeit piecemeal, covering varieties of models of exit and entry, product differentiation, oligopoly and so on. These can be used to pose alternatives in which the idea of determinate equilibrium, as opposed to continuing rivalry, is inappropriate, that all factors cannot be taken into account simultaneously so that an inductive content is necessary, and that the broader context is relevant for what forms competition takes and with what results as opposed to relying upon intra- and inter-firm relations alone. The orthodox, and some heterodox notions of competition can be shown to derive their results by incorporating some aspects of competition at the expense of others. The relationship between competition and economic performance can be located in the wider discussion of the nature of industrial policy, on the one hand, and of industrial transformation (and the developmental state paradigm, say), on the other.

Unlike producer theory (as firms have some sort of lives beyond optimising), as mentioned consumer theory remains remarkably stagnant since the marginalist revolution, a few twists and much sophisticated econometrics aside. This stands in sharp contrast to the postmodernist turn in consumer studies, in which the nature of the consumed (the meaning of goods) and the consumer (the making of identities) have come to the fore quite apart from longstanding theories that totally depart from the reductionist utility maximisation (emulation, distinction, habit-formation, altruism, etc.). This means there is ample opportunity to offer alternatives to orthodoxy from across the social sciences and heterodoxy, with considerable appeal to greater realism and personal experience (why are you wearing what you are wearing?). My own take on handling this has been in part to emphasise the social determinants of consumption, especially those that derive at a distance from consumption itself, with debates over consumer sovereignty offering at most a limited critical point of departure. In case of food, for example, emphasis can be placed on the way in which the food system is based upon underlying compulsions both to eat and to diet, and each individual is faced with how to respond to these pressures giving rise to explanations for the "diseases of affluence" such as eating disorders, obesity, etc., which defy orthodox explanation other than by appeal to an all-encompassing irrationality or intertemporal short-sightedness and discounting. Even here, appeal can be made to history to question to the contrary, why these conditions prevail now, a peculiar aspect of contemporary capitalism.

The fuzzy if non-existent boundaries between micro and macro can also be brought to the fore through focusing on labour markets. The extraordinary influence of human capital theory can be criticised for how it conceives of the definition and gaining of skills as well as how it sees these as being rewarded. On the one hand, the conditioning variables that are necessary for estimating returns to human capital – gender, race, competitiveness of sector, presence of trade unions, pace of technological change, sunset or sunrise – turn out to be more important than what is explained. This leads neatly into segmented labour market theory, and the structural determination of occupational segregation and rewards (although I would add that social factors determine not just how labour markets are segmented but also that each segment operates internally in different ways from one segment to another), and the belated acceptance that labour market structures do exist albeit on the reduced basis of the consequences of market imperfections. But a devastating starting point for reconstructing labour market theory arises out of the minimum wage debate. Essentially, the orthodoxy has attempted to restore an inverse relationship between minimum wages and employment by conditioning the relationship by any variable that might suggest otherwise – choice or work over education as well as trends in productivity or over the cycle, for example. The appropriate response to this is to conclude that labour markets simply do not work in the ways being suggested by the orthodoxy – they are socially constructed as opposed to simply reflecting conditioned interaction of supply and demand.

In the case of macroeconomics, there are many alternative models that can be offered that diverge from orthodoxy but also allow command of it and its techniques. For these, and orthodoxy too, it is imperative to tell students first to find equilibrium for such models as this will tell you much more about them than anything else. Second is to pinpoint how the economy has been disaggregated into which (real and monetary) sectors. Third is to specify how each of these sectors is understood in terms of market clearing and competitiveness or otherwise. Fourth is to understand how these markets interact with one another (if linear, or approximations of such, this will simply be the inverse of the matrix of equations yielding multipliers). As previously mentioned, orthodox and heterodox models share much in common in these respects even if they understand differently how the economic system works. This raises the issue of whether, and to what extent, it can be your model or mine, or whether to argue that complexity and fluidity of macroeconomic relations, structures, processes and agencies render modelling extremely limited for fixing what is not fixed. How, for example, do we handle globalisation, monopolisation, technical change and financialisation which are fundamentally disequilibrating and yet the key mechanisms through which the macroeconomy evolves?

In teaching macro, on top of the history previously delineated, I like to top and tail the course with two models that themselves represent early beginnings and a more contemporary contribution. The Harrod knife-edge (accelerator-multiplier) model offers an excellent starting point for a number of reasons. First, it was itself an orthodoxy in its own time, one seeking to integrate growth with cycles. Second, it fails (other than through artificial introduction of non-linearities dubbed floors and ceilings). Third, it introduces difference equations as a technique (and contrast can be drawn with continuous models). Fourth, the subsequent evolution of macroeconomics can be situated in terms of dropping key assumptions – no money, pricing, adaptive expectations, interest costs and increasing costliness of investment, intertemporal optimisation of production and consumption, and focus on short-run deviations around a given trend. Fifth, this simple model produces dramatic results in terms of the fundamental instability of the capitalist economy. Yet, sixth, all those qualifying assumptions just listed have, whether by accident or design (and with claims of greater realism and generality), the dulling effect of smoothing the course of (the model of) the economy and eliminating the profound instability of the knife edge. Finally, then, this allows for a discussion of whether models are more or less realistic or better understood as offering visions of how a capitalist economy might function if focusing on certain of its aspects with no presumption that the more complex is the more insightful (which can hardly be countered given the orthodoxy's most recent penchant for the new consensus macroeconomics and its three-equation model in place of multi-sector Keynesian modelling).

Dornbusch's overshooting models offer similar perspectives. Whilst there is a literature seeking to test its relevance, this is not the point. Rather, on the basis of the simplest of models with every market clearing (well only two for finance but not the goods market) and full employment at all times (i.e. just one market does not work perfectly but with some stickiness), and with rational expectations as well (i.e. new classicals have almost everything they could possibly wish for), then the exchange rate overshoots in adjusting to a new equilibrium. This totally undermines the motivational thrust of the orthodoxy. For it suggests, and not just for markets for foreign exchange but more generally, that the pride of place occupied by the pricing system in signalling to agents how they should optimise is capable of being totally perverse. The macro-foundations of microeconomics are totally undermined let alone vice-versa. Even worse is that if the assumption of full employment is dropped and output adjusts in response to excess demand, then the overshooting result is tempered and even possibly reversed. In other words, the more Keynesian-like the economy the less it is liable to perverse price movements.

This might be thought to reintroduce a role for Keynesianism and for the state in targeting some form of stability for the economy. As already mentioned, the understanding of the state in modern macroeconomics (and microeconomics for that matter) is severely limited – it is merely a special individual able to move some supply and demand curves and to which individuals can react, thereby potentially nullifying the role of the state in the limit. Alternatives from within heterodox economics and across the social sciences more generally are plentiful, whether in terms of the nature of the state and its relationship to class interests or in terms of the role and functions of the state.

Furthermore, this can all be used to pose alternatives to macroeconomics, microeconomics and the division between the two on a grander scale by contrasting the Keynesian and neoliberal periods of capitalism. When I first began to study economics in the late 1960s, the idea that the post-war boom was anything other than the consequences of Keynesian demand management was considered a heresy, much as the New Consensus Macroeconomics, with its heavy monetarist overtones, projected the conventional wisdom that the state of the macroeconomy and of macroeconomics was more or less settled together with their capacity to regulate the economy. But both periods can be understood in terms of how capitalism is primarily organised for the uneven economic and social restructuring of capitalism as it goes about accumulation. For the Keynesian period, there was a combination of heavy state intervention, extensive welfare provision and internationalisation of capital in all of its forms (multinational production, trade and finance). By contrast, thanks to financialisation, the neoliberal period has been dominated by the increasing role of finance in economic and social restructuring. Whilst this shift has profound implications for macroeconomic policy, not least in terms of austerity and the levels and composition of state expenditure (especially in crisis), this is simply a tip of the iceberg moment again in terms of the ways in which the macroeconomy functions.

In part on a polemical point, not least in offering alternative policies and the means to achieve them, it is worth observing that "macroeconomic" conditions or the "fundamentals" could not have been more favourable to capitalism than under neoliberalism – with the winning of the Cold War, the decline of liberation movements and the strength and organisation of labour and other progressive movements, limitations on increases in economic and social wages, the triumph of neoliberalism in the policy arena, the huge increases in global labour forces (not least with China's turn to capitalism), huge increases in inequality, and the availability of an unprecedented wave of new technologies. Across the areas of microeconomic and macroeconomic policy, this opens up any number of alternatives with a necessary but by no means sufficient condition as the means of achieve them being the bringing of finance under social control.

4. Concluding remarks

In teaching orthodoxy critically and paving the way for alternatives, the psychology of students is of some importance. Being too dismissive of what they have to learn, and may have spent much energy in already having learnt, is liable to be understandably demoralising and courting lack of receptivity. Consequently, a history of thought approach to their subject matter can offer some compensation, allowing them to see how flat earth views of the world can arise even in their own times. Equally, this allows for discussion of how scholarship becomes the way it is – is Keynesianism a product of the Great Depression, for example – and for the relative influence of external events and interests as opposed to inner intellectual momentum (from TA^2, the historical logic of economics imperialism, the incorporation of asymmetric information, etc.). Last, and by no means least, there is the opportunity to discuss the nature of capitalism, its contemporary form as neoliberalism, and the prospects for alternative forms of organisation and policies.

Notes

1 See Fine (2016a) and Fine and Dimakou (2016) where the material suggested here is covered for the purposes of teaching. In what follows, I assume familiarity with such material without the need to offer exposition of it, so this contribution is more teacher- than student-friendly.
2 See Milonakis and Fine (2009) and Fine and Milonakis (2009).
3 But it is worth observing (with students) that how economics is today is itself subject to dispute amongst its opponents, not least whether dissolving from without (Colander 2010), reducible to a social ontology of mathematical deductivism (Lawson 2013), or my own view of expanding application of a suspended technical apparatus and architecture, see below and Fine (2016b) as well as other contributions in the collection in which it appears.
4 One way to view the marginalist revolution, and changes in economics and differences between schools of thought more generally, is as a paradigm shift. This has strengths and weaknesses both as analytical and teaching device but see Fine (2002, 2004) for some discussion. Note, though, that Kuhn's preferred definition of paradigm was as a community of scientists, something which fits the current mainstream extraordinarily well.
5 The terminology underpinning TA^2 comes from a student of mine, Al-Jazaeri (2009).
6 See earlier footnote for reference to discussion of the information-theoretic revolution in economics as a paradigm shift *within* the mainstream.
7 See Fine and Van Waeyenberge (2013).

References

Al-Jazaeri, H. (2009): *Interrogating Technical Change through the History of Economic Thought in the Context of Latecomers' Industrial Development: The Case of the South Korean Microelectronics, Auto and Steel Industries*, PhD thesis, SOAS, University of London.

Colander, D. (2010): 'Moving Beyond the Rhetoric of Pluralism: Suggestions for an 'Inside-the-Mainstream' Heterodoxy,' in W. Garnett, E. Olsen and M. Starr (eds.) *Economic Pluralism*, London and New York: Routledge, pp. 36–47.

Fine, B. (2002): 'Economics Imperialism and the New Development Economics as Kuhnian Paradigm Shift, *World Development*, 30(12), 2057–2570.

Fine, B. (2004): 'Economics Imperialism as Kuhnian Revolution, in Arestis, P. and Sawyer, M. (eds.), *The Rise of the Market*. Camberley: Edward Elgar, 107–144.

Fine, B. (2016a): *Microeconomics: A Critical Companion*. London: Pluto.

Fine, B. (2016b): 'Neoclassical Economics: An Elephant is not a Chimera but Is a Chimera Real?', in Morgan, N. (ed.), *What Is This 'School' Called Neoclassical Economics? Debating the Origins, Meaning and Significance*. London: Routledge, 180–199.

Fine, B. and Dimakou, O. (2016): *Macroeconomics: A Critical Companion*. London: Pluto.

Fine, B. and Milonakis, D. (2009): *From Economics Imperialism to Freakonomics: The Shifting Boundaries between Economics and Other Social Sciences*. London: Routledge.

Fine, B. and Saad-Filho, A. (2016): *Marx's Capital*. London: Pluto Press.

Fine, B. and Van Waeyenberge, E. (2013): 'A Paradigm Shift that Never Was: Justin Lin's New Structural Economics', *Competition and Change*, 17(4), 355–371.

Lawson, T. (2013): 'What Is This 'School' Called Neoclassical Economics?', *Cambridge Journal of Economics*, 37(5), 947–983.

Milonakis, D. and Fine, B. (2009): *From Political Economy to Economics: Method, the Social and the Historical in the Evolution of Economic Theory*. London: Routledge.

5 An outsider's perspective

What can economics teaching learn from history didactics?

Astrid Schwabe

1. Introduction

Modern German history didactics, with its two central categories of historical consciousness ("*Geschichtsbewusstsein*") and historical culture ("*Geschichtskultur*") – we will come back to them later – is understood as the "theory and practice of historical learning" (Baumgärtner 2015, 28). It not only fulfils a pragmatic and empirical purpose, but also has a theoretical and normative function. History didactics, which sees itself explicitly as a sub-discipline of the science of history, demands a didactically "valuable" history education ("*Geschichtsvermittlung*") in general, and learning environments (such as "good" history teaching) or educational media (such as school books) in particular. While German history didactics does not have a clear, generally acknowledged theoretical framework, and the theoretical discourse inside the discipline is rather diverse and controversial, there are, nonetheless, some undisputed central premises or criteria which are consensual for any form of historical education. They purport a normative ideal type of how history is supposed to be taught to create a historical consciousness which "facilitates a sensible social practice and which understands history as a process the human quality of which can be enhanced by human enterprise" ("*eine vernünftige gesellschaftliche Praxis fördert und Geschichte als einen Prozess begreift, dessen humane Qualität durch menschliches Handeln gesteigert werden kann*", Bergmann 1997, 247).

This contribution by an "outsider" will offer a glimpse into an entirely different academic field. Below, I will explain briefly what these consensual premises of history didactics are based on, and how a didactically aspirational representation of history might be affected. In this context, I will outline the concepts of historical consciousness and historical culture, and touch upon the learning and teaching of history. In the relevant literature, we find several but often only slightly different catalogues of criteria or analytical grids which are derived from the theories of history didactics (e.g. Rüsen 1992; Günther-Arndt and Kemnitz 2000; Reeken 2010, 69–83; Schwabe 2012, 57–72; fundamental for these explanations: Schwabe 2012, 39–72).

2. The fundamental understanding of history

A scientific understanding of history must be the basis for the standards set for a "good" history education. This understanding varies greatly from the general public's idea of what constitutes history, which uses history almost synonymously with the past. History is supposedly anything that happened earlier. History is supposed to show "how it actually happened" ("*wie es eigentlich gewesen*," Franz Leopold von Ranke).

This is not at all the case. According to the scientific criteria upon which these reflections are based, history is a special form of human memory which surpasses an individual's lifespan. History is a particular way of thinking and of viewing reality, which is supposed to offer further orientation (Bergmann 2008, 26–27). History means to (re-)construct the highly complex human practices of the past, with all their turns and changes, and to describe those past practices in a way that gives them structure and meaning *("historische Narration")*. This process, which is based on historical records called sources, is motivated by a current interest and looked at from a perspective affected by present circumstances. Working in accordance with the historical critical method ("*historisch-kritische Methode*") means to choose sources, so they might offer answers to current problem/questions (heuristics), to evaluate them (critical review), and to put them into context (interpretation). Dietmar von Reeken 2017, 5) summarises this process very aptly: "History is the process of constructing and re-constructing the past from a present point of view. It is undertaken with the goal to deepen one's own ability to understand present and future social and individual processes, and to gain decision making skills." *("Geschichte ist ein Prozess der Rekonstruktion und Konstruktionsprozess von Vergangenheit aus der Perspektive der Gegenwart. Sie geschieht mit der Zielsetzung, in Gegenwart und Zukunft die eigene Fähigkeit zum Verständnis gesellschaftlicher und individueller Prozesse zu vertiefen und Handlungskompetenz zu gewinnen.")*.

Taking this into consideration, we arrive at the following conclusion: this methodology-guided (re-)construction of history cannot claim to show the truth – the categories "true" and "false" must only be applied very carefully. History is always an interpretation of the past, bound by time and perspective. The view of the past inevitably differs from person to person, who each undeniably have made different experiences over their lifespan and who will each have reached different levels of education and developed varying ideas of morality. History, therefore, is definitely not a reflection of the past, but must rather be understood as a construction of consciousness ("*Bewusstseinskonstrukt*," Jeismann 2000, 51) and as a process of discovering meaning by employing a certain method (Rüsen 1997; Pandel 2006, 153). History is controversial and different historians will reach different conclusions. Yet, the methodology of the science of history allows for an inter-subjective verifiability of these interpretations. Several notions of the validity of these interpretations have been proposed by Jörn Rüsen. He makes a distinction between empirical, normative, and narrative validity. These lead to the following criteria, which a convincing interpretation should fulfill: Are the interpretations compatible with the records employed? Are the interpretations pertinent to the navigation of today's reality? Are the interpretations presented in a fluent and comprehensible narrative?

Consequently, the study of history is, in our context, a critical examination of the past, guided by scientific methodologies. It aims to offer advice for the present or even the future. It could make origins and causes of developments comprehensible or might help to cope with current challenges by examining comparable structures in the past.

3. Historical consciousness, historical culture, and learning history

The term of historical consciousness is pivotal for the understanding of the human interaction with their history or past (the terms are deliberately used synonymously here) from the perspective of history didactics. According to Rüsen (2008, 132), historical consciousness is "the structuring of a narrative and the creation of meaning through the experience of time" ("*narrative Sinnbildung über Zeiterfahrung*"). It is based on the human desire to know the past, to understand the present, and to shape the future. Historical consciousness is a normative term because it represents the ultimate objective of all endeavours of reflective, didactically sensible and guided history teaching. Historical consciousness presumes that one knows that the (re-)construction of the past is necessarily bound to present potential insights, new interpretations and current problems (Jeismann 1997, 42). So, as we can see, this concept, for the differentiation of which history didactics offers a variety of models, is mainly derived from the understanding of history. Finally, the mental structure of an individual historical consciousness encompasses – varying from person to person – cognitive elements, such as "knowledge" about the past, as well as affective components, such as identification.

Closely connected to this is the second fundamental category of history didactics: historical culture. According to Rüsen (1994), historical culture is the articulation of historical consciousness in society ("*praktisch wirksame Artikulation von Geschichtsbewusstsein im Leben einer Gesellschaft*"). Even if it is closely related to the concept of public history, it is based on a slightly different theory. It encompasses all representations of history in a society, to be characterised in different dimensions (i.a. Rüsen 2014). This implicates environments of controlled history teaching, such as schools, and universities, but also museums, monuments and other media, as well as day-to-day occurrences and phenomena, such as street signs or conversations at the dinner table. According to Schönemann (2000), the collective construct of historical culture is affected by various institutions, professions, media, and publications. Each of these areas, among them the science of history, operates according to their own rationale.

The individual construct, historical consciousness, and the collective construct, historical culture, interact and influence each other – they are "two sides of the same coin" (Schönemann 2002, 79). Historical culture impacts the individual historical consciousness: even the shortest interaction with history, be it through films, video games, or political speech, can, and will, affect the individual historical consciousness (i.e. Bergmann 2008, 13; 79–83). This will inevitably launch non-judgmental processes of historical learning. The exact mechanisms are hard to grasp. However, it can be stated, with some certainty, that uncontrolled historical learning can also lead to a fragmented or wrong idea of history and to the development of wrong or, what we could even consider to be dangerous or problematic (re-)construction of the past (Borries 2008, 18–19; Schwabe 2012, 52). In contrast, a historical education that is guided by history didactics – not just at schools or universities –, should facilitate a "good" learning of history, an "elaborated" historical consciousness. It is characterised by the employment of the "competence" of historical thinking. This entails the source-based perception of the human past led by personal perspectives, the understanding of history as a way of making sense of the past, and its contextualisation through a goal-orientated examination of history (i.a. Rüsen 2008, 65–67). So, the promotion of a historical consciousness is about two things: on the one hand, the dissemination of a scientific understanding of history, and on the other hand, a training in the methods necessary for the scientific examination of the past. It is not at all about the accumulation of factual knowledge, but about the appropriation and habitual practice of critical thinking ("*Denkstil*", Pandel 2000, 126).

4. (Historical) didactic criteria for history teaching

Based on these considerations, we must necessarily conclude that all (re-) presentations of history – independently of whether in scientific publications, school textbooks or museums – should fulfil certain (quality) criteria to facilitate a good historical education, to support historical thinking, even if we know that this requirement is deliberately normatively set and follows an ideal. In the following, I will focus on some central aspects of history didactics, which could, in my estimation, offer some especially interesting thought-provoking input on some of the questions about pluralities discussed in this volume (Schwabe 2012, 54–72).

- In history education, it is important to emphasise the **constructed character** of history and the **controversy** which results from the fact that history is only the re-construction of the past from the current point of view. Any (re-)presentation of history should show that historical events are to be considered controversially in the scientific discourse, and that not only plurality, but discussion and even arguments are a "normal" part of that discourse. Different views on and controversial interpretations of past events, acts, and processes are supposed to be presented and compared. Authors should make sure to clarify their view-points and avoid the suggestion of stating the "absolute truth".

- By presenting different, possibly also contradicting, **sources**, a (re-)presentation of history should always enable or even force the recipient to think about the issues themselves, and to arrive at a plausible and sound interpretation. In order to reveal the methods – and possibly limits – of the process of gaining historical knowledge, it is consequently important to integrate different and critically reviewed sources as the basis of any historical findings (i.a. Rohlfes 1989, 603–608; Rüsen 1992, 249). In doing so, it is furthermore important to emphasise that these sources do not indeed reflect past realities. These records only offer one perspective on a section of past events, and were sometimes consciously, sometimes unconsciously, created for a specific purpose. They already include their own evaluation of past events or realities. Sources should never be used as mere illustrations of history (Pandel 2000).
- Since past human perception was bound by viewpoints and perspectives determined by individual social situations, the criterion of **multiperspectivity** ("Multiperspektivität") must be considered in history education. This criterion calls for a historical event to be considered through the eyes of multiple people, if possible, from different social backgrounds and divergent habitus. While the demand for controversy concerns a plurality in the examination of history in the present, multiperspectivity requires a plurality in the historical past. The criterion of multiperspectivity also concerns the abovementioned sources, but not only those (Bergmann 2000, 25–26; Bergmann 2008, 164).
- The criterion of **reality** demands a clear distinction between fact and fiction and the deconstruction of popular myths or misconceptions (Pandel 2005, 11–13). At the same time, it is important to point out that any (re-)construction of history (necessarily) always contains a grain of fictitiousness (Füßmann 1994, 36–37).
- In any case, an academic account of history should always be based on the **most recent research**. It should offer the recipient a clear orientation in **time**, as to the precise point in time, periodisation, chronology of events, continuities, and breaks in developments. The same applies to the orientation in **space**. Reflections on time and space as organising principles should also be integrated. The concepts of continuity and change must also be re-thought in this context, since historical phenomena are always processes. The criterion that requires this to be conveyed is the criterion of **historicity** ("*Historizität*") which also comprises questions on the scope of historical actors' enterprises. The structure of human society-/ies is the main focus of attention; here especially, the aspects of **power and governance**, and **social inequality** (Pandel 1987).
- **Form** and **language** of any historical account must be appropriate to the medium in which history is presented. It should be given clearly and in a way that is adequate to its medium, while using a language that is understandable and does not only suit the intended audience, but is precise and appropriate to the topic.

These aspects of history education also apply to textbooks. In the literature on history didactics, numerous and differentiated lists of such criteria can be found, especially for the teaching medium of schoolbooks (i.a. Rüsen 1992; Rohlfes 1989; Scholle 1997; Borries 2006; Thünemann 2010; Gautschi 2011; Sauer 2012, 254–262). Regardless of minor deviations, the central aim of all these criteria is a historical education which does not only involve the acquisition of historical knowledge, but also a critical approach to the past and its – current and past – interpretations in historical culture. The aim is the advancement of a way of historical thinking which necessarily implies the discussion of different interpretations. This short excursion might offer some valuable impulses for the economic sciences and their didactics. However, others should evaluate this.

References

Baumgärtner, U. (2015): *Wegweiser Geschichtsdidaktik. Historisches Lernen in Der Schule.* Paderborn: Schöningh.

Bergmann, K. (2000): *Multiperspektivität. Geschichte Selber Denken.* Schwalbach a. T.: Wochenschau.

Bergmann, K. (1997[5]): 'Geschichte in Der Didaktischen Reflexion', in Bergmann, K., Fröhlich, K. and Kuhn, A. (eds.), *Handbuch Der Geschichtsdidaktik.* Seelze-Velber: Friedrich, 245–254.

Bergmann, K. (2008[3]): *Geschichtsdidaktik. Beiträge Zu Einer Theorie Historischen Lernens.* Schwalbach a. T.: Wochenschau.

Borries, B. (2006): 'Schulbuch-Gestaltung Und Schulbuch-Benutzung Im Fach Geschichte. Zwischen Empirischen Befunden Und Normativen Überlegungen', in Saskia, H. and Schönemann, B. (eds.), *Geschichtsdidaktische Schulbuchforschung.* Berlin: Lit, 39–52.

Borries, B. (2008): "Orte' Des Geschichtslernens – Trivialität Oder Schlüsselproblem?', in Saskia, H. and Schönemann, B. (eds.), *Orte Historischen Lernens.* Berlin: Lit, 11–35.

Füßmann, K. (1994): 'Historische Formungen. Dimensionen Der Geschichtsdarstellung', in Füßmann, K., Grütter, H.T. and Rüsen, J. (eds.), *Historische Faszination. Geschichtskultur Heute.* Köln: Böhlau, 27–44.

Gautschi, P. (2011): 'Anforderungen an Zukünftige Schulgeschichtsbücher', in Barricelli, M., Becker, A. and Heuer, C. (eds.), *Jede Gegenwart Hat Ihre Gründe. Geschichtsbewusstsein, Historische Lebenswelten Und Zukunftserwartung Im Frühen 21. Jahrhundert. Hans-Jürgen Pandel Zum 70. Geburtstag.* Schwalbach a. T.: Wochenschau, 164–176.

Günther-Arndt, H. and Kemnitz, J. (2000): 'Schreiben Um Zu Lehren? – Geschichtsdidaktische Kategorien in Der Historischen Jugendliteratur', in Staatsbibliothek zu Berlin – Preußischer Kulturbesitz (ed.), *Geschichtsbilder. Historische Jugendbücher Aus Vier Jahrhunderten. Ausstellungskatalog.* Berlin: Staatsbibliothek zu Berlin – Preußischer Kulturbesitz, 240–254.

Jeismann, K.-E. (1997[5]): 'Geschichtsbewusstsein – Theorie', in Bergmann, K., Fröhlich, K. and Kuhn, A. (eds.), *Handbuch Der Geschichtsdidaktik.* Seelze-Velber: Friedrich, 42–44.

Jeismann, K.-E. (2000): "Geschichtsbewusstsein' Als Zentrale Kategorie Der Didaktik Des Geschichtsunterrichts', in Jeismann, K.-E. (ed.), *Geschichte Und Bildung. Beiträge*

Zur Geschichtsdidaktik Und Zur Historischen Bildungsforschung. Paderborn: Schöningh, 46–72.

Pandel, H.-J. (1987): 'Dimensionen Des Geschichtsbewusstseins. Ein Versuch, Seine Struktur Für Empirie Und Pragmatik Diskutierbar Zu Machen', *Geschichtsdidaktik* 12 (2), 130–142.

Pandel, H.-J. (2000): *Quelleninterpretation. Die Schriftliche Quelle Im Geschichtsunterricht.* Schwalbach a. T.: Wochenschau.

Pandel, H.-J. (2005): *Geschichtsunterricht Nach PISA. Kompetenzen, Bildungsstandards Und Kerncurricula.* Schwalbach A. T. Wochenschau.

Pandel, H.-J. (2006). 'Didaktische Darstellungsprinzipien. Ein Alter Sachverhalt Im Neuen Licht', in Bernhardt, M., Henke-Bockschatz, G. and Sauer, M. (eds.), *Bilder – Wahrnehmungen – Konstruktionen. Reflexionen Über Geschichte Und Historisches Lernen. Festschrift Für Ulrich Mayer Zum 65. Geburtstag*. Schwalbach a. T.: Wochenschau, 2006, 152–168.

Reeken, D.V. (2010^{5}): 'Das Historische Jugendbuch', in Pandel, H.-J. and Schneider, G. (eds.), *Handbuch Medien Im Geschichtsunterricht.* Schwalbach a. T.: Wochenschau, 69–83.

Reeken, D.V. (2017^{6}): *Historisches Lernen Im Sachunterricht. Eine Einführung Mit Tipps Für Den Unterricht.* Baltmannsweiler: Schneider.

Rohlfcs, J. (1989): 'Formen Und Maßstäbe Der Darstellung Im Schulgeschichtsbuch', *Geschichte in Wissenschaft Und Unterricht* 40(10), 597–617.

Rüsen, J. (1992): 'Das Ideale Schulbuch. Überlegungen Zum Leitmedium Des Geschichtsunterrichts', *Internationale Schulbuchforschung* 2, 237–250.

Rüsen, J. (1994): 'Was Ist Geschichtskultur? Überlegungen Zu Einer Neuen Art, Über Geschichte Nachzudenken', in Füßmann, K., Grütter, H.T. and Rüsen, J. (eds.), *Historische Faszination. Geschichtskultur Heute.* Köln: Böhlau, 3–26.

Rüsen, J. (1997): 'Objektivität', in Bergmann, K., Fröhlich, K. and Kuhn, A. (eds.), *Handbuch Der Geschichtsdidaktik.* Seelze-Velber: Friedrich, 160–163.

Rüsen, J. (2014): 'Die Fünf Dimensionen Der Geschichtskultur', in Nießer, J. and Tomann, J. (eds.), *Angewandte Geschichte. Neue Perspektiven Auf Geschichte in Der Öffentlichkeit.* Paderborn: Schöningh, 46–57.

Rüsen, J. (2008^{2}): *Historisches Lernen. Grundlagen Und Paradigmen.* Schwalbach a. T.: Wochenschau.

Sauer, M. (2012^{10}): *Geschichte Unterrichten. Eine Einführung in Didaktik Und Methodik.* Seelze: Kallmeyer.

Scholle, D. (1997): 'Schulbuchanalyse', in Bergmann, K., Fröhlich, K. and Kuhn, A. (eds.), *Handbuch Der Geschichtsdidaktik.* Seelze-Velber: Friedrich, 369–375.

Schönemann, B. (2000): 'Geschichtsdidaktik Und Geschichtskultur', in Mütter, B., Schönemann, B. and Uffelmann, U. (eds.), *Geschichtskultur. Theorie – Empirie – Pragmatik.* Weinheim: Beltz, 26–58.

Schönemann, B. (2002): 'Geschichtskultur Als Forschungskonzept Der Geschichtsdidaktik', *Zeitschrift Für Geschichtsdidaktik* 1, 78–86.

Schwabe, A. (2012): *Historisches Lernen Im World Wide Web. Suchen, Flanieren Oder Forschen? Fachdidaktisch-Mediale Konzeption, Praktische Umsetzung Und Empirische Evaluation Der Regionalhistorischen Website Vimu.Info.* Göttingen: Vandenhoeck unipress.

Thünemann, H. (2010): 'Zeitgeschichte Im Schulbuch. Normative Überlegungen, Empirische Befunde Und Pragmatische Konsequenzen', in Popp, S., Sauer, M., Alavi, B., Demantowski, M. and Paul, G. (eds.), *Zeitgeschichte – Medien – Historische Bildung.* Göttingen: Vandenhoeck unipress, 117–132.

Part II

International perspectives on pluralist teaching

6 Issues in teaching of economics and pluralism in Brazil

Rafael Galvão de Almeida and Ian Coelho de Souza Almeida

1. Introduction

The 2007–2008 crisis gave new impetus to a number of international student movements which advocated for change in the teaching of economics. Monistic approaches to economics (see Beckenbach, this volume) reproduce through international standards of teaching, as Kapeller (this volume) writes,

> [the] dominance of a single approach to economic issues is especially relevant in the context of teaching economics, as it allows for the introduction of a set of highly standardised economic textbooks, which, so to say, codify the established knowledge using different degrees of analytical and mathematical complexity.

In other words, an economics textbook can be used in either the United States or Brazil or any other country and it is expected to yield the same results. However, while this allows easy exchanges between different people from different cultures, it also ends up creating a monistic pattern that rules out different approaches (Beckenbach, this volume). On the other hand, it may also create the opportunity for alternative approaches to converge and to become alternatives to the mainstream.

This chapter studies the teaching of economics in Brazil in the light of these dynamics. We conjecture that Brazilian teaching is relatively pluralist, and ask what other countries can learn from Brazil's experience. In the second part of this chapter, we present the history of economic teaching in Brazil and how it evolved in a context of greater relative theoretical pluralism. To argue that economic research in Brazil is relatively pluralist, some aspects of the present structure of Brazilian teaching and research are discussed, including its journal ranking system. The third part studies the perception of economics professors regarding the quality and focus of undergraduate economics studies. We conclude that the Brazilian case shows that pluralism in economic teaching is possible.

2. Economic research and teaching in Brazil: a historical perspective

2.1 Plurality in academic research

One characteristic of Brazilian economics is the presence of many different schools of economic thought, some of them developed in Brazilian traditions (Mantega 1997). This trait is the foundation of our argument about a pluralist environment in Brazilian economics, or, at least, in relative terms when compared to other countries. Fernández and Suprinyak (2016, 2) observe that scholars of heterodox traditions "occupy tenured positions in several of the most prestigious universities in the country, and in a host of smaller academic centres as well, co-existing more or less peacefully with orthodox groups often within the same institutions." Dequech (2014) highlights that non-mainstream economists are able to receive grants and to win national awards, such as the Haralambos Simeonides prize, the most prestigious economics award in the country.[1]

One must concede that this relatively high degree of academic plurality does not necessarily reach the highest levels of economic policy-making. Codato et al. (2016), for example, show that although there was a significant amount of Brazilian Central Bank directors with graduate training from heterodox departments, the vast majority had a mainstream background, and their policy-making and advice was made in accordance with their training. This pluralism of policy-making is different from the one advocated by Dow (this volume), which is related to methodological pluralism of the person responsible for the decisions (e.g. the president of the Central Bank), not necessarily the pluralism in the foundations of the institution. On the other hand, the presence of heterodox economists in such important positions demonstrates the weight of plurality in the economic discourse outside Brazilian academia.

The development of distinct schools of thought is related to the industrialisation of the country, beginning in the Vargas Age (1930–1945).[2] Prior to industrialisation, Brazilian economic thought had a liberal bias, according to Bielschowsky (2001[1989], 37). Sstate-sponsored industrialisation challenged the liberal orthodoxy pre-1930. At the end of the Vargas Age, two approaches disputed the domain of Brazilian economic policy: 1930s neoliberalism,[3] represented by Eugênio Gudin,[4] which defended the insertion of Brazil as a primary products exporter in the international order, following the Ricardian comparative advantage doctrine; and the first developmentalist school, represented by Roberto Simonsen,[5] which defended the continuing industrialisation of the country (Simonsen and Gudin 2013[1977]).[6] Both approaches would shape the policy debates in the following years (and, arguably, today).

2.2 Plurality in economic teaching

The abundance of different approaches is reflected in the different approaches of Brazilian graduate schools. Loureiro and Lima (1994) document the wide range of positions between the graduate centres in Brazil: on one side, the Graduate School of Economics of the Getulio Vargas Foundation (EPGE/FGV) and the Catholic Pontifical University of Rio de Janeiro (PUC-Rio) were the centres of neoclassical orthodoxy, with over 80% of their professors (in 1991–1992) with a PhD from an American university; on the other side, the Economics Institute of the State University of Campinas (IE-Unicamp) and the Federal University of Rio de Janeiro (UFRJ) followed the developmentalist doctrine of the Economic Commission for Latin America and the Caribbean (ECLAC)[7] and had fewer professors with a PhD obtained abroad (the IE-Unicamp had only 8% of their professors with a PhD abroad when Loureiro and Lima conducted their research). In between, there are the eclectic departments, "in the sense that they host both professors that are sympathizers of international mainstream economics and (even if not in the same proportion) others who defend alternative approaches" (Dequech 2014). As examples, we have the Economic Research Institute of the São Paulo University (IPE-USP) and the Centre of Regional Development and Planning of the Federal University of Minas Gerais (CEDEPLAR-UFMG) (Loureiro and Lima 1994, 40). Dequech (2014) concludes that

> the teaching of economics in the set of the most prestigious departments in Brazil is marked by more variety than exists in developed countries, such as the United States, particularly regarding the space that is allowed for alternative approaches to international mainstream economics.
>
> Dequech (2014, 5)

Thus, each school found its own niche and created an environment in which heterodox schools have a relatively greater degree of acceptance than in other countries (Dequech 2014; Fernández and Suprinyak 2014, 2016). Still, there are conflicts between heterodox and mainstream schools. For example, when the IE-Unicamp requested to become a member of the National Association of Graduate Schools in Economics (ANPEC), the EPGE opposed its entrance because it did not consider the research developed in the IE-Unicamp "scientific", due to the centre's heterodox inclination. The request was denied and the EPGE exited ANPEC in protest for a few years (Seminário da USP 1997, 235–236). Fernández and Suprinyak (2016) argue that the return of the EPGE to ANPEC helped to cement the association's role as a mediator of pluralism in Brazil.[8]

One of the sources of this relatively greater plurality today is that economics curricula as well as teaching methods have historically been pluralist. The first official economics college was established in 1945, at the same time as the National College of Economics (and as part of the University of Brazil, future Federal University of Rio de Janeiro). Their curriculum, which featured important contributions by Otávio Gouvêia de Bulhões[9] and Eugênio Gudin, two of the most outstanding Brazilian economists of the time, was the first attempt to create an internationalised curriculum, i.e. one that followed the

American and European curricula. This included an emphasis on economic rationality and scientific rigor and the rejection of "hybrid" curricula (that had too many law and business classes) in favour of mathematics and statistics classes. The model took years to be implemented, though (Loureiro and Lima 1994; Loureiro 1997b).

The formation of economists, especially after the 1930s, was linked to federal administration bodies, and the training focused on preparing them to occupy public positions. According to Seminário da USP (1997), the focus on public careers meant a neglect of private ones. The Superintendence of Credit and Money (SUMOC) and the Department of Public Service Administration (DASP) absorbed the supply of economists (Loureiro 1992). The only way to acquire better training in economics was the ECLAC courses on economic planning (Bielschowsky 2001[1989], 7). Thus, the problems with the teaching of economics continued even after the creation of undergraduate courses in 1945. The first undergraduate classes had low quality: most of the teachers had no formal training in economics because they emigrated from other disciplines, such as Law and Accounting. The low quality created a great level of evasion and led to low demand of economics courses in the following years (Loureiro and Lima 1994).[10]

Those problems persisted for years until the powers that be decided to take action. Since this was not an exclusive problem of economics, in the following years changes we made in the educational system as a whole. Concerned with the improvement of the teaching of economics, the Ford Foundation sponsored the Itaipava Congress in 1966, the first large congress on the situation of teaching of economics in Brazil (Widdicombe 1966), in the city of Itaipava, Rio de Janeiro. The discussions there raised a bleak diagnosis of economic teaching in Brazil.

As for the main suggestions to improve the situation, there was a call to establish a "basic curriculum." In cooperation with foreign teachers, the participants of the congress deliberated the creation of tutorship programmes, a national association of economists, facilitating access to national and international economic research (Delfim Netto 1966), closing low quality schools or transforming them into business schools, replacing the teaching staff, establishing graduate schools[11] (Simonsen 1966), eliminating excessive Law and Accounting classes, expanding *lato sensu* training programmes (Ferreira 1966), reforming hiring methods in the public sector, creating study groups in order to prepare sectorial projects (Velloso 1966), establishing centres of research and research projects, and improving the statistical data system (Kerstenetzky and Chacel 1966). The internationalisation of economic teaching would happen through recommendation to hire foreign faculty in order to tutor future Brazilian teachers.

The changes in the national system of education were also important to the improvement of economic teaching in Brazil. The university reform of 1968 gave momentum to the deliberations of the Itaipava Congress. It started deep modifications in the national pedagogical base and established that universities and colleges should train professionals in order to remedy the lack of human resources.

This was an issue that had been debated before the 1960s (e.g. Cunha 2007). The implemented reform had a strong technical character and was supported and influenced by the United States Agency for Development (USAID)[12] through agreements with the Ministry of Education.

The main proposals were the organisation of teaching institutions in departments, selection of candidates through a unified selection exam (the "vestibular"), the implementation of a common base cycle to many areas, the creation of a credit hour system and the substitution of chairs by disciplines (Rothen 2008). The teaching of economics became more focused on teaching a profession. The reform itself did not impose changes in the standard curricula, which were the responsibility of the Federal Council of Education (CFE). However, it made possible greater changes in the curricula of each university. Almeida (2015) shows how the universities' curricula based on the 1963 model formulated by the CFE have little difference between each other. That changed radically from 1970 onwards with the increasing differentiation between the teachings of the departments of economics.

Regarding graduate studies, the EPGE/FGV was the first economics doctoral programme implemented in Brazil in 1966, led by Mario Henrique Simonsen (Rego 1997). According to Rego, the EPGE method was intimately linked to the US-American methodology, which meant intense use of mathematical content in the disciplines. US-American influence became explicit through the fact that both the EPGE and the IPE received foreign investment and emulated the American model of university management. The National Association of Graduate Schools in Economics (ANPEC), which was established in 1973, also benefited from sponsorship of American institutions, such as the Ford Foundation and USAID (Fernández and Suprinyak 2014).[13]

The modernisation had its critics. Many of the left-inclined professors denounced an "americanisation" of the teaching of economics. "Internationalisation" would be another term for US-American cultural imperialism, which moulded the teaching of economics to US-American demands, not Brazilian ones (Loureiro and Lima 1994).[14] On the other hand, even without changes to the standard curriculum (that would happen only in 1983[15]), the university reform of 1968 brought increased flexibility, allowing each institution to manage their courses based on their own interests. With time, the divergences between the curricula of each institution became apparent for many reasons, among them the political climate. According to Almeida (2015), even in a period of strong social control and repression, none of the professors interviewed for his research claimed to have suffered direct and intentional censorship of the content lectured in the classrooms (not even the Marxist-related content, given the anticommunism of the military government).[16]

2.3 The role of HET and journal rankings

Many authors, including contributors to this volume, have stressed the link between teaching of history of economic thought (HET) and pluralism

(Beckenbach, this volume; Dow 2009; Dow, this volume; Fernández 2011). When an economic education includes training in HET, the argument goes, this facilitates pluralist thinking because students will become acquainted with different approaches to economic research. In the following paragraphs, we show that HET has been an important element of economics curricula in Brazil and argue that this has contributed to the relatively high degree of pluralism in Brazilian economics.

HET has been present in the standard Brazilian curriculum ever since its first inception in 1945, and as a mandatory discipline. None of the later curriculum reforms abandoned this characteristic. Simonsen's model for graduate curricula also included HET as an optional discipline (Simonsen 1966). Similarly, methodology has been an element of some universities' undergraduate curriculum for a long time, and became part of the standard curriculum in 1984, although not as a mandatory discipline (Conselho Nacional de Educação 2004). This is important to notice, because HET is not a required discipline in many countries, such as the United States and Great Britain (O'Brien 2007).

The importance of HET is also related to the journal classification system elaborated by the Coordination for the Improvement of Higher Education Personnel (CAPES). As can be seen in the classification guidelines (CAPES 2016), the classification index follows the system proposed by Combes and Linnemer (2010). CAPES created their index combining Thomas Reuters' Journal Citation Reports (JCR) and other sophisticated indexes. All the ranked journals are allocated among the three upper strata of the classification (A1, A2 and B1).[17]

It should be explained how the CAPES classification is built: for all areas of scientific production, including economics, the CAPES appoints one coordinator, normally an experienced high-level university professor, and she or he chooses six members (also professors). They are responsible for ranking all the journals in which Brazilian professors have published in the last four years. They also have complete autonomy to change the methodology of classification and almost every other rule regarding this process (although they rarely make drastic changes). Additionally, heterodox economists are usually invited to be part of this committee and sometimes even to lead it. Thus, they are able to keep some heterodox journals at a high rank even if they should not be highly ranked according to other methodologies Therefore, the presence of heterogeneity in the CAPES rankings cannot be said to be imposed upon Brazilian professors; rather it is a result of the recognition of the importance of heterogeneity and pluralism in the Brazilian academy.

According to CAPES (2016), this system intends to preserve diversity in economic research. In this manner, important heterodox journals can be classified as top journals, even if their JCR ranking score is not high. For example, all the A1 journals publications have the same weight. In this stratum we have journals like *The American Economic Review* and the *Journal of Political Economy* (traditionally among the most cited journals) along with the *Journal of Post Keynesian Economics*, the *Cambridge Journal of Economics* and *History of Political Economy*. Nevertheless, the vast majority of journals classified as A1 can be considered mainstream. There are other specificities, such as a limit of strata (A2 for foreign and B2 for Brazilian) for journals of areas other than economics. For example, *Science*, the *American Journal of Sociology*, *Nature*, and others cannot be classified as A1 journals in economics.[18]

3. Current issues and challenges in Brazilian teaching: an empirical approach

While the state of economics teaching is a topic of concern in the international literature (for example, Colander and McGoldrick 2009; Coyle 2012; and in this volume), ever since the Itaipava Congress, there has been little attention to topics of teaching economics (with an important exception of Loureiro 1997a).

In an attempt to contribute to understanding the situation, we present an empirical questionnaire-based study.[19] The main topics concerning this research effort were teaching capacitation and its incentives, impressions on the state of economics and its teaching and the role of academics as professors or researchers.

The questionnaire contained 16 questions, ranging from questions about their age, gender, title, current university, teaching experience, incentives to teaching, use of teaching materials, impression teaching and the teaching environment. The later questions (minus the last one) used a Likert scale, ranging from strongly disagree to moderately disagree, neutral, moderately agree and strongly agree. The graphics of their answers are compiled in Figure 6.5. We had 162 replies. The general characteristics of our sample are as follows:

- 71% were men, while 29% were women;
- 52% are less than 41 years old;
- 64% have a doctoral degree (most public universities in Brazil have tighter requirements for hiring such as necessity of a doctoral degree);
- 62% spent the majority or their lecturing time in public faculties;
- on average, they spent 14.7 years lecturing, which may indicate stability in the career.

As for actual experience, it is slightly concentrated in the extremities (high and low experience). About 24.7% have 0 to 5 years of experience, 20.4% have 6 to 10 years of experience, 12.9% have 11 to 15 years, 15.8% have 16 to 20 years and 27% have more than 20 years of experience.

One of the challenged issues related to teaching capacitation. The underlying idea is that if the teacher has a PhD, he or she is automatically prepared to teach (Colander 2004). The result is that PhD students do not consider themselves prepared to teach, to the point where even a superficial training can be helpful for them to feel at ease (McCoy and Milkman 2010). In our results, most of the interviewees had no teaching incentive by their graduate programmes. Nevertheless, as shown in Figure 6.1, this is not a major impact factor on whether the professor actually engaged in those activities or not.

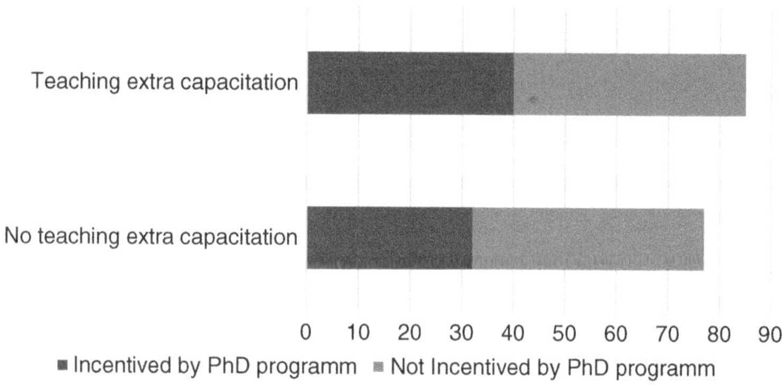

Figure 6.1 Teaching capacitation other than experience

Concerning the curriculum, a well-documented fact of the literature is that the majority of the students do not aim at graduate school and yet the economics curriculum is built as if this was so (e.g., Heyne 1995; Colander 2004; Coyle 2012). In other words, the students learn skills that will help them in graduate school instead of within the organisations for which they are going to work. Thus, we proposed the following questions: "On average, the current curriculum of economics focuses on preparing the student for graduate school instead of the market" and "The current curriculum of *my* college focuses more in preparing the student for graduate school instead of the market." There was a slight agreement with this statement, 26% were neutral, while 25% agreed moderately. In Figures 6.2 and 6.3, we depict these results with a secondary differentiation: whether the respondents spent most of their period as a teacher in a public or private institution. This aspect is important due the current understanding that private and public institutions have different teaching objectives.

The most sensitive information this aspect adds to our study is how private school professors tend to see their institutions' courses as very little inclined towards a graduate focus (about 40% of them marked "1" in the questionnaire). Although 31.5% of the respondents who spent all their career in public institutions "moderately disagree" with the statement, 29.6% of them "moderately agree", keeping us from making any further inference.

Moreover, some researchers argue that there is a trade-off between research and teaching. "If academics have to spend more time teaching, they will spend less time on researching. This lowering of research output hurts the department's reputation and, therefore, its budget." (McMahon 2012). Thus, we posed the following statement: "There is a trade-off between teaching and research". We observed a strong discordance. Over half of them disagreed, either moderately or strongly. This indicates Brazilian economic teachers tend to see the complementarity between research and teaching as important. Again separating the respondents by teaching facilities

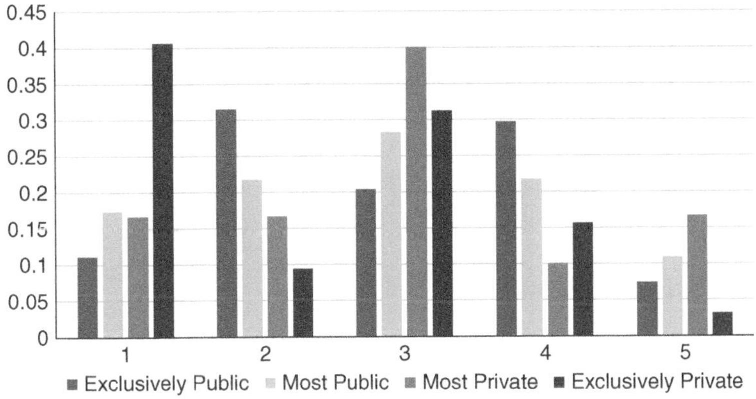

Figure 6.2 Graduate focus perception of own school decomposed by teaching facilities

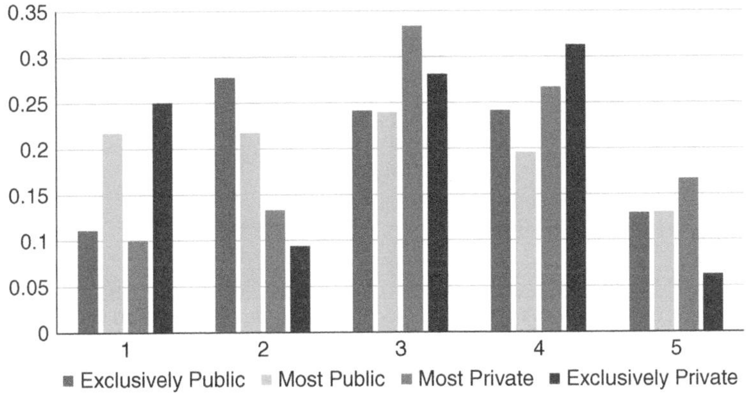

Figure 6.3 Graduate focus perception in general decomposed by teaching facilities

(if either public or private), there was no significant difference; at least 40% of all the four possibilities strongly disagreeing or moderately disagreeing, as can be seen in Figure 6.4.

The research also pointed out that most economics teachers prefer that, in a curriculum reform, both the catalogue of disciplines and their syllabus should be given attention. On the scale, 1 signified it should focus more on the catalogue, 3 should focus equally on them, while 5 meant it should focus on the syllabus. As mentioned above, the compilation of all Likert scale questions can be seen in Figure 6.5.

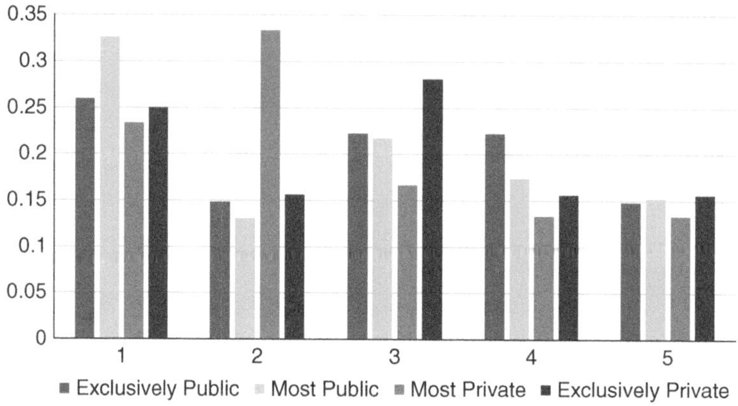

Figure 6.4 Trade off questions results decomposed by teaching facilities

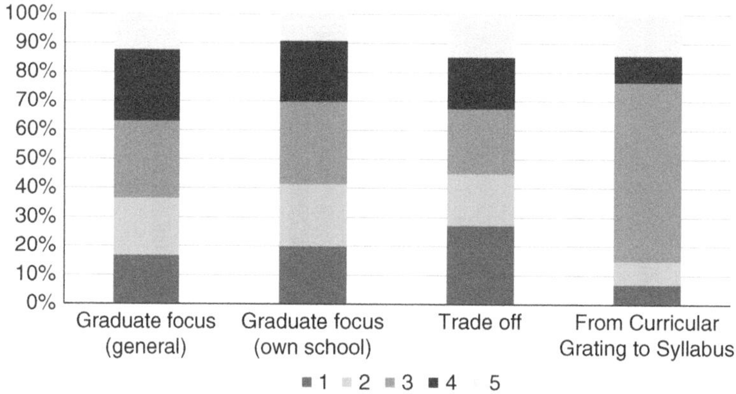

Figure 6.5 Likert scale questions resume

Lastly, we asked the professors to add optional comments regarding teaching economics or any personal experience. It was an open question, allowing for broad answers. Some patterns emerged: a good part of them thought that the courses should be more concerned with applications (some meaning more pro-market teaching, others more mathematical methods or even a Brazilian context to the disciplines). On syllabus reform, pluralism was the most remembered demand, and the intention to open it to the presence of specific subjects (as finance, environmental economics, history, math or behavioural economics) was present. Some also demanded a convergence towards the American curriculum, or even a clearer differentiation among departments, with clear specialisation in each field of economics, in the sense Werlang proposed in Seminário da USP (1997).

However, one of the main problems pointed out by them is the low quality of the high school students that enter college. In the 2012 PISA results, Brazilian students performed below OECD average in mathematics, reading and science (OECD 2012), key disciplines for economics. The survey shows that economics teachers are aware of this underperforming effect. They have to spend more time teaching and re-teaching basic knowledge the students should have mastered in high school and, because of this, little time remains to teach more advanced topics, i.e. the "second high school effect".

4. Conclusion

We argued that the 2007–2008 crisis created opportunities for reevaluation of the teaching of economics. In the end, "all undergraduate economics programs reflect the graduate economics programs that train the undergraduate teachers. People teach what they learn" (Colander and McGoldrick 2009, 31), and if what we teach had an effect in the crisis, even if a small one, then the crisis should be an opportunity for reevaluation and search for alternatives, which is the aim of this volume.

As for Brazil, in general, we are inclined to recognise a tendency towards pluralism in the Brazilian teaching, due to factors such as the tradition of many national schools of thought and the presence of HET, ever since the first undergraduate standard curriculum and the Itaipava model for the graduate curriculum. Both these characteristics dialogue with Beckenbach's (this volume) self-reflectivity argument. In other words, it creates opportunities to question the focus and generalisations of the economic theory developed in the country. While the presence of different national schools of thought represents competitive pluralism, teaching HET fosters complementary pluralism, or at least an attempt. The CAPES classification, by giving a higher level of prestige to heterodox journals, is not only a sign of pluralism, but also an incentive.

Brazil, due to the peculiarity of its economic evolution, is endowed with a *relatively* greater degree of pluralism in the academy. The presence of different approaches allows for more opportunities of creative cross-fertilisation between ideas. However, little is discussed about the state of teaching economics. The concerns of 1966's Itaipava Congress still echo in classrooms. Issues such as lack of updated curricula and teaching technology, low quality of high school graduates, and lack of relevant applications are obstacles that hinder the development of economic teaching in Brazil. The results of our survey point towards some expectations of Brazilian professors regarding a possible change in teaching. Perhaps one of the most important challenges is to improve the educational system while preserving and expanding pluralism in classrooms. Possible reformulation is divided regarding the perception of what should be reformulated, as well as what should be the focus of teaching in economics, although pluralism can be said to be a constant preoccupation of those interviewed. More research in this topic and discussions on strategies to combine the defence of pluralism with improvement of economic learning is warranted.

Acknowledgements

We would like to thank two anonymous referees and our editor, Svenja Flechtner, for their suggestions.

Notes

1 A list of the winners can be seen at http://www.anpec.org.br/downloads/Haralambos.pdf.
2 Getulio Vargas was the President of Brazil on two occasions: 1930–1945 (the "Vargas Age"), which was a dictatorship between 1937 and 1945; and 1951–1954, which ended with his suicide in August 24.
3 It should be noted that the term "neoliberalism" in this context has nothing to do with the modern context of the word. "The neoliberal economists were concerned, primordially, in defending the market system, basic formula of economic efficiency. Therefore, they were mainly liberals. The prefix "neo" has a very precise meaning: it represents the fact that Brazilian liberals, in their majority, started to admit, in the new reality after 1930, the necessity of some state intervention to cure market imperfections, that, according to what they recognised it, affected underdeveloped economies such as the Brazilian." (Bielschowsky 2001 [1989], 37, our translation).
4 Eugênio Gudin (1886–1986) was an engineer turned economist. He was the Minister of Finance during 1954–1955 and the Brazilian representative in Bretton Woods. He was also a director of the EPGE.
5 Roberto Cochrane Simonsen (1889–1948) was also an engineer turned economist. He also managed many companies and had close ties with the Brazilian industrial elite.
6 See Loureiro (2009) for a summary of the debate.
7 Founded in 25 February 1948, The "ECLAC [Economic Commission for Latin America and the Caribbean], which is headquartered in Santiago, Chile, is one of the five regional commissions of the United Nations. It was founded with the purpose of contributing to the economic development of Latin America, coordinating actions directed towards this end, and reinforcing economic ties among countries and with other nations of the world. The promotion of the region's social development was later included among its primary objectives." Source: http://www.cepal.org/en/about.
8 They also stress that this was not ANPEC's original role, but it assumed it accidentally in order to safeguard "the conditions necessary for the open, free-spirited discussion of economics issues" (Fernández and Suprinyak 2016, 14).
9 Otávio Gouveia de Bulhões (1906–1990) was the Brazilian Finance Minister twice: in 1954 (in the interval during Gudin's term) and from 1964 to 1967 (during the Humberto A. Castelo Branco's military presidency).
10 As an example, the Economics Department of the University of São Paulo went through several educational crises in the 1950s. (Canabrava 1984).
11 The curriculum proposed by Simonsen (1966) is still the model for modern graduate programmes.
12 The USAID was created in order to support modernisation in underdevelopment countries, mainly after the Cuban Revolution and the fear of the spread of Communism (Motta 2010).

13 According to Fernández and Suprinyak (2014), the role of the Ford Foundation was beyond the mere organisation of the ANPEC. It established norms for the creation of graduate programmes and facilitated the interchange between Brazilian and foreign institutions, greatly improving the situation of the teaching of economics in Brazil.

14 It should be noted that concerns with ideology started during the establishment of ANPEC. "The thorny moral dilemmas brought by its involvement with applied social science research in the context of an increasingly unsavory military regime seem to have made the Ford Foundation particularly sensitive to the political and ideological implications of its activities in Brazil." (Fernández and Suprinyak 2016, 12).

15 This reform led to the foundation of the National Association for Undergraduate Courses in Economics (ANGE) in the following year and, while not as relevant as the ANPEC, the ANGE helps new undergraduate courses to build their curricula. They encourage pluralism as well. See http://www.ange.org.br/.

16 However, some interviewees did take measures of self-censorship, by not approaching certain issues or not writing about certain themes, fearing reprisals (Almeida 2015).

17 All the strata are: A1, A2, B1, B2, B3, B4, B5 and C. Each one has a corresponding rating that is used as a criterion for funding and classification exams for admission of teachers in graduate programmes (since the programmes depend on the rating of their teachers in order to be well located in the national graduate programme ranking built by CAPES). And the higher the number of articles published in higher strata journals by professors of a centre, the higher will be the grade of the centre and the higher will be the volume of resources the centre will receive.

18 This classification, although created to be used only for ranking academic journals, is being increasingly used as a criterion to hire professors and to select grantees, according to their production in high-ranking journals.

19 See Almeida (2014) for further details.

References

Almeida, I.C.S. (2015): *Disseminação Do Pensamento Marxista Durante a Ditadura Civil-Militar: Uma Abordagem De História Oral*. Master's Dissertation (Economics). Curitiba: Applied Sciences Department, Federal University of Paraná.

Almeida, R.G. (2014): *Desafios Ao Ensino De Economia: Didática, Capacitação E Currículo*. Curso de Especialização em Docência do Ensino Superior. Mogi das Cruzes: Braz Cubas University.

Bielschowsky, R. (2001[1989]): *Pensamento Econômico Brasileiro: O Ciclo Ideológico Do Desenvolvimentismo, 1930-1964*. Rio de Janeiro: Contraponto.

Canabrava, A.P. (ed.) (1984): *História Da Faculdade De Economia E Administração Da Universidade De São Paulo: 1946-1981*. São Paulo: FEA/USP.

CAPES. (2016): 'Critérios De Classificação Qualis – Economia'. *Ministério da Educação*, available at www.capes.gov.br/images/stories/download/avaliacaotrienal/Docs_de_area/qualis/economia.pdf, accessed on 8 June 2016.

Codato, A., Cavalieri, M., Perissinotto, R. and Dantas, E. (2016): 'Economic Mainstream and Power: A Profile Analysis of Central Bank Directors during PSDB and PT Governments in Brazil', *Nova Economia* 26(3), 687–720.

Colander, D. (2004): 'The Art of Teaching Economics', *International Review of Economics Education* 3(1), 63–76.

Colander, D. and McGoldrick, K. (eds.) (2009): *Educating Economists: The Teagle Discussion on Re-Evaluating the Undergraduate Economics Major*. Northampton: Edward Elgar.

Combes, P. and Linnemer, L. (2010): *Inferring Missing Citations: A Quantitative Multi-Criteria Ranking of All Journals in Economics.* GREQAM, Universités d'Aix-Marseille II et III, Document de Travail 2010-2810, available at https://halshs.archives-ouvertes.fr/halshs-00520325 accessed on 8 June 2016.

Conselho Nacional de Educação. (2004): *Parecer Nº 0054.* 'Diretrizes Curriculares Nacionais Para O Curso De Graduação Em Ciências Econômicas', February 18th, 2004, available at http://abmes.org.br/arquivos/legislacoes/Par_CES_54_180204.pdf, accessed on 8 June 2016.

Coyle, D. (ed.). (2012): *What's the Use of Economics: Teaching the Dismal Science after the Crisis*. Kindle edition. London: London Publishing Partnership.

Cunha, J.D. (2007): 'A Política Educacional Da Ditadura Militar E A UFRGS (1964-1970)', in *Anais Da V Mostra De Pesquisa Do Arquivo Público. Do Estado Do Rio Grande Do Sul*, Vol. 1. Porto Alegre: CORAG, 327–338.

Delfim Netto, A. (1966): 'As Oportunidades, Os Problemas e a Estratégia Para Melhorar No Brasil O Treinamento Universitário Em Economia', *Revista Brasileira De Economia* 20(4), 9–18.

Dequech, D. (2014): 'Aplicando O Conceito De Mainstream Economics Fora Dos Estados Unidos E Europa: O Caso Do Brasil Como Um Exemplo De Pluralismo', paper presented at 4th European Society for the History of Economic Thought Latin America Conference (ESHET Latin America). Belo Horizonte.

Dow, S. (2009): 'History of Thought and Methodology in Pluralist Economics Education', *International Review of Economics Education* 8(2), 41–57.

Fernández, R.G. (2011): 'A Metodologia Como Argumento A Favor De Uma Economia Pluralista', in Guilhoto, J., Duarte, P.G. and Silber, S. (eds.), *O Brasil E a Ciência Econômica Em Debate – O Estado Da Arte Em Economia*, Vol. 2. São Paulo: Editora Saraiva, 137–152.

Fernández, R.G. and Suprinyak, C.E. (2014): 'Creating Academic Economics in Brazil: The Ford Foundation and the Beginnings of ANPEC', *Anais Do XLII Encontro Nacional De Economia*, XLII Encontro Nacional De Economia Natal. Niterói: ANPEC.

Fernández, R.G. and Suprinyak, C.E. (2016): 'Manufacturing Pluralism in Brazilian Economics: The Role of ANPEC as Institutional Mediator and Stabilizer', in *Anais Do XLIV Encontro Nacional De Economia*. XLIV Encontro Nacional de Economia, Foz do Iguaçu. Niterói: ANPEC.

Ferreira, M.O. (1966): 'A Formação Do Economista No Brasil', *Revista Brasileira De Economia* 20(4), 29–38.

Heyne, P. (1995): 'Teaching Introductory Economics', *Agenda* 2(2), 149–158.

Kerstenetzky, I. and Chacel, J.M. (1966): 'Reflexões Em Tôrno Dos Problemas Da Investigação Econômica No Brasil', *Revista Brasileira De Economia* 20(4), 47–60.

Loureiro, M.R. (1992): 'Economistas E Elites Dirigentes No Brasil', *Revista Brasileira De Ciências Sociais* 8(20), 47–69.

Loureiro, M.R. (ed.). (1997a): *50 Anos De Ciência Econômica No Brasil: Pensamento, Instituições, Depoimentos*. Petrópolis: Editora Vozes.

Loureiro, M.R. (1997b): 'Introdução', in Loureiro, M.R. (ed.), *50 Anos De Ciência Econômica No Brasil: Pensamento, Instituições, Depoimentos*. Petrópolis: Editora Vozes, 7–14.

Loureiro, M.R. (2009): 'Economists in the Brazilian Government: From Developmentalist State to Neoliberal Policies', in Montecinos, V. and Markoff, J. (eds.), *Economists in the Americas*. Northampton: Edward Elgar, 100–141.

Loureiro, M.R. and Lima, G.T. (1994): 'A Internacionalização Do Ensino De Economia No Brasil', *Revista De Economia Política* 14(3), 31–50.

Mantega, G. (1997): 'O Pensamento Econômico Brasileiro De 60 a 80: Os Anos Rebeldes', in Loureiro, M.R. (ed.), *50 Anos De Ciência Econômica No Brasil: Pensamento, Instituições, Depoimentos*. Petrópolis: Editora Vozes, 109–157.

McCoy, J.P. and Milkman, M.I. (2010): 'Do Recent PhDs Economists Feel Prepared to Teach Economics?', *Journal of Economic Education* 41(2), 211–215.

McMahon, M. (2012): 'Teaching and Research in a UK University, 2012', in Coyle, D. (ed.), *What's the Use of Economics: Teaching the Dismal Science after the Crisis*, Kindle editionpositions. London: London Publishing Partnership, 3122–3282.

Motta, R.P.S. (2010): 'Modernizando a Repressão: A USAID E a Polícia Brasileira', *Revista Brasileira De História* 30, 237–266.

O'Brien, D.P. (2007): *History of Economic Thought as an Intellectual Discipline*. Cheltenham: Edward Elgar.

OECD (2012): *Programme for International Student Assessment (PISA) Results from PISA 2012. Country Note: Brazil*, available at www.oecd.org/education/PISA-2012-results-brazil.pdf, accessed on 12 November 2015.

Rego, J.M. (1997): *Autonomia Dos Centros De Pós-Graduação Em Economia: Uma Abordagem Institucional E De História Oral*. São Paulo: FGV.

Rothen, J.C. (2008): 'Os Bastidores Da Reforma Universitária De 1968', *Educação & Sociedade* 29(103), 453–475.

Seminário da USP. (1997): 'Cinquenta Anos de Ciência Econômica No Brasil', in Loureiro, M.R. (ed.), *50 Anos de Ciência Econômica No Brasil: Pensamento, Instituições, Depoimentos*. Petrópolis: Editora Vozes, 229–313.

Simonsen, M.H. (1966): 'O Ensino De Economia Em Nível De Pós-Graduação No Brasil', *Revista Brasileira De Economia* 20(4), 20–30.

Simonsen, R.C. and Gudin, E.A. (2013[1977]): *Controvérsia Do Planejamento Na Economia Brasileira*. Brasília: IPEA.

Velloso, J.P.R. (1966): 'Treinamento Informal Em Economia E Eficiência Do Setor Govêrno', *Revista Brasileira De Economia* 20(4), 39–46.

Widdicombe S.H. Jr. (1966): 'Introdução Sôbre O Seminário De Itaipava', *Revista Brasileira De Economia* 20(4), 7–8.

7 Economics education in India

From pluralism to neo-liberalism and to '*Hindutva*'

Sudipta Bhattacharyya

1. Introduction

This chapter will analyse how far the rise of neo-classical hegemony in the Western world, especially in US- and UK-centred educational institutions, has also cast its shadow in India and Indian economics education, given a very rich tradition of alternative thinking. Not everyone in India accepted these developments. This chapter will also document the intellectual resistance by some progressive scholars. This chapter supports the view that neo-classicalism is closely associated with neo-liberalism (Dowd 2004, 81–83; Harvey 2009, 1–3). Neo-liberalism emerged as a potent political and economic ideology of capitalism during the early 1980s, along with the concomitant demise of the welfare state. The IMF and World Bank actively imposed neo-liberalism in the less developed countries since 1980 in the form of conditional lending termed 'structural adjustment programmes' (SAPs). India adopted SAPs as the condition of IMF loans in 1991.[1] Additionally, with the collapse of the USSR in 1991, the world suddenly became unipolar. 'There is no alternative' (TINA) became the hypnotic phrase capturing the thought process of many scholars (Kothari 1993). For economists in the West it was convenient to embrace neo-classicalism since it was the favourite framework of neo-liberalism. In India, there was no pressure from the University Grants Commission (UGC) or the Human Resource Development (HRD) ministry to alter the curriculum; but there was a silent transformation of the syllabus and textbooks in some leading economics departments – neoliberal hegemony imported from the US and the UK. However, this tendency has also been resisted in some other university departments, and pluralism still dominates many academic institutions in India, which will be explored in Section 4 of this chapter.

In the following (second) section of this chapter, we analyse the structure of economics education in India from secondary to post-graduate level. Next, in Section 3, we discuss the great pluralistic tradition of teaching economics and social sciences, which was extremely compatible with Indian democracy. Section 4 explains how various institutions related to teaching and research of economics have been reshaped during the post-reform conflicts between neo-classicalism and pluralism. Next, we discuss the UGC guidelines about recruitment and promotion of college and university teachers in India, where there are great possibilities to expand pluralistic ideas in opposition to neo-liberalism. The last section is an introduction to the reader about the present Indian regime based on the major organised religion, namely *Hindutva*. The universities and liberal educational institutions are its prime target of attack through the politics of privatisation and saffronisation.[2]

2. Structure of economics education in India

In India there are three types of school boards. The first type, vernacular medium schools, represents the majority of the schools and is state government funded. There are two other types, which are constituted by the Indian Certificate of Secondary Education (ICSE) and the Central Board of Secondary Education (CBSE) and regulated under by the central government. In India, economics education is neglected in high school. In CBSE, at the IX and X classes, economics is taught as a part of 'social study' together with political science, history, geography and disaster management.[3] Here, economics is taught from an interdisciplinary perspective that is not at all neo-classical. For example, preliminary ideas of globalisation, development, poverty, and food security with special reference to India are covered. However, the CBSE board is basically an English or Hindi medium and is confined within the upper strata of the society and within the organised sector, particularly for the wards of India's Central Government employees. The non-Hindi speaking population in India (around 59% of total population) is not able to study in their mother tongue. The students in the unorganised sector (around 86% of the total population) have narrow access to CBSE-affiliated schools.

The vast majority of school students in India are enrolled in state government affiliated vernacular medium schools with extremely poor infrastructure. Economics is not taught as a compulsory subject in most of these boards.

At the intermediate level, economics is offered as a compulsory elective subject. English and a vernacular language become compulsory for students, but economics is an elective subject among many other electives. However, going through the CBSE and ICSE syllabus,[4] it is very clear that even after two decades of market reforms in India, the intermediate syllabus in India does not have an unnecessary neo-classical bias.

At the university level, economics is offered as an honours as well as a subsidiary subject in graduation (BA/BSc) and a subject of postgraduate (MA/MSc) study. In some Indian universities, economics is conferred as one of the science subjects and economics students are offered BSc and MSc degrees.

Thus, there is a huge difference in the content and quality of economics teaching in India. The standard of education, syllabi, and reference lists vary widely across universities and from state to state. In Delhi or Calcutta University, the syllabus is much advanced, where all the standard global textbooks are followed, such as Varian's (2010) 'intermediate microeconomics', Mankiw's

(2013) 'macroeconomics', etc. On the other hand, in most of the states in India varieties of books (in English or in vernacular languages) written by local authors and published by local publishers are used. In many cases these books are substandard. As a result, the access to academic and policy-making spaces is being occupied by students from good universities like Delhi University, Jawaharlal Nehru University, Calcutta University and Jadavpur University.

Uniformity in the syllabus of various Indian universities is desirable, but despite good intentions from the UGC[5] there has been little progress. Such an on-going discrepancy cannot be explained by overall literacy and progress of basic education, but rather by the size of English educated elite section of the society, which needless to say is much higher in metro-cities like Delhi and Calcutta. Thus, in order to implement a uniform standard among teaching staff in college and universities, UGC has introduced a National Eligibility Test (NET) which we will discuss in the final section.

3. India's rich pluralistic tradition in economics and social science

The Nationalists' interest in economics developed slowly in order to understand the colonial mode of production and nationalist scholars like Dadabhai Nouroji, Ramesh Chandra Datta and Sakharam Ganesh Deuskar tried to understand the British exploitation of the Indian economy, along with the root of exploitation in an otherwise capitalist system. This led to Marxian thinking among Indian scholars who tried to explain colonial India from the Marxist perspective. Rajani Palm Dutt's seminal *India Today* is an exemplary contribution in this regard (Dutt 1949).

Before Indian independence in 1947, a few important institutions related to teaching and research of economics developed slowly, including the Gokhale Institute of Politics and Economics, the Delhi School of Economics, Delhi University and the Indian Statistical Institute, Calcutta. After independence, the Indian education system nurtured a pluralistic approach in all branches of education, including social sciences in general and economics in particular. The founding member of the Delhi school of economics (1948), Professor V.K.R.V. Rao, was a Gandhist and also greatly influenced by the ideas of Swamy Vivekananda, who envisioned a non-violent society with freely available employment (Byres 1998a, 50). Later, eminent economists like Amartya Sen, Jagdish Bhagwati, Sukhomoy Chakravarty and K.N. Raj joined the Delhi School of Economics, where India's current Prime Minister, Manmohan Singh, also taught. During the 1960s and 1970s, the formidable golden age in the Delhi School of Economics had substantial influence all over the globe. The Delhi School of Economics became an eminent institution, largely guided by mainstream paradigm and methodology. However, at that time, the 'mainstream' meant something fundamentally different: the ideology of global capitalism was welfare economics and Soviet economic planning was the guiding principle of Indian policy making. In fact, Amartya Sen's and Sukhamoy Chakravarty's biographies have been included in *A Biographical Dictionary of Dissenting Economists* (Arestis and Sawyer, 1992). K.N. Raj, Jagdish Bhagwati and Manmohan Singh preached the economic ideology of interventionism during the 1950s and 1960s, which they later fundamentally refuted (Byres 1997, 9–11).

On the other hand, the tradition of alternative economic schools developed with immense strength in India. The Centre for Economic Studies and Planning (CESP) at Jawaharlal Nehru University (JNU) was founded by Krishna Bharadwaj, who did her PhD in Bombay University and post-doctoral research with Piero Sraffa. When Bharadwaj joined JNU there was no Economics department. Other distinguished dissenting economists joining CESP include Amit Bhaduri, Prabhat Patnaik, Utsa Patnaik and Sunanda Sen, with Abhijit Sen, Jayati Ghosh and C.P. Chandrasekhar joining later. Most were associated with Cambridge University. The CESP also absorbed the mainstream economist Anjan Mukherjee whose prime research area was general equilibrium. Later many other mainstream scholars joined CESP.

4. The shadow of academic class struggle in economics

The hegemony of neo-classical economics gained momentum after the collapse of the USSR. While neo-classical economics claims to represent simply tools or methodology without bias for or against any particular ideology, there is reason to believe that it gives highest comfort to neo-liberal economic policy and corporate interests (Dowd 2004, 81–83, Harvey 2009, 1–3). In 1991, the Indian Government tried to impose a neo-liberal ideology by inviting Jagadish Bhagwati and T.N. Srinivasan to write an economic reform manifesto in support of the newly appointed finance minister Professor Manmohan Singh (India's former Prime Minister). However, critics (Byres 1998b; Bhattacharyya 2013) argued that the particular manifesto (Bhagwati and Srinivasan 1993) was based more on assertion and less on research. Despite neo-liberalism becoming the dominating policy since 1991, there was no conscious effort by the HRD Ministry, the Government of India or UGC to steamroll neoliberalism in economics and/or social science teaching and research in India. We will discuss this in the next section. Though there was no imposition from above, there was a substantial encroachment of neo-classical economics. At the same time, India never completely relinquished its interventionism by the state; the Planning Commission of India and the Five Year Planning, for example, continued to exist.

'IDEAS: Economics and Finance Research' has attempted to rank economics departments and economists in India; it is evident from the name that they are primarily interested in corporatised economics which is integrated with 'finance'. It is corporatised and 'financed centred' since it is hosted and funded by the Federal Reserve Bank of St. Louis. Not surprisingly, the source of funding determines the ideology used for the ranking which unfortunately leaves no room for heterodox views. In India, dissenting economists have a huge presence in the society, but none are ranked. Another ranking device is the Research Paper in Economics (RePEc) service, based on a limited sample of the research output in Economics and Finance. For the ranking of individual economists, only those registered with the 'RePEc Author Service' are considered. For the rankings of institutions, only those listed in 'EDIRC' (Economics Departments, Institutes and Research Centres in the World) and claimed as affiliation by registered authors can be considered. Thus, this list is by no means based on a complete sample. Following this limited scope, it has ranked only neo-classicals in the top 25% institution and economists in India. Given a department with a strong alternative wing, they are only considered for their fractional mainstream research within the departments, which explains why the CESP ranked 14th.

Although neoclassical ideologues tried to push forward such rankings, they did not receive support from Indian policy makers; this or any similar exercise has not been considered by UGC or the HRD Ministry. UGC has adopted different criteria for promotional norms without any ideological bias to be discussed in Section 6.

The neo-liberal scholars who remained outcasts during the regime of intervention were resuscitated from the newly emerged neo-liberal mainstream. Some scholars who were affiliated to the Left or Centre changed their affiliation, and pressure mounted to change the graduate and undergraduate economics syllabus. For example, in Calcutta University, Ackley's (1969) *Macroeconomics* used to be the standard textbook. The novelty of this book was that the students were able to understand Keynesian economics properly in a comparative manner with classical economics. Once Keynesian economics was understood, they could identify the essential development of Monetarism and supply side macroeconomics that Keynesianism refuted. From the early 1990s, the macroeconomics syllabus of Calcutta University was changed in the light of the chapters of Mankiw (2013). The basic problem with Mankiw is that it obscures Keynesianism and Monetarism. It becomes difficult to understand anything beyond 'short run' and 'long run' aggregate demand/supply and the Phillips Curve, as if there is a monolithic macroeconomics without having any discourse. Another syllabus re-modification occurred with growth theory: the Harrod and Domar growth models were replaced by Solow's Steady State (University of Calcutta 2010, 20). The University even removed Soviet Economic History as a compulsory paper in the undergraduate curriculum – as if with the collapse of the Soviet Union its 70 long years have also vanished from the annals of human history.

Since the 1990s, we have witnessed increased rancour in several university departments and institutions focusing on ideological capture and the recruitment process. Consider the Centre for the Study in Social Sciences Calcutta (CSSSC), a pioneering institute of economics along with other social science subjects in an interdisciplinary ambience. It is also the eastern regional headquarters of the Indian Council for Social Science Research. In fact, the Centre was famous for its radical interdisciplinary research and teaching during the 1970s and 1980s. During the 1990s, the institute hired Sugata Marjit, a trade and general equilibrium economist, and a regular columnist in a vernacular newspaper, who took upa clear anti-Left position. Sugata Marjit opted for a new policy of hire and fire, which was not in the direction of the Centre's convention.

Another fortress of heterodox economics, the Centre for Economic Studies and Planning, suffered a similar fate. JNU in New Delhi had introduced a second MA course in Economics at the International Trade Division of the School of International Studies during the 1990s. While the original MA course instructed students both in mainstream and alternative paradigms, the second MA course, funded by the Indian Ford Foundation, concentrated only on the mainstream. During the 1990s, the CESP began losing its historical character when a neo-classical economist joined CESP as an Associate Professor (in 1995) after his tenure was rejected at the University of California – Riverside. During his headship at CESP, the promotion of faculty with the orientation in alternative economics was detained. He then hired Sugata Marjit from CSSSC, in order to establish neo-classical hegemony. However, after just a few months, Sugata Marjit left CESP to return to CSSSC.

As another example, consider the Economics Department of South Asian University (SAU), based in New Delhi but developed as an international university funded by all member states of the South Asian Association for Regional Cooperation (SAARC). Several young, well-qualified heterodox scholars joined the economics department from various prestigious educational institutes around the globe. However, problems emerged when Professor Partha Sen, strongly opposed to heterodoxy, was hired as Chair. Indian academics witnessed the most severe outrage of neo-classical economics, destroying the harmony and integrity of this pluralistic and heterodox department, and vitiating the once cordial atmosphere.

Another example is *Economic and Political Weekly* (EPW), which had been a heterodox platform since the 1950s, following the vision of its founding editor Sachin Chaudhuri. It accommodated both mainstream and radical scholars. Unfortunately, beginning in 1996, it censored scholars opposing the neo-classical and neo-liberal paradigm. The four leading Left economists of India – Professors Prabhat Patnaik, Utsa Patnaik, Jayati Ghosh and C.P. Chandraekhar – did not contribute any paper in EPW from 2001 to 2004, an unprecedented outcome. It is indeed a bitter truth that only after the demise of Krishna Raj, EPW's editor (in 2004) the four leading dissenting economists of JNU started contributing to EPW again. In my opinion, EPW has recovered from its 1997 to 2004 phase; however, its present character is not as pluralistic as during the 1970s and 1980s.

The Social Scientist is another journal which advocated progressive social science, including economics, since the 1960s under the editorship of Prabhat Patnaik. Since the early 1990s, it has continued a sustained intellectual resistance against neo-liberalism. It is published by Tulika Press (New Delhi) – devoted to publishing books containing Left and progressive ideology. *Leftward Publication* is also devoted to the same goal. *Mainstream* and *Frontline* are two popular magazines that also bring regular updates of Indian economics from a critical perspective, with many radical Indian economists being regular columnists. Similarly, the newspapers *The Hindu* and *The Hindu Businessline* give space to radical economic thinking.

Recently progressive web journals have developed including *Macroscan, Ideas, The Hoot, The Wire, Vikalp,* and *Sanhati.* They are very popular with a substantial impact on students, scholars and policy makers. While *Macroscan* and *Ideas* were developed to promote alternative economics, *Sanhati, Vikalp, The Wire,* and *The Hoot* do not exclusively address economics, though they do publish serious contributions in radical economics.

5. Recruitment and promotion norms in India: no ideological bias involved

In comparison to the UK Research Assessment Exercise (RAE) or in the US, the recruitment and promotional norms introduced in India by UGC involve no ideological bias from either Right or Left. UGC's June 2010 guidelines and its June 2013 and July 2016 amendments generated controversies for giving wrong weights and whether this norm should be implemented retrospectively (Venkataramana 2009). But no one has raised any criticism for ideological bias. Rather, UGC always encourages promoting interdisciplinary and non-conventional research. For the new recruitment as an Assistant Professor (previously lecturer) a candidate must secure at least 55% in Masters (MA or MSc in subject) and qualified in the all India level UGC sponsored written test, called NET for lecturers. The NET syllabus contains a significant portion of Classical and Keynesian macroeconomics. Many topics beyondcontemporary neo-classical economics are covered, e.g. Kaldor-Hicks and Kaldor theory of business cycles, the Harrod and Domer growth model along with the typical Solow model, Marx and Schumpeterian ideas of development etc., along with a substantial section on economic planning; the rise and collapse of Bretton Woods, and the government's positive role in the economy. Also, globalisation and the international debt crisis is an elective subject where a candidate is free to write his/her own analysis. We can therefore say that there is no unwarranted neo-classical bias in the NET syllabus.

6. Gangster neo-liberalism: India's present regime of *Hindutva* – organised attack on universities and institutions of higher education

At the outset, it may be noted that the *Hindutva* regime in India has not interfered in the economics syllabus so far at any level (school, college, university) as they have in other subjects, particularly in the case of history. In the case of the latter, a Hindutva version of history that mixes myths and distorted realities is gaining ground. However, already some so-called Hindu authors have tried to develop a *Hindutva* version of Economics, which is yet to be included in the syllabus. Although an economics syllabus has not so far been particularly affected, there has been a lot of intervention to run education in the desired direction of the *Hindutva* regime.

At the time of independence, India emerged as the sovereign, socialist, secular and federal democratic republic. This reflected the vision of modern India advocated by India's first Prime Minister Jawaharlal Nehru and the constitution maker Babasaheb Ambedkar. There was no effective challenge that came up against these ideological pillars of the constitution except the Leftists' point of view that right to private property and socialism cannot go together. Over almost four decades after independence, Congress or other Centrist parties ruled India and its different states. After 1985, during the Prime Ministership of Rajiv Gandhi from the Congress Party, the forces of *Hindutva* expanded its base and emerged as a big political force. The party advocating *Hindutva*, namely the Bharatiya Janata Party (BJP), captured around 85 parliamentary seats out of 542 in 1989; compared with only two in 1984. The rise of *Hindutva* was based on a communal campaign that demanded that the mosque created by Babar, the first king of Mughal dynasty in Ayodhya, was actually a Hindu temple of Lord Rama, the prime mythical character of the Indian epic Ramayana, popularised at that time through a television serial. The BJP raised the demand for the demolition of the mosque and the construction of a temple on that site. On December 6, 1992, the mosque was demolished during a communal gathering. Riots in the Indian subcontinent and even in other parts of the world, including the UK, followed. After BJP had been able to raise its number of seats and vote share in every election, it ultimately came to central power in 1999. BJP ruled India under the leadership of Atal Behari Bajpayee as the Prime Minister during 1999–2004. BJP lost the election in 2004 and the Congress Party ruled India again from 2004 to 2014 in two consecutive terms under the Prime Ministership of Dr. Manmohan Singh.BJP captured central power in 2014 with a great majority under the leadership of the present Prime Minister Mr. Narendra Modi.

The *Hindutva* regime is trying its best to jeopardise the public education system in India and moved towards privatisation and saffronisation. Ideologically, privatisation and saffronisation are close to each other. Saffronisation cannot go far with a critical mind. Private education trains students rather than educating them. It is extremely difficult to develop somebody's critical mind in private educational institutions. This is the reason that as compared to vote shares, the *Hindutva* regime fails to attract scholars and educationists in their favour. It was not an isolated matter when Saffron Spriritual Guru Sri Sri Ravishankar said public schools are a breeding ground for Ultra-Leftism.

The NDA government first tried its best to abolish public institutions like the University Grants Commission with the mission to control the entire education system from the HRD Ministry. However, they failed to do that, as UGC was constituted by an Act of the Parliament. With the mission to privatise the education system, they halved the UGC funds. As an obvious result there was an increase in tuition fees in universities. At the same time, the government cut Non-NET fellowships for research students (Rs.5000 per month for MPhil and

Rs.8000 per month for PhD students). This created discontent among the students and contributed to the 'Occupy UGC movement'. The students staged a 'sit in' demonstration in front of the UGC office; the protest went on for several months. Since the 'Occupy UGC movement' originated and centred in the JNU, in an unprecedented incident some student leaders were arrested from JNU under the Anti-national Act for 'anti-national slogans'. In a group of students, three persons chanted slogans wearing masks, and some teachers of JNU expressed their belief that they must belong to the state's 'Intelligence Bureau'. A Muslim student of JNU disappeared after he was beaten up by students belonging to the BJP's student wing Akhil Bharatiya Vidyarthi Parishad (ABVP). The HRD minister Irani tried to rule the universities with the slogan of 'nationalism'. She ordered that all the universities must raise the Indian national flag. Additionally, the Indian army is supposed to teach patriotism in the universities. New private universities have been introduced by HRD minister Irani, and some are religious in nature, e.g. Patanjali University, which is run by a *yogaguru*. In fact, the present regime introduced Sanskrit and Yoga syllabi in all institutions of higher education with an objective to saffronise the education sphere. Also the HRD ministry compelled CBSE to drop German as a third language and replaced it with Sanskrit. The regime was pro-active to saffronise most of the syllabi, particularly history. All the statutory boards of education are reconstituted with trusted sympathisers of *Hindutva* politics. The removal of Nobel Laureate economist Professor Amartya Sen from the governing body of Nalanda University marks a preliminary peak in the reconstruction of the educational system. At the same time, school, college and university teachers are under continuous threat from the pay commission. The proposed pay revision reveals the lowest increase in salary among all pay commissions recommendations after Indian independence. In the case of colleges and universities, the government suggested that they will bear 70% of the costs, while the remaining 30% should be covered via private funding. The allocated number of MPhil and PhD were slashed drastically. The two teachers' organisations in the country, namely the Federation of the Central University Teachers' Association (FEDCUTA) and the All India Federation of College and University Teachers' Organisation (AIFUCTO), protested along with other trade unions.

It is clear that the on-going process of neo-liberalisation in India has become faster and more aggressive during the present *Hindutva* regime. The hostility towards old institutions with pluralistic values has become evident, as well as the alliance between corporate and religious fundamentalism. US President Donald Trump declared himself 'a big fan of Hindu' and praised India's nationalist prime minister, Narendra Modi.

7. Conclusions

This chapter gave insights into the conflicts between the rise of neo-classical hegemony on the one hand and the rich tradition of alternative thinking in

Indian economics education on the other. Additionally, the chapter introduced the reader to the present authoritarian developments in the Indian education system under the nationalist *Hindutva* regime.

India had one of the stronger interventionist economies in the world with a robust state intervention executed through Five Year Plans. The experiments of the planned interventionist economy fit well with the political structure of multiparty democracy, which became fertile ground for the emergence of pluralistic teaching and research in most social sciences disciplines. When India enacted neo-liberal reforms in 1991 directed by the IMF, there was a sudden U-turn in Indian policy making. However, there was never any direction from UGC to change the syllabus in neo-classical or neo-liberal fashion, unlike in the US or in the UK, where the Royal Economic Society intervened to reform the economics syllabus in the direction of neo-classicalism through the Research Assessment Exercise.

In India, despite the liberal hegemony influencing Indian intellectuals, there was no directive from policy makers. In fact, the syllabus in Central Government school boards for secondary and higher secondary level is quite heterodox, interdisciplinary and progressive, as Section 3 pointed out. At the same time, in some leading departments of Indian universities, we have witnessed a silent change of textbooks and economics syllabi at least at the graduate level, for example from Ackley's to Mankiw's macroeconomics, and tensions dealing with recruitment and promotion. We have witnessed the shadow of class struggle, as characterised in Section 4. Neo-classicals rank economists and economic departments by means of multilateral institutions like IDEAS and RePEc. We have shown that such a ranking hardly has any basis as it only deals with economists registered on this website.

Pluralism has almost been lost in some prestigious institutions, such as CSSSC. The aggressive expansion of neo-classical economics has tarnished all the pluralistic space in the Economics Department of South Asian University. Also, the heterodox nature of CESP suffered some partial damage. But at the same time, heterodoxy has flourished at Ambedkar University, Delhi, Visva-Bharati and IDSK, although many Indian universities continue to emphasise neo-classical research.

Among print media, EPW had rich legacy of pluralism from its inception in the early 1960s until the mid-1990s. After that, EPW practised a conservative editorial policy till 2004. Ultimately, with the change in editorship, EPW returned to relative pluralism, though not at its former level. A few other print journals and magazines, such as *Social Scientist, Mainstream* or *Frontline*, continue to publish heterodox research. We have analysed the newly introduced recruitment and promotion procedures in India in Section 5 and we conclude that an ideological bias can hardly be found in this realm.

In Section 6, we have discussed the recent attacks of the *Hindutva* regime in India against universities and institutions of higher education. They follow a twin objective: economic privatisation and cultural saffronisation. As a part of this goal, the UGC funding has been halved after the failed attempt to abolish

UGC. Many private universities with a religious character are being founded in India. In order to combat progressive students and teachers on campus, they were branded as anti-national. This has caused imprisonment of student leaders at JNU, suspended by the university on allegations of terrorism instigated by an HRD minister. So far economics syllabi have not been interfered with, but this has happened in other subjects, particularly history. Yoga and Sanskrit were introduced in the university and IIT curriculum as a part of saffronisation. One can expect the economics syllabus may also include saffron content in future.

Acknowledgements

The author expresses gratitude to Saumya Chakrabarti, Jack Reardon and an anonymous referee for useful feedback.

Notes

1 While the Indian Government has persistently explained its compulsion of borrowing from the IMF, it has not explicitly acknowledged that its transition towards neoliberal reform was due to loan conditionality. According to the government, the compulsion was due to the drying up of its erstwhile stable export market in the Soviet Union, stopping of foreign currency inflows from the Gulf due to the first Gulf War and bad harvest (Government of India 1991).

2 Saffron is the colour of flag of the ruling party in India, the Bharatiya Janata Party (BJP). Saffron signifies the Hindutva tradition which is the colour of dress worn by Hindu monks. In contemporary India, saffronisation is a phrase to indicate the ruling parties' attempt to direct the institutions in accordance with Hindutva ideology by means of using government power.

3 See the syllabus of the CBSE for class IX and X: http://media.mycbseguide.com/files/09/social/syllabus/2014_syllabus_09_social_science.pdf, accessed 21 October 2013.

4 See for CBSE syllabus of Class XI and XII: http://media.mycbseguide.com/files/11/eco/syllabus/2014_syllabus_11_economics.pdf http://media.mycbseguide.com/files/12/economics/syllabus/2015_syllabus_12_economics.pdf For ICSE Syllabus of Class XI and XII: http://boards.edurite.com/icse+board+economics+class+11-syllabus~b1Uk-c2lN-s1gb.htmlhttp://boards.edurite.com/icse+board+economics+class+12-syllabus~b1Uk-cgU-s1gb.html All websites under this note accessed on 21 October 2013.

5 Seethalakshmi, S.: 'UGC Proposes One Syllabus for Varsities', *Times of India*, 04.01.2008, available at http://articles.timesofindia.indiatimes.com/2008-01-04/india/27779608_1_ugc-universities-semester-system, accessed 21 October 2013. However, critics pointed out there should be some diversity as well in the syllabus of different universities in India: see Pratap Bhanu Mehta 'One size can't fit all', Indian Express, 07.01.2008; http://www.indianexpress.com/news/one-size-can-t-fit-all/258501/, accessed on 21 October 2013.

References

Ackley, G. (1969): *Macroeconomic Theory*. New York: Macmillan.

Arestis, P. and Sawyer, M. (eds) (1992): *A Biographical Dictionary of Dissenting Economists*. Cheltenham, UK: Edward Elgar.

Bhagwati, J. and Srinivasan, T.N. (1993): *India's Economic Reforms*. New Delhi. Ministry of Finance, Government of India.

Bhattacharyya, S. (2013): 'Introduction: A Critical Look at Two Decades of Market Reform in India', in Bhattacharyya, S. (ed) *Two Decades of Market Reform in India: Some Dissenting Views*. London: Anthem Press, 1–26.

Byres, T.J. (1997): 'Development Planning and the Interventionist State versus Liberalisation and the Neo-Liberal State: India', in Byres, T.J. (ed) *State Development Planning and Liberalisation in India*. New Delhi: Oxford University Press, 1–35.

Byres, T.J. (1998a): 'The Creation of 'Tribe of Pundits Called Economists': Institutions, Institution-Builders and Economic Debate', in Byres, T.J. (ed) *The Indian Economy: Major Debates since Independence*. New Delhi: Oxford University Press, 20–73.

Byres, T.J. (1998b): 'From Ivory Tower to the Belly of the Beast: The Academy, the State, and Economic Debate in Post-Independence India', in Byres, T.J. (ed) *The Indian Economy: Major Debates since Independence*. New Delhi: Oxford University Press, 74–158.

Dowd, D. (2004): *Capitalism and Its Economics: A Critical History*. London: Pluto Press.

Dutt, R.P. (1949): *India Today*. Delhi: People's Publishing House.

Government of India (1991): Economic Survey, 1990–1991. Available at http://indiabudget.nic.in/es1990-91/esmain.htm, accessed 21 October 2013.

Harvey, J.T. (2009): 'Neoliberalism, Neoclassicism and Economic Welfare'. Working Paper No. 09-02. Department of Economics, Texas Christian University.

Kothari, R. (1993): 'The Yawning Vacuum: A World without Alternatives', *Economic and Political Weekly* 28(22), 1100–1107.

Mankiw, N.G. (2013): *Macroeconomics*. New York: Worth Publishers.

University of Calcutta. (2010): *Syllabi for Three-Year Honours and General Degree Courses of Studies: Economics*. Kolkata: The Registrar, University of Calcutta.

Varian, H.R. (2010): *Intermediate Microeconomics: A Modern Approach*. New York: W. W. Norton & Company.

Venkataramana, G. (2009): 'The UGC's Proposal: The Academicians Nightmare', *Economic and Political Weekly* 34(13), 10–12.

8 China's idiosyncratic economics

An emerging unknown monism driven by pluralism

Shuanping Dai

1. Introduction: a Marxist economist's denunciation

China is transforming from a planned economic system to a market-driven economic one, which is also characteristic of its economics education. This chapter starts with a denunciation: "*Some Issues in Economics Teaching and Research*" by a famous Chinese Marxist economist, Liu Guoguang, published in 2005 in the *Economic Research Journal*, which is one of the most influential economic journals in China. Liu's serious denunciation was part of a nonpublic dispute between Marxian economics and mainstream economics (i.e. neoclassical and neoliberal economics) during the transformation period, and reflected a fight between the two paradigms that attempted to lead China's entire economics education. Eventually, over the years, Marxian economics became in danger of complete abandonment by university curricula. Liu earnestly points out that "western economics has been increasingly influential and Marxist economics is weakening in directing current theoretical economics teaching and research [in China]. Such a situation makes us anxious" (Liu 2005, 4).

Furthermore, he argues, "[a]ny intention to enfeeble and abandon Marxism can weaken the leading power of the Communist Party of China (CPC) and may alter the direction of socialism" (Liu 2005, 6). The logic behind this argument is straightforward and easily understandable, if we agree on equalising socialism and Marxism. China, as a socialist country, adheres to socialist principles in its economic development strategy and institutional settings, and especially strives to establish a socialist market economic system that is one of the Party's fundamental pursuits. As neoliberal economics has been increasingly dominating China's economics education, Marxian economics, which used to serve as the only option for students in economics, has increasingly come under existential threat. Liu (2005) therefore offensively criticises neoliberal economics and respective Chinese economists in the field, and concludes that foreign hostile forces are continuously "westernising" China. In addition, his other concern is that international political communism is at a low ebb, which makes Marxian theory suppressed and unpopular in China; meanwhile, Western neoliberal economics has assumed a significant role in

China's transition from a planned economy to a "market economy", hence it is also becoming dominant in economics teaching. Of course, Liu also analyses internal reasons on the Marxian economists' side: some universities have abandoned lectures on Marxian Political Economy, which was partly a result of unclear educational aims and principles in Chinese higher education institutions. In particular, some universities recruited economics professors who only were educated in neoliberal principles rather than in Marxism, which further negatively affected Marxian economics teaching. In addition, China's Marxian economists did not provide attractive economics textbooks for students, as compared to works in neoliberal economics. Nevertheless, some Chinese scholars believe that the invasion of neoliberal economics did not induce Marxian Political Economy's decline, but rather that it happened as a result of China's Marxian economists not possessing comprehensive research in their own field; in particular, they did not understand Marxism well from an economic theoretical perspective (Hu 2008).

Neoliberal economists have never responded to the denunciation. Instead, in the last ten years, neoliberal economics developed much faster than before and has come to dominate most economic departments in China; some universities even abandoned lectures on Marxian political economy, although such (politically incorrect) behaviour cannot survive for long in a centralised education system. Most neoliberal economists in China, however, believe that mainstream economics serves as the only way to integrate and communicate with global economics communities. Hence, they see no incentive to debate with Marxian economists, and do not want to take any risk to compromise their academic reputation in their international networks. This fact may have strong impacts on economics teaching in China. Such segregation, which exists in different economists' groups in China, shows that they are deliberately staying in their own field, and striving for a breakthrough point to be eventually the dominating force in economics education.

The CPC exerts a strong influence in China's social science research, but does not select Marxism as a unique approach and instead keeps open any options that may benefit China's social sciences. Concerning China's idiosyncratic Political Economy as an example, Xi Jinping, the CPC's general secretary, argues that "upholding and developing China's idiosyncratic political economy should be directed by Marxian political economy, and summarize and refine China's practical experience in reform and socialist construction, meanwhile assimilating Western economics' beneficial elements" (Xi 2016).

Since the 1990s, motivated by China's economic success, the establishment of the socialist market economic system, and the reflection of the Soviet Union paradigm and de-doctrinal socialism, Chinese political economists have made efforts to investigate an appropriate theoretical framework to explain China's economic success and to direct further reforms. Along with China's gradual opening, its academic research environment has become free and active, and the former Political Economy paradigm as applied in the past was criticised and abandoned. In this way, neoliberalism, which is deeply attached to the capitalist market economy, came to dominate in economics teaching and research. Such a decline of Political Economic research indeed occurred in other former socialist countries as well. This causes us to think about the connection between Socialist Political Economy and socialist politics, and to discuss what type of idiosyncratic economics has a higher possibility to become successful in China. Socialist market economy, which is the reform objective of the CPC, does not originate in Karl Marx, and has not yet received international acceptance and theoretical support. Hence, establishing China's idiosyncratic economics requires extensive theoretical efforts that might then provide some space for pluralism in economics teaching. Meanwhile, regarding the openness and flexibility of China's economics teaching, any economic thoughts will be optional in classes.

A hidden issue behind the notion of *learning from the West* is that China's economists continue to pursue an approach based on China's reality, which the recent impressive economic success has reinforced. Generally, China's economists have a common sense that China did not follow a single economic theory to guide its reform and development, and believe that China's success can contribute to the further development of economics, although none discloses the character of China's idiosyncratic economics. This chapter will illustrate this ambitious agenda and figure out the opportunities for promoting pluralism in China's economics education. Hence, an unknown, tacit monism might emerge in China, but pluralism may act as a channel for understanding the Chinese economy, and accordingly serve as the essential part of China's idiosyncratic economics, which might be a new monism. However, pluralism also might fail. No totally dominating economic school currently exists and there is space to promote divergent economic approaches; but any effort might face a challenge from the Marxist paradigm and would be influenced by China's political-economic nexus.

2. A brief history of "mainstream forwards, Marxism backwards"

China's economics higher education started at the beginning of the 20th century, when China was learning from Western civilisation, and the economics curriculum system was introduced. Before the translation of *The Wealth of Nations* into Chinese in 1902,[1] China's economics education was almost blank, although the Chinese population had created nearly one-third of global economic production. As an economic entity, China had governed its economy successfully with its conventional wisdom until the closed system was interrupted in the 18th century. Since then, China has started to adapt to the modern Western ways of thinking, their theoretical framework, research methods, and economic terminology (Tan 2000). Such interaction with Western academic systems of thought reflects China's rise and decline, which is partly the reason for Chinese economists' enthusiasm about establishing a Chinese idiosyncratic economics in the context of the recent successful economic development.

Peking University established the first economics department in China in 1912, which paved the way for a modernisation of economics in China. Before 1949, China's economics education and research followed two approaches. One was introduced from Europe, the United States, and Japan. Huge numbers of English and Japanese economic works were translated into Chinese. Many Chinese economists were trained in Western countries, returned to China and dominated economics teaching and research in the universities. The second approach regarded introducing Marxism, which triggered China's revolution and anti-invasion efforts. Starting in the 1930s, *Das Kapital* and other works by Karl Marx were translated (Lin and Hu 2001).

Western mainstream economics education in China was interrupted as the Chinese communist government was established in 1949. Conventional Marxist economics was the only option in the classroom, and almost acted as an ideological education approach, and as a tool for economic planning. Instead, Western mainstream economics was treated and criticised as a decadent capitalist way of thinking. The first textbook was a translation from the *Textbook on Political Economy* in the Soviet Union, with an extra chapter to introduce the economic system in China. From the first version in 1955, this was the chief economics textbook in China for the following twenty years; and since the reform in 1978, Chinese economists have been devoting efforts to establish political economy textbooks with China's economic practice (Liu and Quan 2017).

The fundamental economic reforms during the 1980s brought Western mainstream economics back to the universities, and from the 1990s, economists who were educated in Europe and the United States started to introduce the latest Western economics into China's universities. The majority of their thinking had to be classified as neoliberal, and the popular mainstream economic textbooks and their curriculum came to prevail in China as well. Most economists, including Marxists, welcomed such fundamental changes. The Marxists did this in an effort to absorb Western economics into Marxian economics. However, this eventually made the existing socialist economics education struggle both in research and the classroom, although the CPC still strongly supports Marxist research and teaching.

Several landmark events fundamentally changed China's economics education during that period (1980s–1990s). The initial event, which econometrician Lawrence R. Klein (a Nobel Laureate) organised and led, was the *Summer Palace Econometric Research Training Workshop* in 1980. Approximately 100 junior economists and students attended this training programme. This workshop was considered as an enlightenment in China's economics education and research. Economists such as Klein (University of Pennsylvania), Gregory C. Chow (Princeton University), Lawrence Lau (Stanford University) and Cheng Hsiao (University of Southern California) gave lectures in Econometrics, mainstream macroeconomics and microeconomics. This initial event fundamentally encouraged those Chinese economists who had been well educated before in the United States, and now interrupted their research to return to teach mainstream economics in China.

The second influential project was the "Ford Class". It had 681 graduates in total, and was organised at China's Renmin University (Beijing) and Fudan University (Shanghai) from 1985 to 1995. Considerable financial support came from the Ford Foundation which favours neoliberalism. Within a time span of 11 years, this project invited economics professors, mainly from the United States, to give lectures on 20 different subject fields, including Macroeconomics, Microeconomics, Econometrics, Game Theory, and International Economics. They also designed the curricula according to the neoliberal mainstream given to fresh PhD students, and provided the latest versions of textbooks from the United States. The invitees were top ranking professors at that time, and later Nobel Laureates, such as Angus S. Deaton, Robert F. Engle, Leonid Hurwicz, and Robert A. Mundell, were active in this project. Many students in the Ford Class then went abroad, mainly to the United States, to pursue a doctoral degree in economics, and eventually became the most influential force in China's economics education in the 21st century. In all, the Ford Class project was a major diffusion process of neoliberal economics in China.

Third in the internationalisation process of China's economics education is the important role played by Gregory C. Chow. China's central government frequently invited him to discuss reforming economics education and its relevance to economic reform in the 1980s (for details, see e.g. Chow 1989). Besides the events mentioned above, he also worked closely with the Chinese Ministry of Education (MoE) to select graduate students to study economics in the United States and Canada; for example, sixty American and Canadian universities accepted sixty-three students with his recommendation, and most of them received financial support from the hosting universities, the Chinese government, and the Ford Foundation. Thereafter, more and more students were encouraged to study in the United States, and many of them returned to China after obtaining doctoral degrees or professorships. This was another milestone event: a new round of economics teaching internationalisation through returning economists and their reforms in China. In 1994, Justin Yifu Lin (PhD Chicago, 1986) returned from Yale University and established the *China Center for Economic Research* (CCER) under the Ford Foundation's and the World Bank's initial support. It aims to

> mobilise domestic and international resources for bringing together a group of well-trained economists to contribute to economics education and research at Peking University, (. . .) to contribute to China's market-oriented reform and development, as well as to the development of modern economic theory.
>
> Lin (2007a, 66).

In the same year, Zou Hengfu (PhD Harvard, 1989) established the *Institute for Advanced Economic Study* (two years later, changed to the *Institute for Advanced Study*, IAS) at Wuhan University. The Institute selects the best bachelor students, who are especially talented in mathematics and other natural science fields, for the Double-degree Class of Mathematical Finance and Mathematical Economics, and provides education following the standard curricula of the top universities in the United States.

Other Chinese universities quickly learned such economics education and research patterns, especially after China became more open and liberalised around 2000. Universities started to recruit famous economists from the United States as Deans of economics and business schools, through providing extraordinary salaries, establishing "special reform zones" in economics teaching and research, and recruiting new faculties. Shanghai University of Finance and Economics, for example, employed Tian Guoqiang (PhD Minnesota, 1987, and Professor at Texas A&M University) to reform its economic school in 2004. Tian enjoys high favour in mainstream economics and leads the economics school with a focus on publication in the top-level mainstream economic journals. Similar reforms are very common in other Chinese universities; for instance, with Qian Yingyi (PhD Harvard, 1990, and Professor at the University of California, Berkeley) at Tsinghua University. This new round of reforms in reality helped Chinese universities to integrate into mainstream economics, and meanwhile it changed the entire atmosphere of China's economics teaching and research. Currently, the number of top journal publications has become the most important parameter for almost every economics school in China; therefore, neoclassical and neoliberal economics are developing into the dominating paradigm among economists in order to be able to generate enough top publications.

China has experienced a high level of economic success and deep integration with the world, while Marxist economics is facing serious difficulties in explaining China's economic development. In particular, the transition of former socialist countries into capitalist systems stifled Marxist thought. Hence, the notion of "Mainstream forwards, Marxism backwards" is understandable.

Nevertheless, there are still elements of Marxist economics in Chinese economics curricula. Marxist Political Economy is an introductory course for economics students in Chinese universities, and is a general knowledge course for students with little or no economic background. Moreover, *Das Kapital* and *History of Economic Thought* are compulsory for economics students. On the surface, this may signal that China favours Marxism and pluralism in economics teaching. However, this is not the case, because the main economics courses are neoliberal courses and heterodox courses are isolated from them. Microeconomics and macroeconomics, both introductory courses as well, are to be reinforced and extended in other courses. For example, students may learn price theory in both Marxian Political Economy and neoclassical microeconomics. However, most students may forget what Marx's theory is about after only one course. Instead, the principle of "demand and supply" will become general knowledge, as it leads students to understand the courses in the other three years of their bachelor programme. A coherent curriculum is fundamental to guide economics teaching in the neoclassical/neoliberal direction.

In addition, China's Marxian Political Economy has its own problems. For instance, the teaching content of Political Economy mostly comes from the CPC's documents, and little is adopted from Marx's original work. Political economists are unable to promote research in this field, and the reason behind this is complicated. One reason is that the research evaluation system has been dominated by neoclassical economics. Hence, many scholars, especially the leading scholars, have moved away from Marxist economics. When students consider Marxism as outdated, not all teachers can provide a clear answer to this from an academic perspective. Such a confusing situation makes neoclassical economics even more popular and easier to comprehend, as students learn relatively more about it. Consequently, fewer Marxist economists are sufficiently educated, and in many universities, non-Marxist scholars teach Marxian Political Economy. Since the 1990s, many new concepts, for example, commodity economy, socialist market economy, and so forth, were invented for China's economic reforms; and those new concepts triggered Chinese economists to develop theoretical frameworks and to teach in classes. Those efforts successfully integrated China's practice into political economy theory, but failed to turn the "Mainstream forwards, Marxism backwards" notion around.

All economics schools are nevertheless somewhat inclusive. For instance, in the 1930s, Guo Dali, and Wang Yanan translated *The Wealth of Nations, Das Kapital* and several classical economics books. Such inclusive traditions still are preserved properly. As a whole, China's economics education officially tries to remain open to all economics schools, and dominating neoliberalism cannot alter this. Many non-mainstream scholars can easily survive in the universities where mainstream dominates, but might not attract the majority of students. Courses like *Marxist Political Economy, Das Kapital,* and *History of Economic Thought* are compulsory for bachelor students majoring in economics. Nevertheless, we should not take this as evidence to demonstrate that China's economics education still adheres to the Marxist tradition (see, e.g. Jiang and Lu 2016).

3. A possible way to pluralism in China

Wang (1946) introduced the term "Chinese Economics" in his monograph *The Principle of [the] Chinese Economy*, aiming to establish an original theory which fits Chinese national interests, and to explain Chinese economic and social development. A starting point for establishing Chinese Economics is the consideration of China's characteristics in various aspects of its socio-economic system. In the era of Wang (1946), China was experiencing a transition from a colonial and feudal society to a modern one. Researchers from the existing western paradigms had not done research on that, and therefore could not explain or adapt to such a transition. Concurrently, China's economy was severely underdeveloped and the scientific infrastructure and outputs were deficient as well. Hence, there existed an urgent need to establish a framework to improve China's development. Nevertheless, establishing Chinese Economics did not mean creating a completely new theoretical system, but rather building on and absorbing existing economic theories, grounded on China's economic practices and reality.

China's expanding economic scale generated a rich economic experience, which is a valuable source for enriching economic theory (Lin 2007b; Tian 2016a). Western economists, especially the neoliberalists, have failed to predict China's reform experience. Instead, China has created its own approaches. China's dual-track system during marketisation reforms in the last decades serves as an example here, being beyond the existing theoretical frameworks. This also indicates that any application of theories based on other countries' experiences may lead to flawed results in China.

Hence, many Marxist economists claim that China's success depends highly on its very socialist system and institutional arrangement, rather than Anglo-Saxon neoliberal ideology. In accordance with this argument, China's economic teaching and research should prioritise Marxist Political Economy, and western mainstream economics should be in a subordinate position (Lin 2016). This is one Marxist approach to establish China's idiosyncratic (Marxian Political) economics, because "social science must have a natural and indivisible connection with social institutions, political orientation, and value; it is therefore really misleading to copy the internationalisation approach, which nature science takes, in social science" (Lin 2016, 17). Thus, sinicised Marxism should be the fundamental principle of China's socialist Political Economy (Pang 2012). Neoliberal elements, such as private ownership, a completely free market economy, and nonintervention, were not feasible and were unacceptable in China (Liu 2005).

Another group of economists proposes that China's idiosyncratic economics must be a "marginal innovation" of the new classical economic framework, through absorbing China's experience. China is approaching a market-economy status, which has a "neoclassical, in particular general equilibrium framework" (Tian 2016a, 43). A similar argument comes from Lin and Hu (2001), namely that the straightest way for Chinese economists to be integrated with the world economies is to adopt the "normalised theoretical models and empirical methods". Otherwise, research on China's reform and development will be very limited, especially if the integration issue cannot be solved properly. An ideal scheme, naturally, is to educate the young generation using western mainstream economics, which may ensure that China's economic research integrates with the rest of world to the greatest extent. Indeed, most of China's universities have adopted this approach from the beginning of this century, and the dominating neoliberal economics was highly welcomed soon thereafter, following this logic.

Nevertheless, a common sense among those positions is that western mainstream economics is not the only way to explain China's reform and development experience, and China's special experience may provide a unique channel for economic theory. However, it is still controversial to suggest a particular way to explore a new development model under the assumption of China's speciality. In addition, on how to explain China's development, or to develop a Chinese Economics, or to develop Marxist Political Economy, most Chinese economists have some inclination to monism. This might be rooted in China's academic tradition of always some dominance existing among many schools of thought.

Some economists argue that the process of neoliberalism dominating in China actually reflects the idea that China does not have a historical tradition in economic research, and is now eager to integrate with the western community. However, this appears overstressed. Economics in China has become a purely mathematical game, which lacks deep thinking about what really happens in China (Yang 2016). If we search in the literature for the most influential studies explaining China's development, we find that no Chinese scholars have conducted them. Instead, Chinese scholars have repeated many established western works using Chinese data. At the same time, Marxist economists have not created any significance in developing Marxism, and their activities have a strong connection with how the CPC conceives of Marxism. Currently, Marxists claim that Marxist Political Economy should constitute the dominating economic field in China, because China is a socialist system. Most research regarding this, however, relates to CPC's policies and their arguments. Such highly politically connected research may not be convincing for most students, and thus reform that is more fundamental is needed in economics teaching.

Thanks to the tight connection between Marxism and other western heterodoxies, it would be feasible to introduce heterodox theories in China, and heterodox economists may find more space to follow pluralism in China than they may in other countries. Moreover, China needs pluralism to challenge the dominating role of western mainstream economics (Zhang 2016). For instance, several economists initiated a Research Training School at Jilin University, Jilin province, aiming at integrating heterodox economic theory with Marxiant Political Economy and promoting pluralism in economics teaching.

Many neoliberal economists in leading research institutes and universities also practise pluralism. The CCER, for example, established by Justin Yifu Lin and other neoclassical economists, has an ambitious goal to help China integrate with the world economic communities; however, it also interacts well with complexity economics, feminist economics, and structural economics. In addition, China has a long pluralist tradition, which might provide a fundamental cultural condition. Since *the Spring and Autumn Period* (approximately 771 to 476 BCE) of ancient China, the *Contention of a Hundred Schools of Thought* has profoundly influenced and shaped China's social consciousness up to the present day. The idea of a peaceful coexistence among different school of thought has become a basic social value for Chinese. Until recently, the *Hundred Flowers Movement* of the 1950s had a coherent pursuit similar to 2000 years ago. Regarding evolutionary economics as an example, it has a coherent relation to China's reform experience and traditional wisdom in the way of thinking, and this might be an advantage for Chinese evolutionary and institutionalist economists (Jia 2006).

We propose that China's idiosyncratic economics can serve as a possible way to integrate more economic schools into Chinese academia because of the openness of China's socialist system that shapes China's reform and development strategies. As we observed, although the CPC has a strong will to stick to the socialist system, it also provides adequate freedom for different academic voices in policymaking and education. Pluralism actually is one of the basic values in China. Hence, Marxist Political Economy will be supported at the political level, but will not constitute a dominating economic school in China.

An additional concern will be how to process this fundamental change in economics, if we should attain a common sense of "China's idiosyncratic economics". There must be huge challenges, for instance, in its methodology, theoretical framework, core concepts, as well as in the interactions with the existing theories, and in particular, with mainstream economic thinking. Tian published his microeconomic textbook (Tian 2016b) with the aim to integrate China's practice into the currently prevailing microeconomic theory. He explained the connections between China's reality and practices, and microeconomic theory in several paragraphs, after introducing the theory. However, this is obviously far from China's idiosyncratic economics.

Pluralist economics was introduced in China as soon as the movement for pluralism was initiated in 1970s, although it did not generate any significant influence or propose an operational scheme (Jia and Xu 2009; Yang 2016; Zhang 2016). Furthermore, China's scholars still are invisible in the International Initiative for Promoting Political Economy (IIPPE), the World Economics Association (WEA), and the Institute of New Economic thinking (INET). This is very intriguing. Chinese economists who favour pluralism sometimes strategically connect pluralism with Marxism. For example, Zhang (2016) argues,

> in the next few years, innovative Chinese idiosyncratic economics will become a major concern for Marxists, and China's economic practice will be the cornerstone for these efforts. In the long run, China's economics will become a synonym of Marxist economics, (. . .) and, with innovation in theory based on China's economic practice, becomes a major part of Marxist economics.
>
> Zhang (2016, 18)

Moreover, in the context of criticising the monism of neoliberalism, which "has badly threatened the spread of pluralism in China" (Jia 2006, 59), both sides might have many attitudes in common.

An issue regarding plural economics teaching will be how to create a pluralist culture, which is largely relevant to the academic tradition in universities, as mentioned. For instance, concerning the question of how to reform the existing evaluation system in Chinese universities to generate more pluralism, neoliberalists and Marxists hold different opinions. The former consider publication and citation in the top ranking journals as the core criterion (Tian 2016a). Those top journals form the base for neoliberalism, but the peer review system inherently impedes the publication possibilities of heterodox works, and seriously damages pluralism in economics teaching and research, because the reviewers are usually from the peer group of neoliberals. However, China in particular still has a vigorous trend to support pluralism. For instance, in 2016, the MoE initiated an evaluation programme that counts the publications in top journals; in economics, these comprised 12 journals: *American Economic Review, Econometrica, Journal of Political Economy, Quarterly Journal of Economics, Journal of Finance, Review of Economic Studies, Journal of International Economics, Journal of Econometrics, Journal of Public Economics, Journal of Monetary Economics, Journal of Labor Economics*, and *Review of Economics and Statistics*. This initiative focused on leading scholars to pay more attention to publication quality over quantity. Following this announcement, however, not only Marxist economists but also other scholars immediately expressed strong opposition, which forced the MoE to cancel this evaluation initiative.

4. Conclusion

This chapter discussed the possibility to implement pluralist economics teaching in China by taking the chance to establish China's idiosyncratic economics. Currently, the two most influential economic groups are neoliberals and Marxists, who both have a strong willingness to promote themselves as the dominating group in China. The socialist socio-economic system and the political institutions are most encouraging for the Marxian, who believe the only possible way to achieve socialism and communism is to improve Marxian Socialist Political Economy; whereas the neoliberalists push integration with the western mainstream and insist that neoliberalism is the best way to explain China's story in a formal approach. Both sides are monist and exclusive. Currently, the neoclassical and neoliberal mainstream dominates China's academic economics. Nevertheless, China also has a strong history and present culture, and political practice of theoretical pluralism.

We proposed a way of combining paradigms with pluralism by abandoning ideological constrictions. This is an unknown monism but reflects China's features and current socio-economic development and experience. Based on China's economic education reforms, and academic tradition in universities, we argue that pluralism is a feasible way, and pluralist economics teaching will be helpful for establishing China's idiosyncratic economics and promoting China's further development into new areas of experience.

Note

1 Before the translation of the Wealth of Nations, some Chinese intellectuals and reformists were devoting efforts into learning from the Western economies and translating economics books as well, although the impacts in economics education were limited. For further historical information, see for example Trescott (2016).

References

Chow, G. (1989): 'Economics Education and Economic Reform in China', *Proceedings of the American Philosophical Society 133*(1), 64–74.

Hu, J. (2008): 'Innovative Development and Chinization of Marxist Political Economy', *Economic Perspectives* 4, 20–24 (in Chinese).

Jia, G. (2006): 'China's Economics Revolution', *Social Science Front* 1, 56–71 (in Chinese).

Jia, G. and Xu, S. (2009): *A Research on Post-Autistic Economics Movement*. Beijing, China: Renmin University of China Press (in Chinese).

Jiang, J. and Lu, Y. (2016): 'Does China's Bachelor Economics Education Adhere to Marxism?', *Economists* 5, 13–18 (in Chinese).

Lin, G. (2016): 'Maintaining a Proper Relationship between Marxist Economics and Western Economics', *China Review of Political Economy* 7(1), 16–17 (in Chinese).

Lin, J.Y. (2007a): 'Creating a Market-Oriented Research and Education Institution in a Transition Economy: The Experience of the China Center for Economic Research at Peking University', in Bourguignon, F., Elkana, Y., and Pleskovic, B. (eds.), *Capacity Building in Economics Education and Research*. Washington, DC: World Bank, 65–76.

Lin, J.Y. (2007b): 'Opportunities and Challenges in China's Economics', *Contemporary Economics* 7, 4–5 (in Chinese).

Lin, J.Y. and Hu, S. (2001): 'Economic Research in China: The Last 100 Years', *China Economic Quarterly* 1(1), 1–18 (in Chinese).

Liu, G. (2005): 'Some Issues in Economics Teaching and Research', *Economic Research Journal* 10, 4–11 (in Chinese).

Liu, S. and Quan, L. (2017): 'The Historical Evolution of Chinese Socialist Political Economy Textbooks', *China Review of Political Economy* 8(3), 174–189 (in Chinese).

Pang, J. (2012): 'The Direction and Methods of Chinese Economy', *China Review of Political Economy* 3(4), 3–17 (in Chinese).

Tan, M. (2000): 'The Past and Future of China's Economics', *Economic Research Journal* 4, 57–65 (in Chinese).

Tian, G. (2016a): "Double First-Class' Construction and China's Contribution to Economics Development', *Journal of Finance and Economics* 42(10), 35–49 (in Chinese).

Tian, G. (2016b): *Advanced Microeconomics*. Beijing, China: Renmin University of China Press (in Chinese).

Trescott, P.B. (2016): 'The Diffusion of Western Economics in China', in Warner, M. (ed.), *The Diffusion of Western Economic Ideas in East Asia*. Abingdon, UK: Routledge, 69–93.

Wang, Y. (1946): *The Principle of the Chinese Economy*. Fujian, China: Yongan Press (in Chinese).

Xi, J.P. (2016): *The Speech on the Work Forum of Philosophy and Social Sciences*. May 17, 2016. Available at http://news.xinhuanet.com/politics/2016-05/18/c_1118891128.htm, accessed on November 24, 2017 (in Chinese).

Yang, H. (2016): 'Pluralism in Economics: History, Main Idea and Its Significance to China', *Journal of China's Social Science Evaluation* 1, 37–41 (in Chinese).

Zhang, L. (2016): 'Marxism Economics, Heterodox Economics, and Pluralism of China's Economics', *Social Science Journal* 4, 15–20 (in Chinese).

9 The need for an independent perspective

Teaching economics in Ghana

Hadrat Yusif

1. Introduction

Teaching economics in African countries has been influenced predominantly by mainstream economic ideas that have developed over time in Europe and North America. The dominant schools of thought from the 1950s to the twenty-first century are neoclassical and neo-Keynesian economic ideas. Historical events and processes have resulted in an "export" of these economic ideas from Europe and North America to Africa, namely colonisation, formal independence, structural adjustment programmes, economic globalisation, and the establishment of the African Economic Research Consortium (AERC) in the 1980s. The outstanding issue regarding the teaching of economics in Africa has not been that of mainstream economic ideas but rather of an "imported" economic paradigm from the global north that does not appear to have solved abject poverty, high levels of unemployment, low economic growth rates, inequality and environmental damage. This chapter examines the teaching of economics and economic thinking in Ghana as an exemplary case. It proceeds in four steps: teaching of economics from 1940 to 1957, 1957 to 1988 and from 1988 to the present, and the conclusion.

2. Teaching economics in Ghana: 1940–1957

In Ghana, the teaching of economics started when the University of the Gold Coast (now the University of Ghana, Legon) began to teach undergraduate economics in 1949/1950 based on the syllabus from the University of London. The former was affiliated to the latter and thus granted University of London degrees. Naturally, the undergraduate economics programme was structured along the lines of the programmes in the UK and the academic staff were mainly Europeans: Helen Kimble, Walter Birmingham, Dermot Gatley, T.M. Brown and many others. The textbooks used were those approved by the University of London.[1]

Most of these textbooks concentrated on microeconomics and the topics did not directly address the major economic problems (poverty, unemployment, slow growth rate and inequality) that the economy of Ghana or Africa more widely encountered at that time. The view of some expatriate academic staff in the 1950s was that the principles taught in economics are the same all over the world (Kimble 1969). This view can be accepted because traditional economics teaching practised in Africa had not been documented and was purely oral.

The first cohort of Ghanaian and other African students encountered major challenges regarding the teaching and learning of economics at that time. The materials in these textbooks were drawn from European and North American economies and did not have direct links to Ghanaian or African economies. Marginal concepts, elasticity, market structures and other concepts taught appeared abstract to the Ghanaian and other African students. The "accelerated mathematisation" of economics since the 1920s (Rothbard 1997), as well as the English language of the teaching material, made economics a difficult subject for the Ghanaian and other African students who were being introduced to neoclassical models and theories for the first time.

These shortcomings notwithstanding, the teaching of economics in Ghana intensified, as the economy became more monetised, financial institutions were established and multinational companies opened branches in the major cities. To ensure that data for research into the economic problems of Ghana and Africa and also the teaching of economics were available, a research centre, the Institute of Statistics, was established in 1962 and provided training for statisticians. The scope of the research centre was widened to cover social and economic areas in 1969 (Seck 2010). The mandate was to conduct research in social sciences in order to generate solutions for national development (ISSER 2013). In 1969, the name of the research centre was changed to the Institute for Statistical, Social and Economic Research (ISSER).

The teaching of economics in Ghana in the 1940s and 1950s was not different from other Anglophone countries in West and East Africa including Nigeria, Kenya, Tanzania, Uganda, Zimbabwe, Gambia, and Sierra Leone. Some of the European instructors who taught in West Africa also taught in East Africa and the syllabus used was the same. For Francophone countries, such as Cote d'Ivoire, Senegal, Burkina Faso, Togo and Benin, the teaching of economics was structured along the lines of universities in France. However, the situation in South Africa differed as some public universities were established as far back as the nineteenth century or even earlier (University of Cape Town, Stellenbosch University, and University of Pretoria). The economics departments in these universities were opened many years before the establishment of universities in sub-Saharan Africa.

3. Teaching of economics in post-independence Ghana: 1957–1988

After Ghana gained independence in 1957, several developments influenced the teaching of economics and research. Like many African countries, the new political administration, headed by Kwame Nkrumah, inherited an economy that depended mainly on the export of cocoa and gold for foreign exchange. Other African countries also relied solely on palm oil, tea, bananas, rubber or cotton. The economy was underdeveloped and the government regarded the capitalist economic principles (i.e. profit maximisation and selfishness) that the colonial masters had applied since the 1870s as the primary reason for underdevelopment. Thus in the 1960s and 1970s there was a change in direction, regarding the management of the economy and economic activities. Indeed, government intervention dominated political economic practices in Ghana and many other African countries. This was motivated by the massive inequalities that existed in Ghana and other countries in Africa. As indicated earlier, the government followed left-wing economic theories and price controls were imposed, a fixed exchange rate regime introduced, and a fixed interest rate adopted. The financial sector was tightly regulated.

The general paradigm in the country and many African countries aimed at accelerated economic development. Consequently, dependence on markets and private investment was rejected. The government initiated the ambitious Seven-Year Development Plan (1963–1970). Public enterprises were established (State Transport Corporation, Ghana Railways Corporation, Ghana Airways and many others) and import substitution industries were set up. The objective was to industrialise and reduce dependence on imports and also the export of primary agriculture raw materials and gold.

These developments in Ghana and other African countries informed research in the prestigious universities in Europe and North America. The consensus was that development models for industrialised economies could not be wholly applied to underdeveloped economies in Africa. Textbooks containing economic models that matched developing countries in the 1970s and 1980s were produced.[2] These textbooks were widely used in economics departments. They contained topics that attracted the new political elite in Africa – big push, planning, take-off, and accelerated industrialisation (Killick 1980).

Tony Killick's *Development Economics in Action: a study of economic policies in Ghana* (Killick 1978) had significant impact on research and policy in Ghana. Killick, a Senior Research Associate of the Overseas Development Institute, London, and consultant on development policy issues, had long-standing ties with Ghana and was able to apply economic theory to Ghanaian problems including economic development, economic growth, economic planning, industrialisation, mining, and agriculture. Development economics at this time became very popular among economists. It was taught not only in underdeveloped countries but also in developed countries. Killick (1980) reported that compared with developed countries the teaching of development economics in developing countries was far less satisfactory. In Ghana and other African countries, economics departments and researchers depended largely on textbooks written by Europeans and North Americans (i.a. Nurkse, Arthur Lewis, Kamarck, Meier, Todaro, etc).

From the 1960s to the 1980s, in addition to mainstream economics dominated by neoclassical axioms of rationality and equilibrium (Colander et al. 2004), Marxist economic ideas (scientific socialism) were gradually introduced in the teaching of economics in Ghana and many other African countries. Left-leaning ideas made significant impact on economic policies adopted by some African governments at the time, but their acceptance in economics departments in Ghana and some African universities was marginal. Neoclassical economics and developmental paradigms were widely taught in universities across sub-Saharan Africa. Davis (2006) and Dequech (2007) have argued that neoclassicism remained solidly embedded in economics instruction but its dominance had weakened as a sub-set of mainstream economics. This has not been proven in the African context. In the first two years of university education *n*eoclassical economics remained dominant.

In the 1970s and 1980s, the economic problems of Ghana and other African countries deepened. This macroeconomic instability was attributed to weak institutions, corruption and also socialist economic ideas adopted by governments in the 1960s. Macroeconomic instability had a serious negative impact on economics departments. There were shortages of well-trained staff and even of basic textbooks.

One important development in the 1970s was the recognition by European researchers that economic policies introduced in the 1950s and 1960s (classical ideas in the 1950s and socialist economic ideas in the 1960s) could not address such major economic problems as poverty, unemployment and economic development in Africa. European researchers associated with the African continent quickly filled this gap by the introduction of textbooks in Ghana with topics that related directly to the Ghanaian and African economies. One such example is Ord and Livingstone, *An Introduction to West African Economics* (1969). Ord is from the Department of Economics and Centre of African Studies, University of Edinburgh whilst Livingstone taught at Makerere University in Uganda, the University of Dar es Salam, Tanzania and also at Sheffield and Newcastle upon Tyne. He became a Professor of Economics at the University of East Anglia. They had conducted much research in Africa which influenced their book but neoclassical theories and methodological individualism continued to be the bases of these textbooks. The key topics comprise: factors of production and development; the economic structure of West Africa; the economic system; development planning; money, labour and wages in West Africa; the features of the West African tax system, and other relevant topics. They also wrote *An Introduction to Economics for East Africa* (1968). These books were used widely for both undergraduate economics and also for GCE A level economics in the 1970s and 1980s in Ghana and other English-speaking countries in West and East Africa. The language was simple, the mathematics not very rigorous and students could easily understand the content.

As mentioned earlier, the government of Ghana adopted socialist economic strategies in the 1960s and 1970s with the intention of accelerating the pace of economic development. The intended economic transformation did not materialise, though. Ghana and other African countries encountered significant macroeconomic instabilities i.e. very low real growth rates, high inflation rates, balance of payment problems, rising unemployment and others. The Ghana government contacted the Bretton Woods Institutions (The World

Bank and the International Monetary Fund) for bailout. But the bailout conditions required government to maximise the economic freedom of market participants and reduce the amount of state intervention to the bare minimum. Structural adjustment programmes (SAPs) were implemented and, in this, price controls were abolished, and exchange rates and interest rate were liberalised. The works of Edward Shaw (1973), *Financial Deepening in Economic Development* (Oxford University Press) and Ronald McKinnon (1973), *Money and Capital in Economic Development* (Brookings Institution), through the complementarity hypothesis,[3] had significant influence on policy and teaching of economics in Ghana. SAPs shifted further the teaching of economics towards neoclassical economics and developmental economics.

For the first time, a few Ghanaian economists started writing books that used Ghanaian materials and examples. Kojo Ewusi in 1978 came out with, *The size of the labour force and structure of employment in Ghana*. In 1984, he wrote *The Dimensions and Characteristics of Rural Poverty in Ghana*. ISSER also started annual publication of *The State of the Ghanaian Economy* in 1995. These books have influenced government policies and advanced research.

The effect on economic teaching has been through improved content of courses on the Economy of Ghana offered at undergraduate level. These books are reliable sources of information as regards the various sectors of the Ghanaian economy i.e. government expenditure, revenue, monetary policy, fiscal policy, balance of payment, agriculture, mining, industry and the service sector. However, Ghanaian economists and researchers have not been able to influence the approach to economics in the country. These textbooks by Ghanaians and other African writers were stimulated by neoclassical ideas. This suggests that mainstream economic ideas comprising neoclassical, neo-Keynesian and, to a lesser, extent game theory still dictate the teaching of economics at both undergraduate and graduate levels.

In the 1980s, the composition of the academic staff had changed as Ghanaian economists had taken over economics departments. Much more undergraduate work was done and all students were "fully abreast with mainstream economic thought" (Kimble 1969). Some popular textbooks used in the UK and North American universities were used in Ghana.

According to Davis (2006), changes in economics research generally precede, and ultimately generate, changes in economics instruction. However, in Ghana and sub-Saharan Africa, research output in the 1960s and 1970s was very low. The small amount of research conducted lacked the rigour needed to influence the approach for teaching economics in the country. Consequently, in the 1980s, mainstream economic ideas taught in the most prestigious universities and colleges (Dequech 2007), dominated by neoliberalism which started in the 1970s in Europe and North America, continued to influence the teaching of economics in Ghanaian universities.

The two other public universities in Ghana at that time – the Kwame Nkrumah University of Science and Technology, Kumasi (KNUST) and the University of Cape Coast (UCC) – established economics departments. The main goal was to produce what Kimble (1969) had referred to as "well-rounded social scientists" with a strong economics background. The major courses taught were Principles of Economics, Economy of Ghana, Statistics for Economists, Intermediate Economics, Development Economics, Advanced Economic Theories and Econometrics. Strong emphasis was on mathematical formalisation and the aim was analytical rigour (Dequech 2007).

Between the period 1957 and the early 1980s, the teaching of economics and economic thinking in Ghana and the rest of Africa witnessed increasing trends in developmental models. Development economics was taught not only in developing countries but also in developed countries. However, it was far less satisfactory in developing countries (Killick 1980). This was due to inadequately qualified faculty members in economics departments. Scientific socialism occupied an important place in Africa due to problems of inequality. The introduction of left-leaning ideas did not change the dominance of neoclassical theories and the methodological framework in the teaching of economics in Ghana.. There was also the strengthening of neoclassical economics. The new cohort of European and North American researchers, as well as African writers, used materials and data from Africa but they were inspired by mainstream economic ideas and methodological techniques.

4. Teaching of economics from 1988 to the present

In 1988, the African Economic Research Consortium (AERC) was established. It is a public not-for-profit organisation devoted to the advancement of economic policy research and training. The main goal is to strengthen local capacity for conducting independent, rigorous enquiry into the problems facing the management of economies in sub-Saharan Africa. AERC aims at increasing the output of economists conversant with, and specialists in, African problems. The expectation is that this will lead to the emergence of various theories and African solutions to these problems (abject poverty, unemployment, deepening inequality, slow economic growth rate, migration and environmental damage). There has been reorientation of the teaching of economics at the Masters and PhD levels. The core courses are microeconomics, macroeconomics and econometrics whilst the electives are diverse and carefully selected to benefit African countries. They consist of agriculture, industry, development, trade, labour, environment, monetary, finance, health, public sector, and industrial economics.

There is intensification of the internal coordination of the economics programmes in Ghana and other African countries. Also, what has characterised the teaching of economics in Ghana and the rest of Africa is the narrowing of the differences among universities. Anglophone universities, Francophone universities and universities in South Africa appear to be harmonising economics programmes. Moreover, many economics departments appear to be forging a common research interest and direction through AERC.

The course content for undergraduate programmes do not appear to be significantly different from those in Europe and North American universities. Advances in analytic technology, such as non-linear dynamics which has made it possible for economists and researchers in Europe and North America to study much more complex models and also computing capabilities, and studies with simulations and agent-based models (Colander et al. 2004), have benefitted economics researchers; more so in universities that have capacity to teach advanced economics courses.[4]

AERC has produced an increasing number of well-trained economists in Africa and many find themselves in economics departments in Ghana and other universities on the continent. Presently, the capacity of economics departments in Ghana has significantly improved and roughly 90% of staff have a PhD. Postgraduate programmes comprising MSc, MPhil and PhD are offered in all economics departments. The courses/programmes have been designed to address Ghanaian and African problems. With significant improvement in the capacity of academic staff, research by the economics departments has intensified and basically been driven by "observed development problems and needs of Ghana and other developing countries" (ISSER files 2017).

However, unlike many universities in Europe and North America, where advanced research (PhD research) on new approaches of mainstream economics or programmes like game theory, experimental economics, institutional economics, evolutionary game theory, and behavioural economics has intensified, economics departments in Ghana and many African countries do not have the capacity at present to conduct such research. Perhaps very few public universities, especially in South Africa (Stellenbosch University and the University of Cape Town) may have the capacity to train PhD candidates using the new approaches of mainstream economics that are popular in economics departments in Europe and North America.

There is increasing awareness among African economists that economics should have practical relevance, i.e. economics should lead to policies that will bring rapid development. Evolutionary economics, institutional economics, experimental economics, neuroeconomics and non-linear complexity, which involve significant departures from neoclassical economics (Davis 2006), have not taken a dominant place in economics research in African universities. From the 1980s to date, economists and researchers continue to be interested in agriculture, labour, finance, resources, and industry and monetary. There have been solid treatments of such specialisms as agricultural, industrial, and monetary economics, as well as economic policy and econometrics (Killick 1980). Developments in the economy are dictating the research frontier and what to teach at the undergraduate and graduate levels but the approach of teaching economics has not significantly changed.

Contrary to Europe and North America, where researchers including Colander (2000), Colander et al. (2004), Davis (2006), Hodgson (2007), and Denis (2009) have been investigating developments or approaches in the teaching of economics, i.e. neoclassical, game theory, institutional, evolutionary, experimental, and behavioural, such studies are scarce in Ghana and the rest of Africa. No reference has yet been made to pluralist economic ideas in Ghana and many other African countries. There has not been any discussion between the economic problems facing the continent and the techniques of teaching economics. The key conflict is not one between pluralism and mainstream. The seeming inactivity of African economists and researchers on new approaches to studying economics could be explained by the increasing economic, political and social problems that the continent of Africa is facing and the urgent need to make their research relevant to the individual countries and the African economy in general. The current group of active researchers in Africa see these issues as much more pressing than the approach of studying economics. Mainstream economic theories and techniques of analysis continue to inspire them.

Subsequently, agitation by students for pluralism in economics, both in methods and theories, that had characterised Europe and North America from the 1960s to the present – University of Sydney in Australia, (1971), Ecole Normale Superieure in France, University of Cambridge and University of Manchester in the UK, and Harvard University in the USA – are absent in Ghana and other African countries. In Anglophone Africa (Ghana, Nigeria, Kenya, Tanzania, etc) and Francophone Africa (Senegal, La Cote d'Ivoire, Togo, Mali, etc) and even in South Africa, no such student movement has taken place. However, in Uganda, the Africa's Young Economists Network was formed in August 2015. Their vision has been to make economics accessible, engaging, pluralistic and relevant to Uganda's development needs. Unfortunately, the group has not indicated what is wrong with mainstream economic theories and techniques of analysis and what specifically it is proposing in order to make economics accessible, engaging, pluralistic and relevant to the development of Uganda. Indeed, very little is known about this group on the continent.

One thing that appears to be missing in Africa, and which might have affected economic thinking in Ghana and other countries on the continent, is the absence of Africa's role in the literature of the development of economic thought. Economics schools such as Mercantilism, Physiocrats, the Classical School, the Keynesian School, the Cambridge School, the Chicago School, the Monetarist School, the Austrian School, Institutionalism, and others have shaped economic thinking in Europe and North America. These ideological blocks in economics have had significant influence on the trends of the various economic ideas that characterised the countries they originated from. For example, the Austrian School associated with methodological individualism and radical subjectivism, the Chicago School associated with maximisation, stable preferences, and market equilibrium, dictate the direction of economic thinking in Austria and America respectively. It will be difficult for ideas imported from elsewhere to completely replace these lines of thinking.

Africa does not have such economic ideas properly documented in the past. It was as late as March 1969 that a conference was held in Dar es Salam, Tanzania with the theme *The Teaching of Economics in Africa*. The goal was to come out with an economics syllabus that would suit Africa, but virtually all the contributors were Europeans. This conference did not change much of the economics taught in African universities. There might have been some changes in the economics syllabus in economics department but the approach has not changed. What the 1969 conference achieved was inclusion of African materials in some textbooks, but microeconomics and macroeconomics continued to be based on the mainstream economics that is taught in Europe and North America.

In Ghana, undergraduate programmes continue to be structured on the principles of universities in the UK and the US. Denis (2009) indicated that in the UK undergraduates are taught a core of mainstream textbook microeconomics and macroeconomics in their first two years, alongside courses in mathematics and statistics, and then a range of optional applications of those core specific topics in specialisms like financial economics, industrial economics, labour economics, health economics and monetary economics in the final year. In economics departments in Ghana and many other universities in Africa, the structure is the same.

There is the need for researchers in Africa to develop models that will capture the African way of life. Researchers should consider looking into the good aspects of African culture and tradition. Teaching solely models built by European and American researchers might not solve the problems of Africa. Backhouse (2000) stated that models might be usable to answer some questions but not others. Communities in Africa have the model of togetherness and the extended family system concept. These could be linked to the institutions of chieftaincy that have played key roles on the continent. Researchers should build models that are linked to reality (Backhouse 2000) on the continent.

The generation of economists from the 1950s to the 1980s did not involve themselves in much active research that addressed the economic problems of Ghana and Africa in general. It was from the 1980s, when many economics departments improved upon the capacity and also with the active involvement of the AERC in the teaching and research activities of some universities, that many African economists became much more active in research. The main change in economics departments, not only in Ghana but the whole of Africa, is the increasing volume of publications. This group of researchers appear to be the first generation of researchers in Africa. It is only when the process of change in the research frontier has gone on for some period of time that the bulk of research reflects what is behind the frontier (Davis 2006).

The major economic problems that have characterised African economies since the twentieth century continue to deepen in the twenty-first century: unemployment, poverty and inequality. These problems have been worsened by environmental damage, globalisation and migration. The subsistence sector is still very large. Planning, import substitution industrialisation, the big push, structural adjustment programmes, globalisation, all these models appear to have failed in Ghana and Africa in general.

African researchers have realised that reasoning is impossible without, and inseparable from, its institutional and material context (Hodgson 2007). Since the 1980s, there has been much more engagement in collaborative research aimed at transforming African economies. Researchers in different parts of Africa come together to address the major issues confronting the continent. With teamwork they are likely to find solutions to Africa's economic problems.

5. Concluding remarks

The main goal of this chapter was to examine the approach and ideas that have characterised the teaching of economics in Ghana. Colonisation, independence, structural adjustment programmes, economic globalisation, and the consortium (AERC) have influenced the teaching of economics and economic policies in Ghana and also in sub-Saharan Africa. Anglo-Saxon economics traditions dominated by neoclassical and neo-Keynesian economics ideas have dominated the teaching of economics from 1950 to the present. The emphasis has been on mathematical rigour, general equilibrium and the marginal concepts. The traditional economic values that were in place before contact with European civilisation – i.e. communal spirit, sharing, job creation through learning skills – became inconsistent with mainstream economic values that Colander et al. (2004) have described as the holy trinity (rationality, selfishness and equilibrium). These traditional Ghanaian and African values were abandoned.

Since the 1980s, much progress has been made as regards the teaching of economics in Ghana and other African countries. The capacity of economics departments and data collection have both improved. In Ghana, in 1987, the Ghana Living Standard Survey (GLSS) started the first round of data collection on individual households. The Ghana Statistical Service and other public agencies (e.g. the Bank of Ghana) now engage in the collection of data that will facilitate analysis of the economy. There has been an increasing volume of publications since 1987 but advanced research on new approaches of mainstream economics – i.e. game theory, experimental economics, institutional economics, evolutionary game theory, and behavioural economics – is limited.

Mainstream economic theories and techniques of analysis continue to stimulate teaching and research in economics departments in Ghana and other African universities. Thus, the key conflict is not between pluralism/heterodoxy and mainstream economics but imported knowledge from Europe and North America that is not applicable in the African context versus economic knowledge that is appropriate for Africa.

Notes

1 E. Meade, *Economic Analysis and Policy*, (London, 1936); F. Benham, *Economics* (London, 1940); K.E. Boulding, *Economic Analysis* (New York, 1941); J.R. Hicks, *The Social Framework* (London, 1942); A. Cairncross, *Introduction to Economics* (London, 1944); P.A. Samuelson, *Economics, An Introductory Analysis* (New York, 1948); J.L. Hanson, *Economics for Students* (London, 1949); A.W. Stonier and D.C. Hague, *A Textbook of Economic Theory* (London, 1953); R.G. Lipsey, *An Introduction to Positive Economics* (London, 1963).

2 R. Nurkse, *Problems of Capital Formation in Underdeveloped Countries* (London, 1953); W. Arthur Lewis, *The Theory of Economic Growth* (London, 1955); G.M. Meier, *Leading Issues in Development Economics* (New York, 1964); A.W. Kamarck, *The Economics of African Development* (New York, 1967); M.P. Todaro, *Economic Development in the Third World: An Introduction to Problems and Policies in a Global Perspective* (1977).
3 The complementary hypothesis suggests that in developing countries the demand for real and financial capital are complements but not substitutes.
4 For example University of Cape Town, Stellenbosch University University of Pretoria, University of Witwatersrand in South Africa, University of Benin and University of Ibadan in Nigeria, University of Ghana and Kwame Nkrumah University of Science and Technology, Kumasi, in Ghana, University Nairobi and Jomo Kenyatta University in Kenya and others.

References

Arthur Lewis, W. (1955): *The Theory of Economic Growth*. London: Unwin Hyman.

Backhouse, R.E. (2000): 'Austrian Economics and the Mainstream: View from the Boundary', *The Quarterly Journal of Austrian Economics* 3 (2), 31–43.

Benham, F. (1940): *Economics: A General Textbook for Students*. London: Pitman.

Boulding, K.E. (1941): *Economic Analysis*. New York: Harper and Row.

Cairncross, A. (1944): *Introduction to Economics*. London: Butterworth & Co.

Colander, D. (2000): 'The Death of Neoclassical Economics', *Journal of the History of Economic Thought* 22 (2), 127–144.

Colander, D., Holt, R., Rosser Jr., B. (2004): 'The Changing Face of Mainstream Economics', *Review of Political Economy* 16 (4), 485–499.

Davis, J.B. (2006): 'The Turn in Economics: Neoclassical Dominance to Mainstream Pluralism?', *Journal of Institutional Economics* 2 (1), 1–20.

Denis A. (2009): 'Editorial: Pluralism in Economics Education', *International Review of Economics Education* 8 (2), 6–22.

Dequech, D. (2007): 'Neoclassical, Mainstream, Orthodox, and Heterodox Economics', *Journal of Post Keynesian Economics* 30 (2), 279–303.

Ewusi, K. (1978): *The Size of the Labour Force and Structure of Unemployment in Ghana*. Technical Publications Series No. 37. Legon, Ghana: Institute of Statistical, Social and Economic Research.

Ewusi, K. (1984): *The Dimensions and Characteristics of Rural Poverty in Ghana*. Technical Publications Series No. 43. Legon, Ghana: Institute of Statistical, Social, and Economic Research.

Hanson, J.L. (1949): *Economics for Students*. London: MacDonald and Evans.

Hicks, J.R. (1942): *The Social Framework, An Introduction to Economics*. Oxford: Clarendon Press.

Hodgson, G.M. (2007): 'Evolutionary and Institutional Economics as the New Mainstream?', *Evolutionary and Institutional Economics Review* 4 (1), 7–25.

ISSER. (2013): *The State of the Ghanaian Economy in 2012*. Legon: Institute of Statistical, Social, and Economic Research.

Kamarck, A.W. (1967): *The Economics of African Development*. New York: Praeger.

Killick, T. (1978): *Development Economics in Action: A Study of Economic Policies in Ghana*. London: Heinemann.

Killick, T. (1980): 'Trends in Development Economics and Their Relevance to Africa', *The Journal of Modern African Studies* 18 (3), 367–386.

Kimble, H. (1969): 'On the Teaching of Economics in Africa', *The Journal of Modern African Studies* 7 (4), 713–741.
Lipsey, R.G. (1963): *An Introduction to Positive Economics*. London: Weidenfeld and Nicolson.
McKinnon, R. (1973): *Money and Capital in Economic Development*. Washington, DC: Brookings Institution.
Meade, E. (1936): *Economic Analysis and Policy*. London: Oxford University Press.
Meier, G.M. (1964): *Leading Issues in Development Economics*. New York: Oxford University Press.
Nurkse, R. (1953): *Problems of Capital Formation in Underdeveloped Countries*. New York: Oxford University Press.
Ord, H.W. and Livingstone, I. (1969): *An Introduction to West African Economics*. London: Heinemann.
Rothbard, M.N. (1997): *The Logic of Action I: Method, Money, and the Austrian School*. Cheltenham, UK: Edward Elgar.
Samuelson, P.A. (1948): *Economics: An Introductory Analysis*. New York: McGraw-Hill Inc.
Seck, D. (2010): *Research in Quantitative Economics by National Research Centers: Assessment for Ghana*. Dakar: Centre for Research on Political Economy.
Shaw, E. (1973): *Financial Deepening in Economic Development*. New York: Oxford University Press.
Stonier, A.W. and Hague, D.C. (1953): *A Textbook of Economic Theory*. London: Longmans Green.
Todaro, M.P. (1977): *Economic Development in the Third World: An Introduction to Problems and Policies in a Global Perspective*. London: Longman.

10 Teaching the euro crisis

What do students in Germany and France learn about the causes of Europe's economic crisis?

Philipp Kortendiek and Till van Treeck

1. Introduction

The on-going economic and financial crisis in the eurozone has led to severe social and political consequences which have shaken the European Union to its very foundations. A number of countries, including Cyprus, Greece, Ireland, Portugal and Spain, have had difficulties refinancing their public debt and have had to be "rescued" by means of new and unconventional financing mechanisms provided by the European Central Bank, the International Monetary Fund and European Union member states. Unemployment rates have risen sharply in many countries, reaching sky-high levels of 25% and more in Greece and Spain, but also in other countries such as Italy and France. Meanwhile, political tensions, both within and between eurozone countries, have been on the rise. In many countries, the established political parties have been losing support among the electorate, to the benefit of more radical political movements. At the international level, the degree of mistrust between creditor and debtor countries, and between Germany and Greece in particular, has grown to levels that most European citizens have never seen before. The project of the common currency is clearly in jeopardy.

Given the high degree of controversy in debates about the euro crisis, an important question to ask is: what do students across Europe learn about the origins and consequences of the crisis? Because today's students are tomorrow's decision-makers, their knowledge about and attitudes towards the causes of the euro crisis will be of the utmost importance in shaping the future development of the European project.

In this chapter,[1] we argue that students in France and Germany, Europe's most populous countries, are likely to be confronted with rather different perspectives on the crisis at high-school level. In what follows, we first sketch two archetypical alternative views, grounded in different economic theories, which have dominated the controversial debates about the causes of and suggested remedies for the euro crisis. We then look at selected teaching materials that are likely to be widely used in classrooms in France and Germany, respectively. We cautiously conclude that the "imperative of controversy", in theory the guiding principle of citizenship education, may not be well respected in many teaching materials on the euro crisis.

2. Two tales of a crisis

Both politicians and economists are sharply divided in their interpretations of the causes of the crisis. For simplicity, in this chapter we distinguish between a "neoclassical" and a "Keynesian" narrative of the euro crisis. This is certainly an oversimplification, because many economists combine neoclassical and Keynesian (and other) elements in their attempts to make sense of the crisis. For pedagogical purposes, however, it is useful to identify two archetypical theoretical approaches in order to emphasise the degree of controversy surrounding the crisis. Moreover, the distinctly "neoclassical" or "ordoliberal" approach to the euro crisis of the German government has been widely noted and contrasted with the "new Keynesian" international mainstream (see Dullien and Guérot 2012). In what follows, we focus only on three rather general themes on which the paradigmatic differences between the "neoclassical" and the "Keynesian" views are particularly pronounced. These are: the role of labour and product market deregulation; the causes and consequences of current account deficits and surpluses; and the role of fiscal policy before and during the crisis. We do not discuss in any detail the specific institutional setting of the eurozone which can be seen as an important factor behind the severity of the crisis in Europe, as compared to other regions of the world which were hit by the global economic crisis of 2009. Also, in what follows, we do not discuss in any detail the policy responses to the crisis, but focus instead on the controversial debate about the causes of the crisis. We refer to the period since early 2010, when the first "rescue package" for Greece was initiated, as the euro crisis.

2.1 The "neoclassical" narrative: the crisis is mainly due to inefficient labour and product market regulations, unproductive use of capital inflows, and fiscal profligacy in the crisis countries

A first influential discourse in current debates is grounded in the neoclassical school of thought (see BpB 2014; Dullien and Guérot 2012). The main tenets of neoclassical economics as somewhat simplistically defined here, include the notions that: (1) the level of employment/unemployment is determined in the labour market and that excessive labour market regulation increases structural unemployment; (2) while large current account deficits are not problematic per se and can be due to catching-up effects in countries with a relatively low per capita income, the capital inflows associated with a current account deficit in such countries should be used for productivity-enhancing investment; (3) sustained government deficits are not only unnecessary to maintain high levels of aggregate demand and employment, but high levels of government spending on goods and services crowd out private spending and tend to reduce the overall efficiency of the production process.

According to the typical neoclassical interpretation of the euro crisis, today's crisis countries have lived beyond their means for too long following the introduction of the euro in 1999. This view can be summarised as follows: instead of using the additional inflows of capital at exceptionally low interest rates after the introduction of the euro for productivity-enhancing investments, today's crisis nations used them for consumption. This led to an unsustainable rise in government debt or private debt. Moreover, while the credit-financed demand boom during the period before the crisis temporarily boosted employment and wages, today's crisis countries failed to conduct the structural labour and product market reforms necessary to remain competitive for international capital inflows and to reduce structural unemployment. When the temporary demand boom stopped, the structural deficiencies on the supply side of the Greek, Spanish, Portuguese and other economies became apparent.

In terms of policy implications, this analysis suggests that structural problems in the deficit countries are at the heart of the crisis. It therefore emphasises the need for reforms primarily at the national level in countries such as Greece, Ireland, Spain and Portugal, but also in other countries with competitiveness problems, including France and Italy. These supply-side reforms include labour market deregulation, wage cuts and fiscal austerity measures.

The crisis is also regarded as a public debt crisis. Today's crisis countries have broken the rules of the European Stability and Growth Pact, which says that government deficits shall never exceed 3 per cent of gross domestic product (GDP), while the total government debt-to-GDP ratio shall never exceed 60 per cent. While some countries, like Greece, broke these rules even before the outbreak of the crisis, other countries, like Spain or Ireland, had low public debt just before the crisis, but saw their public deficits and debt rise as a consequence of their governments' attempts to deal with the economic recession and to take over part of the private sector debt once the crisis had hit. Neoclassical economists, especially those of the ordoliberal type dominant in Germany, typically reject the notion that debt-strapped countries ought to be "rescued" through a "bail-out" by the other member states which are financially more secure. Their argument is that a bail-out would undermine the national responsibility of the crisis countries to implement the reforms considered to be necessary. Instead, the adherents of this approach demand that the rules of the Maastricht criteria regarding public deficit and debt levels be strictly applied and tightened.

2.2 The "Keynesian" narrative: fiscal and wage restraint in export surplus countries like Germany are a major part of the problem

A second discourse in the debates about the euro crisis is grounded in Keynesian economics (see BpB 2014; Dullien and Guérot 2012). In contrast to the main tenets of neoclassical economics as defined above, Keynesian economics traditionally is based on the notions that (1) the level of employment/unemployment is determined by the aggregate demand on goods and services, especially in the short term but also in the medium to long term; (2) because export surpluses (deficits) are interpreted as a result of relatively weak (strong) domestic demand, export (current account) surplus countries should be held to stimulate their domestic demand in an environment of overall demand deficiency; (3) fiscal deficits may be necessary over extended periods of time to maintain high levels of employment, when the private sector demand for goods and services is weak.

Keynesian economists have been critical of the "supply-side"-oriented interpretation of the crisis sketched in the previous subsection. In particular, they have argued that the export deficits of today's crisis countries were essentially the flipside of weak domestic demand and excessive dependence on net exports in a number of countries at the "centre" of the eurozone. Clearly, the export surpluses of one group of countries (including Germany, Austria, the Netherlands and some others) have to be matched by export deficits in other countries (including Greece, Spain, Portugal, but also France and Italy). According to the Keynesian analysis, both the stagnation of wages and middle class incomes and fiscal restraint, especially in Germany, by far Europe's largest economy, have contributed to the trade imbalances within the euro area. The reason, according to this interpretation of the crisis, is that wage repression, labour market deregulation and cuts in Germany's social security system have weakened consumption demand, while at the same time the government implemented a pro-cyclical and contractionary fiscal policy during the first years after the introduction of the euro. Because demand and inflation were so low in Germany during the years following the introduction of the euro, the European Central Bank had to keep interest rates low for a long period in order to support aggregate demand in Germany and other countries of the "centre". This contributed to the excessive growth of private debt in particular in the periphery countries.

Hence, according to this Keynesian view, economic policy in Germany contributed in an important way to the problems of the export-deficit countries. This analysis contradicts the neoclassical view, which suggests that all countries should have followed Germany's lead in deregulating labour markets and putting pressure on wages in order to boost employment. The Keynesian answer to this would be that the euro area as a whole would have fallen into a prolonged recession even before the current crisis if domestic demand had been as weak in the rest of the euro area as it was in Germany during the first years after the creation of the monetary union.

From a Keynesian point of view, a decisive contribution to solving the crisis therefore has to come from the surplus countries, which should increase public investment and stop encouraging wage restraint. Austerity is considered to be an inappropriate answer to the crisis, because it worsens the recession and hinders the stabilisation of debt as a result of shrinking incomes and hence tax revenues. Instead, counter-cyclical fiscal policy and expansionary monetary policy are advocated in order to stabilise the economic situation in the euro area. Deeper economic cooperation of the eurozone member states is called for and, ideally, there should be an economic government for the euro area and a common responsibility for public debt that would allow for more discretionary fiscal policies instead of a strictly rules-based approach. At the minimum, the fiscal consolidation measures and wage cuts in the crisis countries should be limited and complemented by higher government spending and wage increases in those countries with export surpluses.

3. Teaching materials in France and Germany

After having briefly delineated the different discourses on the crisis, the remainder of this paper discusses how the euro crisis is taught in French and German secondary schools. It traces the neoclassical and Keynesian arguments on the crisis in a selection of important teaching materials in order to answer the question of whether the different macroeconomic positions are comparably weighted.

3.1 France: the Ministry of Education invites all students nationwide to make a critical assessment of the official economic policy framework in the euro area and to question neoclassical thinking

In France, the National Ministry of Education has published a specific teaching unit entitled "What is the place of the European Union in the global economy?".[2] It was conceived for final year economics and social sciences classes and is intended for use nationwide. Teachers are not formally bound to use this material in their classes, but it is likely that teachers see it as an important and authoritative guideline. The teaching unit comprises three main parts: "key knowledge" that the students have to acquire, "pedagogical activities and resources" and a "complementary bibliography for teachers". The first two parts are evaluated in this chapter.

The "key knowledge" part has a clear Keynesian flavour. The main conclusion to be conveyed to the students includes the view that the "German choice of wage deflation is a non-generalisable model"[3] for Europe. The rationale for this statement is that not every country within Europe can apply a strategy of lowering wages relative to their trading partners: not every country within the euro area can gain a comparative advantage in terms of labour costs and make their economy grow as a result of substantial trade surpluses (unless non-euro area countries are willing to accept deficits). The students are further intended to learn that the "Stability and Growth Pact [...] has not been a good instrument to prevent and to counter the crisis"[4] and are meant to question the decision that was made by European policy-makers to further tighten the rules of the Pact instead of applying "discretionary policies in favour of growth".[5] In particular, teachers are invited to draw their students' attention to various criticisms of the economic policy mix in Europe: in 2011, the US Secretary of the Treasury criticised the failure of the euro area to boost domestic demand by means of expansionary fiscal policy (see Éduscol 2013, 4). Criticism of the European Central Bank, with its strong focus on the fight against inflation (as opposed to a focus on growth), is also highlighted (ibid.).

The "pedagogical activities and resources" include a section on "the sovereign debt crisis: an indicator for the deficient governance of the eurozone."[6] The activity is to be carried out on the basis of two economic papers, "The eurozone: a difficult childhood"[7] (Creel et al. 2008) and "The eurozone: no future?"[8] (Laurent and Le Cacheux 2010), both published by the French Economic Observatory (OFCE), a publicly funded economics research institute. Additionally, a chapter of the book "Can Europe do without an economic government",[9] published by Jean-Francois Jamet in 2011, can be consulted.

The authors of the first economic paper vividly express their criticisms of the pursuit of external competitiveness by countries like Germany, a strategy which they consider to be a "dangerous obsession".[10] In their view, instead of cooperating, the members of the monetary union would be tempted to enter "a race for price competiveness"[11] whose "effects on the overall economic development of the eurozone are very negative".[12] The authors also address the macroeconomic imbalances within the currency union, but they primarily blame not the deficit countries, but the surplus countries as the main contributors to these divergences. They particularly focus on Germany and its "opportunistic national strategies".[13] They criticise the country for its "rigorous pay restraint and tax competition"[14] that has led to a "persistent weakness of German domestic demand"[15] and "sizeable trade surpluses"[16] and for not "honestly engaging in a stimulus programme".[17] The German model, according to the authors, is "not only ineffective, but also costly for the future of the European project that ruins itself in social and fiscal competition".[18] This paper is hence a very obvious rejection of the neoclassical interpretation of the crisis.

The authors of the second economic paper recommended by the National Ministry of Education harshly criticise European decision-makers for having imposed "austerity on Greece in such a brutal and severe way"[19] and conclude that "it can only be counterproductive".[20] With the implementation of austerity measures, the responsible politicians "have [...] spread the crisis all over the continent",[21] so they argue. They "can only weaken domestic demand in the eurozone and hamper the stabilisation of public debt".[22] This is a univocal representation of Keynesian macroeconomics. Laurent and Le Cacheux equally criticise the "German model", which according to them has "in no way proven to be successful in terms of economic growth and the wellbeing of the citizens".[23] They also strongly reject pay restraint in the deficit countries because that would lead Europe "into the deflationary spiral"[24] and be "economically ineffective and dreadfully costly in terms of political and social consequences".[25] Instead, the authors advocate a European economic government which must not be "the occasion to tighten budgetary discipline"[26] as "adherents of orthodoxy"[27] would demand, but an institution open to discretionary policies, rather than strictly adhering to rules, which is "destined to boost growth in the entire eurozone and [...] to reduce the competitive disadvantages which affect its most vulnerable members".[28] The crisis countries, they suggest, are also in desperate need of an investment programme which they could not implement because "they were grabbed by the scruff of the neck when being forced to announce spending cuts in order to ask for forgiveness and show their good will in the fight against the deficits".[29]

The author of the third recommended text likewise criticises the austerity measures, in particular for their negative impact on investment in Europe (see Jamet 2011, 133). According to him, "the experience of structural adjustments [by the International Monetary Fund] has indeed shown that austerity measures have counterproductive effects when they kill investment".[30] Jamet insists that "investment has to be the crucial element of European growth policy in the upcoming years"[31] and argues that the public sector has to play the leading role in the process. Furthermore, he supports the partial collectivisation of the eurozone governments' debt in order to reduce the borrowing costs of those member states who have to deal with high risk premia on their government bonds (see Jamet 2011, 138).

In short, the materials written or recommended by the French National Ministry of Education manifest a considerable lack of pluralism, because they either neglect or reject neoclassical perspectives on the crisis. Clearly, neoclassical economists, and especially those of the ordoliberal variety that is influential in Germany, strongly oppose any kind of collectivisation of state debt within the currency zone because they fear that this would reduce the incentive for highly indebted countries to restore and maintain healthy public finances.

3.2 Germany: towards a privatisation of citizenship education and tendentious teaching materials with an ordoliberal bias

How is the euro crisis taught in Germany? First of all, it is necessary to touch on the organisation of secondary education in Germany. Due to Germany's federal structure, the responsibility for secondary schools lies with each of the country's 16 states ("Bundesländer") individually. Each state keeps a register of accredited schoolbooks which ought to abide by the "imperative of controversy" which is the cornerstone of the so-called "Beutelsbach consensus" (see also the contribution by Urban, this volume), the unofficial constitution of citizenship education in Germany. The problem, however, is that textbooks quickly become outdated, especially in the social sciences where teachers cannot use textbooks published several years ago when discussing topical events like the euro crisis. In North-Rhine Westphalia, for example, the biggest German state, the vast majority of official social sciences schoolbooks do not touch upon the euro crisis because they are simply too old (see Schulministerium NRW 2015). It can also be expected that many schools do not use the most modern textbooks due to cost considerations. As a result, there are many private and public providers of online education materials, including on the euro crisis, which are widely used by teachers. Yet, unlike textbooks, online teaching materials are not subject to official accreditation procedures and hence the question arises as to whether the "imperative of controversy" is respected in such materials. In fact, the dominance of employer-oriented think tanks in the market for online teaching materials has recently been heavily criticised by many observers (see van Treeck 2014).

As it would be beyond the scope of this chapter to provide a comprehensive assessment of every existing teaching unit on the euro crisis published online, we have chosen three units from three different institutions: the first one is public, the second employer-oriented and the third union-affiliated. While this choice is certainly not representative, it reveals that students will get a very different picture about the causes of the euro crisis depending on the teaching materials that are used in class.

The first text "The euro at a crossroads"[32] (Heinemann and Schmuck 2012) was published by the Federal Agency for Civic Education (BpB), which is an institution subordinate to the Federal Ministry of the Interior. The material is published both in print and online as part of the BpB's flagship publication series, "Information for Citizenship Education" (Informationen zur politischen Bildung) which is intensively used by teachers and students. The two authors conceive the euro crisis as a "debt crisis"[33] and therefore conclude that an "enduring confinement of public debt[34]" is inevitable if the crisis is to be resolved. They argue that the Stability and Growth Pact was not "sufficiently effective in limiting public debt"[35] and that countries with high deficits should have been sanctioned earlier. In particular, Germany and France exceeded the 3 per cent deficit level in 2003, but were not sanctioned. However, the authors do not explain why Germany and France were not subject to speculative attacks on their government bonds during the crisis, despite having a much higher initial public debt ratio (above 60 per cent in 2007) than Spain (36 per cent) or Ireland (25 per cent). In addition to the reduction of public debt, the authors consider it imperative to "improve the competiveness of today's crisis countries"[36] in order to solve the crisis. Their focus on public debt and macroeconomic adjustments in the deficit countries clearly reflects a neoclassical approach to the crisis. In contrast to the French authors, Heinemann and Schmuck (2012, 2) make an unequivocally positive assessment of Germany's trade surpluses. According to Heinemann and Schmuck, Germany's trade surpluses show that Germany benefited more than other countries from the common currency and they were one of the reasons for the country's rapid recovery from the Global Economic Crisis of 2008/9 as well as for the overall positive development of the German economy (see ibid.). The Fiscal Compact, which introduces so-called "debt brakes" following the German example in the eurozone member states, and the Euro Plus Pact, which aims at improving "competitiveness" in the member states, are seen as attempts to address the "roots of the problems"[37] of the eurozone. Moreover, the authors approve of the austerity measures in the deficit countries: although leading to "social hardships"[38] and "testing the political stability of these states",[39] the "necessary consolidation of the deficit countries' national budgets"[40] is considered to be indispensable to tackle the debt crisis. The text clearly lacks pluralism in terms of macroeconomic concepts. Whether the austerity measures in Europe are indeed necessary is far from uncontroversial. In many respects, the material published by the German Federal Agency for Civic Education propagates a view of the crisis that is diametrically opposed to the analysis proposed by the French Ministry of Education.

The second teaching unit is a thematic dossier, published online by "IW Medien", a subsidiary of the employer-financed Cologne Institute for Economic Research (IW Köln). It is part of the online platform "Economics/Economy/Business and School" (Wirtschaft und Schule), which was initiated by the employer-financed think tank "New Social Market Economy" (Neue Soziale Marktwirtschaft, INSM). INSM is highly influential in the market for online teaching materials as well as in the public political debate in Germany more generally. The dossier lists three causes of the crisis: the poor competitiveness of the southern European countries, deficits in trade and current account balances and the notion that external imbalances are particularly problematic in a non-optimal currency area (see Wirtschaft und Schule 2011). The first cause refers to the development of unit labour costs within the eurozone. Due to the "moderate" increase in unit labour costs in Germany, the country's "products remained competitive on international markets, while Southern European goods became more expensive."[41] Students also learn that whenever production costs and hence product prices rise, "the international competitiveness of firms or of entire economies deteriorates: Their products can no longer compete with cheaper international competitors."[42] Thus, according to the authors, the obvious consequence is to cut wages in the south of Europe in order to restore competitiveness. By contrast, the argument that wages may be too low in northern Europe is not mentioned. The second cause of the crisis is exemplified by the case of Greece and Germany: "While [. . .] Greece suffered a current account deficit of minus 16% in 2007, Germany had a sizeable surplus of 7.6%".[43] Following this example, the authors explain how southern European countries amassed considerable deficits and why it is necessary that they eliminate their deficits. Meanwhile, no criticism of the very large surpluses of countries like Germany or the Netherlands is raised in this dossier. Again, this is in sharp contrast to Keynesian ideas. The third cause of the crisis refers to the fact that exchange rates no longer exist between the eurozone countries and that member states no longer operate an independent monetary policy (see Wirtschaft und Schule 2011). Hence, states like Greece, for example, can no longer devaluate the drachma in order to cheapen their domestic products. In principle, a real depreciation by the export-deficit countries could be achieved through wage restraint in the less competitive countries, which is what neoclassical economists would typically advocate, or through wage inflation in the surplus countries such as Germany. However the dossier only mentions one solution: pay restraint and deflation in the deficit countries (see ibid.). On the whole, the material published by "IW Medien" has a clear neoclassical bias.

The third teaching unit "Austerity in Europe: vicious circle or act of liberation?"[44] by Peter Neumaier was published by the Hans-Böckler Foundation which is affiliated to the Confederation of German Trade Unions. In the introduction, the author criticises the labelling of the crisis as a debt crisis, citing the examples of Spain and Ireland whose debt levels had been in line with the Maastricht criteria before the crisis started. This argument is often put forward when the tightening of the rules regarding the debt threshold is criticised. He then states that "the cutback in public spending further aggravates the crisis",[45] which reflects a Keynesian logic. In the main section, Neumaier (2012, 3f.) contrasts supply-side and demand-side economics, referring to the underlying economic theories. He outlines both ordoliberal and Keynesian positions on how to resolve the crisis, the first being that the deficit countries like Spain have to get their debt under control and improve competitiveness, the latter being that austerity causes recession and leads to falling tax revenues, which hinders the stabilisation of state debt (Neumaier 2012, 3). By mentioning both Keynesian and neoclassical arguments, the teaching unit shows a clear attempt to respect the "imperative of controversy". However, it is also apparent that the teaching unit is especially concerned with explaining Keynesian reasoning. For example, it contains a text with the title "Austerity in Europe: vicious circle instead of act of liberation"[46] which is a direct and one-sided response to the question asked in the title of the teaching unit. The text is a critique of austerity which is viewed as detrimental to "growth and employment".[47] The author asserts that hardly any empirical evidence exists to prove that "austerity bolsters the confidence of consumers and investors",[48] and that, quite the contrary, it supposedly leads to the collapse of demand from which "all eurozone countries are suffering".[49] The material published by the Hans-Böckler Foundation is certainly the most controversial among those analysed in this chapter, even though it is not entirely pluralistic either.

4. Is this how Europe wants to educate its citizens and its future voters and leaders?

On the whole, the education materials analysed in this paper are unsatisfactory in terms of balancing Keynesian and neoclassical views on the euro crisis. The materials recommended by the French National Ministry of Education are mostly based on Keynesian perspectives on the crisis whereas the German teaching units largely represent neoclassical perspectives, with the exception of the trade union-related material.

Clearly, the discrepancy between the ways in which the euro crisis is presented in the teaching materials in the European Union's two largest member countries, France and Germany, seems to be at odds with its objective to promote international dialogue especially within the young generation. Especially striking are the very different views of the euro crisis propagated in the teaching materials published by the French National Ministry of Education, on the one hand, and the German Federal Agency for Civic Education on the other.

It must be re-emphasised that our choice of teaching materials discussed in this short chapter is by no means representative. For example, the German Federal Agency for Civic Education recently published a new online dossier which informs readers about the ongoing debates over the causes of and potential remedies for the euro crisis in an explicitly and systematically pluralistic fashion (see BpB 2014). While such attempts at controversy and pluralism are to be applauded, the question remains why both the National Ministry of Education and the Federal Agency for Civic Education publish such one-sided accounts of the euro crisis in their guidelines to students and flagship publications, respectively. In the German context, the phenomenon of tendentious teaching materials designed for public school classes and published by private interest groups is a separate, but equally pressing concern.

It would be highly pertinent to examine to what extent the differences in teaching materials actually influence students in Germany and France in their perception of and knowledge about the crisis. It would be deplorable if Europe's students were as one-sided and nationally oriented in their interpretations of the crisis as their current political leaders.

Notes

1 This chapter is based on the BA Thesis "Enseigner la crise/ Die Krise unterrichten - Eine Analyse von deutschen und französischen Unterrichtsmaterialien zur Eurokrise", by Philipp Kortendiek under the supervision of Professor Till van Treeck, University of Duisburg-Essen.

2 "Quelle est la place de l'Union européenne dans l'économie globale ?" (Éduscol 2013, 1).

3 "(. . .) le choix d'une déflation salariale par l'Allemagne qui rend le 'modèle allemand' non généralisable" (Éduscol 2013, 5).

4 "(. . .) le Pacte de Stabilité et de Croissance [. . .] n'a pas été un bon instrument pour prévenir la crise et pour y répondre" (Éduscol 2013, 4).

5 "(. . .) une politique discrétionnaire en faveur de la croissance." (Éduscol 2013, 5).

6 "La crise des dettes souveraines: un révélateur des défauts de gouvernance de la zone euro" (Éduscol 2013, 6).

7 "La zone euro: une enfance difficile" (Creel et al. 2008).

8 "Zone euro: no future ?" (Laurent and Le Cacheux 2010).

9 "L'Europe peut-elle se passer d'un gouvernement économique ?" (Jamet 2011).

10 "(. . .) dangereuse obsession" (Creel et al. 2008, 4).

11 "(. . .) course à la compétitivité-coût" (Creel et al. 2008, 4).

12 "(. . .) dont les effets sur la croissance globale de la zone sont très négatifs" (Creel et al. 2008, 4).

13 "(. . .) stratégies opportunistes nationales" (Creel et al. 2008, 4).

14 "(...) une politique rigoureuse de modération salariale et de concurrence fiscale" (Creel et al. 2008, 4).
15 "(...) une faiblesse persistante de la demande intérieure allemande" (Creel et al. 2008, 4).
16 « (...) des excédents commerciaux considérables" (Creel et al. 2008, 4).
17 « (...) s'engager franchement dans un plan de relance coordonné" (Creel et al. 2008, 4).
18 "(...) non seulement inefficace mais coûteuse pour l'avenir même du projet européen, qui s'abîme dans la concurrence sociale et fiscale." (Creel et al. 2008, 4).
19 "(...) une austérité si brutale et si sévère" (Laurent and Le Cacheux 2010, 1).
20 "(...) sera à coup sûr contre-productive" (Laurent and Le Cacheux 2010, 1).
21 "(...) ont [...] répandu la crise partout sur le continent" (Laurent and Le Cacheux 2010, 1).
22 "(...) ne peuvent que déprimer la demande intérieure de la zone euro, rendant la stabilisation des endettements publics encore plus problématique" (Laurent and Le Cacheux 2010, 2).
23 "(...) aucunement fait la preuve de son succès en termes de croissance économique et de bien-être des citoyens." (Laurent and Le Cacheux 2010, 2).
24 "(...) dans la spirale déflationniste" (Laurent and Le Cacheux 2010, 3).
25 "(...) économiquement inefficace et horriblement coûteux socialement, voire politiquement" (Laurent and Le Cacheux 2010, 4).
26 "(...) l'occasion de renforcer les disciplines budgétaires » (Laurent and Le Cacheux 2010, 2).
27 "(...) tenants de l'orthodoxie" (Laurent and Le Cacheux 2010, 2).
28 "(...) destinées à promouvoir la croissance dans l'ensemble de la zone euro et [...] la réduction des handicaps de compétitivité de ses membres les plus vulnérables" (Laurent and Le Cacheux 2010, 2).
29 "(...) pris au collet par les exigences d'afficher immédiatement des programmes de réduction de dépenses pour faire acte de contrition et de bonne volonté dans la lutte contre les déficits" (Laurent and Le Cacheux 2010, 2).
30 "L'expérience des ajustements structurels du FMI a en effet montré que les politiques d'austérité ont des effets pervers lorsqu'elles tuent l'investissement" (Jamet 2011, 132).
31 "L'investissement doit donc constituer le cœur de la politique européenne de croissance de ces prochaines années..." (Jamet 2011, 133).
32 "Euro am Scheideweg" (Heinemann and Schmuck 2012, 1).
33 "Schuldenkrise" (Heinemann and Schmuck 2012, 1).
34 "die Staatsverschuldung nachhaltig einzudämmen" (Heinemann and Schmuck 2012, 1).
35 "nicht wirksam genug in der Begrenzung von Staatsverschuldung" (Heinemann and Schmuck 2012, 1).
36 "die Wettbewerbsfähigkeit der Krisenländer zu steigern" (Heinemann and Schmuck 2012, 1).
37 "Wurzeln des Problems" (Heinemann and Schmuck 2012, 6).
38 "sozialen Härten" (Heinemann and Schmuck 2012, 6).
39 "politische Stabilität [...] dieser Länder auf eine harte Probe gestellt" (Heinemann and Schmuck 2012, 6).
40 "notwendigen Konsolidierungen der nationalen Haushalte der Defizitländer" (Heinemann and Schmuck 2012, 6).
41 "Deutsche Produkte blieben auf den internationalen Märkten wettbewerbsfähig, südeuropäische Waren wurden teurer" (Wirtschaft und Schule 2011).
42 "Ein Anstieg der Produktionskosten geht in der Regel mit einer Erhöhung des Verkaufspreises einher. Dadurch verschlechtert sich die internationale

Wettbewerbsfähigkeit der betroffenen Firmen oder auch einer ganzen Volkswirtschaft: Ihre Erzeugnisse können preislich nicht mehr mit der günstigeren internationalen Konkurrenz mithalten" (Wirtschaft und Schule 2011).

Technically, this statement is obviously absurd, because it implies that nominal unit labour costs should never increase, but this would imply that either inflation would have to be zero (which would run counter to the inflation target of the European Central Bank of approximately 2 per cent) or the share of wages in the national income would converge to zero over the longer term.

43 "Während [. . .] Griechenland 2007 in der Leistungsbilanz ein Minus von 16 Prozent hinnehmen musste, kam Deutschland auf einen beträchtlichen Überschuss von 7,6 Prozent" (Wirtschaft und Schule 2011).

44 "Europas Sparpolitik – Teufelskreis oder Befreiungsschlag?" (Neumaier 2012, 1).

45 "Die Kürzung staatlicher Ausgaben verschärft die Krise zusätzlich" (Neumaier 2012, 1).

46 "Europas Sparpolitik: Teufelskreisstatt Befreiungsschlag (Neumaier 2012, 7).

47 "Wachstum und Beschäftigung" (Neumaier 2012, 7).

48 "Sparkurs das Vertrauen von Konsumenten und Investoren stärke" (Neumaier 2012, 7).

49 "leiden alle Eurostaaten" (Neumaier 2012, 7).

References

BpB. (2014): 'Europäische Schuldenkrise', available at http://www.bpb.de/politik/wirtschaft/schuldenkrise/, accessed on 21 June 2015.

Creel, J., Fitoussi, J.-P., Laurent, E. and Le Cacheux, J. (2008): 'La zone euro: une enfance difficile', *Lettre de l'OFCE* 304, available at http://www.ofce.sciences-po.fr/pdf/lettres/304.pdf, accessed on 21 June 2015.

Dullien, S. and Guérot, U. (2012): 'The long shadow of ordoliberalism: Germany's approach to the euro crisis', European Council on Foreign Relation, Policy Brief 49/2012.

Éduscol (2013): 'Fiche 2.2: Quelle est la place de l'Union européenne dans l'économie globale?', available at http://cache.media.eduscol.education.fr/file/SES_terminale_allegements/32/6/2.2_UE_ds_l_eco_-_cor_264326.pdf, accessed on 21 June 2015.

Heinemann, F. and Schmuck, O. (2012): 'Euro am Scheideweg?' *Info aktuell*, Bundeszentrale für politische Bildung, available at https://www.bpb.de/system/files/dokument_pdf/Euro_barrierefrei_2.pdf, accessed on 19 September 2017.

Jamet, J.-F. (2011): 'L'Europe peut-elle se passer d'un gouvernement économique?', La documentation française. http://www.ladocumentationfrancaise.fr/catalogue/9782110091734/index.shtml, accessed on 19 September 2017.

Laurent, E. and Le Cacheux, J. (2010): 'Zone euro: no future?', *Lettre de l'OFCE* 320, available at http://www.ofce.sciences-po.fr/pdf/lettres/320.pdf, accessed on 21 June 2015.

Neumaier, P. (2012): 'Europas Sparpolitik– Teufelskreis oder Befreiungsschlag?', Böckler Schule, Unterrichtseinheit Klasse 9 bis Sek II/Eurokrise, available at https://www.boeckler.de/6299.htm?produkt=HBS-005547&chunk=1, accessed on 12 September 2017.

Schulministerium NRW. (2015): 'Verzeichnis der zugelassenen Lernmittel: Gymnasiale Oberstufe, Sozialwissenschaften', available at https://www.schulministerium.nrw.de/docs/Schulsystem/Medien/Lernmittel/Gymnasiale_Oberstufe/index.html#A_30, accessed on 21 June 2015.

van Treeck, T. (2014): 'Wirtschaftsweise im Klassenzimmer', *Capital*, 8 December 2014, available at http://www.capital.de/meinungen/wirtschaftsweise-im-klassenzimmer-3122.html, accessed on 12 September 2017.

Wirtschaft und Schule (2011): 'Die Ursachen der Euro-Schuldenkrise', available at http://www.wirtschaftundschule.de/aktuelle-themen/globalisierungeuropa/schuldenkrise-der-euro-laender/die-ursachen-der-euro-schuldenkrise/, accessed on 21 June 2015.

Part III

Economics textbooks

Failures and new pathways

11 "Waging the war of ideas"

Economics as a textbook science and its possible influence on human minds[1]

Silja Graupe

1. Introduction

Globally, economics is booming as a discipline. By 1995, one and a half million students annually enrolled in the introductory economics course in US colleges and universities alone (Nasar 1995). "This introductory course is both the first and the last brush that most educated Americans have with supply and demand, marginal cost, comparative advantage and other first principles of the dismal science" (ibid). One could make a similar observation about the approximately 540,000 students of economics departments in German universities who make up about twenty percent of all students (Statistisches Bundesamt 2016). Whether enrolled in business or economics study courses, in their introductory microeconomics and macroeconomics classes, students are obliged to confront economic thought. Even if in the past most ambitious economists focused "on the kind of esoteric research that might win them a Nobel Prize," they are now jumping at the chance "to mould the minds of the next generation of political leaders, executives, image makers and other members of the (. . .) elite" (Nasar 1995). We are not simply speaking about the power to shape individual lectures or seminars; rather, the great names in the guild strive to write textbooks powerful enough to *dictate the canons of their discipline to almost all universities around the world.*

To begin with, it is a question of dominance within a giant market. In the United States alone, the market for introductory economics textbooks amounts to about fifty million dollars per year. Of the thirty to forty books that compete for this revenue, a handful secure the lion's share. Of these blockbusters, as the *New York Times* has called them, and not without admiration, each profited from the sale of about 50,000 books annually at about fifty five dollars per book (Nasar 1995). The first fifteen editions of Paul Samuelson's *Economics* (from 1948–1995) sold approximately four million copies, not counting the more than forty translations (Skousen 1997). The careers of other textbook authors have been similarly steep. For example, take Gregory N. Mankiw, who was chairman of the Council of Economic Advisers under President George W. Bush. He was not only paid by Harcourt Publishers a record advance of 1.4 million dollars for his textbook, *Principles of*

Economics, but also received a bonus of twenty-two percent for each copy sold – with sales reaching well beyond a million.[2] Here, too, we are not counting the revenue garnered from over ten translations (Nasar 1995).

Yet the *superstars* of the intro economics textbook business do not simply seek money and wealth. By their own account, they are much more invested in the struggle to secure the best minds in our society. "The top three or four textbooks, even the top 10, are profitable, wildly profitable" admits, for example, Mankiw. He adds: "Besides, economists are proselytizers" (quoted in Nasar 1995). Paul Samuelson formulates the point as follows: "*My interest was not so much in dollars as in influencing minds*" (quoted in Gottesman et al. 2005, 98, my emphasis). Here, as in the fact that authors like Samuelson are, especially in the United States, often treated as "high priests" and their books as "bibles" or "gospels",[3] we find that economists not only desire the massive sale of their standard intro economics textbooks, they also want these to be *read* a million-fold. They wish their content to be actually learned and understood, pushed, if necessary, by the constant pressure of grading and exams.[4] It all comes down to explicitly influencing the ideas, attitudes, and imaginations of each new generation:

> It is hard to gauge the influence of Samuelson's textbook, or in general the impact of introductory courses in economics, on U.S. policymakers or corporate executives. Samuelson has been willing to claim, with tongue only slightly in cheek, a considerable impact. He has made a well-known comment: "I don't care who writes a nation's laws – or crafts its advanced treaties – if I can write its economics textbooks." He has also expressed hope that his textbook would be a reference guide for former students. "When the election of 1984 rolls around," he wrote in 1967, 'all the hours that the artists and editors and I have spent in making the pages as informative and authentic as possible will seem to me well spent if somewhere a voter turns to the old book from which he learned economics for a rereasoning of the economic principle involved.
>
> Skousen (1997, 149–150)

Mankiw writes in his preface to the instructor:

> Economists have a unique way of viewing the world, much of which can be taught in one or two semesters. My goal in this book is to transmit this way of thinking to the widest possible audience and to convince readers that it illuminates much of the world around them.
>
> Mankiw (2001, vii)

Already back in 1955, Samuelson answered the question of why young people should study economics with the following words of John Maynard Keynes:

> The ideas of economists and political philosophers, both when they are right and when they are wrong, are more powerful than is commonly understood. Indeed the world is ruled by little else. Practical men, who believe themselves to be quite exempt from any intellectual influence, are usually the slaves of some defunct economist. Madmen in authority, who hear voices in the air, are distilling their frenzy from some academic scribbler of a few years back. I am sure the power of vested interests is vastly exaggerated compared with the gradual encroachment of ideas.
>
> Samuelson (1955, 12)

This allows us to discover an important thesis about the function of economics as a science: it not only investigates what is (as a positive science) and what should be (as a normative science), but can influence, through its fundamental ideas, what facts and norms are recognised as such in society. It forms something like the base of thought from which we think about the economy and society, without ever reflecting on it in turn. It determines, tacitly, the assumptions of our scientific reason, without, conversely, being interrogated by that reason. Thus, economics immobilises what can appear to us as the most interesting problems or relevant questions in science. Instead, it forms what Ludwik Fleck (1980, 130[5]) would call a *thought style*: "It is readiness for both selective feeling and for correspondingly directed action.... It constrains the individual and determines what cannot be thought in any other way."

2. Economics as a textbook science

Critical economists like Steve Keen see in this nothing less than a campaign of ideological persuasion: "What I had initially thought was an education in economics was in fact little better than an indoctrination" (Keen 2010, xiii). But how can economics education really play a fundamental role in influencing people's opinions? In order to be able to relate to Keen's reproach, we first need to understand how the self-conception of economics as a science has substantially changed over the last seventy years or so. Originally, economics had defined itself by means of its subject matter: it sought to explain the world of commerce (see, for example, Becker 1990). In this way, what economists did was rather well-defined. They were supposed to analyse what were commonly seen as "commercial" or "economic" matters.[6] This limitation in relation to the object of research stood in contrast to a great freedom with regard to the manner of research. Each economist could freely control his methodological approach, and thus how he was to conduct his research. In consequence, economic science conceived itself as a field governed by plurality: it unified a number of perspectives on "economic" phenomena. Modern economics, however, negates this pluralistic self-understanding and inverts the freedom of the researcher into its exact opposite. Gary Becker, a leading figure of the Chicago School of Economics and the Nobel Prize winner in economics in 1992, codified this about-turn as follows: "That which distinguishes economics as a discipline from other disciplines in the social sciences is not its subject matter *but its approach*" (Becker 1990, 5, my emphasis). Scientific freedom means, for Becker, that fundamentally all social subjects may be analysed by the economist: from "fertility, education and the uses of time, crime, marriage, social interactions, and other 'sociological,' 'legal,' and 'political' problems" (ibid., 8). Nothing less than all human behaviour gets reduced to an object of economic research:

> Indeed, I have come to the position that the economic approach is a comprehensive one that is applicable to all human behavior, be it behavior involving money prices or imputed shadow prices, repeated or infrequent decisions, large or minor decisions, emotional or mechanical ends, rich or poor persons, men or women, adults or children, brilliant or stupid persons patients or therapists, businessmen or politicians, teachers or students.
>
> (ibid.)

Under the flag of this economic imperialism,[7] modern economics claims absolute freedom in the choice of its subject matter. Yet this is bought at the price of a substantial limitation of the choice over one's research methods. The economist must (and should!) probe absolutely everything in the world. But he has to approach it from a single angle of vision: that of modern microeconomics or neoclassical theory. Only the "combined assumptions of maximizing behavior, market equilibrium, and stable preferences, used relentlessly and unflinchingly, form the heart of the economic approach" (ibid., 5). While the economist may have become free to analyse everything in the world, he has no choice regarding the rules of thought by which he undertakes this analysis. In order to preserve the unity of economics as a science, he must renounce the multiplicity of conceptual possibilities in order to align himself with a single technique of thinking. In this way, a monoculture of thought is established that extends far beyond the borders of what we usually understand to be "economic" or "commercial."

Often I hear colleagues reply that one can easily exaggerate the power of this monoculture if one ignores, on the one hand, the many directions that are alternative to the economic mainstream, and on the other hand refuses to recognise the extent to which the mainstream itself continually works so as to perfect and refine its approach. These objections might be justified, at most, with respect to research. But in regard to the curriculum, they certainly mistake the actual heart of things. Because in the lecture halls of the world, neoclassical sophistry does not count; nor does its critique. Both are not taught, or only taught to a few Masters students in later semesters. It is much more likely that the following prevails:

> Normal science can keep the student and practitioner on the straight and narrow if there develops an interpretive tradition that makes it unnecessary

> to consult the canonical texts with all their ambiguity, passion, and contingency. The development of textbooks is a hallmark of that interpretive tradition. Teachers of economics sometimes complain that, pedagogical style apart, current economics textbooks are almost all alike. (...) The existence of canonical textbooks is a considerable part of what distinguishes economics from other social sciences.
>
> Pearce and Hoover (1995, 184)

A remark attributed to Paul Samuelson goes: "Economists are said to disagree too much but in ways that are too much alike: If eight sleep in the same bed, you can be sure that, like Eskimos, when they turn over, they'll all turn over together" (quoted in Weinstein 2009). This aptly hits on the superstars of the intro economics textbooks, especially with regard to their microeconomic insights. In this case, it even seems wholly appropriate to say – to remain with Samuelson's image – that all have slept in the same bed for decades, but up to now none of them, either individually or together, has turned over.

Let us look at this more closely: today's economic doctrine is commonly divided into the domains of microeconomics and macroeconomics. To put it a little simply, microeconomics is ascribed the task of explaining, mainly, the individual behaviour of economic actors. Here they divide the social world into two classes: the consumer and the producer. Then they observe the behaviour of a single individual of each class, in order to draw conclusions about all consumers or producers. Thus, microeconomics gives us a methodological individualism[8] in which the behaviour of groups can only be explained from the aggregation of individual actions. On this basis, there arises the image of an ideal market. It is imagined that individual consumers with already given preferences always meet individual suppliers with likewise fixed ideas of profit on markets as though for the first time. Social interaction is considered an end result in this view, but is not seen in turn as the driving force behind individual utility and gain calculi. Modern macroeconomics appropriates the principles of methodological individualism unhesitatingly, in order to dedicate itself to the representation and shaping of the mutual effects of different markets, for example those of commodities, labour and capital. It is understood, in other words, to be micro founded. Already from this rudimentary description we can see the fact that microeconomics fundamentally shapes how human beings and humanity in general are conceived which then bases all further economic descriptions of social interactions on these conceptions. Pprecisely in regard to this subject area the following holds true: even if the macroeconomic content of all standard textbooks already shows "a surprising degree of consensus" (Walstad et al. 1998, 198–199), microeconomics represents precisely that subject area where "the victory of Samuelson's early pedagogy has been most complete and where the beliefs of economists have changed least" (Skousen 1997, 138). Whether in Greek, German, Chinese, Japanese, Hebrew, Serbo-Croatian or Spanish, and under whatever title: in regard to the basic understanding of humanity and human action, all the important economics textbooks of our time establish a single, unified language.

Additionally, current economics textbooks, almost without exception, are based on a single economic theory of human behaviour that was already established in the middle of the 19th century: the neo-classical. In this way, they prevent students of this science from encountering the usual multiplicity of perspectives, visions and ideas:

> More than a decade before I became an undergraduate, a major theoretical battle had broken out over the validity of economic theory. Yet none of this turned up in the standard undergraduate or honours curriculum – unless it was raised by some dissident instructor. There were also entire schools of thought which were antithetical to conventional economics, which again were ignored unless there was a dissident on staff.
>
> Keen (2010, xiii)

In order to trace this phenomenon more precisely, I suggest grasping microeconomics as a textbook or normal science, as described by the famous philosopher of science Thomas S. Kuhn (1996, 17). Textbook science, according to Kuhn, is informed by a pedagogic concept that in essence rests on forgetting history, or more precisely, on an almost complete neglect of one's own intellectual history and history of ideas:

> Textbooks, however, [are] pedagogic vehicles for the perpetuation of normal science. (...) Textbooks thus begin by truncating the scientist's sense of his discipline's history and then proceed to supply a substitute for what they have eliminated. Characteristically, textbooks of science contain just a bit of history, either in an introductory chapter or, more often, in scattered references to the great heroes of an earlier age. From such references both students and professionals come to feel like participants in a long-standing historical tradition. Yet the textbook-derived tradition in which scientists come to sense their participation is one that, in fact, never existed.
>
> Kuhn (1996, 138)

Certainly, Kuhn himself was making this statement simply in regard to the natural sciences. Yet economics has attempted, since its origin in the 18th century, to be a science "which resembles the physico-mathematical sciences in every respect" (Walras 1969, 71). This ambition is mirrored in a neglect of history manifested in the way economics textbooks veil the ancestry and dynamic history of their science and abbreviate it beyond recognition, a process very similar to what Kuhn describes in the case of the natural sciences. For instance, in the first edition of Samuelson's *Economics* we find just a single page dedicated to the history of economics (Samuelson 1955, 12–13). This is presented by Samuelson as an "ancestral portrait gallery," in which he only mentions five economists: John Maynard Keynes and Adam Smith, whom he praises, Karl Marx, whom he refers to as the "black sheep" of the economics profession, as well as David Ricardo and John Stuart Mill.[9] In the newer editions of his textbook, even these rudimentary descriptions have been dropped; instead we find a few disparate references to "important figures in economics" (Samuelson and Nordhaus 2005, xx). If the student already finds it almost impossible to clearly locate scholarly positions and approaches within the original multiplicity of economics opinions and perspectives, other textbooks abandon even these most sporadic remarks on the intellectual history of economics. Mankiw (2001), for instance, does not waste one word on it, and Varian (2007) does just as little.

"The depreciation of historical fact is deeply, and probably functionally, ingrained in the ideology of the scientific profession" (Kuhn 1996, 138). Yet with the loss of one's proper intellectual history, an awareness of the plurality of perspectives and methodological approaches, which once were the glory of the science, vanishes as well. Commerce and society appear differently depending on the perspective from which we envision them. Our "methodological lenses" decide what aspects of the economy we will focus on and how we do so. They also determine what problems remain essentially hidden. Many of the central problems of present day commerce remain completely in the dark as long as we only observe them from the angle of the economic mainstream. Thus, for instance, Norbert Häring in his study "Markt und Macht" ("Power and Markets", Häring 2010) represents how textbook economics systematically obstructs from taking into account the phenomenon of market power. This can similarly be shown for creativity (Brodbeck 1996) or the inherent dynamic of markets (Schumpeter 1942; Sraffa 1926; Keen 2010). In this way, systematic blindness is abetted, which already led Joan Robinson to the following question:

> It is true that we cannot, in the time available, teach everything that we would like. But why do we pick out for treatment just that selection of topics that is least likely to raise any questions of fundamental importance?
>
> quoted in Hill and Myatt 2010, 1

"The point is: The way we think changes things... Freedom of thought depends on the fact that one can choose between different ways of thinking" (Hedtke 2008, 5–6). Correct and important as this insight is, it is just as completely ignored by textbook economics for which "multiple perspectives" is a foreign term that is never mentioned once, even as a possibility. "For every critical economic issue there are competing concepts and theories that lead to different conclusions. The problem is that when they are not missing from textbooks altogether, these theories are almost always summarily dismissed" (Adler 2010, vx). "But if barred from all alternatives, one never realizes that a choice exists between different thought concepts" (Hedtke 2008, 6).

The newer textbooks in particular drive such methodological monism to extremes, in as much as they do not even make their own perspective clear as a means of knowing. There exists a systematic difference between the observer and the observed, or between the knower and the known, and it is the task of an introductory chapter on the scope and methods of science to make the reader aware, at least, of this difference. What commerce looks like to economists, how it appears to them, is not simply equivalent to commercial reality as such. Yet Varian, for instance, simply sweeps aside such reflections as superfluous. He writes explicitly that "it is rather inappropriate to begin the study of the economy with it" (Varian 2007, 1). Mankiw (2001, 3–17) takes this kind of pedagogy even further. At the beginning of his textbook, he explains his "ten principles of economics" so that they appear as simple facts, and not as a higher level, selective description of facts.For example, take Mankiw's fourth principle "people respond to incentives" (Mankiw 2001, 7). This principle essentially tells us to analyse individual behaviour in the framework of a stimulus-response model: we are to preconceive people as if they automatically and unconsciously altered their behaviour in response to changes in market prices. As such, Mankiw essentially leads us to highlight certain characteristics of human beings, i.e. the easily predictable, while erasing others, i.e. the thoughtful, creative and essentially non-determinable aspects of human activity. But Mankiw does not reveal this as a methodological pre-adjustment. He rather pretends to speak about reality as such. He simply tells us that all people factually respond to incentives. Thus he misleads his students into taking a specific view of social reality uncritically as the equivalent of or the substitute for this reality.

At least with Paul Samuelson one can perceive that such leveling is in no way unintended, but is instead a conscious pedagogical programme. In this manner, he confronted millions of students at the beginning of his textbook with the following message :

> We must "firstly develop the faculty in ourselves to see things without partisanship or previous assumptions, that is, to see them as they really are, and without reference to whether that is pleasant or unpleasant to us. (. . .) We know that a doctor passionately interested in stamping out disease must first train himself to observe things as they are. (. . .) Similarly, there are elements of valid reality in a given economic situation, however hard it may be to recognize and isolate them. There is not one theory of economics for Republicans and one theory for Democrats, one for workers and one for employers. . . On many basic principles concerning prices and employment, most – if not all! – economists are in fairly close agreement.[10]
>
> Samuelson 1955, 5–6

These few references may satisfy us in order to show how textbook economics narrows the student's understanding systematically down to a single perspective. Instead of making this limitation known, economics leads the student to apply this perspective to ever more commercial as well as social phenomena, and to describe the latter on this basis in continually more refined detail. Students are thus hindered from developing their own thought, if even completely blocked in regard to the following: They are neither given the tools to critically reflect the basis of the assumptions underlying their own thought, nor to transform them in any way. Kuhn (1996) has made a similar point with regard to the natural sciences. The praxis of science "will seldom evoke overt disagreement over fundamentals" (11). "Given a textbook, ...the creative scientist can begin his research where it leaves off and thus concentrate exclusively on the subtlest and most esoteric aspects of the natural phenomenon that concern his group" (ibid., 20). At the same time, the student is isolated from all social problems that cannot be described with the help of the conceptual instruments of economic textbook science. He is, in other words, compelled to banish all of those problems that cannot be adequately focused within the economic perspective to the realm of the irrational and unscientific – even if they occur to him, as a human being, to be obvious and pressing.

3. The shaping of public opinion and the possible role of economics education

What role can such narrowing of perspective serve within society? The following is concerned with an epistemological clarification of this issue, to which in particular neoliberal thinkers such as Friedrich A. Hayek and Walter Lippmann are considered here to have substantially contributed.[11] Let us shortly turn to the question of "truth" in economics. Paul A. Samuelson's textbook "Economics" purports to impart "enduring truths" (Samuelson and Nordhaus, 2005, xvii). But what are "core truths of economics" in the context of education? According to Hayek, one of the most important representatives of liberalism and neoliberalism in the 20th century, "truth" with regard to economic theories is not about verifying their "truth" or "falsehood" in any empirical sense. What Hayek means in contrast, is that "the power of abstract ideas rests primarily on the fact that they are indeed not consciously accepted as theories but rather that most people receive them as immediately evident truths, which function as silently accepted conditions" (Hayek 1980, 100[12]). People are likely to accept economic theories as true without being able to verify their accuracy. In this sense "truth" is a function of a system of power: those whose theories are accepted as truth are, according to Hayek's thought, the ones who can rule the world. A quick look into the theory and practice of manipulating public opinion, as it has evolved since the beginning of the last century, helps to provide a clearer understanding of what this means from an epistemological point of view. In his seminal work *Propaganda*, published in 1928, Edward Bernays writes:

> The conscious and intelligent manipulation of the organized habits and opinions of the masses is an important element in democratic societies. Those who manipulate this unseen mechanism of society constitute an invisible government which is the true ruling power of our country.
>
> Bernays (2005[1928], 37)

Bernays is considered an essential discoverer of the role played by the unconscious mind in particular with regard to its political significance and instrumentalisation. He created the idea that the collective unconscious (of "the masses") could be influenced and controlled by a few ("the elite"). Walter Lippmann, a close companion of Hayek and founding father of neoliberalism, elaborated on this idea in his work *Public Opinion* Lippmann (1922). According to Lippmann, we are all slaves to the pictures in our heads. He explicitly mentions

> the insertion between man and his environment of a pseudo-environment. To that pseudo-environment his behavior is a response. But because it *is* behavior, the consequences, if they are acts, operate not in the pseudo-environment where the behavior is stimulated, but in the real environment where action eventuates.
>
> Lippmann (1922, 15, emphasis in the original)

Under the circumstances of such insertion of a pseudo-environment, a person cannot be a conscious participant in real world activities. She cannot form her judgments based on the experience made in it. Rather, predetermined pictures of the world keep her detached from reality. The stereotype, as Lippmann describes these pictures, is marked by the fact that "it precedes the use of reason; is a form of perception, imposes a certain character on the data of our senses before the data reach the intelligence" (ibid., 71). As a result it establishes a cognitive barrier between people and the concrete world they live in.

> Real space, real time, real numbers, real connections, real weights are lost. The perspective and the background and the dimensions of actions are clipped and frozen in the stereotype.
>
> (ibid., 110)

Every decision is to be made quasi-automatically based on a particular worldview. "Mental habits", Bernays writes, "create stereotypes just as physical habits create certain definite reflex actions" (Bernays 1961, 162). From this perspective individuals are left with no other choice than to react to the outside world according to predetermined concepts. The simple fact is that it is possible for them to become conscious of these concepts and thus change them, and hence be able to make different decisions based on this ability, is thus ignored or precluded.

While according to Lippmann the phantom worlds influencing behaviour are not to be reflected on by "the masses", the "elites" should, in contrast, be able to formulate them deliberately and thus control the behaviour of the many through creating and influencing the pictures held in the latter's minds. In this regard, scholarship in general and the economic sciences in particular play a significant role. Whether true or false, their theories and methods help to form human reasoning without letting the many catch on to it. Scholarship can, according to Lippmann, "demonstrate the need for interposing some form of expertness between the private citizen and the vast environment in which he is entangled" (ibid., 251) and in this manner clearly delineate what is to be thought and perceived (ibid., 249).

For this, Hayek elucidates, a special type of intellectual is needed "who judge[s] all issues not by their specific merits but ... solely in the light of certain fashionable general ideas" (Hayek 2010[1949], 12). Hayek calls these intellectuals "second-hand dealer in ideas", who are characterised by the "absence of direct responsibility for practical affairs and the consequent absence of first-hand knowledge" (ibid, 13). The scholar is to manoeuvre solely along the lines of firmly established stereotypes which inform all of his statements and decisions. In social resonance, i.e. in interplay between many "second-hand dealers in ideas", a particular "climate of opinion" may emerge – "a set of very general preconceptions by which the intellectual judges the importance of new facts and opinions" (ibid., 17). "Once the more active part of intellectuals has been converted to a set of beliefs, the process by which these become generally accepted is almost automatic and irresistible" (ibid., 13). In other words, intellectuals are to think along the lines of certain stereotypes but never about them and thus to function as "gatekeepers of ideas" (Blundell 2015, 56). As such they are to decide "what views and opinions are to reach us, which facts are important enough to be told to us, and in what form and from what angle they are to be presented" (Hayek 2010[1949], 11). Formulated differently, scholarship is tasked with limiting the scholar's perception to a few abstractions which are "not a product of the mind but rather constitute what the mind is made of" (Hayek 1980, 48). This opens up the possibility of creating a blind adherence and absolute obedience to a particular world view – one that is "not consciously chosen or deliberately selected but [accepted] through a mechanism over which we have no conscious control" (ibid., 49).

The consequence in particular for economics both as a science and an educational matter is that "the market" is not to be researched as a real phenomenon, but the objective is rather to establish a particular way of thinking about it in the heads of people (Ötsch 2009). Its role is to insert abstract, remote economic models between normal people and their real life conditions and between politicians and their actual field of responsibility (see Blundell 2015). As Lippmann clearly outlines, earlier scientific thought offers an example of how this instrumentalisation can be effected: The old economists

> constructed what they sincerely hoped was a simplified diagram, not so different in principle and in veracity from the parallelogram with legs and a head in a child's drawing of a complicated cow. (...) The model worked. The kind of people, which the model assumed, living in the sort of world the model assumed, invariably cooperated harmoniously in the books where the model was described. With modification and embroidery, this pure fiction, used by economists to simplify their thinking, was retailed and popularized until for large sections of the population it prevailed as the economic mythology of the day.
>
> Lippmann (1922, 84)

As a result, abstract economic concepts such as "market balance" or "market mechanisms" that existed as the object and result of theoretical discourse in the 18th and 19th century can be used to facilitate planting stereotypes in the heads of people.

4. Can economic teaching enforce a blind adherence to the market?

In order to elucidate the possible role of narrowing down the student's focus to abstract concepts of the market further, it is, again from a epistemological point of view, interesting to notice that, according to neoliberal think tanks, blind faith in the market is not a natural phenomenon but must rather be brought about through a "war of ideas" as the Institute of Economic Affairs (IEA) co-founded by Hayek menacingly coined it (see Blundell 2015).

> Basic for the struggle to promote personal liberty is the task of persuading our fellow men not only that free market allocation of goods and services is economically efficient and wealth-enhancing but also, and much more importantly, that market allocation is morally superior to other methods of exchange.
>
> Williams (2007, xiii)

In this war, what better way, next to persuasion, could play an essential role than to target education? Its function could simply be to make people "second-hand dealers in ideas" (Blundell 2015, 21). If this were to be the case, an urgent need arises to discuss whether and, if need be, how the current standard of economics teaching may play a significant role in this "war of ideas" – whether intentionally or not. In the following, I would like to outline a few systematic points of departure in response to these questions. At the beginning of this essay I mentioned that today's standard of economics teaching is characterised by detachment from reality, one-sidedness and an uncritical approach. Addressing these points should provide clarity as to their significance in regard to the above mentioned "war" and thus give cause for greater scrutiny.[13]

Detachment from reality: Today's economics teaching primarily rests on a neoclassical theory of economics, which since the 19th century has deliberately presented itself as an "exact science" in the manner of physics and mathematics. As such, it allows its insights to be applied to the world of economic experience, however it does not accept this world as the basis for its insights. Students therefore learn to exclusively negotiate abstract mathematical economic model worlds which as unequivocal calculations are controllable and transmit a harmonised and uniform picture of the economy. What students do not learn here is, first, to take these model worlds and verify them against their own, real experience and second, to form independent, context-specific opinions of economic situations, Moreover, if one were to follow the Council for Economic Education (CEE) for example, one of the most important agents in standardising economics teaching worldwide, there is no need whatsoever for economics to impart any of the basic facts of the American or global economy (Siegfried et al. 2010, vi). In this manner, economics teaching leaves reality completely out of the picture. This situation shows that there is an urgent need for greater research examination: Does standard economic teaching threaten to lose sight of the real world by almost exclusively relying on mathematical models which are independent of experience? Is it possible for teaching to plant economic models as stereotypes in the heads of people?

One-sidedness: As illustrated above, standard economics teaching is based on a form of "economic imperialism" which claims that economics is not to be defined by its object ("the economy") but rather alone through its method, i.e. through a single "approach to all human behavior" (see again Becker 1990) or a "unique view of the world" (see again Mankiw 2001, vii). In short, this means that it is no longer about learning how to look at the world from various perspectives but to view and judge the entire world from one, predetermined perspective alone – an abstract mathematical one. Economic teaching, according to the CEE for instance, should help young people "to develop the capacity to deduce from conclusions from whatever facts are pertinent to the myriad problems they will confront in their lives" (Siegfried et al. 2010, vi). It is about creating by means of one single theory (the neoclassical one) a paradigm that "reflects the assignment to produce a single, coherent set of standards to guide the teaching of economics" (ibid.). In turn, dissenting theories are eliminated from the syllabus for the simple reason that they "would have confused and frustrated teachers and students" (ibid.). But how does such elimination really occur? By which means are neoclassical concepts actually acquired uncritically and without conscious thought on the part of students? How can mental habits as described by Bernays be developed within the teaching process to the point where they almost automatically determine the decisions people make, no matter what the real environment looks like in which they are made? How can thought freeze into stereotypes in this manner?

Uncritical approach: Looking at the standard economics books of today, it is obvious that they rarely touch upon economic theory itself in critical reflection. There is, for instance, a total lack of reference to the history of the economic sciences themselves; they equally fail to explicitly address the assumptions of economic thought. This calls for more detailed research on how economic conceptions in the sense of Lippmann can possibly and invisibly insert themselves between people and their environment. Do people learn to think within these concepts and to not reflect on them?

5. Are there alternatives?

An answer to the above-mentioned questions would involve, as a first issue, how standard economics teaching, operating within the framework of strategies to manipulate "public opinion", can be more efficiently examined and criticised. The second – and perhaps more important – issue concerns the kind of alternatives which can be drawn to counter any blind market adherence informing current economics teaching. Regarding this latter issue, I would like to merely point in a possible direction which is certainly not a novel one, but rather refers to what can be generally described as a humanistic concept of education (Bildung) (Graupe and Schwaetzer 2015). It is also closely related, for example, to demands for social-economic education (Fischer and Zurstrassen 2014). This primarily involves allowing for concrete references to experience, a diversity of perspectives and the ability for independent thought and self-reflection as an integral part of economics studies. Interestingly enough, Hayek himself provides an essential starting-point for this, showing that he himself knew that there could be more to education than simply educating "second-hand dealers in ideas". Hayek calls it learning to become either "original thinkers" or "experts in a particular field of thought" (Hayek 2010 [1949], 10). An original thinker is capable of reflecting on the conditions guiding her thoughts and opinions, thereby reversing, or at least diminishing, the uncritical approach that characterises Hayek's concept of an intellectual. In this regard, the original thinker is capable of critically analysing current stereotypes and recognising that alternatives do exist. As Lippmann notes, education in particular is capable of enabling people to become such original thinkers whenever they attain the capacity to become acutely aware of how deeply the repertory of stereotypes governs the whole process of our perception, making us imagine most things before we experience them (cp. Lippmann 1922, 65). It can also help to realise that stereotypes never possess the quality of irrefutable truth:

> For while men are willing to admit that there are two sides to a 'question, they do not believe that there are two sides to what they regard as a "fact". And they never do believe it until after long critical education, they are fully conscious of how second-hand and subjective is their apprehension of social data.
>
> (ibid., 90)

Enlightened economics teaching should therefore impart historical consciousness which explicitly also takes the development of stereotypes into account, and which would empower students to "know what fairy tale, what school book, what tradition, what novel, play picture, phrase, planted one preconception in this mind, another in that mind" (ibid., 66).

Let us turn our attention to Hayek's second starting-point: enabling people to become experts in a specific field of thought. In short, what this characterises is the very sense of responsibility for real circumstances and their interrelationships as well as the knowledge of concrete things which the "second-hand dealer in ideas" is missing. The expert develops his knowledge and insights according to immediate issues of life. He does not make unconscious judgments based on predetermined concepts about people and situations, but develops his own opinion in direct interaction with these people and situations. As a result, he is capable of dismantling the cognitive barriers which the economic illusory worlds have raised to detach him from his experience, and initiate a productive, perception-altering exchange between himself and the world.

Economics education can enable this sense of responsibility by making explicit reference to students' life realities without pressing their perception into preconceived models. Not least, in order to do this, a diversity of methods must be explicitly taught so that the world can be viewed from various perspectives and people can evolve an adequate and continuously new understanding of the world.

6. Conclusion

What should have become clear is that a concern for enlightened education promoting responsibility for one's own thought pattern stands in direct opposition to education in blind adherence to the market. Those that demand independent thought and self-reflection, reference to reality, controversy and diversity of methods (and their practical application in economics education) are not interested in simply replacing neoliberal stereotypes with other ones. Their interest lies rather in actively undermining any assumptions from the *war of ideas*, propagated by market radical think tanks, which may be guiding economics teaching. In doing so, any ideological persuasion played upon the human intellect is rejected in favour of enabling free and conscious reflection of concrete experiences of social relationships. Hayek and Lippmann were both still aware of these alternatives to manipulative forms of education. Yet the think tanks they established created an economics education that exclusively propagated blind adherence to the market.

In my own experience, alternative ways of economic teaching can in fact encourage students to become conscious of the many ways in which the economic "missionaries" and their "bibles" can be disputed. A critical course in the history of economic ideas empowers them to find their own actual point of view and the reasons for it. "The difficulty lies, not in the *new ideas*, but in escaping from the old ones, which ramify, for those brought up as most of us have been, into every corner of our minds" (Keynes cited in Keen 2011, xii). Yet this escape from old ideas is only possible when one has become truly aware of them. At the least, the discipline's intellectual history should be (re) introduced, as much as an explicit reflection on the concepts of the human being and society underlying economics and its teaching. This could serve as a first step toward ensuring that young generations are no longer brought up as the slaves to dead economists and – let us add Keynes' often cited image – dead or living textbook authors.

Notes

1 "Waging the War of Ideas" is a book title published by the Institute of Economic Affairs (see Blundell 2015).
2 Currently, Mankiw's *Principles* ranks 7th on Amazon's list of 100 best-selling macro-economic textbooks (https://www.amazon.com/Best-Sellers-Books-Macro economics/zgbs/books/2596#1 accessed on 20 March 2017).
3 Compare for instance the obituary notices in the Wall Street Journal (December 13, 2009) published on the occasion of Paul Samuelson's death, where Robert Hall, Professor at Stanford writes: "His book, Foundations of Economic Analysis, was a bible to my generation of economists, trained entirely in the then-new Samuelson mode." Samuelson writes about himself: I was besieged by groupies reminiscent of Talmudic students crowding around famous rabbis. The policeman at the door of the White House whispers, "I am using your book at Georgetown night school." The chap who sells me a newspaper at Harvard Square confides that at Northeastern he studied my book. (. . .) Wherever I go in Europe, Asia, or Latin America, strangers greet me as an old friend or old tormenter. I have never been to India, Russia, or China, but in my MIT office, I am asked to autograph copies of translations" (quoted in Gottesman et al. 2005, 98).
4 Samuelson also invokes another form of pressure. He tells his students to consider the study of economics a factor absolutely decisive to success or failure in the daily struggle for existence: "As we have come to realize, there is one overriding reason for learning the basic lessons of economics: All your life – from the cradle to grave and beyond – *you will run up against the brutal truths of economics*. (. . .) Of course, studying economics cannot make you a genius. *But without economics, the dice of life are loaded against you*" (Samuelson and Nordhaus 2005, 3, my emphasis). In an earlier edition (Samuelson 1955, 3), Samuelson even writes: "Thus, *even from the purely egotistic standpoint of self-interest* [it is important to] find answers to . . . the questions of modern economic life" (my emphasis).
5 Translated by the author.
6 This is to say that economics was believed to simply analyse the production, distribution, and consumption of goods and services or, more specifically, the allocation of limited resources to the satisfaction of mutually exclusive ends. Common to these definitions is that they refer to the objects of economic investigation, but do not prescribe the methods, with which one should investigate these objects.
7 We are not using, here, some insult forged by critics, but the explicit self-understanding, in particular, of a science that has been coloured by the Chicago School of Economics. "I am an economic imperialist. I believe good techniques have a wide application", says, for example, Gary Becker about himself Becker (1993).
8 The concept of "methodological individualism" goes back to Joseph Schumpeter (1908).

9 About Adam Smith, Samuelson writes (Samuelson 1955, 12–13): "First comes *Adam Smith*, a Scotch bachelor with a *powdered wig* like *George Washington*, who gathered together the earlier wisdom of business pamphleteers and philosophic system builders in his Wealth of Nations (1776). He recognised the virtues of free markets, and the times were ripe for his doctrines to become the bible of the rising middle class. About Marx, Samuelson says: "And then our picture gallery comes upon the black sheep, who was beyond the pen of the true classical tradition. Karl Marx, an exile from Germany, worked away in the British Museum vowing that the Bourgeoisie would pay for the suffering his boils cost him as he sat working out his theories of the inevitable collapse of capitalism" (re-translated from the German edition).

10 Re-translated from the German edition.

11 I realise that both authors cannot be placed within the neoclassical spectrum precisely. I also do not claim their proximity to neoclassicism, but I do refer to this school of thought in order to clarify how abstract scientific concepts can function in and for society. My argument is, as stated, epistemological rather than normative. As a result, I do not aim to clarify whether Hayek or Lippman intended or agree with the way current textbooks impart economic principles or the form they take.

12 The original reads: "Die Macht abstrakter Ideen beruht in hohem Maße auf eben der Tatsache, daß sie nicht bewußt als Theorien aufgefaßt, sondern von den meisten Menschen als unmittelbar einleuchtende Wahrheiten angesehen werden, die als stillschweigend angenommene Voraussetzungen fungieren."

13 The other question, whether the instrumentalisation of standard economic teaching is intended, i.e. consciously initiated, will not be answered here.

References

Adler, M. (2010): *Economics for the Rest of Us. Debunking the Science that Makes Life Dismal.* New York: The New Press.

Becker, G.S. (1990): *The Economic Approach to Human Behavior.* Chicago: Chicago University Press.

Becker, G.S. (1993): 'Economic Imperialism. Interview with Gary Becker', *Religion & Liberty* 3(2), available at https://acton.org/pub/religion-liberty/volume-3-number-2/economic-imperialism accessed on 12 September 2017.

Bernays, E. (1961): *Cristallizing Public Opinion.* New York: Liveright Publishing Corporation.

Bernays, E. (2005[1928]): *Propaganda.* New York: H. Liveright, reprinted by Ig Publishing.

Blundell, J. (2015): *Waging the War of Ideas.* London: The Institute of Economic Affairs.

Brodbeck, K.-H. (1996): *Erfolgsfaktor Kreativität. Die Zukunft Unserer Marktwirtschaft.* Darmstadt: Wissenschaftliche Buchgesellschaft.

Statistisches Bundesamt. (2016): Bildung Und KultuR. Studierende an Hochschulen – FS 11 R. 4.1'. Wintersemester 2015/16. Wiesbaden. https://www.destatis.de/DE/Publikationen/Thematisch/BildungForschungKultur/Hochschulen/StudierendeHochschulenEndg2110410167004.pdf?__blob=publicationFile? accessed on 21 September 2017.

Fischer, A. and Zurstrassen, B. (2014, Hrsg.): *Sozioökonomische Bildung.* Bonn: Bundeszentrale für politische Bildung.

Fleck, L. (1980): *Die Entstehung Einer Wissenschaftlichen Tatsache.* Frankfurt am Main: Suhrkamp.

Gottesman, A., Ramrattan, L. and Szenberg, M. (2005): 'Samuelson's Economics: The Continuing Legacy', *Quarterly Journal of Austrian Economics* 8(2), 95–105.

Graupe S. and Schwaetzer, H. (2015, Hrsg.):*Bildung Gestalten. Akademische Aufgaben Der Gegenwart.* Coincidentia, Beiheft 5. Münster: Aschendorff.
Häring, N. (2010): Markt Und Macht. Was Sie Schon Immer Über Die Wirtschaft Wissen Wollten, Aber Bisher Nicht Erfahren Sollten. Stuttgart: Schäffer-Poeschel.
Hayek, F.A. (1980): *Recht, Gesetzgebung Und Freiheit.* Band 1. München: Verlag Moderne Industrie.
Hayek, F.A. (2010[1949]): *The Intellectuals and Socialism.* Whiteish: Kessinger Publishing.
Hedtke, R. (2008): Ökonomische Denkweisen. Eine Einführung. Schwalbach/Ts: Wochenschau Verlag.
Hill, R. and Myatt, T. (2010): *The Economics Anti-Textbook.* London & New York: Zed Books.
Keen, S. (2010): *Debunking Economics. The Naked Emperor of the Social Sciences.* London & New York: Zed Books.
Kuhn, T.S. (1996): *The Structure of Scientific Revolutions.* Chicago and London: University of Chicago.
Lippmann, W. (1922): *Public Opinion.* London: Allen & Unwin.
Mankiw, N.G. (2001): *Principles of Economics.* Fort Worth: Harcourt College.
Nasar, S. (March 14, 1995): 'A Hard Act to Follow? Here Goes', *The New York Times*, available at http://www.nytimes.com/1995/03/14/business/a-hard-act-to-follow-here-goes.html?src=pm, accessed on 4 July 2011.
Ötsch, W. (2009): *Mythos Markt. Marktradikale Propaganda Und Ökonomische Theorie.* Marburg: Metropolis.
Pearce, K.A. and Hoover, K.D. (1995): 'After the Revolution. Paul Samuelson and the Textbook Keynesian Model', *History of Political Economy* 27(Supplement), 183–216.
Samuelson, P.A. (1955): *Volkswirtschaftslehre. Eine Einführung.* Köln: Bund.
Samuelson, P.A. and Nordhaus, W.D. (2005): *Economics.* New York City. McGraw Hill.
Schumpeter, J. (1908): *Das Wesen Und Der Hauptinhalt Der Theoretischen Nationalökonomie.* Leipzig: Duncker & Humblodt.
Schumpeter, J. (1942): *Capitalism, Socialism and Democracy.* New York: Harper & Row.
Siegfried, J., Krueger A., Collins, S., Frank, R., MacDonald, R., McGoldrick K., Taylor, J. and Vredeveld, G. (2010): *Voluntary National Content Standards in Economics.* New York: The Council for Economic Education, http://www.councilforeconed.org/wp/wp-content/uploads/2012/03/voluntary-national-content-standards-2010.pdf accessed on 21 September 2017
Skousen, M. (1997): 'The Perseverance of Paul Samuelson's Economics', *Journal of Economic Perspectives* 11(2), 137–152.
Sraffa, P. (1926): 'The Law of Returns under Competitive Conditions', *The Economic Journal* 36(144), 535–550.
Varian, H.R. (2007): *Grundzüge Der Mikroökonomik.* München and Wien: Oldenbourg.
Walras, L. (1969): *Elements of Pure Economics.* New York: A.M.Kelley.
Walstad, W.B., Watts, M. and Bosshardt, W. (1998): 'The Principles of Economics Textbook. History, Content, and Use', in Walstad, W.B., Saunders, P. (eds.), *Teaching Undergraduate Economics. A Handbook for Instructors.* Boston: McGraw Hill Irwin, 185–205.
Weinstein, M. (December 13, 2009): 'Paul A. Samuelson, Economist, Dies at 94', *The New York Times*, available at http://www.nytimes.com/2009/12/14/business/economy/14samuelson.html?pagewanted=1, accessed on 28 July 2011.
Williams, W.E. (2007): "Foreword to the 3rd edition', in Blundell, J. (ed.), *Waging the War of Ideas.* London: The Institute of Economic Affairs, 11–16.

12 The schoolmaster's voice

How professional identities are formed by textbook discourses in mainstream economics

Jens Maesse

1. Introduction

Textbook economics is, especially by critics, conceived as a dogmatic discourse, based on a neoclassical style of economic reasoning and an almost unchangeable, standardised structure. The market is presented as the ultima ratio for every economic problem. Colander, for example, complained over many years that

> [t]he introductory economics course has become an institution, propagated by a set of textbooks that determine the course structure. These textbooks reflect the desire of reviewers who must teach the course, and these desires generally reflect the structure of existing textbooks. [. . .] The overall structure has developed for a variety of reasons: pedagogical simplicity, need to fit in current issues, and a consensus of what elements of economics are best taught to principle students.
>
> Colander (2003, 82).

As Pahl (2012) has shown, textbook economics is a highly standardised genre of knowledge production that leaves hardly any room for critique or controversy. This is surprising since economics has never been a standardised science. It rather characterised by various controversies, heterogeneous interpretations and multiple perspectives; and even neoclassical models play multiple roles and offer a variety of applications and meanings (Halsmayer 2014). Economics forms a field of conflict that covers several schools and sub-schools from neoclassics to Marxism(s), Keynesianism(s) to ordoliberalism and so forth. However, some studies see an orthodox core at certain elite institutions and established departments, others point to the wide array of heterodox approaches which comment, criticise and challenge the model-based central core (Blaug 2003). Yet, both "orthodoxy" and "heterodoxy" as well as the multiple controversies within the "orthodoxy" camp belong to the economics discipline, even if some schools and paradigms are marginalised whilst others seek to represent and dominate the entire discipline.

Besides the internal conflicts in the academic discipline, many other forms of economic knowledge in economic policy research and in other branches of economic advice and expertise exist (Coats 1993). Economics is not only an academic science, it is also a profession that provides expertise to business and politics (Pechman 1989; Coats 2001). Against this backdrop, the education and training of young economists through university teaching appears to be of particular relevance for academia and society. However, how can we explain this obvious contradiction between a highly heterogeneous field of knowledge prodction in the multiple branches of economics and an apparently strong tendency towards unification, standardisation and canonisation of teaching through textbook economics?

In this chapter, textbook culture is analysed as a special effect of power and exclusion within the economics discipline. The term *textbook culture* will neither refer to every single textbook, nor to every textbook use in economics; it rather takes the ongoing proliferation of standardised undergraduate courses in economics departments as a phenomenological starting point for disclosing the deep structure of mainstream economics as a hegemonic culture. Even if not every course and every department in economics is dominated by the textbook culture, more and more undergraduate courses are influenced by this teaching philosophy, as a survey by Beckenbach et al. (2016) in German economics departments suggests (see the chapters by Almeida, Bhattacharyya, Dai and Yusif, in this volume, for international perspectives).

My chapter will try to explain in what kind of macrosocial and political-economic context the mainstream textbook culture has developed and was institutionalised. Two interrelated explanatory parts will be presented. The first part (Sections 2 and 3) is concerned with the place of textbooks in the *social field of economics*. The particular dynamics and social logics of this field will be outlined in Section 2, first, as hierarchisation-elitisation tendency within academia (Lee et al. 2013) and, second, as a transgressive governmentalisation of economics (Lebaron, 2014). The section shows how the *trans-epistemic social logic* of this field impacts the teaching culture in economics because it facilitates the development of *meritocratic professional values* and *elitist identity concepts* among young economists.

Section 3 explains why the elitist attitudes and the trans-epistemic character of the field of economics relate to the formation of a textbook teaching culture. Values, beliefs, habitus and ethos are fundamental for every academic world. As Fourcade et al. (2014) have shown, economists follow a certain "superiority" ethos. This ethos is based on meritocratic values and an elitist *esprit de corps*. Section 3 will explain these subjective feelings and values as an effect of certain discursive and institutional interrelations.

The second part of the explanation (Section 4) is based on a discourse analysis of textbooks. The discourse analysis will show and explain how and why a textbook culture contributes to the formation of a certain identity that is consistent with the values and beliefs that are prevalent in the discipline. It will be demonstrated how the schoolmaster's voice creates particular social relations for disciples and students alike, and it will be explained why textbooks do not simply teach economic theory in the frist place. I will rather show how textbook discourses provide young academics with a meritocratic and elitist professional habitus. Alternative teaching concepts that will be presented and developed in this volume may use these results for pedagogical reflections.

2. Why do meritocratic values and elitist attitudes result from the trans-epistemic field?

2.1 The governmentalisation of economics and the trans-epistemic field

Textbook economics cannot be reduced to textbooks. Textsbooks are, rather, embedded as a textbook teaching culture within a wider field of academic and non-academic discourses, institutions, evaluation techniques and certain sorts of publication in economics. Different horizontal and vertical forces impact the academic field and constitute it as a heterogeneous *trans*-epistimic field (in contrast to a homogeneous mono-epistmic field). The two axes in Figure 12.1 show how both forces impact the academic knowledge production in the academic subfield.

The trans-epistemic field of knowledge production is important because it serves as an ultimate constitutional framework: even for those micro-practices in economics which have no apparent and obvious connection to the power centres in economics where jobs are offered, academic positions are occupied, scientific reputations are attached and political and other obligations are made. The trans-epistemic field is a social context that makes possible certain circulations and re-appropripriations of symbolic products such as knowledge, reputation, names,

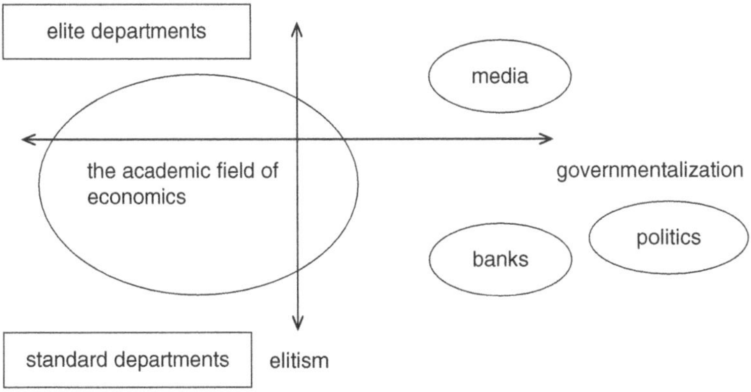

Figure 12.1 Horizontal and vertical forces influence the academic field of economics

group belongings, models and so forth in different social arenas between the media world, politics, banking, businesses and academic institutions.

The trans-epistemic dimension of economics is, in fact, the result of the *governmentalization* of economics (Desrosières 1998; Coats 1993), since the term "governmentalization" refers to the close connection of the economics discipline to (non-academic) apparatuses of power and governance in state, the economy and society. Compared to other disciplines of the social sciences, economics is particularly influenced by those social fields which use economics expertise for their purposes (especially politics, the world of banks and finance, businesses and firms as well as the media) and transform them into means of power and discourse. Economics is not a pure academic science; it is also political discipline, cameralistic tool and hegemonic practice.

Two different but interrelated dynamics of discourse and power account for particular interactions and interdependencies between these subfields: *elitism* and *academism*. Both influence and make possible the multiple translations and circulations of symbolic goods (economic ideas, academic prestige and so forth) between academia and politics, the business world and the media. Furthermore, the entire field is built around four different social sub-fields which are, in contrast to Bourdieu's field theory (Bourdieu 1989), gradually opening up to each other. This field provides a certain institutional terrain (made up of universities, research organisations, businesses, ministries, statistical bureaux, media and so forth) for discursive practices (Foucault 1980) that take place at the interface of these trans-epistemic interrelations.

The academic field is of particular interest in our study of textbook cultures. It is located in the top-left quadrant of the trans-epistemic field (Figure 12.2). Here, economists usually follow academic logics of research and teaching. But this field does not stand alone: it is connected to three other fields where economics expertise and economists as professionals and advisors act. On the right side are the political field and the media field; in the bottom-left quadrant is the business world. These four fields are social contexts that form an institutional arena in which discursive struggles take place over the meaning of economics expertise and other forms of knowledge. Economists are involved in discourses within these different social contexts and they form different professional roles, e.g. as "media experts", "political advisors", "academic researchers", "business consultants" and so forth. Experts do not play singular roles, they are, rather, hybrid beings constructed in and through a heterogeneous socio-discursive space. For example, economic experts in media contexts always rely on their academic status (based on the academic field) and make implicit or explicit reference to their role in the political world (e.g. through certain language use or by mentioning certain positions they used to hold). Symbolic capital from academia is a particularly important power device in the media. For this reason, economic experts never act within each single field.

How are these dynamics related to the textbook culture? In order to be recognised as an "economic expert", a "star economist" or a "distinguished economist" outside academia, symbolic capital must be produced in the academic

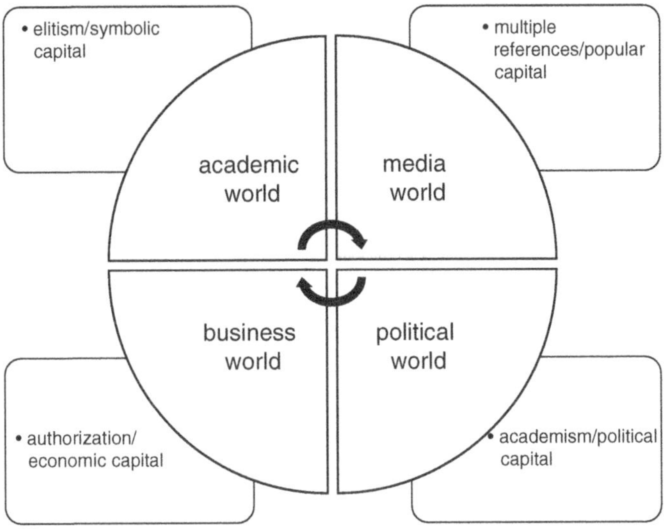

Figure 12.2 The trans-epistemic field of economics
Maesse (2015, 290)

world. This is only possible if academia is able to produce a form of reputation that goes beyond conventional academic prestige (the professor position). Economics can rely not only on the Nobel Prize but also, more importantly, on strong reputational hierarchies. Huge symbolic and material inequalities between "standard researcher" and "big shots" or "star economists" are typically accepted in economics. Academic hierarchies are institutionalised by so-called "elite departments" and universalised beyond the realm of "top departments" by journal rankings. Rankings create an elite myth and an excellence cult. It establishes a meritocratic academic culture that defies comparison with any other social sciences or humanities discipline (for more details see Han 2003).

The dimensions of this elitism culture (Maesse 2017) as well as its impacts on academic graduation processes (Maesse 2018) are explained elsewhere. Section 2.2 will analyse how this elite cult emerged historically, and how it operates systematically. This is important for understanding our argument about the external pressures of the trans-epistemic field for the production of symbolic capital that support the institutionalisation of meritocratic values and an elitist esprit de corps in mainstream economics. Meritocratism and elitist values, in turn, support standardisation, canonisation and unification tendencies, especially in those areas of academia where established researchers meet newcomers. "Teaching" is a particular entry point into the highly complex world of economics. It is the bridge over which non-economists (students) enter the discipline and find themselves thrown into a parrticular professional arena. Textbooks do not teach economic theory in the narrow sense; they rather make the formation of a professional habitus as "economist" possible.

Without the simplifications in textbook economics, this entry would fail because young economists must be properly prepared before being involved in the real conflicts and positioning struggles which take place in the trans-epistemic field. This requires, in the first place, not critical and diversified knowledge about how markets work, fail and can be analysed from different academic perspectives and paradigms. It requires a certain professional identity to participate in academic, political, economic and ideological struggles: the contemporary standard economist is a hybrid being, gradually an academic and gradually a politician (Maesse 2015). The introduction to more research-related issues of knowledge and academic controversies happens after the graduate courses, especially during the PhD period. Before this identity dimension is further discussed in Section 3, the following part will briefly outline what it means to be a member of an academic world characterised by strong hierarchisations and a celebrated elitism.

2.2 Hierarchisation and elitisation within economics

While the trans-epistemic field accounts mainly for the governmentalisation tendency (the external pressures for the production of excellent myths as the *horizontal* impacts on knowledge production in economics), the elitism dispositif will take into account the hierarchising processes. Social hierarchies as the *vertical* dimension have a certain history and are characterised by a dispositif structure that directs most academic activities in economics towards meritocratic values of "excellence" and superiority attitudes of being an "elite" (Fourcade et al. 2014; Lee et al. 2013). Both aspects will be explained with the elitism dispositif, which consists of five characteristics outlined below.

2.2.1 *Academisation: from technical knowledge to academic prestige*

The economics profession has had a strong impact on the formation of the modern nation-state. Economics is used as a discursive tool to intervene in the economy as a field of power and conflict between different social groups over the orientation and direction of social, economic and political development since the end of the nineteenth century (Desrosières 1998; Morgan 2003; Coats 1993). While the first half of the twentieth century was characterised by the foundation of economics institutions (i.e. statistical bureaux, ministries, central banks, think tanks and research institutes), the formation of economic management knowledge (i.e. Keynesian macro-economic theory, expectation utility theory, new Keynesianism, game theory) and the constitution of classification instruments (i.e. statistics, econometrics, GDP), the period after the World War II was dominated by the systematic construction of symbolic capital (reputation and legitimacy), especially through Nobel Prize awards, a prominent role for economists from elite departments in the media, central

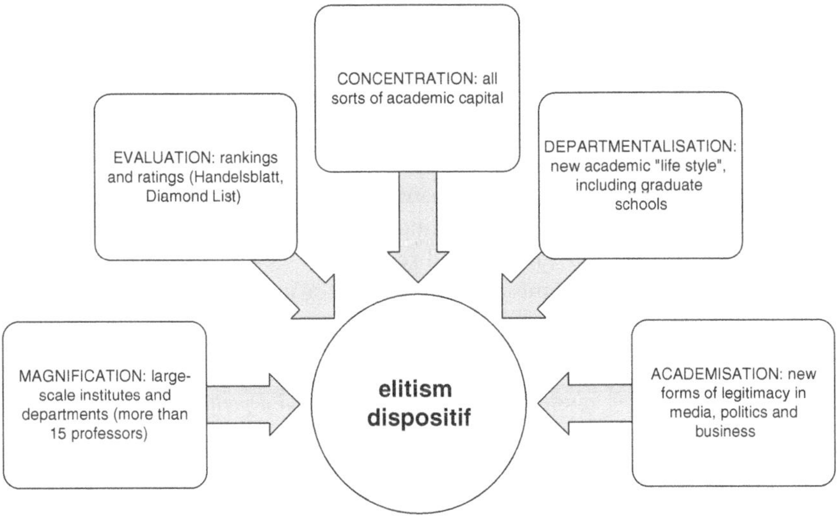

Figure 12.3 Constitution of the elitism dispositif in economics
Maesse (2018, 58)

banks, governments, international organisations and financial markets, and a trend towards excellent orientation and rankings in economics research (MacKenzie 2006; Dezalay and Garth 2009; Hirschman and Berman 2014; Lebaron, 2014). The scientific capital of the first half of the twentieth century would be replaced and substituted by academic capital after 1950. In the course of post-1970 neoliberalisation, economics became even more important for the formation and reconstruction of the economy and nation-state institutions in the course of globalisation (Fourcade 2006). The term "academisation" refers to a change in these legitimation patterns in society (Lebaron 2006). Academic reputations of particular economic experts become relevant in order to perform with credibility and authority, especially in media discourses and political debates. This leads to a growing demand for academic credentials and professional authority from society and accounts for the intensified governmentalisation of the trans-epistemic field of economics (see Section 2.1). "Academic excellence" discourses, understood as symbolic capital, support the formation of professional authority in society as "experts".

2.2.2 Evaluation: "excellence" orientation in research

As a result of the intensified governmentalisation-academisation processes, the academic world of economics began to distinguish more and more between "top research" and "standard research". Academic hierarchies emerged.

Meanwhile, this trend embraced the UK in the 1980s (Lee et al. 2013) and other European countries such as Germany in the 1990s. The introduction of rankings and the paper-journal system has pushed this elite and excellence orientation forward (Laband and Piette 1994). Rankings of journals and publications (Diamond List in the UK, Handelsblatt Ranking in Germany) go hand in hand with a certain style of excellence orientation in academic communication (papers, presentations). "Top publications" and a "quality research" ideology become the ultimate reference frame for research (Lamont 2009: 53–106). Research and publishing as an academic practice that is led by an open-ended search for theories and research outcome, including failures and unforeseeable results, becomes marginalised by a meritocratic academic entrepreneurship that seeks "top publications".

2.2.3 *Magnification: the construction of large institutes and departments*

Rankings and ratings construct symbolic hierarchies between "good" and "bad" research and support a meritocratic ideology. Magnification translates these symbolic hierarchies into material inequalities. In order to realise this translation from symbolic into material hierarchies, two steps are needed. Large institutes and departments must be founded (i.e. Oxford, Frankfurt) or taken over (Munich, LSE). They provide the social context for the production of discourses of excellence. Different strategies of magnification can be detected, as studies in Germany and a comparative study on the UK have shown (Maesse 2016; Maesse 2017). As a result, magnification led, in the UK and Germany, to the formation of between four and six places which are competitive enough to enter into academic elitism. Even if smaller institutes and departments develop an excellence strategy in economics and try to compete with the "top departments", only the large institutes can provide the resources necessary to become "excellent". The concentration of academic capital, as well as the formation of US-style departments, are prerequisites. Thus, the structure of the economics discipline follows the oligpolistic tendencies of global capitalism.

2.2.4 *Concentration: from academic resources to academic capital*

The development of large economics institutes and departments of around 15 or more professorships is the institutional basis for concentration of academic capital. Concentration means putting all kinds of valuable academic resources (funds, competitive research, academic positions, awards and so forth) into these large departments and institutes. When resources become a means for the construction of power and inequalities, they are no longer resources but capital, understood as social power relations (see Bourdieu 1989). Concentration leads to a transformation from academic resources into academic capital. Bigger institutes profit from this change and now have the material opportunities to become "elite" and "excellent", whereas the rest struggles with the status quo. Hierarchies between "elite" and "non-elite" departments are, nevertheless, in Germany, for different reasons, more or less flat. As a study of the distribution of capital between large and small economics institutes has shown (Maesse 2016), large departments have more funds and appoint professors with higher academic positions and higher publication rates in high-level journals. In the UK, for instance, almost all funds distributed by the Research Assessment Exercise (RAE, now REF) are concentrated in a small number of departments. Academic capital is needed to participate in discourses of excellence.

Concentration processes have consequences for the entire discipline, even for those researchers and departments that are excluded from the consecration of being "elite". However, the not yet contested establishment of strong symbolic as well as material hierarchies and inequalities between research and institutes/departments, and the high degree of social acceptance of these hierarchies, contributes to the formation of a certain form of academic competition between researchers (where A-journals count and the content of research outcomes becomes secondary), a particular form of academic biography and career pathways (with an orientation to the top and a certain habitus of resignation and subordination at the periphery), as well as a far-reaching institutionalisation of meritocratic values and a professional *esprit de corps* between members of the economist community (as is well known in other "elite" professions such as medicine and law).

2.2.5 Departmentalisation: organisational change in institutes and colleges

Concentration, magnification, evaluation and academisation processes go hand in hand with organisational and cultural change in economics. This change is called "departmentalisation". It refers to the reorganisation of academic life in universities according to the adoption of US-style departments in the UK and Germany. The national traditions of German humanism (represented by the professor as an autonomous power position) and the British cultural elite (represented by the lecturer at the British "college" as well as the "cultural elite") are replaced by a new type of team-oriented researcher. Departmentalisation processes encompass many changes to the academic culture. The lingua franca is American English, research is published in journals, papers are presented and discussed in standardised sequences in seminars, workshops and conferences, the economic "model" is the cognitive frame of economic thinking, the social-work unit is a supervisor-led network of collaborating professors meeting each other in the department in order to work on papers and prepare the ground for meeting the right people.

The department is the organisational and cultural context for the establishment of the neoclassical model with all its facets. Each professor and researcher is no longer an isolated specialist in their area of expertise, meeting their colleagues only at other institutes and universities, in workshops and at conferences or by email. Rather, departments are places to keep academic collaboration and discussion within a geographical location.

Departments are also places in which meritocratism and community building is socially embedded. Permanent team meetings, brown-bag seminars, invitations and other forms of social interaction arrange forms of interaction and exchange. Members of the department become involved in dense networks of other academic researchers which help each other with career development. The department is a place to form old-boy networks for career promotion and publication. It is important to know what is going on editorial boards, to meet possible reviewers and project collaborators, to discuss special methods and to keep in touch with the recent "research frontier".

To conclude, hierarchisation and elitism in economics consist of the formation of certain places (i.e. Mannheim and Munich, LSE and Oxford and so forth) with a huge amount of academic resources. These places appoint a critical mass of researchers who publish mainly in A-journals, represent meritocratic values and believe in academic elites as a result of excellence in research.

3. What is a textbook culture and why is it related to elitism practices?

Textbook economics cannot be adequately understood without these changes in globalised economics that took place in last few decades. Elitism and hierarchisation provide the environment in which a textbook teaching culture emerged. This context consists of diverse interactions and interrelations between fields, values, practices and institutions. However, elitism has a symbolic-ideological as well as a material-stratificatory dimension. But the main driver of power and inequality in the field of economics does not come from the inner life of the economics discipline itself (Section 2.2); it is, rather, influenced by society to which economics is connected through translations by and within the trans-epistemic field (Section 2.1) (see Figure 12.1).

However, the elitist rituals and excellence cults of the discipline contribute to the production of certain meritocratic values and beliefs as well as to elitist attitudes and group identities. To understand the hidden and complex dynamics, the sociological analysis must try to shed light onto the hidden as well as the obvious interrelations and translations. Meritocratic values of "excellence" and "top research" are not simply motivated by material interests; accordingly, the esprit de corps which supports the entire idea of being "elite" with a group-related ideology has no manifest material basis within economics either. Both phenomena are symbolic effects of the governmentalisation of economics and the trans-epistemic embeddings. They represent a certain tendency to histrionics which attributes a special form of relevance to economics knowledge that is obviously not automatically attached to it. Yet, these complex interrelations, performances, discourses, ideologies and values have strong impacts on teaching. Teaching is the way that laymen as non-members of the profession have to take in order to move into the inner domains of the economics theatre.

Today, the textbook culture has been fully established and institutionalised in economics worldwide. Textbook culture is a particular form of teaching that is characterised by a high degree of standardisation, universalisation and canonisation as well as by a teacher-centred form of interaction between lecturers and students (lectures, lessons, tests and examinations, true-false-questions and so forth). It is mostly found in undergraduate courses and only occasionally in advanced teaching contexts. Textbook culture will neither include all textbooks nor all teaching contexts in which textbooks are read. Today, a textbook culture is not prevalent in all economics institutions. There are many institutes, departments and individual scholars that use distinct sets of teaching practices. In particular, scholars and departments that are involved in interdisciplinary contexts as well as heterodox economists are usually excluded from what I call a textbook culture. Furthermore, I don't talk about all teaching practices in economics. Even if more and more economics departments follow a conventional and canonised teaching structure (see Beckenbach, Daskalakis, Hofmann 2016), non-orthodox forms of teaching and learning still characterise courses of economics in every department, even those that follow a certain elite strategy.

Thus, it is not the aim of this paper to "blame" economists as elitist and snooty academics; rather, I am analytically motivated: what I want to understand is why mainstream economics differs in so many respects from other epistemic cultures in the social sciences.

What my analysis relates to is a certain hegemonic tendency in economics, which had already started by the 1970s (Hesse 2010). This tendency is characterised by: a) a preponderance of lectures and multiple-choice tests instead of writing essays and seminar papers; b) a dominance of the "holy trinity" of micro/macro/math at the expense of a high and uncoordinated diversity of economics theories, paradigms and debates; c) an increasing growth of quantifying assessments in teaching through credit points and rankings instead of qualitative responds to students; and d) an increasing separation between "introductory courses" and "advanced learning", especially between Bachelor/Masters and postgraduate courses. Thus, what I call *textbook teaching culture* captures these tendencies; it includes both the textbook itself and the social contexts of texbook use. The analysis applies only to these aspects. It is not the aim of this chapter to encompass the entire diversity of teaching practices in the field of economics (for example, in mixed departments, interdisciplinary courses and in more heterodox institutions) and the analysis will not represent all sorts of textbooks.

As Figure 12.4 illustrates, the emergence of the textbook culture is not subject to individual and autonomous decisions. It can be explained by its embeddedness within a complex set of discursive and institutional interrelations. These interrelations permeate society and academia and support the construction and institutionalisation of certain values and group formation processes. Accordingly, the academisation processes in the political economy have changed legitimation logics in society towards academic reputation (Box 1 in Figure 12.4). This initiated a deeper governmentalisation of

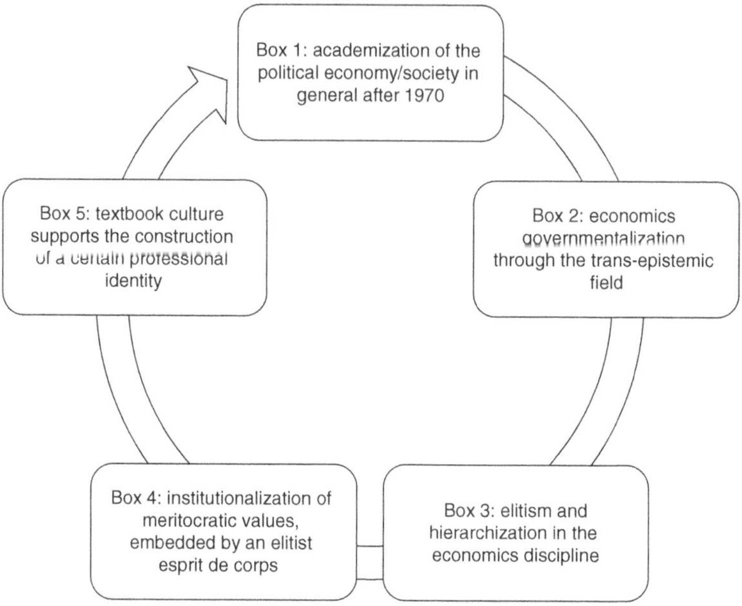

Figure 12.4 Textbook culture as an effect of complex discursive-material interrelations

economics, which has led to a more complex and stronger integration of economics expertise and economic experts into governmental apparatuses involving the state, the media and the economy (Coats 2001) (Box 2). Governmentalisation has initiated a further elitisation and a deeper hierarchisation of social relations in the economics discipline (Box 3), starting especially after 1970 with US departments. It was adopted in the UK, Germany and other European countries after 1980 and 1990. Elitism and hierarchisation have supported the establishment and sedimentation of meritocratic values and collective elitist attitudes (esprit de corps) (Box 4). These values and group formation processes prepared the ground on which textbook teaching culture could be established over recent decades (Box 5). As Hesse (2010) has shown for the German case, the institutionalisation of a standardised curriculum in economics was a highly controversial process, which was only achieved after 1970, in a parallel development with the breakthrough of the elite principle in US departments. Thus, the institutionalisation of textbook economics and the emergence of elitisation/hierarchisation developed simultaneously.

As the next section will show, teaching in economics is not, in the first place, about conceptual learning and cognitive involvement in a disciplinary discourse (that happens many years later, presumably during the PhD period, see Colander 2007; Maesse 2018). It aims rather at constructing a certain professional identity. Identity construction is a form of role-taking, mediated by discourses and social interaction. But not everybody can play every role because role-taking implies identification of the person (the "I" = a personal feeling of identification with a role) with certain social constraints (the "me" = the social expectations associated with the role). Since role-taking implies power mechanisms that coordinate social inclusion/exclusion, role-taking processes will be understood as gatekeeping which regulates the access to the inner world of the economics discipline and profession. Social identity as a gatekeeper moves out those potential members who do not fit with the profession's and the discipline's values and beliefs. But it includes others who might find their way through the world of economics. Thus, what I want to show with the discourse analyis is how textbooks as teaching tools appear to be efficient devices for the recruitment, selection and exclusion of future members of the field of economics.

4. The discursive logic of textbook culture

4.1 Discourse and identity formation

When students decide to study a particular discipline, such as economics, then this decision is prestructured by certain social backgrounds, attitudes toward the world, values and beliefs. Different variables play a role in student's choices. Whereas female students prefer to study psychology or pedagogy, male students dominate engineering and maths. Similar observations can be made for social background, religious belonging and political attitudes. These processes and tendencies continue during the study period and beyond (Schneickert 2013; Lenger 2008; Möller 2015).

A survey of the political attitudes, ethical values and beliefs of economics students would shed light on this topic. However, even if fully fledged results cannot be presented here, we can probably assume that a certain social identity is already selected before students begin textbook courses in economics (Lenger 2016). In addition to these pre-university selection criteria, the interactions between students and teachers at lecture courses in the university have an impact on their professional identity. A certain professional identity will be developed and sedimented through this relation. However, not only do social face-to-face interactions create roles for students but, additionally, *discursive* roles are also created by reading textbooks. While sociological interactionism has shown how role-taking and role-making processes work in face-to-face encounters, discourse analysis has demonstrated that roles are also bound to discourses on the basis of spoken and written language (Flottum 2005; Angermuller 2013; Maesse 2015). Both text-based discursive and face-to-face interactions contribute to the formation of professional identities at university.

This contribution will not focus on face-to-face interactions in classroom and lecture settings but on discursive role creations through textbook discourses. Before we consider these role and identity formations, we will briefly reflect on the general structure of social relations which students encounter when they meet teachers in lectures and on courses. In a typical lecture, let us say in

Microeconomics 1, a few hundred or more students might sit in a lecture hall in front of one professor who will be presenting one slide after another while pointing to a certain textbook that circulates already among the students as a pirate-copy pdf file or whatever. The students are listening to the professor's talk while developing certain learning technologies which will help them to pass the exams. In parallel to the lectures, assistants usually hold exercise courses.

The lectures, courses and autodidactic learning of students have one common goal: passing exams and taking a further step towards graduation. The main goal in this period is not to enjoy intellectual debate and make contact as early as possible with a pleasant lecturer and interesting professors. It is, rather, about getting through the lectures as one among a horde of unknown students and becoming one of those who will actually be selected later by professors and staff. What students probably learn when they study for a bachelor's degree in economics is cramming for one exam after another and coming up as a "winner". Undergraduate economics takes place in a standardised and pre-structured context; it is mostly about competing against hard circumstances, individually and together with others, and also about seeing how some get through and others fail. Thus, a competitive character is formed and confirmed, and the winners are attested to as such by the institution through graduations across the study course. Economics seems to be more about sports, measuring and valuations with clear consequences, whereas sociology, literature studies or history resembles a debating society where students learn to interpret, exchange and balance ideas and interpretations (usually with non-transparent and opaque consequences). This context of competitive learning already impacts the way academic discourses are percieved.

4.2 From "dialogic academia" to "schoolmaster's voice"

Academic discourse is typically organised around a polyphonic game of debates, controversies, schools, theories, approaches, methods and so forth. Polyphony appears in written texts such as papers, books and articles as well as in spoken discourse in workshops, conferences and informal settings. One main characteristic of academic polyphony is the profound democratic and republican[1] character of the academic community. The academic career ladder that leads from PhD candidate to full professor typically represents this. While the selection of members of academic discourse happens on this career ladder, established members usually speak as experts on their research topics, methods and theories. This institutionalised equality between researchers has been called the "academic republic" (Münch 2014). However, even if this republic recognises certain inequalities between "stars" and "unknowns", "icons" and "specialists", "standard researchers" and "distinguished colleagues", the discursive structure which organises academic communication is based on the idea of dialogue within a republican structure of equal members who respect and acknowledge each other (Merton 1938). The following example from economics discourse (Box 12.1) illustrates this democratic-republican dialogic academia.

Box 12.1: Dialogic academia

Expected utility theory has dominated the analysis of decision-making under risk. It has been generally accepted as a normative model of rational choice [24], and widely applied as a descriptive model of economic behaviour, e.g. [15, 4]. Thus, it is assumed that all reasonable people would wish to obey the axioms of the theory [47, 36], and that most people actually do, most of the time. The present paper describes several classes of choice problems in which preferences systematically violate the axioms of expected utility theory. In the light of these observations, we argue that utility theory, as it is commonly interpreted and applied, is not an adequate descriptive model and so we propose an alternative account of choice under risk.

Kahneman and Tversky (1979, 263)

This example from Kahneman and Tversky is strewn with polyphonic markers which refer to other voices of the academic discourse. The footnotes, for example, indicate certain works in relation to which the authors position their theory. But other markers such as "utility theory", "all reasonable people", "most people" and so forth point to other voices in the academic debate as well, which is held by this small excerpt from a well-known paper in economics. However, even if the strong hierarchisation processes and elitisation tendencies in disciplines such as economics restrict the access to important debates in the discipline to a small group of participants who have a chance to get heard, they nevertheless perpetuate this republican logic of academic discourse. Dialogic academia is a characteristic of every academic discourse in current societies, even if the access is sometimes open and sometimes highly exclusive.

But what happens to the voice of the republican when we leave the small and highly restricted world of academic discourse to enter teaching? In disciplines such as sociology (where I was academically socialised) students become introduced to this academic dialogue. I used to read texts by Marx and Weber, Beck and Giddens and so forth and what sociology students learn – among many things – is that sociology is controversy, constructed around multiple research fields, theories and methods where academics have to find a position as a member. The lecturers and professors whom sociology students meet during their studies help them to find their way through the discipline. In this social world, many colleagues have had similar experiences; some believe in stronger hierarchies, others in individual activism, but everybody knows that we live in a world of controversies. However, what happens in economics to the voice of the republican to which academics from the social sciences usually get introduced?

4.3 What is discourse analysis?

In the following analysis, I will argue that, in textbook teaching culture, the voice of the *academic republican* is replaced by the *voice of the schoolmaster*. This switch can be shown in different aspects of textbook discourses. Pahl's narrative analysis of textbooks (Pahl 2011) has elaborated particular elements and characteristics of the interpretative framing of the economic reality through neoclassical market concepts. Particularly significant is the narrative presentation of economics as a *natural science*, in opposition to political science and other social sciences, which studies the economy as a market with scientific methods. Furthermore, economics textbooks operate with *moralisations* of economic policy.

However, my discourse analysis follows Pahl's narrative analysis but extends and deepens it in two directions. First, while Pahl focuses on the knowledge dimension, I will ask how actors are constructed through discourses and how identities are distributed by discursive polyphony. Second, while Pahl seems to follow a certain critique on the epistemological status of mainstream economics knowledge, I will focus on the power dimension in processes of identity construction through discourses. Thus, I will not question the validity of mainstream economics knowledge (even if I share the critique); I will rather show how mainstream economics discourses contribute to the construction of certain professional identities.

Discourse analysis follows an enunciative methodology (see Flottum 2005; Angermuller 2013; Maesse 2015). The main goal of this approach is to ask how the speaker position of a discourse is formed by discursive markers. As the example from Kahneman and Tversky above has already illustrated, discourse analysis is not about analysing the validity or the epistemological statuses of knowledge. It takes the polyphonic organisation of texts into consideration which regulates academic communication processes. Fundamental discursive rules organise these communication processes. Three questions are important: Who speaks in the name of what? Where is the speaker located in time and space? Who is the speaker's other of discourse?

In democratic discourses, speakers usually position themselves in conflicting and dialogical ways within these constellations of positions which span time, space and persons (Bühler 1999 [1934]). Therefore, the speaker as an "academic republican" is presented as one figure among many others with whom s/he enters into collaboration or opposition. The interlocutor, who is the observer of this polyphonic spectacle and the instance to which the discourse is addressed, acts as a referee who must decide (sooner or later) with which camp s/he has sympathy, solidarity, agreement or disagreement. Therefore, the interlocutor is as free as every other actor in the polyphonic game and is invited to become a member of the discursive community. This is only possible because the many other voices of discourse are presented as dialogic figures. If the interlocutor wants to participate in the discourse (and get access to it, which is highly regulated by institutions, hierarchies and other power devices), s/he will develop an identity as a republican as well.

4.4 Three strategies for the constitution of the schoolmaster's voice

When the schoolmaster's voice replaces the republican's position, the polyphonic constellation of the discursive order will be fundamentally transformed. How is the position of the schoolmaster and her/his relation to the student-interlocutor organised by the discourse? The following discourse analysis will point to three techniques which will be applied by the discourse to constitute the schoolmaster's voice: first, the discourse creates a position for the reader (the interlocutor) which works as a *cognitive entry point* to the world of textbook knowledge. This is usually done through a short etymological introduction (economy coming from Greek *oikos*), allegorical allusions (i.e. to households) and comparisons of economic theorems with daily experiences (the scarcity principle with the household budget), or by the enumeration of anecdotes, as the following example (Box 12.2) illustrates.

Box 12.2: Schoolmaster's voice I

Decisions in life are rarely black and white but usually involve shades of gray. When it's time for dinner, the decision you face is not between fasting or eating like a pig, but whether to take that extra spoonful of mashed potatoes. When exams roll around, your decision is not between blowing them off or studying 24 hours a day, but whether to spend an extra hour reviewing your notes instead of watching TV. Economists use the term marginal changes to describe small incremental adjustments to an existing plan of action. Keep in mind that "margin" means "edge," so marginal changes are adjustments around the edges of what you are doing.

Mankiw (2003, 6)

Students can use this place, constructed by several metaphors, allusions, allegories etc. in order to build a cognitive bridge between their daily life world and their possible place in academia. When students obtain this cognitive place, they virtually enter into a communicative contract with the master speaker and declare a certain agreement for further communicative acts. Thus, the entry point is constructed by a cognitive bridge between the daily life experience of middle class students to the opaque world of economics terminology.

Second, after the enumeration of allegories, etymologies, metaphors and so forth, the discourse introduces a *symbolic opposition* which enthrones one perspective and devaluates others. This binary opposition starts already in the realm of metaphors through negations and black/white juxtapositions. Box 12.3 illustrates this binary oppositioning with the same example as in Box 12.3, but now with a focus on binary logic of language structure.

Box 12.3: Schoolmaster's voice II

Decisions in life are rarely black and white but usually involve shades of gray. When it's time for dinner, the decision you face is not between fasting or eating like a pig, but whether to take that extra spoonful of mashed potatoes. When exams roll around, your decision is not between blowing them off or studying 24 hours a day, but whether to spend an extra hour reviewing your notes instead of watching TV. Economists use the term marginal changes to describe small incremental adjustments to an existing plan of action. Keep in mind that "margin" means "edge," so marginal changes are adjustments around the edges of what you are doing.

Mankiw (2003, 6)

This strategy is not only a simplifying methodology for a cognitive (and social) mapping. It furthermore prepares the mind of the interlocutor (students), first, to understand the position of the economist, second, to train (through permanent repetition) how to fix this position, and, third, to learn that several other positions exist but do not belong to the realm of economics. The world appears, step by step, as divided between right and wrong, rational and non-rational, scientific and non-scientific. This oppositioning strategy finally enters into a core oppositioning which usually defines the general status of economics as a "superior position" (Fourcade et al. 2014). This is done by monophonic definitions (Box 12.4) . . .

Box 12.4: Schoolmaster's voice III

Economics is the study of how society manages its scarce resources.

Mankiw (2003, 4)

. . . and it is highlighted by a comparison of the economics perspective with possible competitors, as illustrated by Box 12.5.

Box 12.5: Schoolmaster's voice IV

Every field of study has its own language and its own way of thinking. Mathematicians talk about axioms, integrals, and vector spaces. Psychologists talk about ego, id, and cognitive dissonance. Lawyers talk about venue, torts, and promissory estoppel. Economics is no different. Supply, demand, elasticity, comparative advantage, consumer surplus, deadweight loss – these terms are part of the economist's language. (Mankiw 2003, 19)

The economist as a scientist (Mankiw 2003, 20)

The whole of Chapter 2 is an endless enumeration and equation of economics as a "science" with other natural sciences (physics, biology). Social sciences are not even mentioned as possible alternatives to economics, except in a small application in an appendix to Chapter 3 on page 59. Here, sociology is compared with economics, as presented in Box 12.6.

Box 12.6: Schoolmaster's voice V

Maria can read 20 pages of economics in an hour. She can also read 50 pages of sociology in an hour. She spends 5 hours per day studying.

a. Draw Maria's production possibilities frontier for reading economics and sociology.
b. What is Maria's opportunity cost of reading 100 pages of sociology?

It is, finally, up to the reader to decide what is more complex and theoretically sophisticated: sociology or economics. However, to present sociology as something (apparently not being worthy science) that can be handled as bedtime reading says a lot about the author's knowledge of sociology. More importantly, and this is the core argument presented in this text, it perhaps says something specific about the economist's professional identity. As Fourcade (2009) has outlined, in the US, "science" is something that is particularly prestigious (especially to laymen and other non-intellectuals who have no idea of what happens at university), whereas the social sciences are usually recognised as non-scientific ("sociology", "humanities", "culture", "irrational", "politics" and so forth). However, what we can see with these allusions to "science", and the obvious devaluation of the sociological literature, is that the economics perspective is developed by the discourse as a superior position. The "me" as well as the professional identity of mainstream economists stands in hierarchical opposition and supremacy to the discursive "other". The master leads the student exactly to this superior place which is, of course, fuelled by the superiority of the master position itself. What students learn is not how to study societies as "markets" but how to take a certain position of supremacy and mastery. Therefore, the differences to other perspectives are not created on the horizontal level of symbolic-imaginary differentiation (that includes equality at the vertical level), but on the hierarchical level of stratification.

Last but not least, a third positioning strategy that complements the other two and supports the constitution of the schoolmaster voice is what I would call *pedagogical exemplification*. Pedagogical exemplifications demonstrate what it means to apply a certain form of economic reasoning to a phenomenon or a political problem (see Box 12.7).

Box 12.7: Schoolmaster's voice VI

In Germany in January 1921, a daily newspaper cost 0.30 marks. Less than two years later, in November 1922, the same newspaper cost 70,000,000 marks. All other prices in the economy rose by similar amounts. This episode is one of history's most spectacular examples of inflation, an increase in the overall level of prices in the economy. Although the United States has never experienced inflation even close to that in Germany in the 1920s, inflation has at times been an economic problem. During the 1970s, for instance, the overall level of prices more than doubled, and President Gerald Ford called inflation "public enemy number one." By contrast, inflation in the 1990s was about 3 percent per year; at this rate it would take more than 20 years for prices to double. Because high inflation imposes various costs on society, keeping inflation at a low level is a goal of economic policymakers around the world.

Mankiw (2003, 13/14)

Why contribute this pedagogical exemplification to the constitution of the schoolmaster's voice? First, the problem is presented in a simple way and, second, the solution appears to be obvious. Both constitute a discursive "place of truth". The academic republican voice will work its way through other voices of controversy and opposition. The schoolmaster's "place of truth" appears presumptuous to the republican's mind, because in the republican's discourse, alternatives to the validity of the presented example as well as to the preferred solution will always be visible. The exemplifications of the schoolmaster, in contrast, are pedagogical because they only exemplify a phenomenon (inflation) and a solution (keeping it at a low level), which are valid from the very beginning of the presentation. They are not open to alternative solutions, negotiation and conflicting definitions. They are easy to understand and to learn because they come from the master's mind. He/she has access to the true definition (and exemplification) as well as to the proper political solution. The student-interlocutor must learn to adopt this position in order to get access to the place of truth which is the place of mainstream economics. No wonder that textbook discourses contribute to the formation of the professional identity concept of "superiority" (Fourcade et al. 2014) and elitist attitudes (Lenger 2016).

5. Conclusion

The discourse analysis of the textbook economics culture has studied some aspects of how a schoolmaster's voice develops in discourse. Further research and deeper investigations of different teaching settings and textbook uses in economics should be done in order to work out, differentiate or re-contextualise what I have tried to demonstrate with the schoolmaster's positioning game. In contrast to dialogical academia, the schoolmaster does not speak to an academic community who already has a "sense of judgement", as Immanuel Kant would have put it. The schoolmaster speaks to a student as a "disciple". The (republican) identity of an academic would never allow following a dogmatic system since dialogic academia is based on controversies and the mutual recognition of many other voices. A common solution, fixed consensus or established canon is virtually impossible in the socio-discursive system of the academic republic. However, the disciple replicates, rather, a scholastic system, a tableau of knowledge that is constructed according to fixed rules. This scholastic system cannot be verified, falsified and/or changed by empirical research. Scholasticism aims, rather, at the correct replication of a tableau of traditional knowledge. It is this scholastic logic that rules textbooks and motivates scholars to replicate the free market thesis, even if it is empirically irrelevant. It is precisely for this reason that the idea of the "market" can be used in political struggles as a strong ideological category and as an idiotisation device in public discourse.

Acknowledgements

I would like to thank the two reviewers and the editors of this volume for very helpful comments and critiques.

Note

1 I do not mean the Republican Party but the democratic institution, the *res publica (lat.: public affairs).*

References

Angermuller, J. (2013): 'How to Become a Philosopher. Academic Discourse as a Multi-Levelled Positioning Practice', *Sociología Histórica* 3, 263–289.

Beckenbach, F., Daskalakis, M. and Hofmann, D. (2016): *Zur Pluralität Der Volkswirtschaftlichen Lehre in Deutschland. Eine Empirische Untersuchung Des Lehrangebotes in Den Grundlagenfächern Und Der Einstellung Der Lehrende*. Marburg: Metropolis.

Blaug, M. (2003): 'The Formalist Revolution', in Samuels, W.J., Biddle, J.E. and Davis, J.B. (eds), *A Companion to the History of Economic Thought*. Malden: Blackwell, 395–410.

Bourdieu, P. (1989): *Distinction. A Social Critique of the Judgement of Taste*. London: Routledge.

Bühler, Karl. (1999 [1934]): Sprachtheorie *Die Darstellungsfunktion Der Sprache*. Stuttgart: UTB.

Coats, A.W.B. (1993): *The Sociology and Professionalization of Economics. British and American Economic Essays. Vol. II*. London and New York: Routledge.

Coats, A.W.B. (2001): 'The Role of Economists in Government and International Agencies: A Fresh Look at the Field', *The History of Economics Review* 34(1), 19–32.

Colander, D. (2003): 'Integrating Sex and Drugs into the Principles Course: Market-Failures versus Failures-of-Market Outcomes', *The Journal of Economics Education* 34(1), 82–91.

Colander, D. (2007): *The Making of an Economist, Redux*. Princeton: Princeton University Press.

Desrosières, A. (1998): *The Politics of Large Numbers: A History of Statistical Reasoning*. Cambridge, MA: Oxford University Press.

Dezalay, Y. and Garth, B. (2009): 'National Usages for a 'Global' Science. The Dissemination of New Economic Paradigms as a Strategy for the Reproduction of Governing Elites', in Mallard, G., Paradeise, C. and Peerbaye, A. (eds), *Global Science and National Sovereignty. Studies in Historical Sociology of Science*. New York: Routledge, 143–167.

Flottum, K. (2005): 'The Self and the Others: Polyphonic Visibility in Research Articles', *International Journal of Applied Linguistics* 15(1), 29–44.

Foucault, M. (1980): 'The Confession of the Flesh', in Gordon, C. (ed.), *Power/Knowledge Selected Interviews and Other Writings*. New York: Pantheon Books, 194–228.

Fourcade, M. (2006): 'The Construction of a Global Profession: The Transnationalization of Economics', *American Journal of Sociology* 112(1), 145–194.

Fourcade, M. (2009): *Economists and Societies. Disciplin and Profession in the United States, Britain, and France, 1890s to 1990s*. Princeton: Princeton University Press.

Fourcade, M., Ollion, E., and Algan, Y. (2014): 'The Superiority of Economists'. MaxPo Discussion Paper 14/3. http://www.maxpo.eu/pub/maxpo_dp/maxpodp14-3.pdf

Halsmayer, V. (2014): 'From Exploratory Modeling to Technical Expertise: Solow's Growth Model As a Multipurpose Design', *History of Political Economy* 46, 229–251.

Han, S.-K. (2003): 'Tribal Regimes in Academia: A Comparative Analysis of Market Structure across Disciplines', *Social Networks* (25), 251–280.

Hesse, J.-O. (2010): *Wirtschaft Als Wissenschaft. Die Volkswirtschaftslehre Der Frühen Bundesrepublik*. Frankfurt a. M.: Campus.

Hirschman, D. and Berman, E.P. (2014): 'Do Economists Make Policies? On the Political Effects of Economics', *Socio-Economic Review* 12, 779–811.

Kahneman, D. and Tversky, A. (1979): 'Prospect Theory: An Analysis of Decision under Risk', *Econometrica* 47(2), 263–291.

Laband, D.N. and Piette, M.J. (1994): 'The Relative Impacts of Economics Journals: 1970-1990', *Journal of Economic Literature* 32, 640–666.

Lamont, M. (2009): *How Professors Think. Inside the Curious World of Academic Judgment*. Cambridge, MA: Harvard University Press.

Lebaron, F. (2006): 'Nobel' Economists as Public Intellectuals: The Circulation of Symbolic Capital', *International Journal of Contemporary Sociology* 43(1), 87–101.

Lebaron, F. (2014): 'The World of Economics: A 'Strong Field' - Pegged to the Field of Power', Presentation at the Workshop 'Die Soziologie Ökonomischen Wissens', Jena, Presented at 18. July 2014.

Lee, F.S., Pham, X., Gu, G. (2013): 'The UK Research Assessment Exercise and the Narrowing of UK Economics', *Cambridge Journal of Economics* 37, 693–717.

Lenger, A. (2008): *Die Promotion: Ein Reproduktionsmechanismus Sozialer Ungleichheit.* Konstanz: UVK.

Lenger, A. (2016): 'Der Ökonomische Fachhabitus: Professionsethische Konsequenzen Für Das Studium Der Wirtschaftswissenschaften', in Minnameier, G. (ed.), *Ethik Und Beruf in Der Marktwirtschaft.* Gütersloh: Bertelsmann Verlag, 157 176.

MacKenzie, D. (2006): *An Engine, Not a Camera. How Financial Models Shape Markets.* Cambridge, MA and London: MIT Press.

Maesse, J. (2015): 'Economic Experts. A Discursive Political Economy of Economics', *Journal of Multicultural Discourses* 10(3), 279–305.

Maesse, J. (2016): 'The Power of Myth. The Dialectics between 'Elitism' and 'Academism' in Economic Expert Discourse'', *European Journal of Cross-Cultural Competence and Management* 4(1), 3–20.

Maesse, J. (2017): 'The Elitism Dispositif. Hierarchization, Discourses of Excellence and Organisational Change in European Economics', *Higher Education* 73, 909–927.

Maesse, J. (2018): 'Opening the Black Box of the Elitism Dispositif: Graduate Schools in Economics', in Bloch, R., Mitterle, A., Paradeise, A. and Peter, T (eds), *Universities and the Production of Elites. Discourses, Policies, and Strategies of Excellence and Stratification in Higher Education* Palgrave Studies in Global Higher Education. London: Palgrave Macmillan, 53–79.

Mankiw, G. (2003): *Principles of Economics.* South-Western Cengage Learning.

Merton, R.K. (1938): 'Science and the Social Order', *Philosophy of Science* 5(3), 321–337.

Möller, C. (2015): *Herkunft Zählt (Fast) Immer. Soziale Ungleichheiten Unter Universitätsprofessorinnen Und-Professoren.* Basel and Weinheim: Beltz Juventa.

Morgan, M.S. (2003): 'Economics', in Porter, T. and Ross, D. (eds.), *The Cambridge History of Science.* Cambridge: Cambridge University Press, 275–305.

Münch, R. (2014): *Academic Capitalism: Universities in the Global Struggle for Excellence.* New York: Routledge.

Pahl, H. (2011): 'Textbook Economics. Zur Wissenschaftssoziologie Eines Wirtschaftswissenschaftlichen Genres', *Prokla. Zeitschrift FüR Kritische Sozialwissenschaft* 164, 369–388.

Pahl, H. (2012): 'Die MedialitäT Der Wirtschaftswissenschaften: PfadabhäNgigkeiten, Transferprozesse Kognitiver AutoritäT Und Rhetorische Strategien Im Spannungsfeld Von Research Frontiers Und Textbook Economics', in LäMmle, K., Peltzer, A. and Wagenknecht, A. (eds), *Krise, Cash & Kommunikation – Fallstudien Zur Inszenierung Der Finanzkrise in Informations- Und Unterhaltungsmedien.* Konstanz: UVK, 139–158.

Pechman, J.A. (1989): *The Role of the Economist in Government. An International Perspective.* New York: Harvester Wheatsheaf.

Schneickert. (2013): *Studentische Hilfskräfte Und MitarbeiterInnen. Soziale Herkunft, Geschlecht Und Strategien Auf Dem Wissenschaftlichen Feld.* Konstanz: UVK.

Stichweh, R. (1984): *Zur Entstehung Des Modernen Systems Wissenschaftlicher Disziplinen. Physik in Deutschland 1740–1890.* Frankfurt a. M.: Suhrkamp.

13 Why economics textbooks must, and how they can, be changed into a real-world and pluralist economics

The example of a fundamentally new complexity-economics micro-textbook

Wolfram Elsner

1. Introduction: will this happen?

Colander (2015), among others (e.g. Courvisanos 2016), argued that, in the face of particular uncertainties about correct explanations in the social sciences (including economics), scientific rationality would require a genuine pluralistic approach. This applies particularly to teaching and textbook writing. The argument has also been developed and embedded in larger epistemological and methodological contexts in the previous chapters of this volume and, thus, does not need to be further elaborated and discussed here.

But Colander also argues that mainstream economics textbooks will not change, due to some petrified institutionalisation, however outmoded: their content is "institutionalised", maintaining the human capital of mainstream economists and a social capital among them. Writing and teaching it would provide mainstream economists with larger benefits than they would otherwise achieve, since changing it would involve high transaction costs (or capital depreciation). So they would just pursue a least-effort approach. Mainstream textbooks, thus, became part of the dominant institutional structure.

On top of that, they would receive considerable "external" financial incentives (payments, financial funding) to continue repeating (and only updating within narrow limits) their content. Also, publishers were part of this arrangement; publishers would use reviewers to judge a textbook proposal, who in turn are mainstream – in all, a self-reinforcing system. Thus, apparently, no crisis of the economics profession was recognisable (Colander 2015) – and, we may add, no real-world crisis would be able then to push the mainstream from its commanding position.

This might be considered a coordinated situation that evolved a writing-publishing-teaching-learning system, or, more simply (in Colander's words), it might be "what most students want" and "what the market [sic] wants." We may think of a Pareto-inferior Nash equilibrium, based on some social behavioural rule, emerging in a coordination game (among mainstream economists at least) with Pareto-different equilibria. This analogy may help us understand that individual(istic) agents involved in such an arrangement indeed have no unilateral "rational" incentive to deviate from it – even if change costs might be quickly compensated in the future, when a new and better coordination is attained.

In the case of economics the game's payoffs are not just determined by the teachers/students/publishers/reviewers system, but this mainstream has a larger, exterior role to play for the current economic system and its wealthy and powerful ruling forces. Thus, mainstream economists indeed have a lot to lose, in terms of money and reputation, should they no longer be the providers of the ruling ideas for the vested interests. So, perhaps this is, in fact, an anti-coordination game, a Hawk-Dove game, where the ruling forces support mainstream economists with such high incentives that these always play the dominance and exploitation strategy, the "hawks", and the others, heterodoxers, as long as they remain "anti-coordinated" with the hawks, have to play "dove", remaining the suppressed. Thus, it seems quite possible that the leading textbooks for global higher education will not change.

But 'the times they are a-changin''. The environment of economics evolved since 2008, and the pressure for reform seems to be higher today. In fact, ever more mainstream economists nowadays have realised that at least their research is more exciting, demanding, and rewarding, and that they gain more reputation, when not sticking to simplistic models, but turning to more appealing theories, models, and methods, now that more demanding technologies, methods, models, and theories are available, which can deal with more than simplistic systems with their clear-cut equilibria (or equilibrium paths) as benchmarks (even if dynamic and stochastic).

When the results of more than four decades of neoliberal "market" de-regulation – including unsustainable distribution, exploding richness of the rich, financialisation and financial meltdowns, and the lingering Great Recession – become ever less justifiable, and a litmus test of reality is increasingly required from the economic mainstream, the incentive structure for mainstream economists might change somewhat from the exterior. In fact, some media and many business and political practitioners have become more critical vis-à-vis this mainstream after 2008 (e.g. Mason 2016). Not least, many students of economics have begun to desert the established camp and got together in the *International Student Initiative for Pluralism in Economics* (ISIPE).

Mainstream economists, then, may find it increasingly profitable to enter more complex real-world research with more cutting-edge methods to gain reputation. But many also tend to focus more on reinterpreting their real-world results in favour of the old standard idea, the predetermined, optimal equilibrium (path) of the "market" economy, which will continue to serve the status quo of power and wealth by providing the desired rhetoric.[1]

But is there, nevertheless, space also for behavioural innovators, non-mainstream economists, who deviate from the status quo (or the current Nash equilibrium of economics)? Would critical, heterodox economists not only be able to write fundamentally alternative textbooks (and find some minor critical publisher), but also be able to cut an aisle into the monopoly of mainstream textbook publishing? Under a general requirement to provide real-world analyses and to apply more demanding methods, mainstream research may already have somewhat diversified, as even critical economists suggest (e.g. Colander et al. 2004; Davis 2006).[2] With this, a window may have opened for an upsurge of heterodox and complexity economics, but also for some more real-world, non-simplistic, broader, and more plural textbooks.

In all, in the last 20 years, a number of economists, students, publishers, media, and practitioners have somewhat departed from the former standard-economics camp, searching for new answers, diversifying economics, acknowledging, and making use of, the rich history of economic thought, returning to long-ignored ideas, developing "heterodox" interpretations and textbooks.

It is against that background that we will argue

- that economics textbooks not only have to be changed (from scratch), but also
- that they can be changed, and how we can bring together "critical masses" of research results and teaching experience that make such change feasible at points, even with globally leading established textbook publishers,[3] and, finally, show
- what such critical, real-world, pluralist, history-of-thought-aware "heterodox" textbooks might look like.

Section 2 will briefly describe the problematic situation of the mainstream between research and teaching. Section 3 explains the corresponding problematic structure (in fact, inconsistency) of the mainstream (micro-)textbook. Section 4 presents a case of how a radically new micro-textbook with a heterodox complexity-economics perspective could be published at a world-leading publishing house, and what it looks like. Section 5 briefly concludes.

2. A fundamental dichotomy of the neoclassical/neoliberal "market" mainstream

Economics has been a contested discipline among all scientific branches and a basically multi-paradigmatic science, although heterodoxies have increasingly been eclipsed (e.g. Elsner 1986; Elsner and Lee 2010). Its fundamentals for exact measurement are considerably weaker than in the sciences, and its interweaving with norms thus much more obvious and prevalent and it may easily become ideology-laden and subject to immunisation strategies. Crypto-normativity and immunisation against reality were indeed brought to perfection by the neoclassical school (see the classic methodological critique of "model-platonism" (Albert), e.g. Kapeller 2013), in its historical effort to become the allegedly exact "social physics", the scientific basis for the economy and the socio-economic status quo. Justifying the status quo of the "market economy" was promoted by developing an analogy to the analytical, deterministic and little complex mechanical physics of the early 19th century, deploying a pre-determined equilibrium, being unique, optimal, and self-equilibrating (stable).

Stochastic versions of such relatively simple deterministic systems became systems with "non-organised complexity"[4]: many components and variables, but a presupposition that interactions among these would average out, applying the famous Brownian motion (originally of blossom pollen on a fluid), such as those of molecules of a gas or fluid in a container under static conditions, the idea of mere random distributions (Gaussian normal distributions) of characteristics and events (system motions). This, in turn, justified the assumptions of mean values to be rationally expected, and of an average representative agent. With representative agents, aggregation is just a summation, simple linear characteristics of the system. These assumptions were justified in some natural circumstances, but of course rarely ever in socio-economies with interacting human agents – existing mean values as "rational expectations", easy variances as calculable risk. Mainstream financial market models were based on this until the financial meltdown of 2008, but they were unable to comprehend, expect or forecast major system crises, which did not appear in their smooth normal assumed distributions of agents and events – while real-world self-organised complex adaptive systems, in fact, exhibit highly uneven centrality and power distributions and related motions, so-called right-skewed distributions (and often so-called power-law distributions) with much more problematic dynamic properties implied.

So the critiques have also been permanent and fundamental, establishing the heterodox paradigms, Marxian, Veblenian, Sraffian, or Keynesian, and they further increased with the development of dynamic systems analyses, evolutionary and institutional modeling, physical statistics and social network analysis, and agent-based computational economics in the last two to three decades. The critiques always referred to the heroic and unrealistic neoclassical assumptions, e.g. on "perfect" information and hyper-rationality, required convenient function shapes, non-interdependence among agents, exclusively negative/equilibrating feedback etc., demonstrating computational infeasibility of the predicted perfect equilibrium (e.g. Keen 2001/2011, 2009). For example, alternative approaches to model, analyse, and compute "market economies" under more realistic assumptions than the Walrasian auctioneer – the abstract construction of some central agent required to explain the process of finding equilibrium prices, prohibiting "false trading" (exchange at "non-equilibrium" prices), in all a centralistic, authoritarian, and anti-liberal implication of a perfectly individualistic and "liberal" initial narrative of the "market economy" – looking for a general equilibrium from a direct interaction process, demonstrated an emergence of multiple equilibria, but beyond social optima, most of them exhibiting uneven distributions, which indeed is an essential realistic feature of unequal exchange under capitalism (e.g. Albin and Foley 1998).

Referring to the required function shapes as an example, it is notorious that when required concavities of goal functions (and convexities of isoquants) are not given, "market equilibria" may no longer be feasible. The argument had been developed already by Sraffa in the 1920s, the famous increasing returns argument. In the early 1970s, Sonnenschein, Mantel, and Debreu (SMD, e.g. Sonnenschein 1973) had shown that the assumptions of neoclassical theory on individual demand could not determine unique demand functions as supposed, and, thus, no unique equilibrium of a "market economy". This already signaled, in fact, the exhaustion and end of the neoclassical research programme to prove the historical superiority of a liberal "market economy" – an exhaustion, which, however, is still not taken serious (or even well-known or discussed) in the discipline.[5]

Under continuing attack by multiple "dissenters" and "heterodoxers", the pressure of an upcoming agent-based computational complexity economics, and after the mainstream's exposure to the 2008ff. crisis, many mainstream researchers have moved towards more complex research with its more rewarding methods and more interesting questions – often enough heterodox issues, many of them long-standing ones.

But there are massive extra-scientific forces and incentives to maintain the narratives and models of neoclassicism and neoliberalism, i.e. "market" superiority, de-regulation, minimal state, privatisation, marketisation, and financialisation, a science of the status quo of power and wealth distribution that only neoclassical mainstream economics can provide. Therefore, huge efforts are made, by an "industry" of funded research, towards (re-)interpretations of research results in a pro-"market", pro-status-quo, neoclassical or neoliberal perspective. Unsurprisingly, thus, no serious paradigm change of the mainstream has occurred after the financial crisis or in face of the lingering Great Recession.

In our view, there is only one "residual" explanation, after all "better arguments" have been put forward but could not change anything, for the ongoing dominance of the economic mainstream that has surprised many, and remained a major puzzle for many (for some overview of post-2008 media comments, e.g. Elsner and Lee 2010; Lee and Elsner 2010): Economics has a specific "external" function: it is the generator of the ideological identity and the rhetoric of the socio-economic status-quo and its distributional and power structures.

The neoclassical (and largely neoliberal) mainstream, thus, has remained, and will remain, unswayed by any academic critique, and even by some disregard and disrespect by individual entrepreneurial or political practitioners, except for providing the proper rhetoric, and will even have the resources to counterattack in terms of academic recruitment. Thus, no other discipline nowadays appears non-modern to such an extent, because simplistic rather than complex, as the famous physicist-economist Buchanan (2008) stated.

From this, a fundamental schizophrenia of the mainstream results: its basic research generates in large parts interesting cutting-edge results, often converging in theoretical explanations, models, and methods with broad streams of long-standing heterodoxies. (The latter, on their part, converge into complex systemic micro-macro dynamics, evolutionary and institutional process, social network analysis, agent-based modeling, and complex systems simulation.) But, after proper reinterpretation, its policy advice, its writings and messages in their often privately funded expertise, its public and media statements etc. – all areas, where the mainstream clearly dominates – maintain the standard "market" and neoliberal perspectives (e.g. Elsner 2008, 2011, 2013).

This is even more so in their mass teaching and textbook writing, as in academic recruitment. The same old simplistic, and infeasible, (partial-)"market" model consumes most of the time of the study programmes of generations of BAs, MAs and MBAs – and the largest parts of million-selling textbooks, where allegedly the model sufficiently resembles the economy "out there" (or v.v.).

As stated, the "trick" requires a deliberate, methodologically sophisticated, and (in more than hundred years) elaborated fuzziness of analytic-normative ontology, axioms, assumptions, and propositions. All the more prescriptive and crypto-normative are its political suggestions: if there is only one given optimal point in the universe, then "there-is-no-alternative" for policy – T-i-n-a (Thatcher) – to "market" de-regulation, privatisation etc.

Generation after generation of students worldwide, thus, will be sent into a complex, dynamic reality, with simple static models in their minds and no idea of intricate decision structures, lasting tensions, time, process, evolution, cumulation, and dis-equilibration, or even the transitions from reality to an aspired first-best of the "market".

3. Why this change must happen: the dichotomy, inconsistency, and peculiar outmodedness of the "mainstream"-economics textbook

An earlier critical view on the neoclassical mainstream textbook

Steve Keen, in his much-praised critical economics textbook *Debunking Economics* (2001/2011, 12–15), also started by showing that, why, and how the neoclassically-driven economics orthodoxy was unable to predict even the second most obvious economic crisis in history, the financial meltdown of 2008ff., while, however, a handful of heterodox economists (including himself), running complex (heterodox) models of the economy, did. In fact, the history of real economic crises had never caused the neoclassical mainstream to undergo any paradigm shift (4f.). Keen, thus, vivisects the orthodoxy's higher "education into ignorance" (19), illustrating through calculus, simulations, and empirical data analysis that, among others, there are no such things as a downward-sloping demand curve, a horizontal supply curve, a quickly rising unit-cost curve, an isolated, non-interacting representative agent, or a perfectly "rational" consumer (unless she has a brain as large as the universe, in order to make a "rational" choice among the trillions of alternative good bundles existing in any regular supermarket, or solving infinite-dimensional differential equation systems). But: "Don't tell the children!" (57) As stated, the dismantling of the neoclassical research programme by Sonnenschein, Mantel, and Debreu (see above) has been one of the best-kept secrets of the discipline.

Keen already cited Varian's *Microeconomics* (a recent edition: Varian 2014), showing that it displays a typical neoclassical opacity at critical points. The example was nothing less than the problem of aggregation. Already Varian's language was treacherous: "Suppose that" all individual consumers demand and consume "independent of the level of income of any consumer [and the distribution of those incomes] and also constant across consumers [. . .]" (cited from Keen, ibid.). Ignoring that exactly this eliminates the very core of any real economy and of any micro-macro interaction process, smooth dynamics or crisis, he continues:

> it is sometimes convenient to think of the aggregate demand as the demand of some "representative consumer" who has an income that is just the sum of all individual incomes. The conditions under which this can be done are rather restrictive [sic], but a complete discussion of this issue is beyond the scope of this book.
>
> Varian (2014, 271).

Note that his book has 790+ pages and still cannot explain adequately the fundamental economic problem, or counter one of the classical critiques, e.g. of Sraffa or Keynes, i.e. the (complex) systemic interdependence (and not identical reproduction) of supply and demand functions.

In sum, textbooks and mass teaching play a major role in maintaining the ruling worldview. It is the true tragedy of economics that it dismisses tens of thousands of young people worldwide every year, considered to be academically trained, into a complex world with only simple tools and little strategic, systemic, or procedural understanding.

The dichotomy, inconsistency, and deficient quality of the "mainstream" (micro-) textbook

While the general image of million-selling established (undergraduate) mainstream textbooks, with their often considerable number of editions, the most powerful publishing houses at their back, and lots of nice supplementary online technology, still is one of "standard", "established truth", "disciplinary consensus", "hard science", "solidity" and "reliability", "cutting-edge method" and the like, a closer look at them reveals that their pattern is not only one of extreme arbitrariness, unexplained conventionalism, simple additiveness of diverse critical issues, conventional methodology, mostly relatively simple maths (often the maximum level is the Lagrange algorithm, but with usually no explanation of its theoretical assumptions and restrictions). (For a review of mainstream micro textbooks, e.g. Elsner 2016).

Beyond the display of the standard model in the mainstream textbook, there is a typical trivialisation of new and more recent issues, such as network analysis, different repeated games, network technologies, informational collective goods, social dilemmas, open information and innovation, commons problems, emerging and changing institutions etc., a non-integration of new themes and methods, thus many remaining inconsistencies between these and the standard model of the first half of the book, and, in all, a peculiar inferior quality. Over all, they do not resemble the world out there, but rather they obscure and obvert it.

Thus, the mainstream million-selling textbook (Varian, Mankiw, Pindyck/Rubinfeld and others) has two virtual parts, usually far more than one hundred pages for the standard (comparative-static) partial-"market" equilibrium and its variations, and, depending on how many editions they already have gone through, a second half of additional more recent issues, each of which has the potential to make the first half of the book, the standard model, implode, but not the slightest feedback of all that material over many editions back to that standard model. These remain just "exemptions", "deviations", "curiosa", "varia", "miscellaneous", or "What-else-is-out-there?", including, as stated, externalities, the commons, information technology and network externalities, public/collective goods, or asymmetric information. But the standard message remains: that the "market economy" can be saved, and may help save us, from all these "peculiarities" and "curiosities" in reality.

Thus, students will be dismissed into reality with a world view that there is a "market" out there, which makes everything largely optimal and equilibrated, with, regrettably, some peculiar "disturbing" other isolated aspects on top – which however can be remedied by "more market".

Such textbooks would need a fundamental overhaul, integrating the newer themes and issues, and new methods from scratch, which, however, would make their standard models and message questionable, which, in turn, is unlikely to happen (according to Colander above). So a change of the textbook scenery is unlikely to happen through an endogenous change of the million-sellers. It will happen only through new textbooks. But how can their acceptance by the leading, usually conventional publishing houses, with reviewers representative of the discipline, happen, when the environment overall is adverse, and most curricula still prescribe the received standard?

4. How this can happen: the example of a new, complexity-based, evolutionary-institutionalist and pluralist micro-textbook

The substantial starting point

Luckily, a whole number of critical micro textbooks has come out in recent years, from Bowles (2004) through Himmelweit et al., Goodwin et al., Dollars & Sense, Keen, Dorman, Watkins, Bowles/Foley, Friedman, Fine, Lee and others to Elsner et al. Also, handbooks and collections on critical economics teaching with substantial and methodological teaching concepts have come out (e.g. Mearman 2007). We will briefly focus here on our own (Elsner, Heinrich and Schwardt 2015) to illustrate how this can emerge and what a critical, complexity- and real-world oriented structure may look like.

This micro textbook represents a radical deviation from the usual "demand – supply – market – equilibrium" paradigm, which usually is also pursued by many critical textbooks, either in an effort to criticise in strict parallelism with mainstream textbooks, or to undercut mainstream curricula with the conventional structure, but with critical arguments in detail. This textbook does not display the supply – demand – "market" scheme at all. Its perspective is that "markets" can be all or nothing – being just a decentralised spontaneous mechanisms, where prices play some role. They can be the worst human nightmare and catastrophe or some mechanism serving human needs in some reasonable way, as long as not clearly defined by the institutional arrangement that it represents and is embedded in, and the specific network structure that it in fact is. So the whole perspective is one of the more fundamental needs, motives, incentives, and mechanisms that make agents capable of coordinating (in coordination problems) or cooperation (in social-dilemma problems).[6] This is the classical political-economic research programme of Adam Smith, represented by his main works *Theory of Moral Sentiments* (1759) and *Wealth of Nations* (1776), i.e. first basic institutions, the specifics of the socio-economy. The informal self-organisation mechanisms and the processes of their emergence in complex structures are basic and prior to any "markets" or any other arrangements and allocation systems, which all are better comprehended as network forms, more central or more decentralised. The book integrates the modern issues mentioned so far from scratch.

Nevertheless, we do not change much in the beginning, apparently: we just assume direct interactions among agents that always have different options to act (as modeled in games). But this small change has huge implications for the totality of microeconomics. It quickly implies a phylogenetic approach, considering many 2x2 interactions played (often repeatedly) in populations with heterogeneous agents, behavioural diversification in a then fully-fledged evolutionary process and over historical time (with evolutionary game theory combined with explicit replicator mechanisms). It entails structural emergence, namely endogenously emerging institutions and endogenously evolving network structures and centrality distributions, with, in all, huge variations in outcome. Thus, the whole perspective is one of direct interactions of agents in populations, acting on different topologies, solving different and diverse specific common and collective problems in learning and adaptation processes.

The tools used are game theory from the very start; we start with simple thinking in interaction processes and more or less intricate common and collective decision problems, introduce some easy static standard game-theoretical normal form decision problems, but we quickly proceed to embedding games in careful and appropriate real-world narratives and modeling that make us depart from standard game-theory, entering evolutionary game theory and evolutionary replication. It is easily shown, then, that structures may emerge that are not reducible, i.e. cannot be traced back, to the properties of the individual agents – a basic element of the definition of complex systems and their dynamics.

This is all introduced easily, for undergraduate (1st and 2nd year) studies, where we have taught it for fifteen years. Having worked outside academia for ten years, I quickly apply the first simple technical apparatus to real-world problems of value-added chain coordination, dilemmas in innovation networks, network technologies, open innovation, and other simple coordination and cooperation problems to exercise and practise with (which will be done later at higher levels).

We derive the processes of the real global corporate economy, such as size growth, power-isation, oligopolisation, collusion, as well as standard wars, first-mover strategies, waiting and non-action, but also local clustering, regional systems of innovation, networking and combinations of power/hierarchy with network forms in global hub&spoke supplier networks – all as different, interrelated forms of, progressive or regressive, reaction to increasing complexity of firms' environment, and attempts to reduce such complexity and (re-) gain control over their ecological conditions.

We then proceed, with a real-world focus, to the "markets" part of chapters and contrast the standard neoclassical theory (including critical Lagrange maximisation and general equilibrium) with real-world markets of "size", power, oligopolisation, and the overlap of local oligopolistic network structures into regional, national, and global systems of "market" networks. The well-known oligopoly models form some common ground with neoclassical textbook standard chapters. Neoclassical price theory, then, is contrasted with institutional and post-Keynesian price theory. Sraffian and "Stiglitzian" alternative models of "markets" complete this part. This second part of the book is the only one in which we change our strategy from just teaching the better real-world alternatives to criticising the mainstream, i.e. identifying specific elements that are lacking in the neoclassical approach, and showing how this is problematic and can be addressed and remedied.

We increasingly integrate real-world and theoretical developments of the last decades, dealing with intricate common and collective problem structures, direct interdependence and coordination/cooperation, path-dependent and non-ergodic,[7] and often idiosyncratic[8] process in real (historical) time. After a second batch of chapters introducing formalisms of evolutionary game theory in more detail, and explicit replication, we enter into chapters on agent-based modeling and simulation, and evolutionary and increasingly complex systems, and dynamic analysis of systems more generally, which are considered to be reserved for advanced graduate and PhD-levels.[9]

We proceed with a critical selected history of economic thought that comprises a history of complex economic thinking, starting with Smith's theory of institutional emergence (*Theory of Moral Sentiments*, see above) and the idea of unintended systemic consequences. A chapter on some fifteen selected core models of modern complexity economics follows, which have proved to be important in some broader array of theoretical perspectives, be they critical neoclassical, institutionalist, biological core models, or network models, covering such diverse angles as those of Axelrod, Arthur, Schelling, Kaufman, Ostrom, and Bush. Applied chapters follow with themes such as the size and particularly "meso" dimension of economies, innovation economics, which has usually been the field of complexity economics, information and open information economics, policy implications of complex adaptive systems, and on epistemological reflection. For more detail, see the parts structure below in Box 13.1 and the chapter structure in the appendix.

Box 13.1: The "Microeconomics of Complex Economies" Textbook: Parts Structure

I. BASICS OF THE INTERDEPENDENT ECONOMY AND ITS PROCESSES
II. MARKETS: GENERAL-EQUILIBRIUM THEORY AND REAL-WORLD MARKET STRUCTURES
III. FURTHER TOOLS AND THE ANALYSIS OF COMPLEX ECONOMIES
IV. HISTORY OF THOUGHT AND CONTEMPORARY MODELS IN COMPLEXITY ECONOMICS
V. FURTHER APPLICATIONS: INFORMATION, INNOVATION, POLICY, AND METHODOLOGY

There are few textbooks that meet the demand for high-quality complexity micro, and thus are not obviously a "usual suspect" heterodox book, as many critical and alternative textbooks are, even those that follow the standard structure of "demand – supply – market". Thus, there are few close to our conception, basically only Bowles (2004) and Bowles/Foley (still online only).

Reviews of the book (such as in the *Journal of Economic Methodology*, *Journal of Economic Issues*, or *Mind & Society*) have stressed that we are not just offering

- a cutting-edge complexity micro textbook
- covering undergraduate, graduate and advanced levels
- an array of established courses (micro econ, industrial econ, innovation and information econ, game theory, methods/simulation/ABM, economic philosophy and methodology), and
- a pluralistic one, with neoclassical, evolutionary, institutional, complexity and some other heterodox perspectives, but that here also
- a first heterodox embedding of cutting-edge complexity economics is provided.

The process towards a fully-fledged textbook publication

The book has evolved from fifteen years of teaching micro at undergraduate and graduate levels. The book project itself matured in around five years.

Edward Elgar (in person) was the first I had approached with the idea as early as 1999. A contract was concluded within a year. But Elgar, in fact, was not the right publishing house in the end, not being a fully-fledged textbook publisher in 2011/2012. He did not wish to publish a "big" textbook. So we offered a "light", 250pp. version, which in fact was a selection of more core chapters, a more "conservative" project, which then appeared at Elgar in 2012.

For the fully-fledged, +550pp. version, the usual top addresses were approached in 2013, while we still were working on updates, elaborations, extensions, and rounding off. The top mainstream publishers and even largly "heterodox" publisher, M.E. Sharpe, straightforwardly declined. One of the friendly denial letters said, the book were just "too innovative".

Somewhat surprisingly, Elsevier, the one with the most conservative image, with its textbook branch, Academic Press, was interested. A remarkable, one year-long intense process started. But a very helpful Elsevier book editor managed that process through three stages, always with clear and constructive to-do lists for us. Our first proposal, the then about 70% finished book, was made subject not to the usual two reviewers, not three, not four ... but twelve anonymous reviewers were engaged! They represented, as we could infer from their reviews, the whole spectrum of perspectives from hard-core neoclassicals to some radical. In the first round, we received a huge diversity of comments, most very useful for a future implementation in the main geographical area, USA. A revised proposal was submitted to a second referee round (same reviewers). The reviewers did clearly converge on the supporting side, with two hardcore neoclassical outliers still unswayed, but a clear majority saying "Yes, I would use the book in my course" and "Yes, this book can make it", and some even saying: "This might become one of the future textbooks". The second revision then went into the in-house editors' conference, which took a favorable decision. The final decision was taken by an in-house top-level decision and it was a "Go!", a success after one year of intense struggle. The book is well considered by the publisher now, and said to be selling better than expected (where expectations were rather moderate, we would assume).

What does this adoption process tell us? Let us briefly conclude.

5. Conclusion

A real-world, "post-2008", pluralistic and critical-heterodox, cutting-edge and complexity-oriented teaching and learning of economics is possible, and related textbooks have a chance to appear even at the conventional global first-level of publishers. A consequent break with the simplistic "market" conception and rhetoric, and the usual "demand – supply – market – plus – variations/exemptions" structure can be achieved. Under a changing environment, as described, these publishing houses want to diversify and take on new textbooks of quality with some embedding of advanced formal methods, both conventional and new. Himmelweit et al. (2001), and Bowles (2004), alternative-textbook pioneers (together with Goodwin et al. 2nd edition, 2009), appeared at conservative publishers, Thomson and Sage; Dorman's Micro and Macro textbooks appeared at Springer. Pluralism plus high quality, thus, has some chance under post-2008 conditions (of transition). Critical and heterodox economists have to take themselves seriously and become serious contenders of the mainstream, rather than remaining the "usual suspects" (see also, e.g. Courvisanos 2016). The publishing of heterodox, pluralistic textbooks at conventional top-level publishers rather than courageous minor alternative and critical publishers (like Zed, Verso and others), which, on their part, have a supply of exciting (text-) books (such as Keen), is a step forward in the process of the contested discipline – one little step to the better, not more, but also not less.

Appendix 13.1

The microeconomics of complex economies.
Evolutionary, institutional, neoclassical, and complexity perspectives
W. Elsner, T. Heinrich, H. Schwardt

Table of Contents

V. FURTHER APPLICATIONS: INFORMATION, INNOVATION, POLICY, AND METHODOLOGY

15. The Information Economy and the Open-Source Principle
16. Networks and Innovation – The Networked Firm, Innovation Systems, and Varieties of Capitalism
17. Policy Implications: New Policy Perspectives for Private Agents, Networks, Network Consultants, and Public Policy Agencies
18. How to Deal with Knowledge of Complexity Microeconomics: Theories, Empirics, Applications, and Actions.

Notes

1 This is usually the case, when considerations (analyses, modeling) of the complexity of economic systems as evolving networks end up in a laissez-faire advocacy, restoring a superiority of the "market" then in some (flawed) evolutionary sense of its capacity of long-run selection of the "fittest" (as an example concluding a laissez-faire policy in a Hayekian perspective directly from the financial crisis 2008ff.: Lewin 2014). Other examples include any use of game theory, agent-based modeling, social network analysis etc., applied to oligopoly structures, right-skewed centrality and power distributions in networks etc., but then suggesting that we still are talking about "markets" tending towards equilibrium and defining the optimality benchmark (the leading mainstream textbooks mirror, and do in fact help to establish, this research-to-policy transformation pattern; see below).

2 Consider the theoretical developments of the late K. Arrow (and his role in the Santa Fé Institute) and P. Samuelson, a number of critical presidential speeches of AEA presidents such as, recently, Akerlof or Shiller, many prominent critical keynotes and prominent papers at AEA annual conferences, W. Mosler's and G. Soros's fundings of critical economic research and teaching (within INET, for instance), and other aspects of a melting of the earlier hard-core economic mainstream in research.

3 We are, of course, aware that many critical textbook proposals still are choked off by the mainstream "system".

4 For the distinction among simple systems, systems with non-organised, and with organised complexity, see Weaver 1948.

5 Note that mainstream economists often read the SMD results as conditions, under which aggregation is feasible, which, in turn, shows that the neoclassical case is mostly only an extreme special case of economic systems and states.

6 Note the terminology: Successful coordination is the solution of coordination problems as formally represented by coordination games. As coordination therein is in the immediate interest of the agents, but alternative forms of coordination are possible, the solution requires a learned social rule. In contrast, successfully established cooperation is the solution of social dilemmas as formally represented by prisoners' dilemmas or collective-good games. As defection here is the dominant strategy, cooperation requires the sacrifice of the short-run individualistic maximum (active exploitation) in favour of the longer-run cooperative (mutual) maximum. In order to be able to achieve this, there must be a credible thread among individualistic agents of a mutual punishment (an endogenous sanction, exerted by a trigger strategy like tit-for-tat, leading all agents back into the inferior situation of mutual defection) to incite agents to learn to cooperate in a process. The tool to sustain such cooperation will be a social institution, i.e. a social rule plus an endogenous sanction mechanism.

7 Path-dependent processes are the contrary to random processes. In terms of measurable time series this implies so-called non-stationarity, in terms of system

states this means so-called non-ergodicity, i.e. the distributions of the possible states that a system could basically assume and of the states a system actually assumes over time differ.

8 Idiosyncracy in system dynamics is a particularly heavy volatility of the system against relatively marginal changes of exogenous or endogenous conditions (in an artificial system: a marginal parametrical change). Systems then usually go through so-called phase transitions, and particularly so-called bifurcations, where they may switch among multiple equilibria and even enter so-called chaotic phases, where short-run prediction of the path the system will take is impossible.

9 I owe the idea of the particular relevance of graduate studies to a reviewer: professors teach what they were taught, and investment in mathematics as used by the mainstream can be considerable (see already the introduction above). So few would want to give this up for the sake of more realism. Therefore, graduate education in particular should come in the focus of change. For applied alternative graduate teaching approaches, see many chapters throughout this volume.

References

Albin, P. and Foley, D. (1998): *Barriers and Bounds to Rationality: Essays on Economic Complexity and Dynamics in Interactive Systems*. Princeton: Princeton University Press.

Bowles, S. (2004): *Microeconomics. Behavior, Institutions, and Evolution* New York. Princeton, N.J.: Sage and Princeton University Press.

Buchanan, M. (2008): 'This Economy Does Not Compute', *New York Times*, OP-ED, October 1.

Colander, D. (2015): 'Why Economics Textbooks Should, but Don't, and Won't, Change', *European Journal of Economics and Economic Policy* 12(2), 229–235.

Colander, D., Holt, R. and Rosser, B. (2004): 'The Changing Face of Mainstream Economics', *Review of Political Economy* 16(4), 485–499.

Courvisanos, J. (2016): 'In from the Cold. From Heterodoxy to a New Mainstream Pluralism', in Courvisanos, J., Doughney, J. and Millmow, A. (eds.): *Reclaiming Pluralism in Economics*. New York: Routledge, 303–314.

Davis, J. (2006): 'The Turn in Economics: Neoclassical Dominance to Mainstream Pluralism?', *Journal of Institutional Economics* 2(1), 1–20.

Elsner, W. (1986): *Ökonomische Institutionenanalyse. Paradigmatische Entwicklung Der Ökonomischen Theorie Und Der Sinn Eines Rückgriffs Auf Die Ökonomische Klassik Am Beispiel Der Institutionenanalyse ('Property Rights')* [On Multi-Paradigmatic Development of Economics and the Relevance of a Systematic Recourse to the History of Economic Thought.] (Habilitation Thesis). Berlin: Duncker & Humblot.

Elsner, W. (2008): 'Market and State', in O'Hara, P.A. (ed.), *International Encyclopedia of Public Policy*. Vol. III, *Global Governance and Development – Public Policy*. Perth:: GPERU, 370–389 Available at http://pohara.homestead.com/Encyclopedia/Volume-3.pdf, accessed March 6, 2017.

Elsner, W. (2011): 'Evolutionary Institutionalism. Sources, History and Contemporary Relevance of the Association for Evolutionary Economics – AFEE', *Intervention. European Journal of Economics and Economic Policies* 8(1), 29–41.

Elsner, W. (2013): 'State and Future of the 'Citadel' and of the Heterodoxies in Economics: Challenges and Dangers, Convergences and Cooperation', *European Journal of Economics and Economic Policy* 10(3), 286–298.

Elsner, W. (2016): The Dichotomy, Inconsistency, and Peculiar Outmodedness of the 'Mainstream' Textbook *MPRA Paper no. 70471* available at https://mpra.ub.uni-muenchen.de/70471/1/MPRA_paper_70471.pdf accessed January 30, 2018.
Elsner, W., Heinrich, T. and Schwardt, H. (2015): *Microeconomics of Complex Economies. Evolutionary, Institutional, Neoclassical, and Complexity Perspectives*Oxford: Elsevier/Academic Press.
Elsner, W. and Lee, F.S. (2010): 'Editors' Introduction to 'Evaluating Economic Research in a Contested Discipline. Rankings, Pluralism, and the Future of Heterodox Economics', *Studies in Economic Reform and Social Justice*, Repr. of a Special Issue of *The American Journal of Economics and Sociology* 69(5), 1–12.
Goodwin, N., Nelson, J.A., Ackerman, F. and Weisskopf, T. (2009): *Microeconomics in Context*, 2nd. Armonk, New York: M.E. Sharpe.
Himmelweit S., Simonetti, R. and Trigg, A. (2001): *Microeconomics. Neoclassical and Institutionalist Perspectives on Economic Behaviour* Andover. Hampshire, UK: Thomson Learning.
Kapeller, J. (2013): ''Model Platonism' in Economics: On a Classical Epistemological Critique', *Journal of Institutional Economics* 9(2), 199–221.
Keen, S. (2001/2011): *Debunking Economics. The Naked Emperor Dethroned?* 2nd ed. London: Zed Books.
Keen, S. (2009): 'A Pluralist Approach to Microeconomics', in Reardon, J. (ed.): *The Handbook of Pluralist Economics Education*. London: Routledge, 120–150.
Lee, F.S. and Elsner, W. (2010): 'Assessing Economic Research and the Future of Heterodox Economics. Failures and Alternatives of Journals, Departments, and Scholars Rankings', *Intervention. European Journal of Economics and Economic Policies* (7.1), 31–42.
Lewin, P. (2014): Policy Design and Execution in a Complex World: Can We Learn from the Financial Crisis?. Univ. of Texas Dallas, http://papers.ssrn.com/sol3/papers.cfm?abstract_id=2473258;, accessed March 2, 2017.
Mason, J.W. (2016): 'When We Turn to Concrete Economic Questions, There Isn't Really a 'Mainstream' at All', http://evonomics.com/economist-mason-turn-concrete-economic-questions-isnt-really-mainstream/, accessed March 3, 2017.
McCauley, J.L. (2006): 'Response to 'Worrying Trends in Econophysics'', *Physica A* 371, 601–609.
Mearman, A. (2007): 'Teaching Heterodox Economics Concepts', in: *The Handbook for Economics Lecturers*, https://www.economicsnetwork.ac.uk/handbook, accessed July 7, 2016.
Sonnenschein, H. (1973): 'Do Walras' Identity and Continuity Characterize the Class of Community Excess Demand Functions?', *Journal of Economic Theory* 6(4), 345–354.
Varian, H. (2014): *Intermediate Microeconomics*, 9th ed. New York: W.W. Norton.
Weaver, W. (1948): 'Science and Complexity', *American Scientist* 36(4), 536–544.

14 What can we learn from school economics education?

Janina Urban

1. What economics can learn from school education

Teaching a plurality of perspectives in civic education is considered a standard in German schools. The *Beutelsbacher* consensus of 1976, agreed upon above party and confessional lines, holds that the plurality of society and politics must be reflected in teaching content. Key principles include, besides this claim for pluralism or controversy, the consideration of the student's interests and the prohibition of overwhelming the student (Reinhardt 2016). For university education, it is widely held that its content should cover core results of what has been developed under the freedom of science (Deutscher Hochschulverband 1999). School and university curricula and textbooks reflect these different ideals while, at the same time, both fields have undergone major shifts towards more internationalisation, regulation, and external influence. In this comment, I aim to show, on the one hand, how pluralism is a natural part of civic education, especially when looking at teaching material. On the other hand, I point to developments in school and university curricula and teaching material which reveal a problematic one-sidedness of theoretical and political positions. In order to preserve pluralism in schools and to achieve it in universities, there seems to be a need for more transparency and stronger institutional support for critical voices.

2. Debates on the direction of (economic) education and pluralism in teaching material

School and university education as well as culture are the major policy fields of the German states. Together with students, teachers and academia, the conference of the state ministries for education and culture inter alia aims to achieve quality standards as well as the unity and comparability of certificates between states and nations (KMK 2016). The bad results of German students in the OECD-wide PISA test in 2000 motivated the introduction of education standards and an increasing output orientation in teaching, which is still regarded as a somewhat controversial development for two main reasons. Firstly, the PISA test itself is perceived to diminish diversity in education and to make students primarily fit the requirements of an international labour market (Graupe and Krautz 2014, 140–141). Secondly, standards differ according to school type, which can be regarded as cementing the already high selectivity of the German school system (Wernstedt and John-Ohnesorg 2009, 5–6).

While for civic education national standards are still in the process of formulation, curricula and teaching material determined by the states continue to be the major field of differing education concepts and practices. A claim for the further inclusion of *economic* education in schools has been widely received in the public debate, with some scientists and practitioners calling for a separate subject "economy" and for teaching more of the standard neoclassical concepts like the homo oeconomicus, efficiency and market equilibrium (Kaminski and Burkard 2008; degöb 2011). Others have shown how economic content is already part of the subject civic education as well as geography, recommending to strengthen the existing socioeconomic content between subjects and within an embedded understanding of economic phenomena (Hedtke 2016a, i, 1; Iböb, Initiative für eine bessere ökonomische Bildung 2016). Researchers of the socioeconomic education tradition have set up principles which reflect the *Beutelsbacher* consensus and in some points overlap with the call for pluralism in economics in universities raised by students and professors (e.g. Thielemann et al. 2012; Netzwerk Plurale Ökonomik 2012; ISIPE, International Student Initiative for Pluralism in Economics 2014). These principles for socio-economic education include orientation towards and relevance for the life situation of the student, contextualisation of economic phenomena, analysis and reflection of theoretical, political, normative, methodological and practical plurality, including the plurality of agents and forms of knowledge, critique and orientation towards multiparadigmatic, scientific concepts (Hedtke 2016a, 4–5; Iböb, Initiative für eine bessere ökonomische Bildung 2016).

An in-depth analysis of civic education school books has until now only dealt with attitudes towards entrepreneurism, the state and the social market economy (Grindel and Lässig 2007; Lenz 2010), and not with pluralism in economics in particular. For the purpose of an explorative analysis for this comment, the two most relevant books from the authorised book list for civic education of the ministry of education of North Rhine-Westphalia have been chosen (MSW Ministerium für Schule und Weiterbildung Nordrhein-Westfalen 2016). A look at these books of the specialisation phase reveals that the principles of the *Beutelsbacher* consensus are widely fulfilled. In most parts of the books analysed, two conflicting points of view or points of departure are presented, for example on wage and unemployment (Floren 2015, 52–53; Stiller 2015, 86–87), on the role of the state in the economy (Floren 2015, 121–129, 173–181, 224–236; Stiller 2015, 48–61, 89–91, 135–139), on the goals of monetary policy (Floren 2015, 245–256; Stiller 2015, 139–140), on current account surpluses (Floren 2015, 221–222; Stiller 2015, 69–72), on growth (Floren 2015, 149–152; Stiller 2015, 39–40), on free trade (Floren 2015, 419–430; Stiller 2015, 154–162, 193–203), on taxation (Floren 2015, 262–261, 270; Stiller 2015, 244–245, 307–310), on income and wealth inequality (Floren 2015, 68–76; Stiller 2015, 302–310), on environmental issues (Floren 2015, 276–278; Stiller 2015, 344–347) and on European integration and crises (Floren 2015, 339–341, 352–355; Stiller 2015, 415–420). Although sparingly, Keynesian, Schumpeterian and Marxian theory appear as valid theoretical starting points for analysing current economic and political issues (Floren 2015, 86, 173, 224–228; Stiller 2015, 44, 48–50, 283–284).

This acknowledgement of a meaningful variety of perspectives on economic and political issues in schoolbooks differs clearly from what recent book reviews find in university economics textbooks. Here, economic issues are exclusively explained by the mainstream paradigm (neoclassic economics, the New Keynesian Consensus and behavioural economics) (van Treeck and Urban 2016). As this paradigm also forms the core of university economic education for future school teachers, it is not surprising that concepts which break down socially and politically negotiable economic issues into questions of market (dis-)functions and incentives are also widespread in schoolbooks. The goals of public policies, for example, are identified as lying in allocation, distribution, correcting market failures, stability and growth (Stiller 2015, 28), or as having to weigh positive against normative arguments (Floren 2015, 154–156). Looking at free trade, the Heckscher-Ohlin model is taken as the scientific benchmark (Floren 2015, 423–425; Stiller 2015, 156–157) while path dependencies in development and financial market instabilities are not mentioned. Environmental issues are only conceptualized as problems of market failure by Floren (2015, 275–279). Furthermore, concepts like the business location of Germany (Floren 2015, 457–465; critically Stiller 2015, 68–77) and Germany's inflation experiences (Floren 2015, 180–194; Stiller 2015, 96–101) are partly discussed at greater length, which may evoke an overly strong identification with the nation or the national economic model.

3. Limited plurality and external influence

The trend towards a superficial plurality – in which the starting point is neoclassical economics with variations – can also be observed in other teaching material and curricula of civic education. Schoolbooks of the introductory phase start with the homo oeconomicus and deviations, taken from behavioural economics, continue with "the market", market failures, the German social market economy and the functioning of corporations (Floren 2014, 5; more contextualized and differentiated Stiller 2014, 4–5). A further source of increasingly one-sided and even manipulative content is the material offered online and for free by third parties like insurance companies, banks, other companies, but also the chambers of commerce and institutes. A study which looks at the transparency, controversy and student orientation of such online resources shows that material offered by corporations receives the worst grades of all suppliers examined (VZBV 2014). This rising influence of third parties can said to be due to digitalisation and the need to keep education material up to date, but also due to the increased claim for an economically-oriented education and lobby interests. A recent examination of the civic education curricula of all school forms in North Rhine-Westphalia uncovers that there has been a strengthening of ordoliberal concepts in recent years, and a questionable microeconomic focus for lower and more practically-oriented school forms and levels, alongside more macroeconomic content for higher levels. Concepts from the scientific fields of political economy, economic policies and macroeconomics are lacking throughout. This trend of presenting economic and political issues to the majority of students only through the lenses of consumers and corporations, according to Hedtke "depoliticizes the perspective on the economy and withdraws one central policy field from the democratic process" (Hedtke 2016a, 49; Hedtke 2016b).

4. Monoparadigmatic dominance and diversity reducing competition in universities

While schools moved towards a stronger output orientation at the turn of the millennium, the Bologna process demarked a similar shift for universities. After the democratisation of universities in the 1970s, the 1980s and 1990s saw the entry of corporate mechanisms into universities. This turn was accompanied by protests and concerns over how third-party funds, university rankings and excellence initiatives would influence the aim of knowledge generation (Grammes 2009, 4–5; Merkt 2014, 95–102). This orientation towards what Grammes calls "the rule of the secondary" (Grammes 2009, 5) seems to have created an especially problematic situation in economics, in which recent scientific work still deviates little from the neoclassic paradigmatic core (Dobusch and Kapeller 2009; Grimm et al. 2016).

Looking at the module handbooks of introductory economic courses and results of 406 interviews with university lecturers in Germany, a recent study finds that the plurality in curricula and practical teaching is very limited. Only 17.2 percent of the interviewed report teaching concepts other than mainstream in undergraduate introductory courses, though with rising figures in higher level courses. Furthermore, bigger universities tend to have more strongly specified guidelines with mainly orthodox concepts, while smaller universities tend to have less specified ones, potentially leaving room for pluralism in teaching. In some cases, like at the universities of Bremen or Lueneburg, more strongly specified module handbooks already stipulate theoretical and methodological pluralism (Beckenbach et al. 2016). As mentioned before, the limited plurality in curricula is accompanied by the dominance of a number of US textbooks which in their baseline message do not deviate much from the theoretically and empirically challenged conclusions drawn from neoclassical standard models (van Treeck and Urban 2016).

5. Conclusion

What can we learn for the academic discipline by looking at how economics is taught in schools (Table 14.1)? Clearly, the recent meta-analyses of economics teaching and research make a vital contribution to the discussion of whether the current structures in education in fact improve knowledge. Such meta-analyses have always been in place for school education and even constitute their own academic field. Module handbooks could move further to the centre of attention, either calling on universities to leave lecturers enough room for good economic teaching, or by inscribing more pluralism into curricula. Since adapting the curricula is already a sensible task for schools, offering more pluralistic teaching material has been chosen by a variety of actors to meet the demand for a greater variety in perspectives (e.g. Jäger and Springler 2012; van Staveren 2014; Exploring Economics[1]).

Despite these positive developments in the field of economics, recent trends in school and university economics education hint to a disproportion of scientific and political positions which should be reflected upon. Ordoliberal and microeconomic neoclassical concepts come to dominate school material and curricula. This seems to be somewhat connected to the fact that 50 percent of German professors do research in the field of microeconomics, while macroeconomic aspects appear to be underrepresented, and that a relative majority is or was active in rather ordoliberal and neoliberal think tanks (Kapeller et al. 2016). Although other studies show that economists are generally open towards more pluralistic approaches in their field (Beckenbach et al. 2016; Fricke 2016), the structures of universities currently seem to limit potential. What is problematic in the university context is even more worrying

Table 14.1 Comparison of teaching material, curricula and meta-analyses in school and university economic education

	University economic education	*School civic education*
Meta-analyses of institutions, curricula and material	– no, only very recent studies on the state of economic education (and research) with regard to the aim of increasing knowledge	– yes, a continued evaluation of teaching institutions, content and methods, with regard to the state of the art of the correspondent scientific fields, student orientation and pluralism
Plurality in curricula	– no/yes, mainly orthodox concepts and rather strongly specified curricula, but some room for pluralistic teaching	– yes/no, still concepts from the pluralistic socio-economic tradition, but stronger ordoliberal focus
Plurality in teaching material	– no, but increasingly pluralistic or heterodox content offered by non-mainstream authors and by students	– yes, but increasingly more neo-classical and ordoliberal content and manipulative external material

in the school environment, since the standards of the *Beutelsbacher* Consensus are increasingly violated, knowingly and unknowingly, by interest groups and schools themselves. The – a reaction of schools and universities to these developments could thus involve an increased effort and debate about how and if a claim for plurality can be fulfilled with more determination.

Note

1 Exploring Economics is an online teaching and learning platform for pluralist economics. Available at https://www.exploring-economics.org/de/.

References

Beckenbach, F., Daskalakis, M. and Hofman, D. (2016): *Zur Pluralität Der Volkswirtschaftlichen Lehre in Deutschland.* Marburg: Metropolis.

degöb, Deutsche Gesellschaft für ökonomische Bildung (2011): *Forderungen Zur Ökonomischen Bildung an Allgemein Bildenden Schulen.* Available at http://degoeb.de/index.php?page=forderungen, accessed 9 December 2016.

Deutscher Hochschulverband (1999): 'Zur Zukunft Der Deutschen Universität'. Resolution Des 49. Hochschulverbandstages 1999. Available at https://www.hochschulverband.de/537.html#, accessed on 25 November, 2016.

Dobusch, L. and Kapeller, J. (2009): 'Why Is Economics Not an Evolutionary Science? New Answers to Veblen's Old Question', *Journal of Economic Issues* 43(4), 867–898.

Floren, F.J. (2014): *Politik, Gesellschaft, Wirtschaft. Sozialwissenschaften in Der Gymnasialen Oberstufe* Band 1 (Einführungsphase). Paderborn: Schöningh.

Floren, F.J. (2015): *Politik, Gesellschaft, Wirtschaft. Sozialwissenschaften in Der Gymnasialen Oberstufe* Band 2 (Qualifikationsphase). Paderborn: Schöningh.

Fricke, T. (2016): *Wenn Wirtschaftsweise Den Erkenntnisfortschritt Bremsen* FGW-Impuls Neues ökonomisches Denken 02. Düsseldorf: FGW.

Grammes, T. (2009): 'Editorial: Ausbildungsdidaktiken – Themen Und Aufgaben Einer Hochschulfachdidaktik Der Sozialwissenschaften in Der Lehrerausbildung', *Journal of Social Science Education* 8(2), 2–22.

Graupe, S. and Krautz, J. (2014): 'Die Macht Der Messung. Wie Die OECD Mit PISA Ein Neues Bildungskonzept Durchsetzt', *Coincidentia* Beiheft 4, 139–146.

Grimm, C., Kapeller, J., and Pühringer, S. (2016): 'Zum Profil Der Deutschsprachigen Volkswirtschaftslehre – Paradigmatische Ausrichtung Und Politische Orientierung Deutschsprachiger Ökonom_Innen', FGW-Publikation Neues ökonomisches Denken, 02. Düsseldorf: FGW.

Grindel, S. and Lässig, S. (2007): 'Unternehmer Und Staat in Europäischen Schulbüchern. Deutschland, England Und Schweden Im Vergleich', Studie Im Auftrag Der Initiative Neue Soziale Marktwirtschaft. Braunschweig: Georg-Eckert-Institut für internationale Schulbuchforschung.

Hedtke, R. (2016a): *Paradigmatische Parteilichkeit, Lückenhafte Lehrpläne Und Tendenziöses Unterrichtsmaterial? Eine Studie Zu Gestalt Und Gehalt Sozio/Ökonomischer Bildung* FGW-Studie Neues ökonomisches Denken 01. Düsseldorf: FGW.

Hedtke, R. (2016b): *Paradigmatische Parteilichkeit, Lückenhafte Lehrpläne Und Tendenziöses Unterrichtsmaterial? Ergebnisse Einer Studie Zu Gestalt Und Gehalt Sozio/Ökonomischer Bildung* FGW-Impuls Neues Ökonomisches Denken 01. Düsseldorf: FGW.

Iböb, Initiative für eine bessere ökonomische Bildung (2016): *Für Eine Bessere Ökonomische Bildung!* Available at https://www.iboeb.org/ueber-uns, accessed 9 of December 2016.

ISIPE, International Student Initiative for Pluralism in Economics (2014): 'An International Student Call for Pluralism in Economics'. Available at http://www.isipe.net/open-letter/, accessed on 9 December 2016.

Jäger, J., and Springler, E. (2012): *Ökonomie Der Internationalen Entwicklung: Eine Kritische Einführung in Die Volkswirtschaftslehre.* Wien: Mandelbaum.

Kaminski, H. and Burkard, K.-J. (2008): *Konzeption Für Die Ökonomische Bildung Als Allgemeinbildung Von Der Primarstufe Bis Zur Sekundarstuge II.* Berlin: Im Auftrag des Bundesverbandes deutscher Banken.

Kapeller, J., Pühringer, S. and Grimm, C. (2016): *Zum Profil Der Deutschsprachigen Volkswirtschaftslehre – Eine Bestandsaufnahme* FGW-Impuls Neues Ökonomisches Denken 03. Düsseldorf: FGW.

Kmk, Kultusministerkonferenz (2016): 'Aufgaben Der Kultusministerkonferenz'. Available at https://www.kmk.org/kmk/aufgaben.html, accessed on 25 November 2016.

Lenz, J. (2010): *Die Darstellung Von Marktwirtschafts Und Unternehmertum in Schulbüchern in Deutschland Und in Der Deutschsprachigen Schweiz* Studie im Auftrag des Liberalen Instituts der Friedrich-Naumann-Stiftung für die Freiheit. Erfurt: Staatswissenschaftlichen Fakultät der Universität Erfurt.

Merkt, M. (2014): 'Hochschuldidaktik Und Hochschulforschung. Eine Annäherung Über Schnittmengen', *Die Hochschule. Journal Für Wissenschaft Und Bildung* 23(1), 92–105.

MSW Ministerium für Schule und Weiterbildung Nordrhein-Westfalen (2016): *Verzeichnis Der Zugelassenen Lernmittel: Gymnasiale Oberstufe.* Available at https://www.schulministerium.nrw.de/docs/Schulsystem/Unterricht/Lernmittel/Gymnasiale_Oberstufe/index.html, accessed on 9 February 2018.

Netzwerk Plurale Ökonomik (2012): 'Offener Brief an Den Verein Für Socialpolitik'. Available at https://www.plurale-oekonomik.de/projekte/offener-brief/, accessed on 9 December 2016.

Reinhardt, S. (2016): 'The Beutelsbach Consensus', *Journal of Social Science Education* 15(2), 11–13.

Stiller, E. (eds.). (2014): *Dialog Sowi 1. Unterrichtswerk Für Sozialwissenschaften.* Bamberg: C.C. Buchner.

Stiller, E. (eds.). (2015): *Dialog Sowi 2. Unterrichtswerk Für Sozialwissenschaften.* Bamberg: C.C. Buchner.

Thielemann, U., von Egan-Krieger, T. and Thieme, S. (2012): 'Für Eine Erneuerung Der Ökonomie. Memorandum Besorgter Wissenschaftlerinnen Und Wissenschaftler'. Available at http://www.mem-wirtschaftsethik.de/memorandum-2012/, accessed on 9 December 2016.

van Staveren, I. (2014): *Economics after the Crisis. An Introduction to Economics from a Pluralist and Global Perspective.* London: Routledge.

van Treeck, T. and Urban, J. (eds.). (2016): *Ökonomie Neu Denken. Blinde Flecken Der Lehrbuchökonomie.* Berlin: irights media.

Vzbv, Verbraucherzentrale Bundesverband (2014): *Unterrichtsmaterial Unter Der Lupe. Wie Weit Geht Der Lobbyismus in Schulen? Eine Qualitätsanalyse Von Lehrmaterialien Verschiedener Anbieter Und Interessensvertreter Des Verbraucherzentrale Bundesverbands (Vzbv).* Available at http://www.verbraucherbildung.de/sites/default/files/downloads/2014-01-30_unterrichtsmaterialien_unter_der_lupe_korr.pdf, accessed on 9 December 2016.

Wernstedt, R. and John-Ohnesorg, M. (eds.). (2009): *Bildungsstandards Als Instrument Schulischer Qualitätsentwicklung. Zementierung Des Selektionsprinzips Oder Mittel Zur Chancengerechtigkeit?* Berlin: Friedrich Ebert Stiftung.

Part IV

The prospects of pluralism in economics

15 Explaining difference and diversity in an increasingly complex economics

John Davis

1. Normative and descriptive pluralism

Many advocates of pluralism in economics treat pluralism as a *normative concept.* They believe economics is insufficiently pluralistic, and argue there ought to be greater pluralism in economics. Pluralism, however, also functions as a *descriptive concept* when used to describe the nature and extent of difference and diversity in the world – in effect, how 'pluralistic' the world actually is. This involves explaining:

i the differences between different types of things
ii the relationships between different types of things
iii the extent of different types of things and their relationships in the world
iv how (i), (ii), and (iii) change over time.

It seems fair to say, then, that *descriptive pluralism* underlies *normative pluralism,* since it makes little sense to recommend more pluralism if one cannot say what more pluralism would involve. Presumably, however, what advocates of pluralism mean when they recommend greater pluralism in economics is (iii) – that the extent or diversity of different types of things in the world should be greater – where 'different types of things' in economics specifically refers to different types of approaches.

Yet this leaves open what advocates of pluralism think about (i), (ii), and (iv). Thus,

- How do they explain differences between different types of approaches in economics?
- How do they explain the relationships between different types of approaches in economics?
- How do they explain the change in difference and diversity in economics over time?

More broadly, how might advocates of pluralism in economics understand the nature and evolution of difference and diversity in economics?

2. A social-ecological perspective on difference and its evolution in economics

A social-ecological perspective on the nature of difference (i) and its evolution (iv) can be developed in terms of the connected concepts of specialisation and species, where the latter term refers to all kinds of things, not just natural kinds. *Suppose, then, that specialisation is a fundamental process in the world.* Then, in the social economic world, specialisation in different forms of activity continually produces different kinds of things or different kinds of species. Similarly, in the natural world, the range of species continually increases due to the process of specialisation in nature. Thus, a social-ecological perspective on difference framed in terms of the concepts of specialisation and species describes a world in which a process of specialisation continually leads to increases in the number of kinds of things or species that exists, causing the extent or diversity of different types of things in the world (iii) to continually increase.

Extending this to economics, species can then be taken to be different kinds of approaches in economics. Thus, the process of specialisation in economics continually increases the number of approaches in economics, so that the extent or diversity of different types of approaches in economics continually increases. This also implies, with respect to (ii), that the multitude of relationships between different approaches continually increases, making economics' landscape increasingly complex through a proliferation of overlapping and cross-cutting relationships between an increasing number of approaches. Putting (i) through (iv) together, on this social-ecological view, economics has become increasingly diverse through specialisation and will become still more diverse over time.

This view is contrary to what many advocates of pluralism in economics believe, especially heterodox economists, namely, that economics is becoming less pluralistic and less diverse. Their response is often to argue for greater specialisation in economics.

However, there is evidence that greater specialisation and further increase in the number of approaches in economics is well under way. The history of the *Journal of Economic Literature* (JEL) classification code of different kinds of approaches in economics shows that the number of approaches in economics has increased continually over time (Cherrier 2017). Heterodox economists believe the JEL code under-represents non-mainstream and heterodox economics, but there is also evidence that the number of approaches in heterodox economics has increased continually over time (Lee 2009). With respect to the relationship between the mainstream and heterodoxy, I have argued that the post-1980 movement of research programmes from outside economics and from other sciences into economics has also increased diversity within mainstream economics by creating a more complex 'mainstream pluralism' that blurs the lines between orthodox and heterodox (Davis 2008). Thus, contrary to the view of many advocates of pluralism, the evidence seems to indicate that economics has become and will continue to become more pluralistic over time.

It is interesting that pluralism only became a significant methodological concern and active research subject relatively recently, arguably about two decades ago in the late 1990s, prior to which the idea was rarely discussed (Salanti and Screpanti 1997; Samuels 1998). This could have occurred for various reasons, but one cause could be that its emergence was more a reaction to the proliferation of different approaches in economics. From this perspective, normative pluralism might somehow reflect an awareness that economics is becoming increasingly pluralistic and diverse rather than a concern that economics is becoming less pluralistic and less diverse, despite what many advocates believe. If this is so, then while one should still advocate greater pluralism, that advocacy risks not appreciating the particular issues associated with the nature of change in an increasingly complex economics if based on a mis-apprehension of the state of pluralism in economics. Thus, if economics is becoming more pluralistic, what specifically should advocates of pluralism be calling for?

3. Reorienting normative pluralism: a complexity view

One way to proceed is to take a complexity view of pluralism, and think holistically in terms of the many overlapping, cross-cutting relationships between different types of approaches in economics – the subject of (ii) above, the relationships between different types of things. This shifts the focus from the process of specialisation and the continual development of different approaches to the increasing connectedness between kinds of specialisation and approaches, and thus to the subjects of (iii) and (iv) above, the extent of difference and diversity in economics and how it is evolving.

From this complexity-holism perspective, advocating for pluralism is then a matter of advocating for the viability of entire systems with many approaches with many interconnections. As was demonstrated by the recent financial crisis (e.g., Haldane 2009), complex systems can be robust or fragile depending on how well different activities coordinate with one another. Moreover, when complex systems break down, not only do the connections between different types of activities break down, but specialisation also declines, since specialisation occurs within a context in which activities and approaches differentiate themselves from each other. So heterodox economists' advocacy for greater specialisation in economics is more likely to be successful when it involves advocacy for robust systems of specialisation.

Decline in formerly robust systems of specialisation has been extensively investigated in connection with the loss of biodiversity in natural systems, particularly associated with the Earth's current sixth wave of species extinction (Wilson 2016). One thing that biologists seem to agree on, then, is that complex systems are so highly interconnected that the loss of any given species – whatever its seeming importance – can jeopardise the balance and viability of an entire ecosystem. Thus, advocates of pluralism in economics ought to be able to argue, to those from all approaches who may have developed no special interest in normative pluralism, that diversity should generally be promoted.

That argument would broadly emphasise a shared need across the spectrum of approaches in economics for high rates of specialisation across the field. It would emphasise the unpredictable and possibly damaging effects on economics of declines in diversity in the field, and would emphasise the evolutionary nature of economics as a science, much like other sciences.

What advocates of pluralism might avoid are non-holistic specialisation arguments formulated in terms of the relative merits of different approaches – long a mainstay of heterodox calls for pluralism and a defense of heterodoxy. Certainly, proponents of all approaches in economics – mainstream and heterodox – are entitled to believe and argue that their own approaches each have special merit and value vis-à-vis other approaches. That is the essence of specialisation. However, arguments of this kind tend to base pluralism on the advance of some approaches at the expense of others, and consequently are unlikely to provide common ground for proponents of different approaches. Thus, they probably do not promote pluralism in economics as a whole.

In any event, however one judges these conclusions, what this brief comment has attempted to show is that normative pluralism in economics needs a basis in an understanding and explanation of the nature of difference and diversity in economics. The particular conclusions reached here reflect one such explanation. In the spirit of pluralism, hopefully this comment will stimulate advocates of pluralism to further develop their thinking in this regard.

References

Cherrier, B. (2017): 'Classifying Economics: A History of the JEL Codes', *Journal of Economic Literature* 55(2), 545–579.

Davis, J. (2008): 'The Turn in Recent Economics and Return of Orthodoxy', *Cambridge Journal of Economics* 32, 349–366.

Haldane, A.G. (2009): 'Rethinking the Financial Network', speech on 29 April 2009. Available at https://www.bis.org/review/r090505e.pdf, accessed on 20 February 2018.

Lee, F. (2009): *A History of Heterodox Economics: Challenging the Mainstream in the Twentieth Century*. London: Routledge.

Salanti, A. and Screpanti, E. (eds) (1997): *Pluralism in Economics*. Brookfield, VT: Edward Elgar.

Samuels, W. (1998): 'Methodological Pluralism', in J. Davis, Hands, D.W. and Mäki, U. (eds), *The Handbook of Economic Methodology*. Cheltenham: Edward Elgar, 300–303.

Wilson, E.O. (2016): *Half-Earth: Our Planet's Fight for Life*. New York: Norton.

16 Towards a critical and transdisciplinary economic science?

Samuel Decker

1. Introduction

Where is economics heading? Ten years after the outbreak of the Great Recession, this question seems more difficult to answer than ever. On the one hand, the discipline became exposed to an unprecedented degree of criticism, arguing that (neoclassical) mainstream economics[1] had been without means to predict the crisis, or even to be an integral part of its causes (Ötsch and Kapeller 2012). With demands for change coming even from high-ranking policy makers and formerly orthodox institutions, the state of the discipline moved more and more into the attention of the general public, not least because of numerous student initiatives that started to organise internationally and to demand pluralism in economics (ISIPE International Student Initiative for Pluralism in Economics 2014). With the *Institute for New Economic Thinking* (INET), a financially strong actor emerged in response to the crisis, which holds ties to young researchers and has co-financed a much-noticed curriculum reform project (Core-Econ 2017; Losse and Esterházy 2017). In addition, the discipline of economics became a subject of scientific enquiry itself, with an unprecedented growth of literature exploring the concept of pluralism as a framework for teaching and research.

Are we thus witnessing the end of mainstream economics, or even a transition towards pluralism? While some observers provide indications of such a claim (Davis 2008; Fontana 2014), others have pointed out that non-mainstream approaches were not able to overcome their institutional marginalisation and fragmentation in order to offer a positive alternative to the dominant narratives of the mainstream (Stilwell 2016; Lee et al. 2013). As empirical studies indicate, the "long fall of heterodox economics" (Heise and Thieme 2016), which began in the 1980s, continued during and after the Great Recession in an unbroken fashion, while mainstream economists held their dominant position within social sciences and policy advice (Pühringer 2016). This "strange non-crisis of economics" (Pühringer 2015) converges, regarding critical observers, with a continued marginalisation of alternative paradigms – even in self-acclaimed pleas for reform.[2]

As I will argue in this chapter, economics neither undergoes a linear development towards pluralism, nor is pre-crisis economics, or "business as usual" (Stilwell 2016), persisting. Economics is in a period of transition, in which manifold actors, networks, concepts and strategies compete for hegemony. A *Gramscian* theoretical framework provides useful insights into the current change processes in economics in the broader context of contemporary capitalism. The analysis put forward in the second section of the chapter makes sense of the post-2008 period as an "organic crisis" of the neoliberal consensus that manifests itself in the discipline of economics. Two ideal-types of transition strategies can be distinguished: "passive revolution" and "counter-hegemony". The third section will discuss the potentials and limits of the concept of pluralism regarding its capacities to offer a genuine renewal of economic science in a counter-hegemonic fashion.

With this contribution, I intend to address two aspects that are normally neglected in the pluralism debate in economics: first, the political-historical context of the current change processes in economics in the highly dynamic phase of political and economic restructuring after the financial crisis; and second, the issue of strategy and realistic possibilities for a transformation of economics.

My central thesis is that pluralism is a necessary, but not sufficient demand for a comprehensive transformation of economics. Pluralism opens up an interesting epistemic field, but then remains blurred.[3] Though there are intrinsic reasons to advocate for pluralism both as an pedagogic principle as well as a means of scientific development, it lacks the political and strategical capacities to link discursive-institutional change in economics to a broader process of societal change.

2. From organic crisis to counter-hegemony

The concepts of civil society, hegemony, organic crisis, passive revolution and counter-hegemony, which were developed by Antonio Gramsci more than 80 years ago, are best understood as categories of change, which provide a powerful analytical schema to interpret processes of transition in times of crisis (Merkens 2002). In this section, I will firstly conceptualise economics as a sphere of (transnational) civil society in which an interior hegemony of neoclassical and pro-market discourses consolidated itself from the 1970s (2.1). The current situation is best understood as an organic crisis of global capitalism (2.2), in which two ideal-types of transition strategies can be distinguished: "passive revolution" and "counter-hegemony" (2.3).

2.1 Economics as a sphere of (transnational) civil society

In Gramsci's analysis, economic crises do not necessarily lead to structural ruptures on the discursive and institutional-political level. In "progressive states", Gramsci writes, "civil society" has "developed into a very complex...

and resistant structure" that mediates – in abstract terms – between society, state power and capital accumulation (*Prison Notebooks*, quoted from Candeias 2013, 3). Civil society can be understood as the "complex whole of institutions, ideologies, and practices" (Candeias 2013, 6), as a permanently reconstructed epistemic terrain which is intertwined with state power and parliamentary democracy.[4] On the discursive-political terrain of civil society, Gramsci's argument goes, a moral-intellectual hegemony consolidates if and to the extent that certain social groups are able to generalise their individual interests and to armour them by material concessions and legitimate force. Hegemony thus describes a modern type of (state) domination under the complex conditions of developed class-divided sociability, in which a contested and preliminary "consensus" frames a dominant political paradigm and cushions the state structure against social and economic tensions. In parliamentary democracy, domination does not present itself primarily as a coercive power, "rather, it appears to be based on the consent of the majority, expressed in the so-called organs of public opinion" (Gramsci, *Prison Notebooks*, quoted from Thomas 2009, 164).

The concept of hegemony has been applied to international politics by Neo-Gramscian scholars. According to the Neo-Gramscian view, the international dispersion of (neoliberal) capitalism since the 1970s went hand-in-hand with the transnationalisation of civil society and the manifestation of a neoliberal hegemony in international organisations, think tanks and elite networks (Cox and Sinclair 1996). "Economics" can be conceptualised as a sphere of civil society on national and transnational scales. Economics departments, academics and journals are part of a much broader network of economic knowledge creation, taking place in think tanks, political parties, public media, etc. This extended field of economics with its various institutions, discourses and public intellectuals plays a key role in providing ideas and policy advice; it shapes public decision-making and understandings of "sound" policies (see Figure 16.1).

Within the extended field of economics as a sphere of national and transnational civil society, an interior hegemony of neoclassical and pro-market discourses consolidated itself since the 1970s. The neoliberal consensus in national and international politics and the neoclassical hegemony within the extended field of economics stand in a complicated relationship with each other that is not reducible to one side. As Joan Robinson (1962, 7) put it eloquently: economics has "always been partly a vehicle for the ruling ideology for each period as well as partly a method of scientific investigation". Though modern mainstream economics is not reducible to neoclassical economics, and various types of "dissenters" can be found within the discipline, it is nevertheless justified to speak of the extended field of economics as a particular point of condensation of neoliberal hegemony within (transnational) civil society.[5]

2.2 An organic crisis of global capitalism

In the Gramscian concept of civil society, an economic crisis can lead to a deep political crisis if and to the extent that the prevailing political and

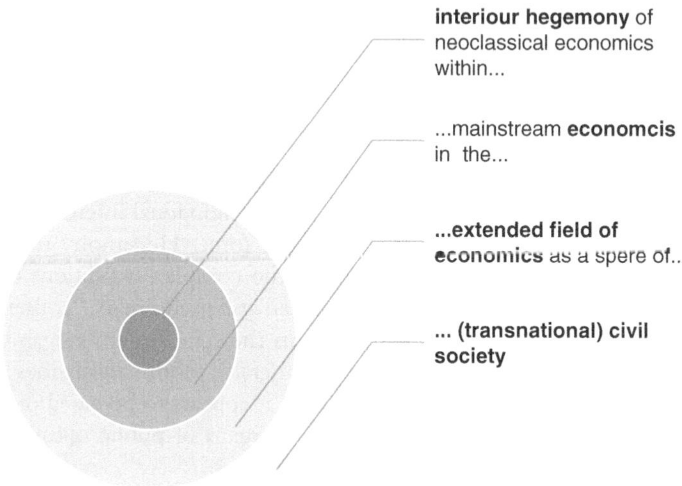

Figure 16.1 Economics and civil society. Own representation.

intellectual hegemony is not capable of absorbing the crisis via its established political and discursive tools. In the vocabulary of regulation theory, the accumulation regime (the current type of capitalist development) and the regulation regime (the current type of political governance and coordination on different scales) enter a combined and mutually reinforcing crisis. In such an organic crisis of capitalism that shows itself as a sobering crisis of the prevailing cultural and intellectual hegemony, the terrain of civil society can open up for new intellectual and political projects. The "organic" character of the crisis, however, inhibits a smooth paradigm shift, since political and intellectual alternatives have to develop organically from below and cannot just be implemented into existing state apparatuses. This leads to an ambivalent situation, in which "[t]hose in power cannot solve the crisis; yet they wield the power which prevents other groups from solving the crisis. As such, the only power they have is the power to prolong the crisis" (Gramsci, *Prison Notebooks*, quoted from Carroll 2010, 170).

Can we make sense of the current political-economic configuration with the help of the concept of "organic crisis", which was developed more than 80 years ago? While a thorough examination of this question goes beyond the scope of this paper, a few preliminary observations can be made: The financial and economic crisis of 2007–2009 was the sharpest contraction in world GDP since the Great Depression and was followed by continuing symptoms of crisis or stagnation, e.g. in the Euro currency area since 2010 and the emerging economies since 2015. After a period of massive and internationally coordinated fiscal intervention as an immediate response to the collapse of mortgage lending in the US and a historical loose monetary policy maintained until today, the crisis has officially morphed into a recovery – however the weakest in recent history (IIPPE International Initiative for Promoting Political Economy 2015). It becomes increasingly clear that the current, crisis-prone recovery is different from previous ones and that structural problems of public and private debt, international imbalances, financial fragility and over-accumulation are to persist (e.g. McNally 2009; Kotz 2009; IMF 2015). Crucially, the established fiscal and monetary policy tools have lost their former functionality (Rasmus 2010) and previous means to absorb economic crisis (such as the expansion of credit) are becoming a factor of crisis themselves. Taking additional dimensions of crisis into account, as the crisis of societal nature-relations, it seems justified to speak of a multiple crisis of capitalism (Demirović et al. 2011).

The particular focus of the concept of organic crisis rests on the interaction of problems of reproduction in the circulation of capital, problems of absorbing the crisis via established means and the problems of reproducing hegemony on the terrain of civil society. It becomes more and more obvious that the structural crisis of the post-Fordist, finance-dominated mode of accumulation is accompanied by a deepening political crisis, a crisis of the relationship between the representatives and the represented in a number of countries. On the one hand, the political programme of neoliberalism is still dominating. Political-economic processes, such as debt creation, financialisation, transnationalisation and concentration of capital, dismantling of social security systems and – despite protectionist rhetoric – free trade policies continue to dominate the political agenda (Crouch 2011; Mirowski 2013). On the other hand, there are indications that the neoliberal programme is losing its general acceptance, that it is still dominant but no longer hegemonic. Social inequality, austerity and free trade policies, the dismantling of democracy and humanitarian and ecological crises provide the background for a growing dissident spectre (Carroll and Sapinski 2017). However, typically for an organic crisis, not only socially-oriented and emancipatory but also reactionary, far-right and fascist forces emerge, leading to an era of political polarisation.

2.3 Passive revolution and counter hegemony

The concepts of passive revolution and counter-hegemony are analytical tools to ascertain patterns and development trajectories within the multi-layered and complex processes of political and economic restructuring in times of crisis. These two concepts can be understood as two (ideal-type) opposite patterns of political-economic change that potentially unfold on the terrain of civil society in the context of an organic crisis of capitalism.

Tough justified criticism against an arbitrary application of the concept of passive revolution has been raised (Callinicos 2010),; it can be applied as a useful ideal-type of societal change, in which the ruling hegemony selectively integrates political and intellectual elements of oppositional forces without giving away its power. Just as hegemony depicts a modern type of domination under developed capitalism, passive revolution can be understood as a modern, capitalist type of transition, in which modernisation "from above" restores the legitimacy, profitability and stability of the political-economic order in times of crisis (Merkens 2002). Passive revolution occurs when political-economic relations are reorganised due to economic and popular pressures, "but ultimately, popular initiatives are neutralised" (Hesketh 2017, 14).

The historical examples Gramsci referred to as "passive revolutions" were the state-induced creation of industrial capitalism in the 19th century as well as the emergence of the Fordist regime of accumulation in the early 20th century (ibid.: 11). As Hesketh has pointed out, "seemingly discrepant phenomenon such as Keynesianism and Fascism can both be interpreted within the broader logic of passive revolution" (ibid., 1). The concept has also been applied to the emergence of neoliberal capitalism in response to the crisis of Fordism in the 1970s (Morton 2010). For the present organic crisis, distinct new types of accumulation regimes are imaginable, centring, for example, around digitalisation, surveillance, "green growth" and climate change (adaptation), frontier technology, or defence. On the political level, an increasingly authoritarian and manipulative character of neoliberal governance can be observed (Bruff 2014).[6] The crucial characteristic of any economic or political mechanism of passive revolution lies in the restoration of profitability and political stability via incorporating and neutralising oppositional intellectual elements.

The (ideal-type) opposite possibility for political-economic change in the state of organic crisis is counter-hegemony. To grasp the core idea behind the concept of counter-hegemony, it is important to distinguish it accurately from the concept of hegemony. As indicated above, hegemony refers to a type of cultural leadership under capitalism, which, via a combination of (legal) force and (intellectual) persuasion, legitimises and naturalises the existing political order under a ruling paradigm. It is important to bear in mind that in Gramsci's vocabulary hegemonic ideas (and the popular consent they build on) are "'spontaneous' in the sense that they are not the mere result of any systematic educational activity on the part of an already conscious leading group, but have been formed through everyday experience illuminated by 'common sense'" (Gramsci 1971, 199). This means that counter-hegemony does not coincide with a replacement of the existing hegemony by a new "political programme" that universalises new individual (ruling) interests by a combination of force and persuasion.

Counter-hegemony is not limited to a change of political contents, but intents to transform the form of political power. The intellectual and persuasive elements developed in the process of counter-hegemony are not supposed to impart general acceptance to particular interests, but to provide a truly democratic terrain of (scientific) knowledge creation and (political) decision-making. Counter-hegemony is not restricted to proposals of political reform, but refers to "molecular" processes of collective societal learning and experiencing, in which new patterns of societal reproduction are developed. In today's context, the project of counter-hegemony describes the full process in which alternative concepts and practices, modes of living and production, institutions and networks are developed within different spectres of civil society (social movements, NGOs, media, science and education, parties, unions, etc.) and brought together in a pluralist, non-hierarchical "mosaic" that carries out an emancipatory, social-ecological transformation of fossil and neoliberal capitalism.[7]

3. The potentials (and limits) of pluralism

In this section, I will discuss the strategic capabilities of the concept of pluralism to overcome the interior hegemony of neoclassical economics as part of a wider counter-hegemonic project of social-ecological transformation. I will firstly outline the historical context of the pluralism debate in economics (3.1). Secondly, I will apply the ideal-type patterns of passive revolution and counter-hegemony on the current processes of discursive-institutional change in economics (3.2). With the help of these clarifications, I will then discuss the counter-hegemonic potentials of pluralism (3.3).

3.1 The historical context of the pluralism debate

In the historical evolution and development of economic science, different paradigms acquired the status of interior hegemony. Already the rise of (classical) political economy at the end of the 18th and the beginning of the 19th century – arguing for the potentially positive impact of markets and accumulation for societal development – can be situated in the context of an emerging bourgeoisie that came into conflict with the political-economic restrictions set by feudalism and mercantilism (Jäger and Springler 2015). The classical political economists followed a pre-disciplinary understanding of science and dealt with philosophical issues and state affairs (Shah 2014; Jessop and Sum 2001).

Marx's "critique of political economy" adopted core assumptions of classical political economy, as the labour theory of value, but also formulated a powerful political critique of the existing societal relations that were taken up by the rising workers' movement and social democracy at that time. The class-based classical view of the economy as a capitalist system of accumulation, in which value results from human labour, can be understood as an inherently political (critical) scientific approach that came into conflict with the development of capitalism and the legitimational needs of the bourgeoisie in the second half of the 19th century (Jäger and Springler 2015).

The neoclassical paradigm that started to supersede the classical paradigm alongside with the institutionalisation of "economics" as an academic discipline in the 1870s, provided an a-political, deductive-mathematical model that naturalised the "economy" as an autonomous sphere strictly separated from history, politics and social issues (ibid.). Both the "disciplining" of the social sciences and the marginalisation of political-economic (critical) approaches characterised the formation of "modern" social sciences and their mainstream biases during the 20th century.

In response to the deep and connected crisis of both laissez-faire capitalism and neoclassicism in the 1930s, the (so-called) Keynesian paradigm consolidated its interior hegemony hand-in-hand with the expansion of the Fordist mode of accumulation.[8] The Keynesian intellectual "revolution", however, did not call into question the disciplinary closure of economics, and was furthermore appropriated by the neoclassical paradigm already by the end of the 1930s (ibid.).

The structural crisis of the Fordist mode of accumulation and the failure of Keynesian economic policy during 1970s led to a massive revaluation of neoclassical approaches, which had never disappeared under the Keynesian paradigm. While the monetarist innovations as well as the political project of neoliberalism had already been formulated, the ideas of Hayek and Friedman did not receive sufficient political support in the 1950s and 1960s due to the negative experiences with laissez-faire capitalism (Brand 2010). The crises in the 1970s provided a window of opportunity for the re-formation of the interior hegemony of neoclassical and pro-market discourses in the extended field of economics, which, as pointed out above, went hand-in-hand with the consolidation of the neoliberal consensus in national and international politics. With the incorporation of concepts such as informational economics, game theory, agent theory, behavioural economics, complexity economics, statistical procedures and the spread of neoclassical methods to the realm of neighbouring disciplines, the modern mainstream developed.

Since the consolidation and differentiation of neoclassical economics, no paradigm has truly challenged its interior hegemony. Nevertheless, the growing spectre of 'heterodox economics since the 1980s – as well as the emergence of critical theories of International Relations (Van Der Pijl 2012) – should be interpreted as an episode in the more fundamental, historical line of societal conflict that is inherent in all social sciences as important arenas of civil society. The proliferation of alternative paradigms and initiatives – as heterodox, post-autistic, real world or pluralist economics – plays a key role in challenging the interior hegemony of neoclassical economics. Those "labels matter" as Stilwell (2016, 42) put it, since they "construct imagery and signal strategic choices". Paradigms have an intrinsically political function since they organise cooperation and conflict of different actors within civil society and thus are crucial in the process of consolidating and dissolving hegemony.

Heterodox economics became a reservoir for critical and transdisciplinary economic thinking from the 1980s on. The "community of heterodox economists as manifested through their graduate programs, conferences, journals and identity" (Lee 2012, 337) developed into a relevant alternative to "orthodox" approaches, but never into a common counter-hegemonic project. The self-marginalisation and the highlighting of differences inherent in the concept of "heterodoxy", as well as the paralysing discussion about its characeristics and associated schools, made "heterodox economics" both a vehicle and an impediment for the proliferation of alternative economic approaches.. The concept of heterodox economics neither politicises the disciplinary closure of economics nor resonates in a collective subjectivity that could challenge the interior hegemony of neoclassical economics.

The petition from a small number of economics students that demanded a "post-autistic" economic curriculum in Paris in the year 2000 represented a crucial intervention not only due to the subsequent international spread of the "post-autistic" movement (Peacon Post-Autistic Economics Network 2017; Netzwerk Plurale Ökonomik 2017), but also because it articulated *of* a common line of conflict. Crucially for challenging the interior hegemony of neoclassical approaches within the extended field of economics, the demand for a reflective, plural and embedded economic science politicised the disciplinary closure of economics and highlighted common interests and features of non-mainstream approaches.

Also, the concept of real world economics, which partly developed in parallel to the "post-autistic" movement, partly devolved from it, emphasised the common claim of heterodox approaches to put forward a more realistic description of economic reality than the isolated, deductive-axiomatic world of mainstream economics. With the emphasis on alternative truth claims, the concept of real world economics contributes to an important sharpening of the conflict in the sense that the opposing analytical views of mainstream and non-mainstream approaches and the disproving of core elements of mainstream theories were addressed. On the other hand, the focus on "better" or "truer" theory shifts the debate on technical, empirical aspects and appears debatable from a critical realist view, arguing that any type of truth claim can be neither universal nor clean of power-relations. Successfully challenging mainstream economics cannot, as Stilwell (2016, 45) puts it, "be just a matter of developing 'better' economic models (claiming higher values for explanatory capacity). It also has to be a political process".

The concept of pluralism, finally, represents the most comprehensive as well as the most widespread meta-paradigmatic approach to reform economics. Though the demand for pluralism has a long history (Heise 2016), both the scientific and political use of the concept has taken on a new quality since the outbreak of the Great Recession.

3.2 Counter-hegemony in economics?

As pointed out above, the extended field of economics as a sphere of national and transnational civil society – in which an interior hegemony of neoclassical, pro-market approaches has consolidated itself in a complex relationship with the emergence of neoliberal hegemony in national and international politics – depicts a central place of contestation of the neoliberal "consensus" and the articulation of alternatives. Can we discover patterns of passive revolution or counter-hegemony within the field of economics after the crisis?

The "non-event" (in mainstream theory) of the Great Recession partially opened up the epistemic terrain of economic policy advice, journalism and education. Though textbooks and teaching have not altered fundamentally after the crisis, the shift in the public discourse is nevertheless remarkable. Financial fragility and social inequality became important topics of scientific and public debate. "Public economists", such as Thomas Picketty, Joseph Stieglitz, Paul Krugman or Yanis Varoufakis, played an important role in questioning neoliberal wisdoms and austerity policies in the aftermath of the crisis. Left-wing parties and governments built directly and indirectly on the insights of New-Keynesian or even heterodox economists. Students' initiatives and the demand for pluralism indicate that not only the content, but also the pedagogical form of mainstream economics is called into question. These developments could be considered as elements of an emerging, counter-hegemonic spectre in the extended field of economics within (transnational) civil society.

These elements remain incomplete and underdeveloped, however, since it remains unclear in what way they could combine in a comprehensive transformation of economics. Recalling the genesis of mainstream economics outlined in section 3.1, a counter-hegemonic transformation cannot restrict itself to a pushback of mainstream theories, but has to overcome the a-political and mono-disciplinary nature of economics itself. The a-political, deductive and formalised method of mainstream economics has to be replaced by a critical method that reflects upon the role of science within society and hegemonic discourses. Thus, a counter-hegemonic approach to mainstream economics should be envisaged as a critical and transdisciplinary economic science. Following the reasoning in section 2.1, any interior hegemony develops in complex interaction with the wider hegemony that manifests itself on the terrain of (transnational) civil society. Thus, the success of any challenger of mainstream economics depends on its ability to link discursive-institutional change in economics to a broader process of societal change.

Considering the two criteria of counter-hegemonic change in economics – overcoming the a-political and mono-disciplinary nature of economics and making the change in economics part of a wider, transformative project – relatively little has happened in economics. The INET, which holds ties to young academics (Rethinking Economics and Young Scholars Initiative) and co-financed a much-noticed curriculum reform project (Core-Econ 2017; Losse and Esterházy 2017), serves as a good example for the complicated and contradictory nature of the current change process in economics. While its creation was crucial in starting a debate about economics reform, heterodox and critical approaches remain marginalised in CORE (AHE Association for Heterodox Economics 2014). At the same time, behavioural approaches, evolutionary game theory, neuro-economics, complexity agent-based economics, and experimental economics make considerable inroads into mainstream economics, leading to a form of "mainstream pluralism" (Fontana 2014; Fontana and Cedrini 2015).

This can be considered a nascent form of passive revolution in economics, where demands for change and so far excluded intellectual elements are integrated into the mainstream corpus without challenging the core assumptions of mainstream economics and its underlying, pro-marked bias. In a probable future scenario, one could assume a progressive inclusion of Keynesian, behavioural, complexity and evolutionary approaches, in combination with an altered thematic focus on destabilising inequality and debt levels, financial fragility and ecological issues. This thematic focus could be complemented by narratives of "green growth" or "technological solutions", which in turn are linked to specific investment strategies. In this highly speculative scenario, more critical heterodox perspectives and qualitative approaches would remain excluded.

3.3 Pluralism and counter-hegemony

What is the role of the pluralism demand in the current change processes in economics, which are in turn part of a broader intellectual crisis of the prevailing hegemony? How could pluralism contribute to a counter-hegemonic project in economics that challenges the un-political and mono-disciplinary closure of economics and at the same time links to a wider, transformative project? Two aspects have to be addressed here, a theoretical and a practical one.

In theory, the concept of pluralism clearly implies a thorough transformation of economics. It could only be realised through profound curriculum reform. Institutionalist and critical approaches – as Post-Keynesian economics, feminist economics, post-growth economics and Critical Political Economy – would have to be strengthened. Qualitative and quantitative methods of various kinds as well as neighbouring disciplines and new didactic concepts would have to make their entry to research and teaching. Beyond that, the method of pluralism as a way of presenting and solving scientific questions represents a counter model to the monist and one-sided form of how economic knowledge is created and processed under the dominance of mainstream economics. An economic education based on the assumption that there are totally different theories as part of different world views, with their respective strengths and weaknesses to explain economic phenomena, would encourage self-determined learning, make the students intellectually more independent from the teachers and convey tolerance and respect. In addition to this ethical and emancipatory aspect, pluralism can be understood as a scientific attitude in the face of an inherently complex, open and irreducible social and economic reality, in which only a multifarious interplay of diverse theories and methods produces the best results. Pluralism in this way represents a means of scientific development that, as emphasised above, adheres to the idea of scientific progress, meaning a relative increase in truth.[9]

It becomes clear that pluralism – as an ethical and emancipatory principle as well as a means of scientific development – is a far-reaching proposal that aims not only at a complete redesign of the curriculum, but at changing the way economic knowledge is produced and processed. Pluralism can be understood as a necessary condition for a comprehensive transformation of economics. But, turning to the practical aspect of the question posed above, to what extent can the proposal of (critical) pluralism be realised or has it been realised already? Is pluralist economics the challenger that will end the decades long interior hegemony of neoclassical economics?[10] Following the argumentation put forward in section 2 of this chapter, any interior hegemony develops in complex interaction with the wider hegemony that manifests itself on the terrain of (transnational) civil society, of which the extended field of economics is a particular sphere. As the emergence of historical materialism in the 19th century or Keynesianism in the 20th exemplify, the emergence new paradigms is not an encapsulated academic matter that then spreads to society; it is deeply interwoven with the political, societal and economic struggles in the respective period. The extended field of economics as introduced in chapter two plays a mediating role between the interior hegemony within economics and the wider hegemony within civil society. The counter-hegemonic potential of pluralist economics thus depends on its ability to link discursive-institutional change in economics to a broader process of societal change.

This is the weak spot of pluralist economics. Even though the demand for pluralism receives support from economic schools far beyond the heterodox community, it has so far not led to the creation of robust alliances among its supporters, which range from Marxist to Austrian economists. An effective displacement of mainstream economics and the institutionalisation of a pluralist discipline would practically require a sufficiently close coordination of scientists, intellectuals, students, research departments and universities, as well as journals and publishers, research networks and institutes, think tanks, foundations and non-governmental organisations, politicians, parties, journalists and media organisations, etc. – in other words: a science-political actor that bridges the scientific terrain with the broader terrain of civil society.

The demand for pluralism, however, runs counter to the broader societal searching processes for alternatives to neoliberalism in the context of an unfolding organic crisis of global capitalism. There are left- as well as right-wing forces that make use of heterodox economic thought (Becker and Weissenbacher 2016). The project of pluralism, however, cannot ally with any particular political force without undermining the concept of pluralism itself. Political neutrality is not a promising starting point for building transformative alliances across civil society that can compete with the powerful political network of mainstream economics. This is the "paradox of pluralism" (De Langhe 2010, 795, emphasis in the original), meaning "that pluralism is *self-defeating* because it cannot claim its own truth lest it be inconsistent".

There exists the tacit argument, however, that via increasing the space for critical, left-leaning theories and the integration of Keynesian or Marxist arguments in a neutral political subtext, the proposal of pluralism functions de facto as a progressive force. Crucially for successfully applying this (justifiable) strategy of discourse transmission via translating so far marginalised arguments in a novel way and integrating them in a new framework, however, is the linkage between new, compatible frameworks and already existing, marginalised contents – in other words: the organisation of a contradiction. Via dissecting themselves from any political content or power, the initiatives for pluralism cannot organise this contradiction in the long run and gradually lose their transformative potential. Without these linkages between science and the wider field of civil society, the concept of pluralism can be easily instrumentalised, e.g. by ordo-liberal, Keynesian or even mainstream forces. Though pluralism is a desirable and highly advanced proposal, it lacks the political and strategic capacities to link discursive-institutional change in economics to a broader process of societal change.

The practical realisation of pluralism is complicated by a further aspect. As pointed out in section 3.1, the foundations for the current interior hegemony of neoclassical economics were already set in the late 19th century, when the neoclassical paradigm crowded out the classical paradigm alongside with the institutionalisation of "economics" as an academic discipline and the separation of social sciences. Section 3.2 concluded that a counter-hegemonic challenge of neoclassicism has to question the modern scientific division of labour and put forward the vision of a truly transdisciplinary, historical and critical economic science. Many heterodox schools orientate themselves in a trans- or post-disciplinary framework, but the demand for pluralism is restricted to the discipline of economics. Though "interdisciplinary pluralism" is part of the demand for pluralism (ISIPE International Student Initiative for Pluralism in Economics 2014), the concept of pluralist economics quickly encounters the limits of the discipline. This can be understood as a second paradox of pluralism. The realisation of the concept of pluralism would imply a transformation of the disciplinary organisation of social sciences itself.

To sum up, pluralism is a far-reaching and desirable aim in theory, but is hard to realise in practice. Two paradoxes are built into the concept of pluralism. First, such a far-reaching transformation of economics would be dependent on a political alliance that bridges the institutionalised scientific realm with the broader terrain of civil society. However, the concept of pluralism is obliged to maintain a neutral position and cannot become an element in a broader, transformative project. Second, the concept of pluralist economics demands "interdisciplinary pluralism", but restricts itself to the discipline of economics. Tackling the roots of mainstream economics and its dominance, however, would require transcending the disciplinary boundaries between social sciences themselves.

Thus, the concept of pluralism does not have the potential to politically push back mainstream economics and only in part contributes to a more critical and transdisciplinary economic science. Even if the concept of pluralism should receive more attention in the future, it will most likely proliferate a form of pluralism that treats critical and transdisciplinary approaches not on equal footage. Economics textbooks, study programmes and institutions that take up the name of pluralism without realising the underlying idea could possibly absorb the criticism of student initiatives and the general public and at the same time re-organise the interior hegemony of neoclassical economic thinking in the form of a passive revolution.

4. Conclusion

With this contribution, I intended to address two aspects that are normally neglected in the pluralism debate in economics: first, the political-historical context of the current change processes in economics in the highly dynamic phase of political and economic restructuring after the financial crisis; and second, the issue of strategy and realistic possibilities for a transformation of economics as part of a progressive transformation of neoliberal and fossil capitalism.

In section 2, economics has been described as a sphere of (transnational) civil society in which an interior hegemony of neoclassical and pro-market discourses consolidated itself since the 1970s. In the ongoing organic crisis of global capitalism, two ideal-types of transition strategies can be distinguished ("passive revolution" and "counter-hegemony"). Based on an historical contextualisation, it became clear that a counter-hegemonic transformation of mainstream economics would mean overcoming the (superficially) a-political and mono-disciplinary nature of economics and to establish a critical and transdisciplinary economic science. Currently, however, a nascent form of passive revolution can be observed in economics, where demands for change and so far excluded intellectual elements are integrated into the mainstream corpus without challenging the core assumptions of mainstream economics and its underlying pro-marked bias.

Section 3 considered the potentials of pluralism to overcome the interior hegemony of neoclassical economics and to extend the space for critical and transdisciplinary economic thought. I concluded that pluralism – as an ethical and emancipatory principle as well as a means of scientific development – is a far-reaching proposal that aims not only at a complete redesign of the curriculum, but at changing the way economic knowledge is produced and processed. Though pluralism is an important and desirable aim in theory, it is hard to be realised in practice. Due to the two paradoxes that are built into the concept of pluralist economics (the impossibility of political partisanship despite being a political project; the impossibility to realise pluralism within the discipline of economics despite restricting itself to economics), it is incapable of overcoming the a-political and mono-disciplinary nature of economics. It lacks the political and strategic capacities to link discursive-institutional change in economics to a broader process of societal change.

The main finding of this chapter is that the demand for pluralism is no sufficient strategy to transform economics. It has to be complemented by concepts such as (Critical/Global) Political Economy or Transformative Science which could be more successful in building transformative alliances and overcoming the mono-disciplinary closure of economics. Crucially, pluralism, Political Economy and Transformative Science should not be understood as mutually exclusive concepts, but as complementary elements in a comprehensive strategy to transform economics. Pluralism for itself, however, is not sufficient to push back the political network of mainstream economics, and rather runs the risk of becoming an element in a passive revolution that re-stabilises economics as an un-critical and mono-disciplinary science.

Overcoming mainstream economics has to be understood as a deeply political project that should be connected to the emergence of new collective subjectivities in the context of an organic crisis of global capitalism. Any strategy of transformation of economics should locate itself in this broader historical and political context and question the disciplinary organisation of economics itself. As Freeman (2016, 27) has pointed out, economics "as a distinct subject or discipline did not even exist until the early twentieth century, and there is no reason to suppose that it will inevitably continue to do so".

Acknowledgements

I would like to thank my friends and colleagues from the Netzwerk Plurale Ökonomik for countless engaged and friendly discussions that contributed considerably to this article.

Notes

1 Following Heise (2016), Lawson (2013) and Arnsperger and Varoufakis (2006), (neoclassical) "mainstream economics" can be defined as a positivist, taxonomic, mathematical-deductive paradigmatic approach that follows the three axioms of methodological individualism, instrumentalism and equilibration. Advanced general equilibrium modeling (DSGE) and Neo-Keynesianism are included in this definition as well as evolutionary game theory, non-Walrasian equilibrium theory, social choice theory, industrial economics, economic geography, new political economy, public choice economics or environmental economics.

2 See AHE Association for Heterodox Economics (2014) on CORE.

3 Brand and Daiber (2012) applied this formulation to describe the discourse on (social-ecological) transformation.

4 Despite its discursive appearance, civil society nevertheless should be understood as a material structure. It consists of the economically and legally co-constituted networks of public decision-making, government, mass communication, science, education, pedagogy and penalisation. News agencies, universities, schools, courts and non-governmental associations constitute important dots of the network of civil society that creates the discursive terrain on which moral concepts, world-views and common "truths" are both reproduced and contested.

5 Regarding the complicated relationship between neoclassical economics and neoliberalism, see Plehwe and Mirowski (2009).

6 Not only the rise of openly authoritarian and far-right parties and heads of government are implicated here. The concept of "authoritarian neoliberalism" covers more subtle aspects, such as the constitutional solidification of neoliberal policy or the rise of a new type of "special" (but not necessarily openly authoritarian) politician.

7 This specific interpretation of the concept of counter-hegemony rests on the considerations by Carroll and Ratner (1994). It is important to point out that Gramsci was influenced by a Leninist tradition and saw a special position for parties and their leaders in counter-hegemonic strategies.

8 Following Regulation Theory, a "mode of accumulation" can be understood as a relatively stable mode of capitalist development and growth that persists for several decades. Regulation Theory distinguished between a Fordist mode of accumulation, which rested on workers' consumption and growing wage rates and a post-Fordist mode of accumulation since the 1970s, resting on transnationlisation of production, wage suppression, financialisation and debt creation (see Brand 2010, Decker and Sablowski (2017).

9 I am building on the concept of Critical Pluralism that has been formulated by Freeman and Kliman (2005). It has to be stressed that, following a Critical Realist epistemology, "truth" in this context by no means refers to an accurate representation of "reality" in the form of language. "Truth" or "theories" are linguistic constructions that can establish contingent yet relatively durable relations between signifiers and their referents in the objective world. Still, truth is a societal phenomenon which is subject to historical change. Truth claims can never be universal nor clean of power relations (Caroll and Rathner 1994).

10 Though the concept of pluralism does not advantage any particular school of thought, the realisation of pluralism still depicts a counter-hegemonic project. Pluralism would have to become the established standard in economics and protected by institutional structures (and sanctions).

References

AHE Association for Heterodox Economics (2014): 'Pluralism, Heterodoxy, and the Prospects for a New Economics Curriculum: Assessing the Potential of INET, What's the Use of Economics, and the Core Project?', Association for Heterodox Economics, Available at http://www.hetecon.net/documents/The_prospects_for_a_new_economic_curriculum.pdf, accessed on 1 February 2017.

Arnsperger, C. and Varoufakis, G. (2006): 'What Is Neoclassical Economics? The three axioms responsible for its theoretical oeuvre, practical irrelevance and, thus, discursive power', *Panoeconomicus* 1, 5–18.

Becker, J. and Weissenbacher, R. (2016): 'Heterodoxy from the Right: Economic Policy Concepts of the Nationalist Right in Europe', Working Paper. Vienna University of Economics and Business. (August 2016). Vienna. Available at http://www2.euromemorandum.eu/uploads/becker_heterodoxy_from_the_right.pdf accessed on 1 February 2017.

Brand, U. (2010): 'Internationale Politik', in Sieder, R. and Langtaler, E. (eds), *Globalgeschichte 1800–2010*. Wien: Böhlau, 213–260.

Brand, U. and Daiber, B. (2012): 'Socialecological Tranformations', *Austrian Journal of Development Studies* 28(3), 4–6.

Bruff, I. (2014): 'The Rise of Authoritarian Neoliberalism', *Rethinking Marxism: A Journal of Economics, Culture and Society* 26, 113–129.

Callinicos, A. (2010): 'The Limits of Passive Revolution', *Capital and Class* 34, 491–507.

Candeias, M. (2013): Gramscian Constellations. Hegemony and the Realisation of New Ways of Production and Living. Online-Publication, Rosa Luxemburg Foundation. July 2013. Berlin. Available at https://www.rosalux.de/fileadmin/rls_uploads/pdfs/allg_Texte/Gramscian_Constellations.pdf accessed on 1 February 2017.

Carroll, W.K. (2010): 'Crisis, Movements, Counter-Hegemony: In Search of the New', *Interface: a Journal for and about Social Movements* 2, 168–198.

Carroll, W.K. and Ratner, R.S. (1994): 'Between Leninism and Radical Pluralism: Gramscian Reflections on Counter-Hegemony and the New Social Movements', *Critical Sociology* 20, 3–26.

Carroll, W.K. and Sapinski, J.P. (2017). 'Transnational Alternative Policy Groups in Global Civil Society: Enablers of Post-Capitalist Alternatives or Carriers of NGOisation?', *Critical Sociology* 43, 1–18.

CORE Core-Econ (2017): 'Economics for a Changing Word', Available at http://core-econ.org/, accessed on 1 February 2017.

Cox, R.W. and Sinclair, T. (eds.) (1996): *Approaches to World Order*. Cambridge: Cambridge University Press.

Crouch, C. (2011): *The Strange Non-Death of Neo-Liberalism*. Cambridge: Polity Press.

Davis, J.B. (2008): 'The Turn in Recent Economics and Return of Orthodoxy', *Cambridge Journal of Economics* 32, 249–366.

De Langhe, R. (2010): 'How Monist Is Heterodoxy?', *Cambridge Journal of Economics* 34 (4), 793–805.

Decker, S. and Sablowski, T. (2017): 'Die G20 Und Die Krise Des Globalen Kapitalismus', Study on Behalf of the Rosa-Luxemburg-Stiftung 4/2017(May), 2017.

Demirović, A., Dück, J., Becker, F. and Bader, P. (eds.) (2011): *VielfachKrise. Im Finanzmarktdominierten Kapitalismus*. Hamburg: VSA Verlag.

Fontana, M. (2014): 'Pluralism(s) in Economics: Lessons from Complexity and Innovation', *Journal of Evolutionary Economics* 24(1), 189–204.

Fontana, M. and Cedrini, M. (2015): Mainstreaming. Reflections on the Origins and Fate of Mainstream Pluralism. CESMEP Working Paper 1/2015 University of Turin. Turin. Available at https://ideas.repec.org/p/uto/cesmep/201501.html accessed on 1 February 2017.

Freeman, A. (2016): 'Economics and Its Discontents: Comments on George DeMartino's the Economist's Oath', *Rethinking Marxism* 28(1), 25–37.

Freeman, A. and Kliman, A. (2005): 'Beyond Talking the Talk: Towards a Critical Pluralist Practice', *Post-Autistic Economics Review* 40, 26–53.

Gramsci, A. (1971): *Selections from the Prison Notebooks*. London: Lawrence and Wishart.

Heise, A. (2016): 'Pluralism in Economics. Inquiries into a Daedalean Concept', *Discussion Papers*, Zentrum für Ökonomische und Soziologische Studien, No. 51. Available at https://www.econstor.eu/bitstream/10419/141825/1/860401677.pdf, accessed on 1 February 2017).

Heise, A. and Thieme, S. (2016): 'The Short Rise and Long Fall of Heterodox Economics in Germany after the 1970s. Explorations in a Scientific Field of Power and Struggle', *Journal of Economic Issues 50(4)*, 1105–1130.

Hesketh, C. (2017): 'Passive Revolution. A Universal Concept with Geographical Seats', *Review of International Studies* 3, 1–20.

IIPPE International Initiative for Promoting Political Economy. (2015): '6th Annual Conference in Political Economy', available at http://iippe.org/wp/?page_id=2470, accessed on 5 February 2015.

IMF International Monetary Fund (2015): 'Lagarde: Prevent 'New Mediocre' From Becoming 'New Reality', IMF-World Bank Spring Meetings, IMF Survey, April 9 2015. Available at http://www.imf.org/external/pubs/ft/survey/so/2015/NEW040915A.htm, accessed on 1 September 2016.

ISIPE International Student Initiative for Pluralism in Economics (2014): 'An International Student Call for Pluralism in Economics', May 5 2014. Available at http://www.isipe.net/, accessed on 1 February 2017.

Jäger, J. and Springler, E. (2015): *Ökonomie Der Internationalen Entwicklung. Eine Kritische Einführung in Die Volkswirtschaftslehre*. Wien: Mandelbaum Verlag.

Jessop, B. and Sum, N.-L. (2001): 'Pre-Disciplinary and Post-Disciplinary Perspectives in Political Economy', *New Political Economy* 6(1), 89–101.

Kotz, D.M. (2009): 'The Financial and Economic Crisis of 2008: A Systemic Crisis of Neoliberal Capitalism', *Review of Radical Political Economics* 41(3), 305–317.

Lawson, T. (2013): 'What Is This 'School' Called Neoclassical Economics?', *Cambridge Journal of Economics* 37(4), 947–983.

Lee, F.S. (2012): 'Heterodox Economics and Its Critics', *Review of Political Economy* 24(2), 337–351.

Lee, F.S., Pham, X. and Gu, G. (2013): 'The UK Research Assessment Exercise and the Narrowing of UK Economics', *Cambridge Journal of Economics* 37(4), 693–717.

Losse, B. and Esterházy, Y. (2017): 'Plurale Ökonomen: Neue Lehren Für Die Volkswirtschaft', *Wirtschaftswoche*, 14.05.2017, available at http://www.wiwo.de/erfolg/campus-mba/plurale-oekonomen-neue-lehren-fuer-die-volkswirtschaft/19752700.html, accessed on 14 May 2017.

McNally, D. (2009): 'From Financial Crisis to World Slump: Accumulation, Financialisation and the Global Slowdown', *Historical Materialism* 17, 35–83.

Merkens, A. (2002): 'Neoliberalismus, Passive Revolution Und Umbau Des Bildungswesens. Zur Hegemonie PostFordistischer Bildung', in Merkens, A., Meyer-Siebert, J. Nowak, I., Rego Diaz, Victor Rego Diaz V (eds), *Die Unruhe Des Denkens Nutzen. Emanzipatorische Standpunkte Im Neoliberalismus*. Hamburg: Argument, 171–182.

Mirowski, P. (2013): *Never Let a Serious Crisis Go to Waste. How Neoliberalism Survived the Financial Meltdown*. London: Verso Books.

Morton, A.D. (2010): 'The Continuum of Passive Revolution', *Capital and Class* 34(3), 315–342.

Netzwerk Plurale Ökonomik (2017): 'Die Geschichte Des Netzwerks', Available at https://www.plurale-oekonomik.de/das-netzwerk/geschichte-des-netzwerkes/, accessed on 1 February 2017.

Ötsch, W. and Kapeller, J. (2012): 'Perpetuating the Failure: Economic Education and the Current Crisis', *Journal of Social Science Education* 9(2), 16–25.

Peacon Post-Autistic Economics Network (2017): 'A Brief History of the Post-Autistic Economics Movement', available at http://www.paecon.net/HistoryPAE.htm, accessed on 1 February 2017.

Plehwe, D. and Mirowski, P. (eds) (2009): *The Road from Mont Pèlerin. The Making of the Neoliberal Thought Collective*. Cambridge, MA: Harvard University Press.

Pühringer, S. (2015): *The Strange Non-Crisis of Economics. Economic Crisis and the Crisis Policies in Economic and Political Discourses*. Dissertation. Johannes Kepler University Linz. Linz.

Pühringer, S. (2016): Still the Queen of the Social Sciences? (Post-)Crisis Power Balances of 'Public Economists' in Germany, *ICAE Working Paper Series* 52 Linz.

Rasmus, J. (2010): 'Value, Price and Epic Recession', *Critique* 38, 445–464.

Robinson, J. (1962): *Economic Philosophy*. London: C. A. Watts.
Shah, A. (2014): Jenseits Der Neoklassik Oder Jenseits Der Volkswirtschaftslehre? Plurale Ökonomik Und Kritische Gesellschaftsforschung. presentation at the IMK Workshop 'Pluralismus in der Ökonomik' 8-10 August 2014 Berlin.
Stilwell, F. (2016): 'Heterodox Economics or Political Economy?', *Real-World Economics Review* 74, 42–47.
Thomas, P.D. (2009): *The Gramscian Moment. Philosophy, Hegemony, Marxism*. Leiden: Brill.
Van Der Pijl, K. (2012): 'The Limits of Discipline, or How to Make Sense of the State of the World', *Global Change, Peace and Security* 24(1), 25–30.

A pluralist economics teaching is practicable and illuminating

A conclusion

Samuel Decker, Wolfram Elsner and Svenja Flechtner

The contributions to the present volume have provided

(1) epistemological and methodological foundations and a number of building blocks, in terms of
(2) didactical approaches
(3) country studies, and
(4) alternative textbook conceptions

to develop pluralism in economics teaching. The chapters in this way have addressed the major challenges of pluralism in economics teaching, the meta-theoretical foundations, the international perspective, the alternatives to the mainstream textbooks system, and conceptions for a didactics of pluralist teaching. We have focused on teaching and textbook production as the realm of the academic discipline least developed towards differentiation, variety, and pluralism. Higher economic education, therefore, also has to be a crucial point of leverage for transformations aiming to advance a pluralism debate in economics and make the discipline as a whole more real-world, more relevant, and more effective in increasing the social knowledge stock.

1. Pluralism and cognition: meta-theoretical foundations

The contributions in the first part have elaborated on the necessity, the ways, forms, and expected effects of pluralism, to enable the discipline to teach a serious social science, which may have a chance to substantially and continuously increase societal knowledge. The contributions have provided meta-theoretical as well as pedagogical and first practical answers to the question of how a pluralist economics can be conceptualised and implemented. But the relations among the different meta-theoretical frameworks, be it a "structured pluralism" (Dow), a "competitive pluralism" (Beckenbach), or some "interested pluralism" (Kapeller), still need to be further explored and developed. All these approaches are standing on a fruitful middle ground between the current paradigmatic monism and an "anything goes" pluralism. As they vary in their epistemological rationales, they indicate a potential diversity of meta-theoretical approaches to pluralism, a second-order pluralism, so to speak. Future meta-theoretical work may compare, relate, and perhaps even integrate them. In any case, pluralism researchers and pluralist lecturers should develop and disclose the meta-theoretical grounds on which they develop, advocate, and practice pluralism.

The chapters of this part have shown that there is no consensus yet regarding the current state of pluralism in economics and its mainstream, and the role of the concept of transformation of economics. The links between the concepts of pluralism and of transformative science will have to be discussed further.

A particular (and perhaps more practical) problem is the (perceived) need to teach mainstream economics, even if in a critical, heterodox, pluralist, and transformative motivation and perspective (often following flat university or school enforcements), to equip students with the ability to understand and discuss the prevailing paradigm and everyday ways of thinking, rhetoric, and discourse (as Fine and others have argued). In any way, such a "first mover" problem favouring the mainstream needs innovative solutions and further discussion and intelligent embedding. Taking pluralism seriously might require to strongly reduce the amount of mainstream teaching contents in favour of so far excluded paradigms.

2. International perspectives on pluralist teaching

The contributions in the second part have offered inspiring, and in parts also worrying, insights into the teaching of economics in Brazil, China, India, and Ghana. These perspectives may further help to move away from the Euro-centric viewpoint that still largely characterises the mainstream (and in parts also heterodox) economics. However, to overcome the current dominance of a few countries and universities in the Global North in determining research, theories, rhetoric, ideologies, and discourse, much more has to follow. A pluralist higher economics education at the international level should be understood as a fifth dimension of pluralism, adding to the meta-theoretical, theoretical, pedagogical, and disciplinary pluralisms (e.g., ISIPE International Student Initiative for Pluralism in Economics 2014).

3. A textbook science – and beyond

The chapters in the third part have put forth a critique of the normalising and normative role of the rigid textbook system and corresponding dogmatic and scholastic teaching and learning culture in economics, and offered examples of alternatives. The structural problem that remains and requires the combined efforts of teachers, students, associations, and publishers is to develop and disseminate not only alternative textbooks but also new networks and platforms for teaching plural contents in general. For instance, the platform exploring economics (https://www.exploring-economics.com/) may serve as a model and nucleus of a pluralist teaching platform that collects teaching material and overcomes the outdated format of the classical purely printed textbook. Combinations of both, including print and interactive online materials, often standard already with the big mainstream directive-style textbooks, will have to be developed in particular for a pluralist teaching and learning.

4. Pluralism as a long-term transformative project

In the current situation in which mainstream economics appears to have regained its stability and predominance after the financial (and, with this, its very own) crisis, it seems critical that the pluralist (epistemological as well as pedagogical and textbook-based) approaches are consolidated and established as a well-advanced, feasible, practicable and practised alternative. A pushing back of the largely ossified mainstream monopoly and the implementation of pluralism in research, public discourse, teaching and textbook production has to be comprehended as a long-term transformative project. This, in fact, already started towards the end of the 20th century and will obviously extend into the future.

It seems helpful to consider waves of the public demand for pluralism, which may follow their own particular dynamic, but may build on one another and together form a transition cycle that will span several decades. Olsen and Starr (2010), for instance, have distinguished different waves of pluralism: the first started by the end of the 1970s, when Austrian, Marxian, Sraffian, Post-Keynesian, and evolutionary-institutional economists challenged the post-war monism in economics in the US (and elsewhere) and established or re-established their respective paradigms. These alternatives, however, stood in relative isolation to each other and sought little institutional cooperation.

Distinct from that, the petition of 44 leading economists in the *American Economic Review* marked a second wave of pluralism (Abramovitz et al. 1992). It denounced the monism in economics and acknowledged the establishment of pluralist associations. Among those had been the *Association for Social Economics* (ASE), the *Association of Evolutionary Economics* (AFEE), the *Union for Radical Political Economy* (URPE), the *European Association for Evolutionary Political Economy* (EAEPE), the *International Association for Feminist Economics* (IAFFE) or the *International Confederation of Associations for Pluralism in Economics* (ICAPE); somewhat later appeared the *Association for Heterodox Economics* (AHE), the *International Initiative for the Promotion of Political Economics* (IIPPE) and others.

On top of those two waves, the famous public letter by French students in 2000, demanding a post-autistic economics education, could be considered the beginning of a third wave of pluralism demand, in which student groups have assumed a role in challenging the mainstream. Accelerated by the financial crisis and Great Recession, and accompanied by an increasing public interest in the failure of the economic mainstream, the public letter by the *International Student Initiative for Pluralism in Economics* (ISIPE International Student Initiative for Pluralism in Economics 2014) marked a peak in this phase. In this stylised periodisation, we might currently be situated in the offshoots of that third wave.

Several basic questions still are not fully answered: Has mainstream economics really survived unswayed the shock of 2008 and regained its old dominance and stability? Or is some sort of mainstream pluralism underway? If yes, how would the selective inclusion of so far marginalised paradigms into the mainstream change the movement for pluralism? If so, is this evenly reflected in research and teaching? Or is there rather a mainstream schizophrenia between increasingly specialised, and perhaps even fragmented, complex research and its outcomes – often converging with heterodox positions – on the one hand, and its subsequent reinterpretation in favour of "market", "optimality", and "equilibrium" simplicism, particularly in standard textbooks and in higher economics education and their curricula, on the other (e.g., Elsner 2016)?

Further, will the associations and professional networks that drove the second wave, and the student initiatives that began to play a role in the third wave of pluralism be able to combine their efforts and really transform mainstream economics and implement a pluralist higher economics education in favour of a more effective cognition and learning? Will social movements that share the critiques of mainstream economics come to play some role in this process? Among these, the Promoting Economic Pluralism (PEP) initiative (https://www.economicpluralism.org/aboutus) has recently figured prominently.

Finally, will those politicians and top administrators of the science system, who also have begun to share some critiques of mainstream economics in the last decade, take up their responsibilities and start playing some supportive role as well? There is a whole list of urgent things to do in science policies to stop ongoing ideological cleansing in the economics faculties, not least by virtue of the ranking industry and its mistaken approach towards comparative academic performance in economics.

The lesson that can be learnt from the history of public demand for economic pluralism is that the idea of a pluralist economic science and a pluralist higher economic education is not an abstract and trivial issue, but a political and a practical project. Pluralism in economics is necessary for an innovative and transformative economic science that is capable of addressing complex real economic problems, systemic problems, multiple crisis symptoms, and profound socio-economic change. With the contributions in this volume that expound the meta-scientific foundations, the international perspective, the alternatives to the mainstream textbooks, and some practical options of pluralism, we intend to improve the conditions for economics pluralism and the contestations on it that lay ahead. In the corresponding forthcoming volume *Principles and Pluralist Approaches in Teaching Economics: Towards a Transformative Science*, we will provide an international compilation of already practised pluralism in economics teaching and its implications for future efforts in the discipline.

References

Abramovitz, M., et al. (1992): 'Plea for a Pluralist and Rigorous Economics', *American Economic Review* 82(2), XXXV.

Elsner, W. (2016): 'The Dichotomy, Inconsistency, and Peculiar Outmodedness of the 'Mainstream' Textbook. The Example of Institutions', *MPRA Paper* no. 70471.

Available at https://mpra.ub.uni-muenchen.de/70471/1/MPRA_paper_70471.pdf, accessed on 30 January 2018.

ISIPE International Student Initiative for Pluralism in Economics (2014): 'An International Student Call for Pluralism in Economics', May 5 2014. Available at http://www.isipe.net/, accessed on 1 February 2017.

Garnett, R.F. Jr., Olsen, E.K. and Starr, M. (eds.) (2010): *Economic Pluralism*. New York and Abingdon: Routledge.

Index

Note: Italicized page numbers indicate a figure. Bold page numbers indicate a table.